CLASSICAL PERSIAN LITERATURE

BY A. J. ARBERRY

Sufism
The Holy Koran
Scheherezade
The Koran Interpreted
Revelation and Reason in Islam
The Seven Odes

A. J. ARBERRY
Litt.D., F.B.A.

CLASSICAL PERSIAN LITERATURE

B1

NEW YORK
THE MACMILLAN COMPANY

FIRST PUBLISHED IN 1958

PRINTED IN GREAT BRITAIN

CONTENTS

ONE

Introduction

WHEN the Arabs carrying the Koran in their breasts overran Persia in the middle years of the seventh century and destroyed the once-powerful Sāsānian empire they swept out of existence, though not out of memory, almost all vestiges of a literature which had behind it a thousand years of varied and changeful history. With the scanty remnants of that pre-Islamic culture, recovered painstakingly from imperishable rock and tattered leaves of widely scattered codices, this book is not concerned. Here it is proposed to tell the story of the first rebirth of a national literature in the national language, and to trace the course of its development and full maturity from the beginning of the ninth to the end of the fifteenth century. This story has of course been told before, both briefly and at length: briefly, as by Reuben Levy in his *Persian Literature* (London, 1923); at length, as by Edward Granville Browne in his *Literary History of Persia* (four volumes, Cambridge, 1928)—those are the best-known and most reliable guides to this extensive territory in English, but many other books and monographs in many languages have surveyed the same scene in general or in particular. However, since Browne and Levy wrote, much new material has been published both in Persia and elsewhere which, without affecting seriously the broad picture painted by them, has modified very considerably our perspective of many parts of that picture. It therefore seemed opportune to compile a new history of classical Persian literature, within the compass and following the proportions appropriate to a single volume work, for the assistance of students coming newly to the subject, as well as for the enjoyment of the wider public interested to discover the sum of what the poets and writers of Persia produced during the golden age.

Before setting out on our long journey and tracing the waymarks century by century, it will be helpful to sketch the political history of Persia during the period under review, and to examine in a comprehensive fashion the nature and scope of Persian literature. A knowledge of the political history is essential to an understanding of the characteristics of the literature and its noticeable limitations, for it has almost invariably been associated with kings and princes and has owed nearly everything to patronage. It is necessary also to glance at the main trends of Arabic literature, for in many respects Persian authorship has been derivative, at all events in the primary phases, the principal models having been supplied by Arabic poetry and prose writing. The conquerors imposed their language and literary conventions on the vanquished along with their religion; the subject people proved themselves complacent to conform and quick to learn, and many of the most eminent Arabic scholars and authors during the first centuries of Islam were men of Persian blood and birth. It was only when political control of the Persian provinces loosened, a natural sequel to the weakening of the central administration, that the Persian language re-emerged, with a modified morphology and vocabulary, to serve once more as vehicle for the display of the Persian genius.

'The political situation of Persia,' writes E. Berthels, 'whose rulers were trying to cast off the Arab yoke, and the gradual exhaustion of the caliphate demanded not only political opposition to the Arabs but also the ending of the domination of the Arabic language in the field of literature. But the 150 years of the supremacy of Arabic did not pass without leaving a trace. Pahlavi had become a dead language; there was therefore only Persian to oppose to Arabic as a literary language. On the other hand, there prevailed, especially in poetry, Arabic forms (*ḳaṣīda*, *ghazal*) and the Arabic quantitative metre (*'arūḍ*), which so firmly established rhyme, probably foreign to Pahlavi, that a return to the poetical technique of the Sāsānian period was impossible.' These words were published over twenty years ago, when the question of what constituted Pahlavi poetry was being actively discussed. In 1950 Professor H. B. Henning could still record that 'the formal problems, the problems of rhythm, metre, and rhyme, remain in the dark. It seems doubtful whether the material at hand is capable of leading us to definite conclusions.' The result which he reached in his careful investigation was that Pahlavi verse was accentual and not, as some had supposed, syllabic; he added that 'even the most cautious will not be able to deny the presence of conscious rhyme in a Pahlavi poem that to the present has remained unnoticed.' Even so, Henning felt obliged to hesitate, asking whether the verses examined by him belonged in fact to 'an ancient poem, or merely an imitation of Persian models.' Berthels' statement therefore stands in need of little if any modification.

The *qaṣīda*, a long poem in monorhyme which has been called 'ode' in these pages, was a creation of pre-Islamic Arabia which the Arabs ever afterwards esteemed as their highest form of poetic expression. A frequently quoted description by the Arab critic Ibn Qutaiba, who died at Baghdad about the year 888, brings out well the narrow conventions within which the ancient poets were pleased to work.

'I have heard a certain man of letters remark, that the author of a *qaṣīda* began always by mentioning the encampment, the dung-heaps and other relics. He then wept complainingly, addressed the deserted site and begged his companion to halt, in order that he might furnish an occasion for mentioning the folk who once dwelt there but were now departed. . . . To this he joined the amatory prelude; he complained of the violence of his sentiments and the pain of separation, as well as the extremity of his passion and yearning, so as to incline men's hearts towards him and win the attention of their eyes and ears; for love poetry is very near to the soul and readily cleaves to the heart. . . . When he was confident that he had secured a hearing, he followed all this up by affirming his rights: in his poetry he mounted the saddle, complained of weariness and sleeplessness, of long journeying by night and through the heat of the noonday; he described the exhaustion of his riding-beast or his camel. When he was conscious that he had sufficiently affirmed to his patron the right he had for hoping and the guarantee he felt entitled to that his desires would be gratified, and that he had convinced him of the sufferings he had endured upon the journey, he began the panegyric, inciting his patron to be generous and bestirring him to compensate him adequately; he extolled him above his peers, and belittled them in comparison with his superior worth.'

The precise definition here outlined has been accepted by Arab poets of the conservative school down to modern times, so that F. Krenkow could report that he had 'specimens by poets still living where we find the absurdity of a description of a desert-ride by persons who live in Cairo and travel by railway and steamer.' Even from the beginning however it was permitted to vary the prescription to the extent of substituting satire for panegyric, though elegy, albeit protracted to equal length, was thought to be excluded from the strict canon. The element of flattery was increasingly stressed as the competition for royal favour became keener, and by the time the Persians started writing odes in their mother-tongue panegyric had been brought to a very fine art indeed. Meanwhile a revolution had taken place in poetic style. The exiguous repertory of themes having been exhausted, virtuosity applied itself to the problem of discovering novelty in the manner of expressing threadbare topics. The resources of simile and metaphor had been fully exploited; now rhetorical embellishment came to deliver the creative impulse out of utter stagnation. Even the most ancient poets had indulged in punning and similar forms of word-play, but sparingly; the Arabic language lent itself most obligingly to all manner of verbal jugglery, and the 'new style' on which the caliph's son Ibn al-Mu'tazz (d. 908) was the first to theorize required that every line should have its quota of cunning artifice. The formal ode reached its apogee of perfection in the work of al-Mutanabbī (d. 965). In due course the Persian court-poets followed suit with their brilliant sallies of artificial wit, overcoming easily the handicap of using a language less amenable to such gymnastics.

It was a half-Persian, Abū Nuwās (d. about 810), who led the revolt against the classical ode in Arabic.

> O sing me not the old songs—let others if they must
> Make melody of ruins, all desolate and dust.

In one poem, as R. A. Nicholson, its translator, has put it, 'he gives a description of the desert and its people which recalls some of Dr. Johnson's sallies at the expense of Scotland and Scotsmen.'

> Let the south wind moisten with rain the desolate scene
> And Time efface what once was so fresh and green!
> Make the camel driver free of a desert space
> Where high-bred camels trot with unwearied pace;
> Where only mimosas and thistles flourish, and where,
> For hunting, wolves and hyenas are nowise rare!
> Amongst the Bedouins seek not enjoyment out:
> What do they enjoy? They live in hunger and drought.
> Let them drink their bowls of milk and leave them alone,
> To whom life's finer pleasures are all unknown.

His ideal of enjoyment was something quite different.

> Four things there be that life impart
> To soul, to body, and to heart—
> A running stream, a flowered glade,
> A jar of wine, a lovely maid.

Was this Persian blood calling over the centuries to Persian blood?

> A Book of Verses underneath the Bough,
> A Jug of Wine, a Loaf of Bread—and Thou
>   Beside me singing in the Wilderness—
> Oh, Wilderness were Paradise enow!

For Abū Nuwās not only simplified the stilted and archaic vocabulary of the formal ode; he also specialized in short bacchanalian poems which are the ancestors of many Persian lyrics. Yet a century before this 'Umar ibn Abī Rabī'a of Mecca (d. about 715) had been about the same business, though to different purpose; he took the dramatic step of detaching from the ode its amatory prelude which he developed into a love-poem in its own right, thus supplying the other main constituent of the Persian *ghazal*. But before discussing this delightful art-form further, let us recall some of the new uses to which the ode was being put. Abu 'l-'Atāhiya (d. 805), harking back to the sententious asides of some of the old Bedouin poets, wrote almost exclusively on philosophical and didactic themes, thus preparing the way for Persian moralists like Nāṣir-i Khusrau. The rise of Ṣūfism, the mystical movement within Islam, led to the evolution of the mystical ode, perfected by Ibn al-Fāriḍ of Cairo (d. 1235) in time to affect the rapturous outpourings of Rūmī. The occasions for which formal odes were composed also affected their contents, though panegyric always remained the predominant note. The *ḥabsīya* or 'prison-poem' had been admirably worked out by Abū Firās al-Ḥamdānī (d. 968) during his long captivity in Constantinople, so that Mas'ūd-i Sa'd-i Salmān had a good model to imitate when he found himself in gaol. The spring festival, the tournament, the hunt, the banquet—these were among the royal occasions which along with military triumphs challenged the ingenuity of the ambitious poet, awake to every opportunity of pleasing his sovereign. All these items duly reappeared in the programme of the Persian panegyrists.

Though countless lyric-like poems were composed in Arabic from the seventh century onwards, it was left to the Persians to recognize this kind of writing as belonging to a separate genre and to call it *ghazal*. When precisely this division took place is not clear; the most characteristic feature of the classical *ghazal* is not so much its comparative shortness (between four and fourteen couplets) as the convention that the poet should affix his pen-name in the concluding verse, and we find that many lyrics of Sanā'ī, for instance, are without such a signature, whereas from 'Aṭṭār onwards (who signs himself sometimes 'Aṭṭār, sometimes Farīd) the rule is strictly followed. It therefore seems reasonable to conclude that the *ghazal* as such was largely a Persian invention; certainly its prestige was far higher in Persian than ever in Arabic literature.

The quatrain (*rubā'ī*) with its peculiar metre was undoubtedly a Persian creation, as will be shown in a later chapter; its most famous practitioner was of course 'Umar Khaiyām. Its brevity matched admirably the Persian fondness for proverbs and the Persian genius for epigram. The epic, though not entirely unknown in Arabic—Abān ibn 'Abd al-Ḥamīd al-Lāḥiqī for instance, who died about 815, wrote *muzdawij* (couplet) versions of the *Kalīla wa-Dimna* and the *Bilauhar wa-Būdāsāf* as well as the adventures of Sindbād and Mazdak and the romances of Ardashīr and Anūshīrwān, but these were never popular and have not survived—attracted few Arab poets. The simple rhyming couplet was felt by the Arabs to be a poor sort of jingle, good enough for mnemonic exercises to assist the schoolboy in his grammar, his elementary law, his rules for reciting the Koran, but not sufficiently dignified to be mistaken for serious poetry. The Persians fortunately did not suffer from any such inhibition; from Firdausī's times throughout all the classical period the epic in the grand manner, and its rather shorter variety the idyll, continued to please patrons and to be a challenge to poets. The *mathnavī*, as the rhyming couplet was called in Persian, served not only for heroic and romantic narratives but also for didactic compositions; among its greatest exponents were Sanā'ī, Niẓāmī, Rūmī, Sa'dī and Jāmī.

The composition of prose was not attended at first by any considerable complexities, once the Arabic monopoly had been broken; the short and straightforward periods of the earliest writers could not have been far removed from ordinary educated speech. So too it had been in the beginning with Arabic, though the Bedouin love of pregnant brevity had produced a natural rhetoric long before desert men knew the use of ink and paper. When 'Abd al-Ḥamīd al-Kātib (d. 750), chief secretary to the last Umaiyad caliph Marwān II, applied his Persian ingenuity to the invention of Arabic epistolary style, he fell back upon Sāsānian models and, as al-'Askarī expresses the matter, 'extracted from the Persian tongue the modes of secretarial composition which he illustrated, and transposed them into the Arabic tongue.' The development of artistic prose in Arabic was taken a stage further by another Persian, 'Abd al-Ḥamīd's pupil Ibn al-Muqaffa' who was executed in 757 on suspicion of being a Zoroastrian renegade. On the other hand the use of *saj'*, 'a peculiar mode of rhetoric in which at short intervals words occur which rhyme'—the term signifies literally the cooing of a dove—mounts right back to pagan Arabia and the sphinx-like utterances of the soothsayers; it reached its culmination in the *maqāma*, a literary genre invented by the Persian Badī' al-Zamān al-Hamadhānī (d. 1007). F. Krenkow, who had no great admiration for this highly artificial form of writing, observed that *saj'* 'invaded other branches of literature, even the chronicles, of which conspicuous specimens are in Arabic the *Ta'rīkh al-Yamīnī* and 'Imād al-Dīn's writings and in Persian the history of Waṣṣāf. In both works everything is sacrificed for the jingling rhymes. This exuberance of *saj'* may be due to the bad taste of the Persians who from 'Abbāsid times increasingly took a larger share in Arabic letters; the disease seems to spread gradually towards the West and has become one of the main causes why so much of Muhammadan literature, whether Arabic, Persian,

Turkish or any other language under their influence, does not appeal to European taste.' We shall see later that the acknowledged master of Persian rhythmical and rhyming prose was Sa'dī in his *Gulistān*.

Though the Persian genius had broken the close fetters of Arab convention in poetry by inventing the quatrain and the epic, and by greatly enhancing the lyric, in prose the limitations inherited from Sāsānian times and reinforced by Arab influence were never transcended until the most recent period. The drama, which was the chief glory of Greek literature and enjoyed a considerable vogue in Sanskrit, did not strike roots in Persia; the great inspiration of the stage was entirely lacking. The novel, so rich and fascinating a part of the Chinese heritage and so promising—though too belated—a development of late Hellenistic writing, also failed to awaken any response; yet the animal fable of India and the fantastic adventure of the *Arabian Nights* cycle to some extent gave scope to the creative imagination, and anecdote was always in demand. But in the main Persian prose treated of serious and learned topics; the purpose of the author was to inform and to uplift rather than to amuse. The branches of literature most assiduously cultivated were history and philosophy, including political theory and popular ethics. History indeed employed the energies of many writers, and that for a diversity of reasons. It enabled the Persian patriot to nurse his wounded pride by recalling the splendour of that ancient civilization which had preceded the Arab conquest. It furnished the propagandist for this or that local or nation-wide dynasty with the means to leave on record a version of events favourable to the masters whom he served, and who might be expected to reward him if he appeared to have succeeded in his major aim, and in doing so adroitly combined the functions of the chronicler with those of the panegyrist.

The increasing sophistication of prose style showed itself in all kinds of writing; eventually the point was reached when every sentence needed to be planned and constructed in conformity with the elaborate rules of rhetorical theory. The rhymed and rhythmical periods, their measured cadences charming and beguiling the attentive ear, were lavishly ornamented with snatches of Arabic—quotations from the Koran and the Traditions of the Prophet, well-loved proverbs and well-worn clichés—and frequently interspersed with fragments of poetry. Niẓāmī the Prosodist's definition of poetry might apply equally well to artistic prose: 'Poetry is that art whereby the poet arranges imaginary propositions, and adapts the deductions, with the result that he can make a little thing appear great and a great thing small, or cause good to appear in the garb of evil and evil in the garb of good. By acting on the imagination, he excites the faculties of anger and concupiscence in such a way that by his suggestion men's temperaments become affected with exultation or depression; whereby he conduces to the accomplishment of great things in the order of the world.' These words were written in the middle of the twelfth century, by a man of many talents who served one royal house for nearly fifty years.

It was in the reign of the liberal al-Ma'mūn (813–33), whose mother was a Persian slave called Marājil (his father being the great Hārūn al-Rashīd), that there began, as J. H. Kramers describes it, that 'political loosening of Khurāsān and neighbouring provinces from the 'Abbāsid caliphate, not by the action of the ancient Persian nobles, nor by Khārijite or 'Alid propaganda, but by the action of Persian-Muḥammadan governors not of ancient noble lineage, but nevertheless animated by national feelings, preparing in this way the Persian-Muḥammadan political and cultural renaissance.' It is significant that 'Persian sources profess to consider the fragments that survive of a *ḳaṣīda* by 'Abbās Marwazī said to have been composed in Marw (809) in honour of Ma'mūn as the oldest poem in Persian. Unfortunately,' adds E. Berthels, 'it is still somewhat difficult to express a definite opinion on the genuineness of these lines.' In 820 al-Ma'mūn appointed as governor of Khurāsān his general Ṭāhir called Dhu 'l-Yamīnain ('the man with the two right hands'), descended from a Persian slave, and he established the Ṭāhirid dynasty which maintained a semi-independent status, while acknowledging vassalage to Baghdad, for just over fifty years. The fifth of the line, Muḥammad by name, tamely surrendered his fiefdom in 873 to Ya'qūb ibn Laith, a coppersmith (Ṣaffār) who had begun his public career as a bandit chief, but converted from thief to policeman when Ṣāliḥ, the caliph's governor of Sīstān, put him in charge of his gendarmerie. Before 868 he had made himself governor, and then embarked boldly upon a campaign of aggrandizement which took into his Ṣaffārid dominions Harāt, Fārs, Balkh, Ṭukhāristān and all the Ṭāhirid lands; being finally refused recognition by the caliph al-Mu'tamid, he marched against the capital of Islam but suffered defeat at the hands of al-Muwaffaq and died in 879.

What had been denied to Ya'qūb was readily conceded to his brother 'Amr; and the Ṣaffārids ruled their stolen kingdom for three generations. But Baghdad mistrusted this upstart house, and in 900 encouraged Ismā'īl the Sāmānid to attack 'Amr ibn Laith. This incitement brought into prominence a family chosen to revive something of the glory of the Sāsānians. The founder of the Sāmānid fortunes was a certain Sāmān or Sāmānkhudāt, a noble of Balkh claiming for ancestor the famous Sāsānian general Bahrām Chūbīn; being obliged to flee from his estates, he had found refuge with Asad the governor of Khurāsān and gratefully turned Muslim. This was all back in the eighth century; Sāmān had four sons, and about 820 al-Ma'mūn made them all local governors—Nūḥ of Samarqand, Aḥmad of Farghāna, Yaḥyā of Shāsh and Ilyās of Harāt. Aḥmad proved himself the ablest of the brothers; he took over Nūḥ's territory, added Kāshghar, and begot Ismā'īl who wrested Khurāsān from the Ṣaffārids in 903. Further campaigns established his sovereignty over an area extending from 'the Great Desert to the Persian Gulf, and from the borders of India to near Baghdad.' The tenth century was the century of the Sāmānids, who ruled their wide dominions through fluctuations of fortune in the following order:

Ismā'īl ibn Aḥmad	892–907
Aḥmad ibn Ismā'īl	907–13
Naṣr ibn Aḥmad	913–43
Nūḥ I ibn Naṣr	943–54
'Abd al-Malik I ibn Nūḥ I	954–61
Manṣūr I ibn Nūḥ I	961–76
Nūḥ II ibn Manṣūr I	976–97
Manṣūr II ibn Nūḥ II	997–99
'Abd al-Malik II ibn Nūḥ II	999

The brilliant Sāmānid court with its twin capitals of Bukhārā and Samarqand inspired a mighty upsurge of Persian national consciousness. Under the benevolent patronage of these enlightened rulers, imitated by wealthy landowners who prospered in this comparatively peaceful kingdom, Persian letters passed from its auspicious infancy into the early promise of strenuous maturity. The great philosopher and scientist Ibn Sīnā (Avicenna), born in 980 towards the end of the Sāmānid century, has left us a graphic description of the royal library which had been built up in Bukhārā for the benefit of serious students.

'Now the Sulṭān of Bukhārā at that time was Nūḥ ibn Manṣūr, and it happened that he fell sick of a malady which baffled all the physicians. My name was famous among them because of the breadth of my reading; they therefore mentioned me in his presence, and begged him to summon me. I attended the sick-room, and collaborated with them in treating the royal patient. So I came to be enrolled in his service. One day I asked his leave to enter their library, to examine the contents and read the books on medicine; he granted my request, and I entered a mansion with many chambers, each chamber having chests of books piled one upon another. In one apartment were books on language and poetry, in another law, and so on; each apartment was set aside for books on a single science. I glanced through the catalogue of the works of the ancient Greeks, and asked for those which I required; and I saw books whose very names are as yet unknown to many—works which I had never seen before and have not seen since. I read these books, taking notes of their contents; I came to realize the place each man occupied in his particular science. So by the time I reached my eighteenth year I had exhausted all these sciences.'

With the Sāmānids are associated the names of many poets and men of letters, as will be set out in some detail in the next chapter. Here it is sufficient to mention Rūdakī the panegyrist of Naṣr ibn Aḥmad and the first major poet in Persian literature, Manṣūr ibn Nūḥ's vizier Abū 'Alī Bal'amī who translated Ṭabarī into Persian and so largely created Persian prose style, and Firdausī who composed the greater part of his *Shāh-nāma* under the protective shadow of this great house, but had the ill luck to be obliged to offer it to its destroyer. Yet the Sāmānids were not the only Persian dynasts of their time. In the west of the country, along the southern shores of the Caspian Sea, the Ziyārid brigands-turned-princes carved out a kingdom for themselves which at its widest extent included Raiy, Iṣfahān and Ahvāz; in the end, which came in 1042, they had been pushed back to Ṭabaristān. To this house belonged Shams al-Ma'ālī Qābūs (976–1012) whose grandson Kai-Kā'ūs composed and named after him that famous 'Mirror of Princes' the *Qābūs-nāma*. Southern Persia and Iraq were simultaneously in the hands of the Buwaihids (932–1055), sprung as they pretended of royal Persian stock; the three sons of Buwaih, 'Alī, Ḥasan and Aḥmad, divided these territories between themselves and forced the caliph al-Mustakfī to grant them patents of nobility and high-sounding titles. Later the confederates fell out, making it easy for the Ghaznavids and the Saljūqs to swallow their dominions piecemeal.

For a new constellation was rising in the eastern sky; Persia, together with Iraq and Asia Minor, was about to capitulate to Turkish conquerors. The first blow fell from Ghazna where Alptigīn, a Turkish slave promoted to high office by 'Abd al-

Malik I the Sāmānid, had entrenched himself when he decided that the time had come to lead an independent life. But the true founder of the Ghaznavid empire was his slave and son-in-law Subuktagīn, whom Nūḥ II appointed governor of Khurāsān in 994; though he was content to call himself the faithful servant of the Sāmānids, in reality his power was greater than theirs as his son Maḥmūd soon proved after his accession in 997. Going over the heads of his nominal liege-lords, he demanded and obtained from the caliph al-Qādir a diploma confirming him as king of Ghazna and Khurāsān. The Sāmānids, weakened by internal quarrels and aggressions from without, collapsed into utter ruin; their royal library went up in flames. Maḥmūd then turned eastwards, raiding and devastating deep into India twelve times between 1001 and 1024; between whiles he was expanding his kingdom to take in Samarqand and Iṣfahān. But the Ghaznavids were not to rule in Persia proper for long; Maḥmūd's son Mas'ūd was driven out of Transoxiana by the Saljūqs, and his successors down to 1186 contented themselves with Afghanistan and the Panjab. Yet though Maḥmūd was a Turk and a fanatical Sunnī, he too patronized Persian letters in a truly royal manner; his laureate was 'Unṣurī, whose pupils included Farrukhī and Minūchihrī. The Persian tradition was fully maintained by the later Ghaznavids, who handed it on to their Muslim successors in India; Hujvīrī the Ṣūfī theorist resided in Lahore, and Mas'ūd-i Sa'd-i Salmān and Abu 'l-Faraj Rūnī were natives of that city; Sanā'ī dedicated his greatest poem to Bahrām Shāh.

'The advent of the Seljūḳian Turks forms a notable epoch in Moḥammedan history.' This sentence introduces S. Lane-Poole's masterly unravelling of the tangled skein of the Saljūq dynasties, which continues:

'At the time of their appearance the Empire of the Caliphate had vanished. What had once been a realm united under a sole Moḥammedan ruler was now a collection of scattered dynasties, not one of which, save perhaps the Fāṭimids of Egypt (and they were schismatics) was capable of imperial sway. Spain and Africa, including the important province of Egypt, had long been lost to the Caliphs of Baghdād; northern Syria and Mesopotamia were in the hands of turbulent Arab chiefs, some of whom had founded dynasties; Persia was split up into the numerous governments of the Buwayhid princes (whose Shī'ite opinions left little respect for the puppet Caliphs of their time), or was held by sundry insignificant dynasts, each ready to attack the other and thus contribute to the general weakness. The prevalence of schism increased the disunion of the various provinces of the vanished Empire. A drastic remedy was needed, and it was found in the invasion of the Turks. These rude nomads, unspoilt by town life and civilized indifference to religion, embraced Islam with all the fervour of their uncouth souls. They came to the rescue of a dying State, and revived it. They swarmed over Persia, Mesopotamia, Syria, and Asia Minor, devastating the country, and exterminating every dynasty that existed there; and, as the result, they once more reunited Moḥammedan Asia, from the western frontier of Afghānistān to the Mediterranean, under one sovereign; they put a new life into the expiring zeal of the Muslims, drove back the re-encroaching Byzantines, and bred up a generation of fanatical Moḥammedan warriors, to whom, more than to anything else, the Crusaders owed their repeated failure.'

The founder of the family fortune was Ṭughril Beg (1037–63), grandson of that Saljūq who had migrated from the Kirghiz steppe to Jand in the province of Bukhārā, where he and his clan embraced Islam. Within seventeen years from his seizure of Nīshāpūr and his first collision with the Ghaznavids Ṭughril had mastered all northern Persia, destroyed the Ziyārids and the Buwaihids, and entered Baghdad in 1055, to be saluted as 'King of the East and of the West.' Other Turkish tribes poured down to reinforce his Ghuzz warriors, and 'the whole of western Asia, from the borders of Afghānistān to the frontier of the Greek Empire in Asia Minor and the Fāṭimid Caliphate of Egypt, became united under the rule of the Seljūḳs before 1077.' Lane-Poole summarizes as follows the subsequent history of this powerful house.

'Tughril Beg, Alp-Arslān and Malik Shāh held supreme sway over the whole of this vast Empire, but after the death of the last, civil war sprang up between the brothers Bargiyāruḳ and Moḥammad, and separate branches of the Seljūḳ family attained virtual independence in different parts of the widely scattered dominions, although the main line still preserved a nominal suzerainty down to the death of Sinjar, the last 'Great Seljūḳ' (whose rule was almost confined to Khurāsān) in 1157. The Seljūḳs of Kirmān, of 'Irāḳ, of Syria, and of Rūm or Asia Minor, were the chief sub-divisions of the family, but individual members of it ruled in Adharbījān, Tukhāristān, and other provinces. In the East, the Seljūḳ empire succumbed before the attack of the Khwārizm Shāh; in Adharbījān, Fārs, Mesopotamia, and Diyār-Bakr it was supplanted by dynasties founded by Seljūḳ officers, or Atābegs, but in Rūm it survived until the beginning of the power of the 'Othmānlī Turks in 1300.'

The succession of the Great Saljūqs down to their replacement by the Khvārizm-Shāhs may be conveniently tabulated.

Rukn al-Dīn Ṭughril Beg	1037–63
'Aḍud al-Dīn Alp Arslān	1063–72
Jalāl al-Dīn Malik Shāh I	1072–92
Nāṣir al-Dīn Maḥmūd	1092–4
Rukn al-Dīn Barkiyārūq	1094–1104
Malik Shāh II	1104
Ghiyāth al-Dīn Muḥammad	1104–17
Mu'izz al-Dīn Sanjar	1117–57

It was under the Saljūqs that court poetry reached its zenith, though as E. Berthels remarks, 'the simplicity and the vigour and freshness of colour which so delight us in the Sāmānid poets gradually disappear; the *ḳaṣīda* becomes more arid, but attains more and more technical dexterity, which finds expression on the one hand in the accumulation of poetical artifice and on the other in the utilization of all branches of scholastic learning to create choice and unusual images.' The triumph of the Arabic 'new style' was complete. Panegyric being a profitable profession with proud and lofty-minded Turks on the throne, professional encomiasts crowd the pages of Persian literary history during the eleventh and twelfth centuries; only a selection of the outstanding figures will be considered in these pages. The greatest of them all, Anvarī, served Sanjar and survived the collapse of the Great Saljūqs. Mu'izzī enjoyed the favour of Malik Shāh before Sanjar liberally rewarded him. Adīb Ṣābir was sent by Sanjar on a diplomatic mission to Atsīz the Khvārizm-Shāh, which proved the end of him. Khāqānī lauded the Saljūq vassal Minūchihr the Shīrvān-Shāh. Ẓahīr al-Dīn Fāryābī wrote panegyrics for Qizil Arslān the Atābeg of Iraq. These men and many others explored and fully exploited all the possibilities of flattering hyperbole. The greatest composer of idylls Niẓāmī, coming towards the end of the Saljūq period, also found it necessary to seek his sustenance from Shīrvān-Shāh and Atābeg rulers. 'Umar Khaiyām, whom Malik Shāh invited to reform the calendar, wrote his immortal quatrains for his own amusement. Nāṣir-i Khusrau, who had sold his pen to Ismā'īlī propaganda, wrote tirelessly in verse and prose to advance that cause, but without much political success.

The Saljūqs were also prepared to pay for good prose, provided that it furthered their ends. Malik Shāh's able minister Niẓām al-Mulk, who devoted his energies to re-establishing orthodox Islam in territories which had been torn by schism, was not only himself a patron of religious learning and sound teaching but wrote a famous manual of practical politics. Historiography was always encouraged by Persian rulers, for reasons that have been given already; the Saljūqs were no exceptions. Ibn al-Balkhī dedicated his epitome of world-history to Ghiyāth al-Dīn

Muḥammad, Rāvandī sketched out his Saljūq chronicle while serving Sanjar. The Ghaznavids also saw the value of this kind of writing; Baihaqī worked for Mas'ūd and 'Abd al-Rashīd and thus gained a first-hand knowledge of the political events which he afterwards recorded. When Naṣr Allāh translated into elegant Persian the *Kalīla wa-Dimna* of Ibn al-Muqaffa', he offered the product to Bahrām Shāh; the animal fables cloak a wide variety of political aphorisms.

The end of the Great Saljūqs came in 1157; the Ghaznavids were extinguished in 1186. Kirmān had had its independence under its own Saljūq rulers since about 1070, but they were ousted by Ghuzz Turkumāns in 1187. The Salghurid Atābegs of Fārs, ancestors of Sa'dī's patron Abū Bakr ibn Sa'd ibn Zangī, were also originally Turkumān brigands. The bonds of empire were loosening and breaking rapidly, as if in preparation for the cataclysm that was to overwhelm eastern Islam in the thirteenth century. In Khvārizm to the far north-east Malik Shāh had appointed as governor a Turkish slave who formerly waited upon him with the wine-cup; his grandson Atsīz successfully defied Sanjar and laid the foundations of a powerful but short-lived realm. 'Alā' al-Dīn Muḥammad, who acceded in 1199, 'reduced the greater part of Persia by the year 1210, subdued Bukhārā and Samarḳand, and invading the territory of the Gūr-Khān of Ḳarā-Khitay, seized his capital Otrār. In 1214 he entered Afghānistān and took Ghazna, and then, having adopted the 'Alid heresy, prepared to put an end to the 'Abbāsid Caliphate. His career of conquest was suddenly cut short by the appearance of the Mongol hordes of Chingiz Khān on his northern borders. Moḥammad fled incontinently before this appalling swarm, and died in despair on an island of the Caspian Sea, 1220.' The Ghūrids of Afghanistan and northern India, who had long ago been tributaries in Ghūr of the Ghaznavids, but incurred the anger and tasted the cruelty of Bahrām Shāh, under 'Alā' al-Dīn Ḥusain nicknamed Jahān-sūz ('World-Burner') revolted against their masters and sacked Ghazna. Waves of Ghuzz raiders for a time converted both the Ghaznavid and the Ghūrid realms to anarchy, but Muḥammad Ghūrī rallied his followers, drove the last of the Ghaznavids out of Lahore, and mastered successively Gwalior, Bundelkund, Bihar and Bengal. Having repulsed Muḥammad Khvārizmshāh, who had seized Afghanistan and was now invading the Panjab, he was meanly assassinated by a conspiracy of Ghakkars in 1206. His empire broke up soon afterwards into the kingdoms of Sind, Bengal and Delhi, which escaped the full impact of the Mongol onslaught and all encouraged Persian letters.

The twelfth century had belonged to the Saljūqs, as the eleventh to the Ghaznavids and the tenth to the Sāmānids. Persian and Turkish dynasts had strutted across the stage of empire, attended by their trains of eager encomiasts who by now had created a great literary tradition. The thirteenth century opened the gates of Persia to invaders from far Mongolia, and city after city was reduced to ashes; pyramids of skulls marked the trail of the ferocious horsemen. Chingiz Khān had inherited from his father no more than forty thousand tents north of the Gobi Desert; by the time he chased Muḥammad Khvārizmshāh out of Persia he had mastered all the Karaits and Uighurs, begun the conquest of China and absorbed into his rapid empire the old Turkish kingdom of Qarā-Khitāi, Kāshghar, Khotan and Yārghand. When he died in 1227 his armies were already fanning out over the Russian steppes, and the subjugation of China was proceeding apace. Persia now became merely one out of the many provinces of the Mongol Empire, willed by Chingiz to his son Ogotāy (1227–41) who ravaged Europe as far as Hungary. Kuyuk returned from his westbound excursion to succeed his father in 1246, but enjoyed his elevation only two years, the empire then passing to the line of his uncle Tulūy. Mangū reigned from 1251 to 1257, long enough to despatch his brother Hūlāgū to Persia as Īl-Khān. He speedily liquidated the assortment of pretenders who had been striving to build fugitive principalities on the smoking ruins left by the first holocaust. In 1256 Hūlāgū destroyed the stubborn Ismā'īlī stronghold of Alamūt; in 1258 he massacred Baghdad and terminated the 'Abbāsid caliphate. Riding still westwards, his soldiers were halted in Syria by the Mamlūks who had wrested Egypt from the Fāṭimids, and the Saljūqs of Rūm were able to offer a safe shelter to such fugitives as Jalāl al-Dīn Rūmī who preferred freedom in exile to the quisling prosperity at home that Naṣīr al-Dīn Ṭūsī chose. Hūlāgū Khān died in 1265, and thereafter (to quote Lane-Poole again) 'for nearly a century his dynasty reigned in practical independence, whilst rendering a certain feudal homage to the remote Khāḳaān in China. Save for an occasional contest over the succession, the country was quietly and peaceably governed, and the Īl-khāns showed a praiseworthy desire to emulate the examples of earlier rulers of Persia in the encouragement of science and letters. In the reign of Abū-Sa'īd, however, the dynasty was undermined by the same causes which had previously destroyed the power of the Caliphs and the Seljūḳs, and were destined at last to bring about the downfall of the Mamlūks in Egypt: rival amīrs, generals, ministers, fanatics, began to take a large share in the government of the country, and in their jealousies and animosities lay the prime danger of the Īl-khāns. After Abū-Sa'īd's death the throne of Persia became the toadstool on which the puppet sovereigns set up by rival amīrs seated themselves only to find it crumbling beneath them.'

Hūlāgū	1256–65
Abāqā	1265–81
Aḥmad	1281–4
Arghūn	1284–91
Gāikhātū	1291–5
Bāidū	1295
Ghāzān	1295–1304
Ūljāitū	1304–16
Abū Sa'īd	1316–35
Arpa	1335–6
Mūsā	1336

The greatest poet of the thirteenth century, Rūmī, wrote all his Persian in what is now Turkey under the protection of the Saljūqs of Rūm, who had received and encouraged an earlier refugee, Najm al-Dīn Dāya, also a mystic but a writer of prose. Sa'dī, driven by the terror to see the world, returned home to Shīrāz where the Atābegs were now Mongol vassals to impart the wisdom and relate the anecdotes garnered during his long wanderings. Naṣīr al-Dīn Ṭūsī, who had betrayed his Ismā'īlī masters into the hands of Hūlāgū Khān, extracted from his new and far more powerful patron the promise to build a splendid observatory where he might watch the movements of the heavenly bodies that rule all human destinies; he was the first of many Persian scholars and authors who delightedly discovered that the Mongol overlords were as ready as any of their predecessors to loosen their purse-strings for the benefit of literature. Historians especially benefited from this new and greater source of wealth. Juvainī served the savage conquerors and extolled in eloquent and measured prose the career of Chingiz Khān, his forebears and successors. Rashīd al-Dīn Faḍl Allāh, who was Ghāzān Khān's minister and rose to even higher rank under Ūljāitū, compiled a great history of the world but was executed by Abū Sa'īd, having in the meantime secured the advancement of the turgid Vaṣṣāf. Poetry, except for Sa'dī and a cluster of lesser luminaries, did not shine so brightly in the homeland yet awhile. But as Rūmī had soared to glory in a western sky, so presently Amīr Khusrau poured forth his flood of song for the delectation of Indian rulers. As the Īl-Khān power sagged and crumbled, court-poetry joined hands with court-history to produce the acceptable epic of Ḥamd Allāh Mustaufī.

Persia was now split into fragments again, and uneasily awaited the descent of another conqueror who should ravage and then heal her broken body. 'In these chaotic times,' writes J. H. Kramers, 'when the authority of political power was waning, the more popular and, in a way, democratic elements in Persia gained more opportunity of asserting themselves, as may be seen from the rather independent way in which the citizens of different towns behaved towards the quarrelling rulers. This self-assertion of democratic elements is also to be observed in Asia Minor, but on the culturally more fertilized soil of western Īrān, it bore the fruit of a brilliant literary development in the fourteenth and fifteenth centuries, which at first sight may seem astonishing in such unfavourable political surroundings.' The provincial squabbles of Jalā'irids (Iraq, Azerbaijan) and Muẓaffarids (Fārs, Kirmān and Kurdistān) with which students of Ḥāfiẓ need to be familiar, the more distant rivalries of the Sarbadārids (Khurāsān) and the Karts (Harāt)—all these noisy tumults were silenced towards the close of the fourteenth century when Tīmūr Lang thundered out of the north. Between 1380 and 1387 he overran Khurāsān, Jurjān, Māzandarān, Sijistān, Afghanistan, Fārs, Azerbaijan and Kurdistān. Baghdad fell in 1393; in 1398 Delhi was raided. Six years later he was at Ankara, taking prisoner the Ottoman Bāyazīd I. Syria had already saluted him as liege lord, displacing the Mamlūk; and in 1405 he was planning the conquest of China when he died on the march in Central Asia.

'If Persian literature in the Mongol period had fallen into a kind of lethargic trance, under Tīmūr and his successors it experienced a renaissance.' Berthels continues: 'The reason for this is probably that, with the decline of Mongol sovereignty, a large number of petty local dynasties arose who were all anxious to restore the ancient usages of court life and to adorn their courts with poets. This period therefore became a new flowering-time of Persian poetry and it may well be called the second classical period. Although the greater part of its poetry lacks the freshness and vigour of the pre-Mongol period, some of its poets succeeded in surpassing their predecessors.' A striking new development of this epoch, no doubt a reaction against the demoralizing sequence of rising and falling empires, was the emergence of satire and parody, as in the writings of 'Ubaid-i Zākānī and Busḥāq. History retained its power to enrich, and each successive court awarded its professional chroniclers. Tīmūr's conquests were glorified by

Niẓām al-Dīn Shāmī and 'Alī Yazdī; Shāh-Rukh employed Ḥāfiẓ-i Abrū to relate his family record to the previous history of the world, and later in his reign 'Abd al-Razzāq began work on his majestic canvas of Tīmūrid Empire. Rashīd al-Dīn Faḍl Allāh's gigantic universal annals yielded at Harāt to Mīr Khvānd's elephantine tomes. In the field of political science Ṭūsī's ethical analysis found a successor in the meditations of Davvānī writing for Uzun Ḥasan of the 'White Sheep'; Ibn al-Muqaffa' stimulated the rhetorical verbosity of Ḥusain Vā'iẓ Kāshifī. The increasing influence of Ṣūfī mysticism is attested by the poetry of Auḥadī, Maghribī, Ni'mat Allāh Valī and Qāsim-i Anvār, while Ibn Yamīn showed what could be made of the cult of occasional verse.

One crowded lifetime had created yet another vast empire; Tīmūr's descendents quarrelled among themselves, and although Shāh-Rukh contrived to hold the far-flung provinces together, his death was the signal for the kaleidoscope to turn once more. The full greatness of the Tīmūrid house would be realized in Mogul India; Persia, divided between the Black Sheep and the White Sheep Turkumāns—Jāmī's gracious patron Sulṭān Ḥusain Bāiqarā had his splendid capital in Harāt—found deliverance and unity for many years when the Ṣafavids fought their way to the throne. In their days merchants and diplomats arrived from Europe, heralding the dawn of modern times.

TWO

From the Beginnings to Firdausī

'It is necessary to know that the first person to compose Persian poetry was Bahrām Gūr.' Such is the assured statement of Muḥammad 'Aufī, thirteenth-century author of the oldest extant history of Persian literature. His assertion was repeated by Daulatshāh more than two hundred years later: it has remained for modern critical scholarship to raise incredulous eyebrows at so improbable a pronouncement. However, the Arab writers had long claimed Adam as the inventor of Arabic poetry, so that the Persian pretension seems by comparison surprisingly modest. 'Aufī was in fact not the originator of the legend; he drew his information about the poetic outburst of 'that great Hunter' of Sāsānian times from Tha'ālibī the Arabic-writing but Persian-born polymath who died in 1038, and Tha'ālibī himself acknowledges his debt to the ninth-century geographer Ibn Khurdādhbih. The alleged first-fruits of the Persian literary genius amount indeed to very little—a couplet of princely boasting that may be rendered speculatively (for the text is naturally corrupt) somewhat as follows:

> I am that vengeful lion, I am that mighty tiger,
> I am that Bahrām Gūr, I am that Bū Jabala.

These verses, if genuine, would have preceded the Muslim conquest of Persia, like the two lines in *mutaqārib* metre but 'ancient' script said to have been found inscribed on the ruined walls of Qaṣr-i Shīrīn. Thereafter, according to the popular record, no Persian poetry was composed until the 'Abbāsid caliph al-Ma'mūn, whose mother was a Persian slave, came to Marv in the year 809, there to be eulogized in his mother's tongue by a certain 'Abbās. It is a pity that the spirited ode attributed to him displays the style of poets of at least a century later, for otherwise we must concede a far earlier flourishing of Persian poetry than the sum of reliable evidence allows. A single verse quoted in the name of Abū Ḥafṣ Sughdī is much more antique, and while some writers allege that he lived in the seventh century, others date him two hundred years later. It is still not possible to do more than echo the view expressed by E. Berthels regarding the scanty scraps preserved by the lexicographers and historians: 'Some may possibly be as early as the eighth century. These fragments however are but miserable remnants, which give evidence of the existence of poetry but do not enable us to obtain a clear idea of Persian verse in its earliest period.'

The remnants surviving from the times of the semi-independent Ṭāhirid and Ṣaffārid dynasties (820–900) are exiguous indeed; yet they have an importance out of proportion to their bulk, for they provide solid proof of the emergence by the middle of the ninth century of a polished and eloquent poetic style. In view of the widely propagated opinion that these old relics of Persian verse are characterized by an almost complete absence of words derived from Arabic, it is interesting to consider the famous lines composed by Ḥanẓala of Badghīs, who lived in Nīshāpūr in the reign of 'Abd Allāh ibn Ṭāhir (d. 844).

Mihtarī gar ba-kām-i shīr° dar ast
Shū khaṭar kun ẓi kām-i shīr° bi-jūy;
Yā buẓurgī u 'iẓẓ u ni'mat u jāh
Yā chu mardān-t° murg° rūyārūy.

If Honour lies within the Lion's jaws,
Go, greatly dare, seek Honour in that place;
Strive after Grandeur, Riches, Ease, Applause,
Or manly meet Disaster face to face.

In this short poem of twenty-six words no fewer than four of Arabic origin occur, though one (*jāh*) is admittedly derived from Persian. But it was under the Sāmānids (875–999) that Persian poetry grew out of infancy into vigorous youth. Many names are recorded in the anthologies, most of them credited with only a handful of lines; the magnitude of their output, now irrecoverably lost, may be assessed from what is reported of the greatest of them.

Abū 'Abd Allāh Ja'far ibn Muḥammad, called Rūdakī, was born in the district of Rūdak near Samarqand, and according to some authorities he was blind from birth. Of the details of his life little is recorded; we know from his poems that he enjoyed for many years the patronage of the Sāmānid Amīr Naṣr ibn Aḥmad (reigned 914–43), finally to be banished from court in 937; he died three years later in his native village of Bannuj. A famous anecdote describes picturesquely the emotive quality of his poetic art. The ruler, whose capital was Bukhārā, made it his custom to pass the spring and summer on a royal progress through his kingdom, returning to his palace at the onset of winter. On one occasion however he outstayed the winter in the south, and showed every sign of prolonging his absence into the following summer. What happened then is related by Niẓāmī of Samarqand (*fl.* 1150) in his *Chahār maqāla*, as translated by E. G. Browne.

'Then the captains of the army and courtiers of the King went to Abú 'Abdu'lláh Rúdagí, than whom there was none more honoured of the King's intimates, and none whose words found so ready an acceptance. And they said to him: "We will present thee with five thousand dinars if thou wilt contrive some artifice whereby the King may be induced to depart hence, for our hearts are dying for desire of our wives and children, and our souls are like to leave us for longing after Bukhárá." Rúdagí agreed; and since he had felt the Amír's pulse and understood his temper, he perceived that prose would not affect him, and so had recourse to verse. He therefore composed a *qaṣída*; and, when the Amír had taken his morning cup, came in and did obeisance, and sat down in his place; and, when the musicians ceased, he took up the harp, and, playing the "Lover's air," began this elegy:

> The Jú-yi-Múliyán we call to mind,
> We long for those dear friends long left behind.

'Then he strikes a lower key, and sings:

> The sands of Oxus, toilsome though they be,
> Beneath my feet were soft as silk to me.
> Glad at the friend's return, the Oxus deep
> Up to our girths in laughing waves shall leap.
> Long live Bukhárá! Be thou of good cheer!
> Joyous towards thee hasteth our Amír!
> The Moon's the Prince, Bukhárá is the sky;
> O Sky, the Moon shall light thee by and bye!
> Bukhárá is the mead, the Cypress he;
> Receive at last, O Mead, thy Cypress-tree!

When Rúdagí reached this verse, the Amír was so much affected that he descended from his throne, bestrode the horse which was on sentry-duty, and set off for Bukhárá so precipitately that they carried his riding-boots after him for two parasangs, as far as Burúna, and only then did he put them on; nor did he draw rein anywhere till he reached Bukhárá, and Rúdagí received from the army the double of that five thousand dinars.'

The verses in the original are indeed of striking beauty, their tones of sweet melancholy being contrived by astonishingly skilful assonances. Yet Daulatshāh expresses his amazement at the success they achieved. 'It is a simple poem, barren of all artifice, ornament and vigour. If any composer uttered such words today in an assembly of sultans and princes he would merit the disapprobation of all.' His remarks epitomize the change in literary taste wrought by the intervening centuries.

Rūdakī's output was evidently immense, even if we discount

as exaggerated the estimate of 1,300,000 verses given by some biographers. In addition to a large number of panegyrical odes and lyrics he is stated to have composed six idylls and, at Amīr Naṣr's request, to have versified the famous *Kalīla wa-Dimna* animal fables which the Persian Ibn al-Muqaffa' (d. 759) had made out of Pahlavi into Arabic. Of all this productivity little indeed has survived the ravages of time, but enough to confirm the judgment of the old Persian critics that he was the first great poet of his country. His gift for bacchic verse, which the half-Persian Abū Nuwās had long ago popularized in Arabic, is attested by his sparkling description of ruby wine: the version is by E. B. Cowell, Edward FitzGerald's Persian master.

Bring me yon wine which thou might'st call a melted ruby in its cup,
Or like a scimitar unsheathed, in the sun's noon-tide light held up.
'Tis the rose-water, thou might'st say, yea, thence distilled for purity;
Its sweetness falls as sleep's own balm steals o'er the vigil-wearied eye.
Thou mightest call the cup the cloud, the wine the raindrop from it cast,
Or say the joy that fills the heart whose prayer long looked-for comes at last.
Were there no wine all hearts would be a desert waste, forlorn and black,
But were our last life-breath extinct, the sight of wine would bring it back.
O if an eagle would but stoop, and bear the wine up to the sky,
Far out of reach of all the base, who would not shout 'Well done!' as I?

An even greater praiser of wine, 'Umar Khaiyām, would later

be pleased to take up Rūdaki's opening simile and exquisitely to refine it.

Wine is a ruby liquified,
  Quarried within the hollow bowl;
  The cup's a body, and its soul
The liquor's coruscating tide.

Yon gleaming glass of crystal clear
  Now laughing with the crimson wine
  Enshrines the life-blood of the vine,
And all its glitter is a tear.

But the days of love and laughter came to an end all too soon, leaving the exiled laureate in his old age to utter a pitiful lament, sympathetically interpreted by A. V. Williams Jackson:

Every tooth, ah me! has crumbled, dropped and fallen in decay!
Tooth it was not, nay say rather, 'twas a brilliant lamp's bright ray;
Each was white and silvery-flashing, pearl and coral in the light,
Glistening like the stars of morning or the raindrop sparkling bright;
Not a one remaineth to me, lost through weakness and decay.
Whose the fault? ''Twas surely Saturn's planetary rule,' you say.
No, the fault of Saturn 'twas not, nor the long, long lapse of days;
'What then?' I will truly answer: 'Providence which God displays.'
Ever like to this the world is,—ball of dust as in the past,
Ball of dust for aye remaining, long as its great law doth last. . . .

The poem continues in this mournful strain for many couplets, and set a fashion of 'protesting against the infirmities of old age' copied by countless later composers: Jāmī plays on the same theme in his *Salāmān u Absāl* more than five centuries afterwards, and FitzGerald makes him say:

My teeth fall out—my two eyes see no more
Till by Ferenghi glasses turn'd to four;
Pain sits with me sitting behind my knees,
From which I hardly rise unhelpt of hand;
I bow down to my root, and like a Child
Yearn, as is likely, to my Mother Earth,
Upon whose bosom I shall cease to weep,
And on my Mother's bosom fall asleep.

Among the minor poets of the Sāmānid court mention may be made of three: Abū Shakūr of Balkh, Abu 'l-Ḥasan Shahīd, and Kisā'ī of Marv. Abū Shakūr, who enjoyed the favour of Amīr Nūḥ I (reigned 943–54), was among the first to compose in the *mathnavī* style of rhyming couplets. A well-known verse of his is perhaps the earliest expression of that agnostic attitude which is so characteristic of the Persian outlook down the centuries.

To this point does my knowledge go:
I only know I nothing know.

He published in 948 a long poem entitled the *Āfarīn-nāma* which, to judge by the few extracts we now possess, anticipated the gnomic writings of Nāṣir-i Khusrau and Sa'dī.

A tree whose temperament is bitter,
if you should plant it in the garden of Paradise
and out of the river of Heaven sprinkle
its roots with pure and unadulterated honey,
in the end its nature will assert itself:
bitter will be all the fruits it bears.

Shahīd, also of Balkh, was a master of Arabic as well as Persian verse; he was also an accomplished philosopher, and is said to have disputed with Abū Bakr al-Rāzī (Rhazes) himself who died at Raiy in 925. He too admitted disillusionment at the end of much study, though the cause of his conturbation seems to have been material rather than intellectual.

Knowledge and wealth are like narcissus and rose,
they never blossom in one place together:
the man of knowledge possesses no wealth,
the wealthy man has scant store of knowledge.

He expresses his disappointment in another bitter epigram.

If grief gave off smoke the same as fire
the world would be darkened for evermore;
if you went about this world from end to end
you wouldn't find one wise man who was happy.

Rūdakī himself composed an elegy for Shahīd when he died, probably in 937.

Shahīd's caravan has gone on ahead:
take it from me that mine has gone on also.
As the eye counts, there's one body the fewer;
as the mind counts, the loss runs into thousands.

Kisā'ī, who may have been born about 904 (though some assign him a rather later date), is put forward as the pioneer of religious poetry, a full-blooded man who turned to austerer pleasures in his later years. His fragments reveal a sensitive appreciation of natural beauty, and R. A. Nicholson's version of his poem on roses brings out well his lyrical powers.

Roses are a gift of price
Sent to us from Paradise;
More divine our nature grows
In the Eden of the rose.

Roses why for silver sell?
O rose-merchant, fairly tell
What you buy instead of those
That is costlier than the rose.

It was surely this thought that inspired 'Umar Khaiyām (and FitzGerald) to say:

I often wonder what the Vintners buy
One half so precious as the ware they sell.

It makes sad reading to turn from this youthful gaiety to the lament of Kisā'ī's decline.

The turn of the years has reached now three hundred and forty-one;
Wednesday the day is; three days more, and Shauwāl is done.
Into this mortal world I came to utter and to do—what?
To sing songs and make merry with such wealth as I'd got.
So like any brute beast I've passed the whole of my life,
And now I'm a slave to my kinsfolk, a bondsman to children and wife.
What do I have in my hand for the fifty years of my score?
A fine balance-sheet, truly—ten thousand sins, and more!
How can I hope to break even when I come to the end of the game,
Seeing I started with lies, and am like to finish in shame?

Rūdakī's banishment from the Sāmānid court coincided with the fall of his protector, the vizier Abu 'l-Faḍl Bal'amī who had been so partial as to declare that 'Rūdakī has no equal amongst the Arabs or the Persians.' It was this minister's son Abū 'Alī Bal'amī, vizier to the Sāmānid Manṣūr ibn Nūḥ (reigned 961–76), who composed the earliest extant book in Persian prose. The origins of prose are even more obscure than the beginnings of poetry; Arabic was the language of learning, letters, administration and prestige throughout the first three centuries of the conquest, though Persian must surely have been used to a certain extent in private correspondence; with the rise of the semi-independent principalities local chieftains began to write to one another officially in Persian. There are some grounds for supposing that at an early date, perhaps in the first half of the eighth century, a prose epic existed recording the exploits of Ḥamza ibn ‘Abd Allāh the Khārijite who rebelled unsuccessfully against Hārūn al-Rashīd. When however Abū ‘Alī Bal‘amī made a Persian version of the famous *Universal History* compiled in Arabic by his compatriot Ṭabarī (d. 923), he served notice that his native language was thenceforward to be reckoned with as a respectable medium of self-expression for all loyal Persians and for all high purposes. This translation, which contains some passages not to be found in the original—notably the legend of Bahrām Chūbīn, presumably drawn from some lost, perhaps oral Persian source—has survived in two recensions, one ancient and patently authentic, the other a revision by a later editor who looked askance at the rugged simplicity of Bal‘amī's pioneering prose and sprinkled his simple sentences with a liberal seasoning of Arabic words. A comparison of the opening sequence in the two versions illustrates well this adulteration: words of Arabic origin are underlined.

OLDER RECENSION

In tārīkh-nāma-yi buzurgast gird āvarda-yi Abī Ja‘far Muḥammad ibn Jarīr-i Yazīd al-Ṭabarī raḥimahu llah ki malik-i Khurāsān Abū Ṣāliḥ Manṣūr ibn Nūḥ farmān dād dastūr-i khyīsh-rā Abū ‘Alī Muḥammad ibn Muḥammad ibn al-Bal‘amī-rā ki īn tārīkh-nāma-rā ki az ān-i pisar-i Jarīr ast pārsī gardān har-chi nīkūtar chunān-ki andar vai nuqṣānī na-y-uftad.

YOUNGER RECENSION

In tārīkhīst mu‘tabar ki Abū Ja‘far Muḥammad ibn Jarīr-i Yazīd-i Ṭabarī farāham namūd u Abū Ṣāliḥ Manṣūr ibn Nūḥ Abū ‘Alī Muḥammad ibn Muḥammad Bal‘amī vazīr-i khvud-rā farmān dād ki dar zabān-i pārsī ba-kamāl-i salāmat tarjama sāzad ba-nau‘ī ki dar aṣl-i maṭālib nuqṣānī rāh na-yābad.

Bal'amī began his translation of Ṭabarī in the year 963, more than two decades after the death of Rūdakī. It seems that it was at the same time, or very near it, that a group of scholars from Transoxiana, at the behest of the same Sāmānid ruler, took in hand to put into Persian Ṭabarī's other great work, his immense *Commentary on the Koran*. The exordium of this version is of much interest for the justification given for translating a religious book; it may be surmised that the fashion of compiling interlineary Persian interpretations of the Koran goes back to about this period. 'This book is the great *Commentary* related by Muḥammad ibn Jarīr al-Ṭabarī (God's mercy be upon him), translated into correct and straightforward Persian,' the text begins. 'They brought this book from Baghdad: it was forty volumes, written in Arabic and furnished with long chains of authority. They brought it to the victorious lord Amīr Abū Ṣāliḥ Manṣūr ibn Nūḥ ibn Naṣr ibn Aḥmad ibn Ismā'īl (God's mercy be upon them all). Then it proved difficult to read and interpret this book in the Arabic language, and so he desired that it should be translated into Persian. Then he assembled the ulema of Transoxiana and sought from them a legal pronouncement: "Would it be lawful for us to turn this book into the Persian tongue?" They said: "It would be lawful to read and write the *Commentary of the Koran* in Persian for the benefit of those who do not know Arabic, since God Most High has said:

> We have sent no Messenger
> save with the tongue of his people.

Moreover Persian has been understood from antiquity, from the time of Adam down to the time of Ishmael (upon whom be peace). All the prophets and kings of the earth have spoken Persian: the first to speak Arabic was the prophet Ishmael (upon whom be peace). Our own prophet (God bless him) came forth from the Arabs, and this Koran was sent to him in the language of the Arabs. In this region the language is Persian, and the kings of these parts are Persian kings." Then the victorious King Abū Ṣāliḥ commanded that the ulema of Transoxiana should be brought from Bukhārā, Balkh, the gates of India, Farghāna and every city of Transoxiana, and they all consented to the translation of this book, declaring: "This is the right way." Then the victorious King, the lord Amīr Ṣāliḥ ordered this assembly of ulema to choose from among themselves the most learned and erudite, so that they might translate this book. Then they translated it.'

It was in the reign of Amīr Manṣūr and of his son Nūḥ II (reigned 976–99) that the first great experiment in epic poetry was attempted, and the first and last great Persian epic was largely drafted. Abū Manṣūr Muḥammad ibn Aḥmad Daqīqī, probably a native of Balkh, has been thought by some scholars, among them Ethé and Nöldeke, to have been a confessed Zoroastrian because he concluded a lyric on the beauty of spring with the following lines:

> Daqīqī has chosen four properties
> out of all the world's beauty and ugliness:
> the ruby-coloured lip, the lament of the lute,
> the bright red wine, the Zoroastrian faith.

E. G. Browne however thought that 'Daqíqí's admiration for "Zoroaster's creed" was probably confined to one single point—its sanction of wine-drinking.' If the poem is genuine, and that is by no means certain, it may well be that the Sāmānid poet's boldness was symptomatic of the prevailing reaction against Arab domination and reflected a court policy of reviving the memory of Persia's past greatness. Certainly it was at Amīr Nūḥ's instigation that the old panegyrist—for Daqīqī had long used his gift of words to praise the living Chosroes—proceeded with the congenial task of celebrating the ancient emperors of Iran. He had only completed a thousand couplets, however, when he was murdered by his favourite Turkish slave.

Daqīqī was not in fact the earliest epic poet of Persia, though his verses, incorporated in the work of his successor Firdausī, exceed by far the paltry fragments surviving from the *Shāh-nāma* of his obscure forerunner Mas'ūdī of Marv. The foundations upon which these men built were laid for them nearly two centuries earlier, when the ill-fated Ibn al-Muqaffa', who was executed in 759, translated out of Pahlavi into Arabic the Sāsānian *Khvadāi-nāmak*. Others followed his example in rescuing from oblivion the contents of the pre-Islamic books, until in Persian we hear of prose *Shāh-nāmahs* in the names of Abu 'l-Mu'aiyad Balkhī, Abū 'Alī Balkhī and Abū Manṣūr Ṭūsī, all compiled in the first half of the tenth century. Of these the last was the most ambitious and influential; and though the work, which must have been on a massive scale, has long since vanished out of existence, its preface has by chance been preserved. Abū Manṣūr Ṭūsī when he was governor of Khurāsān commissioned (rather than executed) the enterprise, entrusting the research to four learned Zoroastrians under the direction of Abū Manṣūr Ma'marī. An analysis of the language of the preface shows that no more than two per cent of its vocabulary is derived from Arabic. This was certainly no accident: the translations of Ṭabarī exhibit similar features. It is surely insufficient to explain the matter by seeing in the common style a mere desire to write simple Persian; the earlier poetry from Ḥanẓala to Rūdakī had drawn much more extensively on the conquerors' speech. It is perhaps not too rash to conclude that Amīr Manṣūr and Amīr Nūḥ II aimed to advertise their political independence by purging the written language so far as possible of those intrusive elements which were a constant reminder of national defeat and humiliation. A thousand years later some ardent patriots were promoting the same programme.

The scene was now set for the appearance on the stage of an actor of heroic stature, a poet of supreme genius who should be a living embodiment of the rebirth of Persian pride, of Persian self-respect, of Persian consciousness. That genius was born in miraculous Ṭūs, birthplace of so many famous men, about the year 940. The city was at that time the fief of Abū Manṣūr Ṭūsī, ambitious and reluctant subject of Nūḥ I and his son Manṣūr. It was in 957 that Abū Manṣūr put on foot his project of a prose *Shāh-nāma*. Abu 'l-Qāsim Manṣūr (Ḥasan? Aḥmad?) ibn Ḥasan (Aḥmad? 'Alī? Isḥāq?) called Firdausī, whose father was a prosperous landowner, grew up in circumstances of ease; according to report he enjoyed the favour of Abū Manṣūr, and it seems that he exercised himself early in epic. These essays were doubtless encouraged by Abū Manṣūr; yet it was apparently only after the death of Daqīqī in about 980 that Firdausī addressed himself in earnest to the labour which was to occupy him some thirty years. In the interval his fortunes had changed; the Sāmānid dynasty moved to its close; civil war made literature an unrewarding profession. By the time Firdausī had completed his *Shāh-nāma* in its final form (*circa* 1010) not only had he exhausted his patrimony, but a new royal house of Turkish blood was firmly established in Transoxiana. Maḥmūd the Ghaznavid, a fanatical conformist, dedicated himself to the high cause of rooting out heresy and infidelity wherever they were to be found. When Firdausī presented his vast epic in praise of Zoroastrian Persia to this man, hoping for imperial bounty to repair his impoverished estate, the auspices were inexorably adverse. Maḥmūd, who had already proved himself a great patron of science and letters acceptable to orthodoxy, failed to recognize the merits of Firdausī's masterpiece and offered an insultingly small reward. Though the poet, in pardonable anticipation of favours to come, had prefixed a handsome panegyric to 'that prince whose like was never seen, not since the Creator created the world,' he now relieved his feelings by penning a savage satire. Joseph Champion's version in eighteenth-century couplets would not have done discredit to Alexander Pope.

Had worth or judgment glimmer'd in your soul,
You had not basely all my honour stole.
Had royal blood flow'd in your grov'ling veins,
A monarch's laurels had adorn'd my strains;

Or were your mother not ignobly base,
The slave of lust—thou first of all thy race—
A poet's merit had inspir'd thy mind,
By science tutor'd, and by worth refin'd.
Such as thou art, the vileness of thy birth
Precludes each generous sentiment of worth:
Nor Kingly origin, nor noble race,
Warms thy low heart, the offspring of disgrace.

After that Firdausī had to run for shelter, which he found in his old age at the provincial court of Ṭabaristān. There, some say, he composed the romantic idyll *Yūsuf u Zulaikhā*, a Koranic theme to atone for so many years wasted on the extolling of pagandom: in modern times this ascription has been shrewdly contested. Finally Firdausī returned to his native Ṭūs, to die there in 1020 or 1025. The story that Maḥmūd repented of his niggardliness and sent, too late, a load of precious indigo to the poet—'even as the camels entered the Rúdbár Gate, the corpse of Firdawsí was borne forth from the Gate of Razán'—this story makes an ideally dramatic ending, but is difficult to reconcile with the publication of that satire.

The plan conceived by Firdausī for his great work was sufficiently ambitious: he would recount in song the entire history of his motherland, from the creation of man down to the fall of the Sāsānian Empire. This plan he completely carried through, in some 60,000 *mutaqārib* couplets. His chief source was the prose *Shāh-nāma* of Abū Manṣūr, but other writings, and some oral informants, contributed to the filling in of his massive picture. The quasi-historical design presents a somewhat ramshackle appearance to readers familiar with the neater and more confined pattern of the *Iliad*, the *Odyssey*, the *Aeneid*: it is more satisfactory to judge the *Shāh-nāma* for what it actually is, a series of self-contained idylls composed at different times over a long period and loosely strung together within a chronological framework. If a central theme is sought, then it is to be recognized easily enough; it is the perennial glory of Persia and its great heroes. As for the 'unnecessary monotony of the similes' which E. G. Browne found so wearisome, does not this feature also reflect a deliberate purpose, to prove one and unchanging the seemingly kaleidoscopic scene which the poet is painting?

'It is on the *Sháhnáma*, of course, that Firdawsí's great reputation as a poet rests,' E. G. Browne observes. 'In their high estimate of the literary value of this gigantic poem Eastern and Western critics are almost unanimous, and I therefore feel great diffidence in confessing that I have never been able entirely to share this enthusiasm. The *Sháhnáma* cannot, in my opinion, for one moment be placed on the same level as the Arabian *Mu'allaqát*; and though it is the prototype and model of all epic poetry in the lands of Islám, it cannot, as I think, compare for beauty, feeling, and grace with the work of the best didactic, romantic, and lyric poetry of the Persians.' The writer of these words was certainly the greatest Persian scholar ever produced in the West, and the most enthusiastic and informed admirer of Persian literature. To understand why the Persians themselves rank Firdausī as their national poet, and incidentally to see how Persians today feel about their classical poetry, it is profitable to read the observations cast in the form of a letter which were made by Browne's old friend and admirer Mīrzā Muḥammad 'Alī Furūghī, later Prime Minister, on the occasion when Persia was celebrating the millenary of Firdausī's birth.

'My dear Friend,

'You wish to know what my feelings are towards the *Shāh-nāma* and what I think of Firdausī. If you are content to have a concise and exact answer, it is this: I love the *Shāh-nāma*, and I am truly devoted to Firdausī. If you are not satisfied with this brief statement, why, "the true lover always has his proof in his sleeve," and I could talk for a long time and produce endless arguments in support of my declaration with regard to the *Shāh-nāma*. But please don't get anxious: I haven't any such intention, and I'll try to be as short as possible, without however omitting anything essential.

'Firdausī's *Shāh-nāma*, considered both quantitatively and qualitatively, is the greatest work in Persian literature and poetry; indeed, one can say that it's one of the world's literary masterpieces. If it weren't that I always follow the safer course and don't wish to sound extravagant, I would cast all caution aside and assert that the *Shāh-nāma* is the grandest monument in the literature of mankind. But I'm afraid people will criticize me, saying I'm not capable of appreciating the fine qualities and beauties of the literary works of all ancient and modern tribes and nations, and therefore haven't the right to make such a claim. So I'll let that go; besides, I don't wish to offend the susceptibilities of Maulānā Jalāl al-Dīn Rūmī, Shaikh Sa'dī and Khvāja Ḥāfiẓ. I will therefore concede that if we wish to be absolutely just and truthful we must allow these three men to stand side by side with Firdausī, and call them the four pillars of the Persian language and literature, the four elements making up the culture and national character of the Persian people. But I don't want this letter to drag out interminably, and so I'll now restrain myself from paying compliments to the *Mathnawī* of Rūmī, the *Kullīyāt* of Sa'dī and the *Ghazalīyāt* of Ḥāfiẓ and try merely to put forward my reasons for being so partial to Firdausī, which is the subject of our present enquiry—besides the fact that Firdausī came before the other three in point of time, and therefore possesses at least the merit of precedence over them.

'The first great obligation we owe to Firdausī is for his having rescued from oblivion and preserved for all time our national history. Although the actual compilation of this history was not done by Firdausī, his work being to put into verse a book which had been assembled before him, nevertheless this fact is quite sufficient for him to be reckoned the reviver of the past greatness of Persia. . . . Your sound judgment and rich common sense will confirm that if he had not made the *Shāh-nāma* into poetry, then there's a strong probability that the same torrent of mighty events which has continuously swept over our oppressed country would have carried away those narratives too, and washed clean that record. And even assuming that it had not been lost but had survived in books like Bal'amī's *History*, the result would have been that not one person in a hundred thousand would have read or even seen such a work. . . . In any case books of that kind would never have had such a deep and penetrating influence on the minds of the Persians as these narratives have exercised through the medium of Firdausī's poetry. You certainly know that from the very beginning the charm of Firdausī's *Shāh-nāma* has fascinated all whose mother-tongue was Persian. Everyone who could read has always read the *Shāh-nāma*, while those who couldn't read would throng to listen with enjoyment to the recitation of its rhapsodes. Very few indeed were the Persians who were ignorant of these stories and didn't know the *Shāh-nāma* by heart. . . . In my opinion it is the duty of every Persian first, to familiarize himself with the *Shāh-nāma* and secondly, to encourage and provide the means for his fellow-countrymen to become familiar also with this book. In short, Firdausī composed the title-deeds of the Persian nation's nobility: this statement renders it needless for me to labour any further this aspect of his greatness. . . .

'Our second obligation to Firdausī is for his having rescued from oblivion and preserved for all time our Persian language. I don't need to pursue this topic any further, because I've never met anyone who would venture to deny the fact. But I just take this opportunity of recalling that rhythmical and harmonious speech, which is admired and cultivated by all peoples, makes a very special impression on the Iranian nature. Most Persians possess the faculty of composing rhythmical speech; you will find very few indeed who will not on all appropriate—and sometimes even on inappropriate—occasions ornament their discourse with rhyme. One might say that in the Persian view, speech without rhythm and rhyme is not worthy of attention. The need for rhyme and rhythm in the speech of children and the common people is readily observable. It is for this reason that great monuments of prose in the Persian language are very limited in number, and those writers too who have sought to make their prose popular have inevitably rhymed it and decorated it with various rhetorical ornaments. Consequently it is poetry that has preserved the Persian language. But this result could not accrue from any and every sort of verse: poetry that is to preserve the language should not only comprise the proper poetical embellishments, it must also not be remote from the understanding of the common people and it must speak of things that appeal to them. Very few of our poets before Shaikh Sa'dī and Khvāja Ḥāfiẓ fulfil these conditions to the extent that Firdausī does, and of course the very size of the *Shāh-nāma* has an important bearing on the achievement of this result.

'The virtues of the *Shāh-nāma* and the reasons for Firdausī's popularity are not confined to what I have already stated. The time you spend in reading the *Shāh-nāma* is by no means wasted: it is really a part of life itself. Apart from the fact that patriotism and loyalty to throne and country are the necessary consequences resulting to everyone who reads the *Shāh-nāma*, it is the best of recreations and the healthiest of amusements. Its language is as solid as iron, yet smooth as running water; like a beautiful face that requires not "the borrow'd gloss of art" it is extremely simple and unadorned. It contains no weak or flaccid lines; from beginning to end the style of the *Shāh-nāma* is uniform and consistent. Events and topics are expounded and objects described with the maximum of brevity and conciseness, yet with perfect clarity. Certainly there is a good deal of longwindedness and repetition in the *Shāh-nāma*. But the fault is not Firdausī's; he was fettered by the book he had undertaken to versify; he relates whatever lies before him, and omits nothing. It's as though he regarded it as his sacred duty to record these stories, and to a certain extent sacrificed his poetic art in the discharge of this obligation. He repeatedly shows signs of being afraid that he won't live long enough to complete his task, and so he is generally satisfied simply to make his discourse metrical and gives less rein to his poetic imagination. He refrains strictly from adding to or subtracting from his original. From this point of view one must indeed be sorry; for while every verse and fragment of the *Shāh-nāma* is extremely vigorous and beautiful, each time Firdausī reveals anything from the treasure-house of his inner nature and private thoughts under the impact of special impressions—as for example in the preludes to certain stories, and in his reflexions on the death of kings and great men—these are all glittering jewels that dazzle the inward eye. What a pity it is that he didn't do more of that kind! But at all events it's clear that he felt a personal attachment to these stories, and performed this task as a true labour of love; and that's the chief reason why his words have such a hold on our hearts.

Words that issue from the soul
Cannot but the heart control.'

Furūghī concluded his candid and revealing appreciation as follows:

'One mustn't lose sight of a particularly subtle point. It should always be borne in mind that Firdausī in his own person is a perfect embodiment of all that is meant by a Persian: he comprises all the characteristics of our Persian race. When you assess Firdausī in regard to his emotions, his character, his beliefs, his feelings as revealed in his utterances, it's exactly as though you were weighing the emotions of the Persian nation. Of all the Persians who have ever lived I know of no one bar Sa'dī who stands comparison with Firdausī in this respect. I truly do not know whether my affection for these great men springs from the fact that I discern in them an all-revealing mirror of the Persian race, or whether my love for the Persian people arises from my having seen its emotions incarnated in them. However the case may be, one of the attributes of Firdausī to which I would draw special attention is that his patriotism and partisanship for all things Persian, though standing at the peak of perfection, is not based on self-worship or narrow-mindedness or xenophobia. His only hostility is for evil and wickedness. He loves utterly the whole of the human race; his compassionate heart bleeds for every man who is unfortunate or afflicted, whether he be kinsman or stranger, and he draws a lesson from his experience. He never rejoices over the unhappiness of anyone, even if he be an enemy. He does not despise or belittle any people or party; he does not show hatred or malice towards any community. . . . My final recommendation to you is simply this: Read the *Shāh-nāma*. Read it from beginning to end, even though its end is not so very pleasant!'

These words written by a modern Persian who was both profoundly steeped in Persian culture, and played a leading part in his nation's affairs, deserve to be pondered with attention and respect: they reveal, better than many chapters of erudite criticism, the authentic Persian attitude to the nature and function of poetry. The criteria Furūghī sets up will perhaps be considered defective, even at times immature, by western readers accustomed to other and more complex standards of judgment. But if one wishes to understand and appreciate what Persian poets and writers have been trying to do down the centuries, it is juster to assess their achievements against the background of their traditions and ideals, than according to the impact made by their productions upon our so differently conditioned minds. Even less has one the right to pontificate upon the merits and shortcomings of Persian literature, if one's knowledge of it is confined to what may be gleaned from translations. Nevertheless some lustre of Firdausī's glowing style succeeds in shining through the dull vessel of scholars' versions (for no poet has yet attempted him), and the European reader has a sufficiently wide variety of these to choose between. In English the most successful experiment so far is still that made early last century by J. Atkinson, and his rendering of the episode of Suhrāb and Rustam can be enjoyed by those familiar with Matthew Arnold's later free treatment of that noble theme. The passage following describes

Rustam's recognition of his son Suhrāb after he has fatally wounded him in single combat.

The loosened mail unfolds the bracelet bright,
Unhappy gift! to Rustem's wildered sight;
Prostrate he falls—'By my unnatural hand,
My son, my son is slain—and from the land
Uprooted.' Frantic, in the dust his hair
He rends in agony and deep despair;
The western sun had disappeared in gloom,
And still the Champion wept his cruel doom;
His wondering legions marked the long delay,
And, seeing Rakush riderless astray,
The rumour quick to Persia's Monarch spread,
And there described the mighty Rustem dead.
Káús, alarmed, the fatal tidings hears;
His bosom quivers with increasing fears.
'Speed, speed, and see what has befallen to-day
To cause these groans and tears—what fatal fray!
If he be lost, if breathless on the ground,
And this young warrior with the conquest crowned—
Then must I, humbled, from my kingdom torn,
Wander like Jemshíd, through the world forlorn.'
  The army roused, rushed o'er the dusty plain,
Urged by the Monarch to revenge the slain;
Wild consternation saddened every face,
Tús winged with horror sought the fatal place,
And there beheld the agonizing sight—
The murderous end of that unnatural fight.
Sohráb, still breathing, hears the shrill alarms,
His gentle speech suspends the clang of arms:
'My light of life now fluttering sinks in shade,
Let vengeance sleep, and peaceful vows be made.
Beseech the King to spare this Tartar host,
For they are guiltless, all to them is lost;

I led them on, their souls with glory fired,
While mad ambition all my thoughts inspired.
In search of thee, the world before my eyes,
War was my choice, and thou the sacred prize;
With thee, my sire! in virtuous league combined,
No tyrant King should persecute mankind.
That hope is past—the storm has ceased to rave—
My ripening honours wither in the grave;
Then let no vengeance on my comrades fall,
Mine was the guilt, and mine the sorrow, all;
How often have I sought thee—oft my mind
Figured thee to my sight—o'erjoyed to find
My mother's token; disappointment came,
When thou deniedst thy lineage and thy name;
Oh! still o'er thee my soul impassioned hung,
Still to my Father fond affection clung!
But Fate, remorseless, all my hopes withstood,
And stained thy reeking hands in kindred blood.'
His faltering breath protracted speech denied:
Still from his eyelids flowed a gushing tide;
Through Rustem's soul redoubled horror ran,
Heart-rending thoughts subdued the mighty man.
And now, at last, with joy-illumined eye,
The Zábul bands their glorious Chief descry;
But when they saw his pale and haggard look,
Knew from what mournful cause he gazed and shook,
With downcast mien they moaned and wept aloud;
While Rustem thus addressed the weeping crowd:
'Here ends the war! let gentle peace succeed,
Enough of death, I—I have done the deed!'
Then to his brother, groaning deep, he said:
'Oh what a curse upon a parent's head!
But go—and to the Tartar say—no more
Let war between us steep the earth with gore.'

THREE

The Ghaznavids and Early Saljūqs

'Sulṭān Maḥmud was such a king, that his name stands as a frontispiece to the scroll of world-empire by reason of his noble qualities and proud exploits; the robe of glory and grandeur was richly embroidered by his virtues and triumphs. From the centre of his kingdom, like a circle's circumference he encompassed all the climes of earth; his bidding and forbidding embraced in absolute authority every land and sea. Omnipotent as heaven straddling the earth, the whole world shone in the reflected splendour of his sun. Though his lofty zeal was dedicated to the cause of showing forth the truth and raising high the banners of Islam, so that by its mighty aid many thousands of pagan temples were converted into mosques and shrines where true believers might worship, and though he conquered the greater part of India and the evidences of his triumph are plain to see in all those territories, despite all these preoccupations he did not neglect for a moment to care for the learned and the eminent. For their conversation he entertained a sincere passion, and he always sought every occasion to associate with them. He lavished noble gifts and splendid prizes upon poets, so that inevitably every one according to the limits of his capacity strove to immortalize his fair fame and goodly name, filling many volumes of Arabic and Persian verse and prose with the record of his laudable attributes and mighty achievements.'

Muḥammad 'Aufī's sonorous periods echo the chorus of extravagant adulation to which the supplanter of the Sāmānids complacently listened in his gorgeous palace at Ghazna. The tale is taken up again by Daulatshāh: 'They say that in the cavalcade of Sulṭān Maḥmūd—may God illumine his proof—four hundred appointed poets were constantly in attendance. The leader and commander of this regiment of poets was Master 'Unṣurī; all acknowledged and confessed themselves to be his pupils. He enjoyed at the Sulṭān's court the combined rank of companion and poet, and was continuously engaged in commemorating in verse the Sulṭān's progresses and campaigns. . . . Sulṭān Maḥmūd finally invested Master 'Unṣurī with the title of laureate of his domains, ordaining that every poet and every man gifted with eloquence dwelling within his territories should submit his compositions first to Master 'Unṣurī; when the Master had separated the wheat from the chaff, only then would he offer the effusion to the royal presence.'

Abu 'l-Qāsim Ḥasan ibn Aḥmad of Balkh, called 'Unṣurī, was the greatest of the panegyrists thronging Manṣūr's court. The recorded details of his life are meagre, as is usual with Persian authors; the most probable date of his death is 1050, by which time Maḥmūd, Mas'ūd, Muḥammad and Maudūd were all laid with their fathers. It would have been his authority, if the story of his appointment as literary arbiter is to be believed, which set the fashion for that multiplication of rhetorical embellishment which characterizes the poetry of the Ghaznavid and post-Ghaznavid period. In Arabic the same tendency had long since gained the upper hand; it may be that its invasion of Persian literature had been retarded by the antiquarian policy of the Sāmānids. Maḥmūd the orthodox Sunnī once more opened the floodgates of foreign influence; Ghazna developed into a greater centre of Arabic learning than Bukhārā had ever been, and Persian writers now loaded their language increasingly with Arabic words and Arabic conceits; it is significant that 'Unṣurī's contemporary Farrukhī (d. 1038) was nicknamed the Persian Mutanabbī. A typical and admired example of 'Unṣurī's euphuistic wit may be read in E. G. Browne's version of his 'Question and Answer' ode in praise of Maḥmūd's brother. The brilliance of his invention, coupled to an astonishing fluency and euphony of language, defies adequate translation: consider this description of a sword.

Chīst° ān ābī chu ātish v-āhanī chūn parniyān,
bī ravān tan-paikarī, pākīza khūn dar tan ravān?

What is that aqueous thing like fire, that steely thing like painted silk,
In form a body sans a soul, blood coursing purely through its veins?
Stir it, and it is like a stream; shake it, and it's a lightning-flash;
Hurl it, and it's an arrow sped; bend it, and it is like a bow.
Behold, it is a looking-glass besprinkled with minutest pearls;
See how the chips of diamond are interwoven in the silk!

The concluding couplet is a miracle of mesmeric eloquence; the poet has made his skilful transition, converting a descriptive poem into a royal panegyric.

Shādi ū shāhī tu dārī: shād° bāsh ū shāh° bāsh!
Jāma-yí shādī tu pūsh, ū nāma-yí shāhī tu khvān!

Kingship and happiness are yours: be happy then, and be a king!
Put on the robe of happiness, recite the scroll of royalty!

With 'Unṣurī the names of three other poets are closely associated: Farrukhī, Minūchihrī and Asadī. E. G. Browne has given clever metrical versions of the most celebrated odes of all three: Farrukhī's brilliant picture of the branding of the colts, Minūchihrī's ingenious description of a candle, and Asadī's curious 'strife-poem' in which Night and Day are depicted as competing in a kind of medieval disputation. Minūchihrī in the course of his ode pays a striking and doubtless rewarding compliment to Maḥmūd's laureate.

'Unṣurí, the greatest master of the day in this our art,
Soul of faith, of stainless honour, great in wisdom, pure in
heart,
He whose voice is like his wit, alike original and free;
While his wit is like his verse in grace and spontaneity.

Another of Minūchihrī's panegyrics begins with a remarkable bacchic sequence enigmatically describing a vat of wine.

'Jamshīd's daughter is living yet':
So I read in a book to-day;
'Above eight hundred years it will be
In her prison she doth stay.
In the house of the worshippers of fire
She stands, like a cypress-tree,
Nor sits her down, nor ever at all
On a pillow her side rests she:
Never of food nor drink she takes,
Nor her long, lone silence breaks.'

Now as I thought upon this screed,
It gave me small merriment;
Swiftly as one that maketh trial
To that ancient house I went,
And I saw a house all of black stone,
Like a hoop its passage bent.
With magic craft I opened the door,
And thief-like a fire I lit;
A lamp I took, like a dagger's head
Golden the shine of it.
And in the house I saw there stood
A doll, full huge and round
Like a standing camel; by God's grace
No gold or gems I found,

But earthen girdles seven or eight,
And a fine veil o'er its head,
Its belly swollen, as great with child,
Its brow like a palm outspread.
Much dust was gathered upon its brow,
On its head was a clay crown put,
Thick as an elephant's thigh its neck,
Round as a shield its foot.

As a sister unto a sister runs,
So fondly I ran to her,
And I gently took from her brow the veil
Finer than gossamer.
With my sleeve I softly swept her face
Of the dust and ashes grey;
Like a warrior's helmet from her head
I lifted the crown of clay.
Beneath the crown was a mouth agape,
And a throat below the mouth,
And her lips were thick as a negro's lips,
Or a camel's in the drowth;
Sweet musk was her breath, as frankincense
Smoked in a brazier.
With the love of a dark-eyed fairy fey
I was seized by the wine of her,
And I ravished her, my maiden fair,
And a cup of her wine I drew
Whereof on my palm trickled a drop
Till my palm as Kausar grew;
And I smelt my wrist, and of that scent
Jasmined my every hair;
And I set my lips to the goblet's rim,
And sweetness I tasted there.

Asadī, who seems to have specialized in the *tenzone* style—

an ancient convention, still practised even to-day—is probably to be distinguished from another Asadī (though some have doubted the distinction), son of the older poet and author of an epic *Garshāsp-nāma* which was completed in 1066. The younger Asadī also compiled a *Persian Lexicon* of great philological interest and some literary value, in that it contains brief quotations from early poets whose work is otherwise lost. By chance we possess a specimen of his handwriting, for it was he who transcribed in 1056 the precious Vienna manuscript of the *Pharmacology* of Abū Manṣūr Muvaffaq, itself one of the earliest examples of Persian scientific prose.

Farrukhī was without doubt the most gifted of 'Unṣurī's 'disciples': a native of Sīstān, he joined Maḥmūd's entourage after serving his apprenticeship at the provincial court of Chaghāniyān. He composed a large quantity of panegyric and descriptive poetry of high quality, much of which has survived. It has often been stated that he performed an equally notable service to letters by compiling the earliest treatise in Persian on rhetoric, but the *Tarjumān al-balāgha* generally credited to him has recently been proved to be the work of a later and much more obscure author. Farrukhī is admired for the elegance of his amatory sequences and his mastery in describing natural scenes; his picture of a sudden storm, the prelude to a famous ode in praise of Maḥmūd, is considered to be without equal.

An indigo-tinted cloud came up from over an indigo-tinted sea,
swirling around like a lover's thoughts, distraught like the mind of a lovelorn lad;
there in the midst of the sleeping waves a sudden, twisting torrent surged,
dark and astonished as the dust spinning about a squall of wind.
Down it rained; then it split apart and hurtled headlong through the sky,
a herd of elephants stampeding, lost in an indigo wilderness.

A tenderer mood is revealed in his lovely elegiac verses.

Loving in the time of youth—
That is happiness, in sooth;
Happiness, at love to play
With the lovely all the day;
Happiness, to sit apart
With companions of one heart,
And in harmony divine
To imbibe the purple wine.
Best it is in youth for thee
To be loving instantly,
Since, when thou art aged grown,
All thy virtue will be gone.
To be young, and wary of
The intemperance of love—
What is that, if it not be
Weariness, and misery?
If a man be young and strong,
And not love the whole day long,
O the pity and the ruth
Of the season of his youth!

While the scientist Bīrūnī was well content to serve Maḥmūd and to write exclusively in Arabic, the philosopher Ibn Sīnā (Avicenna), who had once enjoyed the favour of the Sāmānids and scorned to transfer his allegiance to conforming Ghazna, though using Arabic for most of his voluminous output also composed an encyclopaedia in Persian. The *Dānish-nāma-yi 'Alā'ī*, dedicated to 'Alā' al-Dīn of the short-lived Kākūyid dynasty whose Prime Minister he was at the time of his death in 1037, shows Avicenna as a coiner of many Persian philosophical terms, most of which were afterwards rejected in favour of the dominant Arabic. His Persian style is as free and lucid as his Arabic; it belongs however to the history of philosophy rather than of literature. The gigantic *Dhakhīra-yi Khvārizmshāhī* of a later age, along with the anonymous *Ḥudūd al-ʻālam*, though interesting as specimens of how Persian prose served the needs of physicians and geographers, hardly rank as examples of *belles lettres*.

The middle of the eleventh century saw the appearance of three important historical works. The emergence of the Saljūqs encouraged an unknown author to write a *History of Sīstān*; a later hand or hands continued it down to the fourteenth century. The original core of the book resembles the prose of Balʻamī; its unpretentious simplicity gives it a refreshing charm, as in the account of the birth of the prophet Muḥammad. The words are put into the mouth of Ḥalīma, Muḥammad's nurse; the author's Arabic source was the lost *History* of Muḥammad ibn Mūsā al-Khwārizmī the mathematician (d. *circa* 850) which Ṭabarī had also used; the percentage of Arabic words in his vocabulary is between six and seven.

'In that year there was a great famine, and I suffered much. On the night of Muḥammad's birth I dreamed that an angel seized me and carried me into the air, and I saw a spring of water the like of which I had never seen before. The angel said, "Drink of this," and I drank. He said, "Drink again," and I drank again. He said, "Now your milk will become plentiful. A suckling is coming to you who is the Lord of former and of latter men." Then I awoke, and saw that my milk was plentiful and my strength great; no trace of hunger remained in me. The next day the women of the Banū Saʻd said to me, "Ḥalīma, to-day you will be like the daughter of a king!" I said nothing, till I went to the mountain to search for fuel and dried grass. After a time a voice proclaimed, "Why don't you go to Mecca and the Sacred Territory, and take the Lord of former and of latter men and give him milk, so that your labours may be good in both worlds?" Those women, and I too with them, came down and set off on the road. At every point that I lagged behind alone, all the herbs and stones would say to me, "You have found the best of created beings; now fear no more!" By the time I came down all the women of the Banū Sa'd had gone off towards Mecca. I said to my friend, "We must also go." I had a she-ass; I sat on it and went, I and my companion, towards Mecca. By the time I reached there these women were already gone into Mecca and had seized every child that had a mother and a father. I saw a majestic-looking man, tall as a date-tree, who came out of the midst of the mountain. He said to me, "Ḥalīma, that has remained for you. Seek out the Lord of the Arabs." Then when I arrived there I said to my companion, "Who is the Lord of the Arabs?" She said, " 'Abd al-Muṭṭalib." Then I went into Mecca. I saw the women who had seized the children of Quraish; each had found something and returned. I saw 'Abd al-Muṭṭalib who said, "Which of the women of the Banū Sa'd is it who will nourish my child?" I said, "I am the one." He said, "What's your name?" I said, "Ḥalīma." He said, "Fine, fine! Truly you'll nourish him." I said, "Though he hasn't any father, this dream and what I've seen with my own eyes and what I've been told can't be wrong." I went with him, and he sweeping the ground with his skirts went on before me to Āmina's apartment. He opened the door, so that I would have said the door of Paradise was opened, so sweet was the scent. He brought me in. I saw Āmina like the full moon or a glittering star. They took me into that apartment. The sweet perfume came to my head, so that I said, "Perhaps I was dead and have now returned to life, and this is the Spirit." I looked, and saw Muḥammad asleep wrapped in white wool, that you'd have known at once was never made by mortal hands, and folded in green silk; the scent and sheen of every garment proclaimed it to be the handiwork of God, not of any created being. He was fast asleep. When I saw that light and radiance of his, I wanted to lay down my life before him. I hadn't the heart to wake him. I wanted to put my breast against his lips. He laughed and opened his eyes; a light came forth from his eyes and mounted to heaven. I became stupified, and kissed him between the eyes, and gave him my right breast. He drank. I wanted to give him my left breast; he refused, and didn't take it.'

It was in the reign of Sulṭān Farrukhzād (d. 1059) that Abu 'l-Faḍl Muḥammad ibn Ḥusain Baihaqī (996–1077) composed the greater part of his thirty-volume *History of the Ghaznavids*; of this one-sixth has survived, covering the reign of Sulṭān Mas'ūd I (1030–41). Baihaqī was a civil servant for most of his active life; yet his style was not corrupted by the tortuous phraseology so popular in government offices. An equal simplicity invests the *Zain al-akhbār* of Abū Sa'īd 'Abd al-Ḥaiy ibn Ḍaḥḥāk Gardīzī, a succint history of Persia with excursuses on related topics, which was composed while 'Abd al-Rashīd (1049–53) was on the Ghaznavid throne. The following extract is Gardīzī's description of how Ya'qūb the Ṣaffārid took Nīshāpūr in 873.

'When Ya'qūb reached Farhādhān, three stages from Nīshāpūr, Muḥammad's generals and cousins came out to meet him and did him obeisance, all except Ibrāhīm ibn Aḥmad, and Ya'qūb came with them to Nīshāpūr. Then Muḥammad ibn Ṭāhir sent Ibrāhīm ibn Ṣāliḥ al-Marwazī to Ya'qūb with this message: "If you have come to me by order of the Commander of the Faithful, present your credentials so that I may hand the province over to you. If not, then go back." When the messenger reached Ya'qūb and delivered the message, Ya'qūb drew out his sword from under his prayer-mat saying, "This is my charter and my standard." So Ya'qūb came to Nīshāpūr and alighted at Shādhiyākh. He seized Muḥammad and brought him before him and reviled him much; he took all his treasuries. This capture of Muḥammad was on 2 Shauwāl of the year 259. Then Ya'qūb summoned Ibrāhīm ibn Aḥmad and said, "All the retinue came out to meet me. Why didn't you come?" Ibrāhīm said, "God save the Prince! I hadn't the honour of knowing you, otherwise I'd have come out to meet you or sent a letter. I hadn't any grievance against Amīr Muḥammad, that I should desert him, and I didn't think it right to betray my liege lord. Treachery was no way to repay him and his father." This pleased Ya'qūb; he honoured him and made him stand near him saying, "I need subjects like you." As for those who had gone out to greet him, he amerced them and seized all their goods.'

Avicenna's invention of Persian philosophical prose opened the way for further developments in the exploitation of the national language. The time had not yet come for theology proper to be written in Persian; but towards 1050 Abu 'l-Ḥasan 'Alī ibn 'Uthmān of Ghazna, better known as Hujvīrī, composed the first treatise on mysticism in the mother tongue. The preface to his *Kashf al-maḥjūb*, which has been translated by R. A. Nicholson, throws light on the piratical practices of those early times, when the writing of a book was evidently so much of a rarity as to make literary theft a worthwhile crime. 'Two considerations have impelled me to put my name at the beginning of the book: one particular, the other general. As regards the latter, when persons ignorant of this science see a new book, in which the author's name is not set down in several places, they attribute his work to themselves, and thus the author's aim is defeated, since books are compiled, composed, and written only to the end that the author's name may be kept alive and that readers and students may pronounce a blessing on him. This misfortune has already befallen me twice. A certain individual borrowed my poetical works, of which there was no other copy, and retained the manuscript in his possession, and circulated it, and struck out my name which stood at its head, and caused all my labour to be lost. May God forgive him! I also composed another book, entitled *The Highway of Religion*, on the method of Ṣúfiism—may God make it flourish! A shallow pretender, whose words carry no weight, erased my name from the title page and gave out to the public that he was the author, notwithstanding that connoisseurs laughed at his assertion. God, however, brought home to him the unblessedness of this act and erased *his* name from the register of those who seek to enter the Divine portal.'

Works on Ṣūfism had hitherto been written exclusively in Arabic, and it fell to Hujvīrī to invent Persian equivalents for many technical terms; yet his vocabulary contains a considerably higher proportion of Arabic words than that of the contemporary historians. This was inevitable in dealing with a subject of such a specialized kind; but one may also remark in Hujvīrī's theoretical discussions a trend towards a greater complexity of style. Glancing towards the later years of the century, it is convenient to notice here the Persian writings of another mystic, who also composed in Arabic. Abū Ismā'īl 'Abd Allāh ibn Muḥammad al-Anṣārī, who was born at Quhandiz in 1005 and died at Harāt in 1088, is famous as the author of a very concise sketch of the Ṣūfī path entitled *Manāzil al-sā'irīn*; this treatise was written in Arabic, and has attracted the attention of numerous commentators. In Persian he compiled a biographical dictionary of saints and mystics called the *Ṭabaqāt al-ṣūfīya*, basing himself upon the Arabic work of Abū 'Abd al-Raḥmān al-Sulamī (d. 1021); this text, as yet unpublished, is of much philological interest since it was composed in the old dialect spoken about Harāt in his time. Anṣārī's most popular book however is his *Munājāt*, a small but charming collection of prayers in rhymed and rhythmical prose interspersed with short poems. The following version of its opening passage imitates this style, which afterwards enjoyed a long vogue.

Thou, Whose breath is sweetest perfume to the spent and anguished heart,
Thy remembrance to Thy lovers bringeth ease for every smart.
Multitudes like Moses, reeling, cry to earth's remotest place:
'Give me sight, O Lord!' they clamour, seeking to behold Thy face.
Multitudes no man has numbered, lovers, and afflicted all,
Stumbling on the way of anguish, 'Allah! Allah!' loudly call.

And the fire of separation sears the heart and burns the breast,
And their eyes are wet with weeping for a love that gives not rest.
'Poverty's my pride'—Thy lovers raise to heav'n their battle-cry,
Gladly meeting men's derision, letting all the world go by.
Such a fire of passion's potion Pīr-i Anṣār quaffing feels
That distraught, like Lailā's lover, through a ruined world he reels.

O Generous, Who bounty givest!
O Wise, Who sins forgivest!
O Eternal, Who to our senses comest not near!
O One, Who art in essence and quality without peer!
O Powerful, Who of Godhead worthy art!
O Creator, Who showest the way to every erring heart!
To my soul give Thou of Thy own spotlessness,
and to my eyes of Thy own luminousness;
and unto us, of Thy bounty and goodness, whatever may be best
make Thou that Thy bequest!

O Lord, in mercy grant my soul to live,
And patience grant, that hurt I may not grieve:
How shall I know what thing is best to seek?
Thou only knowest: what Thou knowest, give!

Meanwhile another and more gifted writer, one of the greatest of the Persian poets, had also been using prose for philosophical and religious purposes. Abū Mu'īn Nāṣir ibn Khusrau ibn Ḥārith, famous as Nāṣir-i Khusrau, was born in 1003 at Qubādhiyān, a village in the district of Balkh. A Shī'ite by upbringing, he nevertheless obtained employment in the Saljūq government of Khurāsān. In 1050, as he relates, he saw the Prophet in a dream and was so moved by the experience that he resolved to give up wine-drinking and to make the pilgrimage to Mecca. His westward journey continued on to Egypt, at that time prosperous under the Fāṭimid anti-caliph al-Mustanṣir; there he became a convert to the Ismā'īlī sect and was promoted to the rank of Ḥujja. Full of zeal for the cause he had newly espoused, he returned to Balkh in 1053 with the ambition to win Persia to Ismā'īlism. Not unnaturally his former Saljūq employers were displeased with his missionary activities; he fled for his life, which he preserved for a few years in the mountains of Badakhshān; there he died in 1060 or 1061. In a poem written in premature old age he cried:

> Look not upon this feeble body of mine, for my written words excel in number yonder sphere with its complement of stars.

This boast did not lack for substance altogether. In poetry Nāṣir-i Khusrau is credited with 30,000 verses, of which more than 11,000 are extant; in prose he wrote some fifteen books, many recovered and published in recent years. The great bulk of his verse is cast in the form of lengthy odes; but whereas his predecessors had employed this instrument to play elaborate paeans to kings and princes, his panegyric was directed towards very different themes—the unity and majesty of God, the religious life, the pursuit of virtue, the praise of good learning and good doing. To these topics he dedicated unwearyingly his poetic skill; his odes taken in large samples make monotonous reading, but he was undoubtedly a supreme master of his chosen medium, and Persian critics rightly acclaim him as one of the greatest poets of their language. 'Despite all differences of individual inclination and preference, despite the general divergence of opinion entertained by people on most matters, practically all are agreed on this one question; that the greatest poets of the Persian language since the coming of Islam to the present time (each one in his special variety) are the six following—Firdausī, Khaiyām, Anvarī, Rūmī, Sa'dī, Ḥāfiẓ. In my view, one can confidently add to these six the great philosopher Nāṣir-i Khusrau, since all the characteristic merits and artistic qualities that have established these six in the front rank of Persian poets are completely and in every respect present in the poems of Nāṣir-i Khusrau.' That was the verdict delivered by Mīrzā Muḥammad Qazvīnī, and his judgment commands unquestioning assent. The technical virtuosity of Nāṣir-i Khusrau is dazzling in the extreme; no other poet has shown a greater rhyming dexterity, none has written clearer, richer or purer Persian. These are qualities which unfortunately vanish in translation; and that lofty sententiousness, expressed in prolific eloquence, which commends him so highly to his compatriots appeals less strongly to western taste. His *Raushanā'ī-nāma*, a long moralizing sequence in rhyming couplets which looks back to Abū Shakūr's *Āfarīn-nāma* and forward to the *Būstān* of Sa'dī, resists successful interpretation as stubbornly as the *Būstān* itself. This is the section on self-knowledge:

Know yourself; for if you know yourself
you will also know the difference between good and evil.
First become intimate with your own inner being,
then become the commander of the whole company.
When you know yourself, you know everything;
when you know that, you have escaped from all evil.
You don't know your own worth, because you are like
  this;
you see God Himself, if you see yourself.
The nine spheres and seven stars are your slaves,
yet you are your body's servant: that's a pity!
Don't be fettered to bestial pleasures
if you are a seeker of that supreme blessedness.
Be a real man, and abandon sleep and feasting;
pilgrim-like, make a journey into yourself.
What are sleep and feasting? The business of brute
  beasts;
it is by knowledge that your soul subsists.
Be wakeful for once: how long have you been sleeping?
Look at yourself: you're something wonderful enough.
Reflect now; regard from where you've come
and why you are now in this prison.

Break the cage; depart to your own celestial station;
be an idol-breaker like Abraham, Azar's son.
You were created after this fashion for a purpose;
it will be a shame, if you neglect that purpose.
It is a shame for an angel to take orders from a devil;
it is a shame for a king to be servant to a doorkeeper.
Why must Jesus be blind?
It is wrong for Karun to be one-eyed.
You have snakes coiled over your treasure:
kill those snakes, and be free of pain.
But if you feed them, you will become fearful,
you'll have nothing of that boundless treasure.
There's a treasure in your house, yet you're a beggar;
you've a salve in your hand, yet your heart is wounded.
You are asleep; how will you reach journey's end?
You weave charms, and are heedless of the treasure.
Quick, break the charm and take the treasure:
take a little pains, and rid yourself of pain.

The remark that 'it is a shame for an angel to take orders from a devil' appears in its context to be nothing extraordinary; it is only when we set it beside a passage in Nāṣir-i Khusrau's *Jāmi' al-ḥikmatain*—a long prose essay to reconcile reason and revelation—that its wider significance becomes apparent. 'It is the rational soul in every man that is the potential angel, and the potential soul is a fairy, as we have said. The appetitive and passionate souls in every person are a pair of potential demons. Every man whose rational soul brings his passionate and appetitive souls to obedience becomes an angel; every man whose passionate and appetitive souls control his rational soul becomes an actual demon. This is what the Prophet meant when he said, "Every man has two devils that beguile him." He was asked, "O Prophet, do you also have these two demons?" He replied, "I had two devils, but God succoured me against them and they surrendered." We have therefore made it clear that in every man there is an angel and a demon, while he himself is a fairy. The demon was not created by God, but owes its existence to man's disobedience. Fairies are potential angels, and become actual angels by obedience; they also become actual demons by disobedience. Men are thus potential angels and potential demons; and the other world is full of actual angels and actual demons.'

Nāṣir-i Khusrau's best-known prose work is his *Safar-nāma*, a fascinating account of his journey to Egypt, available to readers of French in C. Schefer's version, and partly rendered into English by G. Le Strange. His other books are of a more limited appeal, though of great importance to students of Islamic philosophy and sectarian theology. His style resembles that of Avicenna, yet he would have had at his disposal an even older model; for we now possess in the *Kashf al-maḥjūb* of Abū Ya'qūb Sijistānī a specimen of Persian Ismā'īlī prose going back to the tenth century. It is however by his odes that Nāṣir-i Khusrau proves his title to greatness; the following version shows him treating an unusual subject.

The pilgrims came with reverence,
grateful for the mercy of God the Merciful,
came to Mecca from 'Arafāt
crying the pilgrim *Labbaika* of reverence.
Weary of the toil and trial of Hejaz,
delivered out of hell and dire chastisement,
pilgrimage accomplished, visitation done
back they returned home, safe and sound.
I went out awhile to welcome them,
thrusting my foot outside my blanket.
In the midst of the caravan there came
a friend of mine, true and well-beloved.
I said to him, 'Tell me how you escaped
out of this journey of anguish and fear.
When I remained behind from you so long
repining was always the companion of my thoughts.

I am happy, now you have made the pil-
  grimage;
  there is none like you in all this region.
Tell me now, after what manner did you
  hallow that most holy sanctuary?
When you resolved to put on pilgrim garb
  with what intention did you robe yourself?
Had you forbidden to yourself all things
  save only one, the Almighty Maker?'
'No,' he replied. I said, 'Did you cry
  Labbaika knowingly and with reverence?
Did you hear the summoning voice of God
  and so answer as did Moses before you?'
'No,' he replied. I said, 'When on 'Arafāt
  you stood, and made offering unto God,
did you know God, and unknow yourself?
  Did the breeze of gnosis then blow on you?'
'No,' he replied. I said, 'When you went
  into the Sanctuary, like the men of the Cave,
were you secure from your own soul's evil,
  the pangs of burning, the anguish of Hell?'
'No,' he replied. I said, 'When you cast
  your handful of stones at the accursed Satan,
did you then cast utterly from yourself
  all evil habits and blameworthy acts?'
'No,' he replied. I said, 'When you slew
  the sheep for the sake of captive and orphan,
did you first see God near, and slay
  in sacrifice your mean and worthless soul?'
'No,' he replied. I said, 'When you stood
  high on the hill where Abraham once prayed,
did you then truly in faith sure and certain
  surrender to God your most inward self?'
'No,' he replied. I said, 'When you circled
  the Holy House, running like an ostrich,

did you remember the holy angels
all circling about the mighty Throne of God?'
'No,' he replied. I said, 'When you hastened
from Safa to Marwa, hurrying to and fro,
did you see in your soul's glass all creation,
was your heart heedless of Hell and Heaven?'
'No,' he replied. I said, 'When you returned,
your heart torn at forsaking the Kaaba,
did you then commit your self to the tomb,
are you now as if already your bones crumbled?'
'Of all whereon you have spoken,' he answered,
'I knew nothing, whether well or ill.'
'Then, friend,' I said, 'you have made no pilgrimage;
you did not dwell in the station of effacement.
You went; you saw Mecca; you returned,
purchasing for much silver the toil of the desert.
If hereafter you would be pilgrim again,
let it be so as I have now taught you.'

The period which saw the beginnings of prose literature on mysticism also witnessed the first Ṣūfī outpouring in Persian verse. The earliest poets were of no great productivity, or at all events their compositions have not survived in any considerable quantity. Concerning Abū Sa'īd ibn Abi 'l-Khair (967–1049) it has been questioned by an eminent authority whether we have any genuine poetry of his at all, though more than six hundred poems have been published in his name. 'It is doubtful,' states R. A. Nicholson in his valuable monograph on this saint, 'whether Abū Sa'īd is the author of any of these poems, and we may be sure that in the main they are not his work and were never even quoted by him. To repeat what has been already said, they form a miscellaneous anthology drawn from a great number of poets who flourished at different periods, and consequently they reflect the typical ideas of Persian mysticism as a whole.' Nevertheless in recent years the Persian scholar Sa'īd Nafīsī has defended the authenticity of several hundreds of these poems, which he has collected in print.

The problem is all the more interesting, and involved, because the poems are composed in the form called *rubāʿī* (quatrain), so familiar to western readers through FitzGerald's famous paraphrase of ʿUmar Khaiyām. The legend of the origin of this uniquely Persian creation has been told often, but merits repetition. Shams-i Qais the prosodist, writing in 1220, relates that one of the early Persian poets—'I think it was Rūdakī, but God knows best'—was walking one festival day in a pleasure garden at Ghazna, and paused to join a crowd of idlers watching some children playing at nuts. His attention was particularly engaged by a handsome boy of ten to fifteen years 'with ringlets and cheeks like hyacinths twined about anemones,' who presently threw a walnut along a groove in such a way that it jumped out, and then rolled back again. The child thereupon shouted, '*Ghaltān ghaltān hamī ravad tā bun-i gau.*' The poet recognized in the cry the invention of a new metre of the *hazaj* group; by repeating the hemistich four times, with the appropriate rhyming, he produced the *rubāʿī*. Daulatshāh, who tells much the same story, takes the incident back to a century earlier and improbably identifies the child-inventor with a son of Yaʿqūb ibn Laith (d. 879) the founder of the Ṣaffārid dynasty.

Whatever the truth behind all this may be, there seems no doubt that by the end of the tenth century the *rubāʿī* had established itself as a great favourite, especially for extempore composition. The poem could be used for all manner of subjects and occasions. 'Noble and commoner alike were entranced by this form, scholar and illiterate equally enamoured of this poetry; ascetic and reprobate each had a share in it, pious and wicked each had an affection for it.' Such is Shams-i Qais's account, and he adds: 'Men of crooked temperament, who could not make out verse from prose, and had no knowledge of metre and stress, found an excuse in the song for dancing; men whose hearts were dead, so that they could not distinguish between the melody of the pipes and the braying of a donkey, and were removed a thousand leagues from the delight of the lute's strains, were ready to yield up their souls for a quatrain. Many a cloistered girl there is who out of passion for a song has broken to pieces the door and wall of her chastity; many a matron out of love for a quatrain has loosed the warp and woof of her continence.' Yet if legend and Sa'īd Nafīsī (reverting to Ethé's view) are to be believed, it was the pious and ascetic Abū Sa'īd who first composed *rubā'īyāt* on a large scale; specimens of these verses may be read in E. G. Browne's *Literary History of Persia.*

The *rubā'ī*, as has been stated, is marked off from all other poetry by its unique and complicated rhythm. Another form of quatrain, called *dū-baitī*, having the same A A B A rhyming-scheme but a simpler version of the *hazaj* metre, was employed by a wandering mystic of Abū Sa'īd's times called Bābā Ṭāhir 'the Naked.' His poems exhibit the further peculiarity of being composed in a rustic dialect; in this respect they resemble the seven hundred popular songs in the same metre collected and published by the modern scholar Kūhī Kirmānī. But whereas these anonymous quatrains display the same variety of themes which Shams-i Qais observed seven centuries ago, Bābā Ṭāhir played on only one string, and that doleful; he was the distracted lover of God whose sufferings wrung from him a monotonous protest.

A nameless, homeless braggart,
  A Kalendar am I:
By day the world's my parish,
  At night with weary sigh
  On bed of stones I lie.

No moth e'er knew such burning,
  No madman bore such dree:
Ants have their nests for shelter,
  For serpents holes there be,
  But roof is none for me.

The stony earth for pillow,
For coverlet the air;
My only sin was loving—
Do all Thy lovers share
This torment that I bear?

The art of Abū Sa'īd and Bābā Ṭāhir was natural and unforced, though within a very narrow scale conforming to the conventional imagery already accepted. Much greater poets graced the royal audiences of the early Saljūqs and the minor dynasts of their age; their work will be considered in the following chapter. Here will be noticed four important prose-works all composed in the last years of the eleventh or the early years of the twelfth century. First is one of the most remarkable documents in Persian literature, a treatise on the art of government written by a man who served for many years as Prime Minister of a powerful kingdom. Niẓām al-Mulk, vizier successively to Alp Arslān (d. 1072) and his son Malik Shāh (d. 1092), not only secured the political stability of the house he served but also promoted an ambitious programme of religious education aimed at destroying the insidious propaganda of the Isma'īlīs and re-establishing the paramountcy of orthodox Sunnī doctrine. It was therefore natural that he should be singled out as a prime target by the fanatical Assassins, who contrived his murder in October 1092. He left behind him, in addition to a number of well-endowed academies and schools, the political testament generally known as the *Siyāsat-nāma*. This work, composed in the last year of his life, is made up of fifty chapters of advice to rulers, varied with illustrative anecdotes; it has been characterized as 'in a sense a survey of what he had failed to accomplish' as vizier. Niẓām al-Mulk's prose is 'a mixture between the *History* of Bal'amī and the *History* of Baihaqī.' This is the diagnosis of Muḥammad Taqī Bahār, who picks on the following passage as exhibiting a masterly economy of style: 'Nūḥ said to his father, "Mount, and let us both proceed to the palace of the commander-in-chief and take with us the huntsman's bag (in which the head of the rebellious commander had been placed). Then do you in the presence of the generals disembarrass yourself of the kingship and make me your heir, so that I may answer them and the kingship may remain in our house, for this army will never come to terms with you; then at least you will die a natural death." ' A longer quotation gives a clearer idea of the contents of this typically Persian book; the author is speaking on the need of the ruler to consult with men of learning and mature years, and it is not difficult to recognize that it was in his own direction that he was pointing.

'To take counsel in one's affairs is a mark of strongmindedness, perfect intelligence and common prudence. Every man has some knowledge, and every man knows something, but one man knows more, another less; one man possesses a certain knowledge but has had no practical experience, while another man possesses the same knowledge and has gained practical experience as well. It is just the same with medicine: one man has read in a book how to treat pains and ailments and knows by heart the names of all those remedies, but nothing more; another man knows the same remedies, but has also tried them out and tested them many times. The former will never be as good as the latter. Similarly one man has made many journeys and seen much of the world; he has tasted warm and cold in plenty, and has been in the middle of things. It is impossible for him to be equalled by the other man who has never travelled, never seen foreign parts, never been in the middle of things. That is why they have said that it is necessary to govern with the help of men of learning and mature years who have seen the world. Besides, one man has a quicker wit and can see into things rapidly, while another man is slow of understanding. The wise have said that single-handed government is like the strength of a single man; two-man government is like the strength of two; ten-man government is like the strength of ten; the more, the stronger. One man's strength is less than that of two men; in the same way government by ten men is stronger than government by three. It is generally agreed that of all who have ever lived, none has excelled in wisdom the Prophet (God bless him and grant him peace); he could see as well behind as before, indeed nothing in earth and heaven was hidden from him—Throne, Carpet, Tablet, Pen, Heaven, Hell and all. Gabriel was constantly coming to him with revelations from God, informing him what was and what was not. Yet despite all these advantages and miraculous powers that he possessed, God Most High said to him:

"And take counsel with them in the affair."

'Seeing that the Prophet himself was bidden to take counsel, how can you possibly not need advice?'

Niẓām al-Mulk completed his *Siyāsat-nāma* in 1092, very shortly before his death. Ten years earlier a man of lighter weight but also lighter wit had finished writing a somewhat more cynical manual on the art of government. Kai-Kā'ūs, son of Iskandar, son of Qābūs, son of Washmgīr, a prince of the Ziyārid house that ruled south of the Caspian Sea, in the fullness of his sixty-three years decided to exercise the Persian ruler's immemorial privilege and for the benefit of his son and heir to distil into words the wisdom read in ancient books and added to by long experience. The *Qābūs-nāma* is a delightful book, richly revealing and full of shrewd asides; it can be savoured at leisure in Professor R. Levy's *A Mirror for Princes*. 'Never seek the friendship of fools; a foolish friend in his unwisdom can do such harm to you as a clever enemy could not. Rather cultivate the friendship of men who have talent, are faithful to their trust and are good-natured; you will thus become known and praised for the same virtues as those for which your friends are known and praised. Further, bear in mind that solitude is preferable to evil associates.' *C'est mieux d'être seul que mal accompagné.*

Reference has already been made to the false ascription to the poet Farrukhī of the earliest Persian treatise on rhetoric. The *Tarjumān al-balāgha*, well known in earlier times but long believed lost, has recently been rediscovered in a unique manuscript compiled in 1114. This precious codex, now edited by the Turkish scholar Ahmed Ateş, gives the name of the author as Muḥammad ibn ʿUmar al-Rādūyānī; internal evidence proves that the book could not have been written earlier than 1088. Rādūyānī states that he had never seen any work on rhetoric composed in Persian; all existing treatments of the subject known to him were in Arabic. Modelling himself upon the *Maḥāsin al-kalām* of Naṣr ibn al-Ḥasan al-Marghīnānī, an Arab poet-scholar of the eleventh century, he divided his discourse into seventy-three chapters setting forth all the varieties of rhetorical ornament employed by the poets. Rādūyānī chose his illustrations from Persian authors, so that his book has the added value of containing much old poetry otherwise unrecorded.

Nāṣir-i Khusrau had chosen Persian as his medium of propaganda, clearly desiring to secure as large a public as possible for his sectarian teaching. A similar motive must have led Abū Ḥāmid Muḥammad ibn Muḥammad al-Ghazālī (d. 1111) towards the end of his prodigiously fruitful life to compose the *Kīmiyā-yi saʿādat*, a Persian digest of his famous treatise on ascetic theology, the *Iḥyāʾ ʿulūm al-dīn*. But while Ghazālī writes a simple and fluent Persian, well calculated to attract the casual reader, it is noticeable that in using Arabic technical terms he follows Hujvīrī rather than Nāṣir-i Khusrau. His style has therefore a certain severity, an impression of erudition; yet it is by no means lacking in poetic charm. Ghazālī lightens his argument with a frequent recourse to anecdote, and shows a great fondness for and skill in the invention of apposite similes. His discussion of the mystery of the unknowableness of God is a fine example of his didactic method.

'Know, that there are two reasons why a given thing may be unknowable: either it may be covered and so not be clear, or it may be clear to such a degree that the eye cannot support it. That is why the bat sees nothing by day, but does see at night: it is not that at night things become manifest, but because by day they are exceedingly manifest, only the bat's eye is weak.

The difficulty of knowing God is therefore due to brightness: He is so bright that men's hearts have not the strength to perceive it. You will realize how bright and manifest God is from a simple analogy. If you see a line of writing or a sewn garment, nothing is clearer to you than the power, knowledge, vitality and will of the writer or the tailor; that handiwork of his reveals his inner qualities to you so clearly that you know them necessarily. If God had created nothing in the whole world except a single bird, everyone looking at it would perforce realize God's perfect knowledge, power, majesty and grandeur. That proof is more evident even than the proof which the line provides of the writer. But everything that exists—heaven, earth, living creatures, plants, stones, clods—everything that has been created or comes into the imagination and fantasy, all is of one quality and bears unanimous witness to the beauty of the Maker. And it is only because of the very abundance of proof and evidential clearness that He is hidden. If certain things only had been His handiwork and other things not, then He would have been manifest; but because all things are of one quality, He remains hidden. Consider a parallel. There is nothing brighter than the sun, for through it all things become manifest; yet if the sun did not go down by night, or if it were not veiled by reason of the shade, no one would realize that there is such a thing as light on the face of the earth. Seeing nothing but white and green and the other colours, they would say that nothing more exists. However, they have realized that light is a thing outside colours, the colours becoming manifest through it, because at night the colours are hidden, and are obscurer in the shade than in the sun: they have apprehended light through its opposite. Similarly if it were possible for the Creator to vanish out of existence, the heavens and earth would dash together and be annihilated: then they would apprehend Him of necessity. But because all things are of one quality in respect of bearing witness, and this witness is continuous and uninterrupted, God is too clear: He is hidden by His very brightness.'

FOUR

The Middle Saljūqs

THE twelfth century was the golden age of the panegyric in Persia. The profession of verbal flattery which Rūdakī had found so profitable under the Sāmānids, and 'Unṣurī and his 'school' under the Ghaznavids, rose to new heights of prosperity in the reigns of Alp Arslān, Malik Shāh, Barkiyārūq, and above all Sanjar. The lesser ruling houses of these times competed with the greater in offering prizes for men of words, and the gilded cage of singing-birds now gathered songsters from as far afield as Lahore. The long history of Indo-Persian literature opened.

Qaṭrān ibn Maḥmūd (d. 1072) served well the Saljūq nominees who governed north-western Persia. Nāṣir-i Khusrau met him on his passage through Tabrīz and remarked that 'he wrote good poetry, but did not know Persian well.' This was a prejudiced view, however, the contempt of a metropolitan for a provincial; for Qaṭrān (whose large *Dīvān* has now been published) is recognized as among the great masters of the formal ode. Jāmī, who was well qualified to judge, four centuries later observed:

> Qaṭrān was a savant of subtlety, a master of magic:
> a single drop from his pen was an ocean of mystery.

Indeed, his style is as brilliantly artificial and elaborate as the most jaded appetite for rhetorical embellishment could desire. At the same time he was skilful in descriptive verse; his picture of Tabrīz destroyed in the earthquake of 1042 is famous.

God hurled destruction upon the men of Tabrīz:
God chose for Tabrīz, instead of prosperity, ruin,
Highland was turned to lowland, lowland to highland,
the sands were turned to ashes, the ashes to sands.
The earth was rent asunder, the trees bent like bows,
the swelling waters hissed, the mountains marched.

This backward glance at early Saljūq times brings into view a poem which exercised influence beyond the frontiers of Persia. Fakhr al-Dīn As'ad Gurgānī, an otherwise obscure figure, in 1048 or thereabouts dedicated to Ṭughril's vizier Abu 'l-Fatḥ Muẓaffar the *Vīs u Rāmīn*, a romantic epic on an ancient Persian theme which was compared by Ethé with the story of Tristan and Iseult. This composition has not been translated into any European language; but a twelfth-century Georgian version was put into English by Sir Oliver Wardrop. An interesting feature of this charming poem in simple Persian is a series of ten letters addressed by Vīs to Rāmīn in which he runs through all the repertory of passionate emotions; he concludes with an eloquent benediction:

I send you blessings past all reckoning,
Blessings more numerous than the flowers of spring,
More than the sands of mountain and of plain,
More than the drops of ocean and of rain,
More than the herbs that grow on dale and hill,
The living things that land and water fill,
More than the circling days that hurry by,
More than the stars that throng the wheeling sky,
More than the multifarious seeds of earth,
The males and females owing Adam birth,
The hairs of beasts, the feathers of all birds,
The many-folio'd volume's sum of words,
More than the anxious thoughts within my heart,
More than my fantasy, my faith, my art:

I send you blessings everlastingly,
Knowing your love and your fidelity,
I send you blessings as a lover's right,
Seeing your beauty fills my soul with light.
Blessings ten thousand times as such again
I pray good fortune rain on you. Amen.

Lahore (not, as Daulatshāh alleges, Gurgān) produced a far more eminent poet in Mas'ūd-i Sa'd-i Salmān (1047–1121), who chose the more orthodox and lucrative medium of the ode to win the favour of princes. His father had gained lands in the Panjab capital from his Ghaznavid employers, and Mas'ūd's early years were passed in pleasurable prosperity. But presently his protector fell from grace, and the poet with his fellow intimates of the governor were arrested; his estates were confiscated. A long term of imprisonment followed, and it was during those years that he perfected the *Ḥabsīya* ('jail-poem') which offered scope for complaint, hopeful pleading and manly fortitude. When Sulṭān Ibrāhīm was succeeded in 1099 by his son Sulṭān Mas'ūd, there came a change in Mas'ūd-i Sa'd's fortunes; he was released and allowed to return to Lahore; his possessions were restored to him. But this luck did not last; envied and maligned by his less prosperous rivals, he was soon thrown into prison again, where he languished for a further eight years. In 1113 he was set free once more, an old and broken man; he regained his estates, but had no further taste for composing panegyric, preferring to spend his last years in obscure but safe retirement.

Since I have seen with the eye of certitude
that this world is an abode of desolation,
that all the generous men of goodly presence
hide now their faces in the curtain of shame,
that heaven, like an inequitable mate,
is set upon sly tricks and wearisomeness,

my heart is bruised and broken, like a grain
crushed by the mill-stone of the emerald sky.
Thanks be to God, my temper, that was sick,
has risen at last from the pillow of ambition
and, in the drug-store of good penitence,
sought the sweet antidote of sincerity.
That tongue, which erstwhile sang the praises of kings,
hymns panegyrics to the Presence of God:
long while enough I passed in applauding princes,
now is the watch of worship and earnest prayer.

Mas'ūd's printed *Dīvān*, edited by the poet Rashīd Yāsimī, occupies 736 pages. Though a very large part of these is taken up with panegyric, whose eloquence one can admire but whose hyperboles become a little wearisome, many passages of great beauty and transparent sincerity invite the attention of the sympathetic interpreter. He wrote only a handful of lyrics, but these make rewarding reading; some four hundred quatrains also are attributed to him. It was a captive who had felt the chains and fetters that composed this melancholy little song.

I knew, my love, as clear as day I knew
You would at last desert me; and when you
  Resolved to part, no, not with bands of steel
Could I then bind you to my breast anew.

But it is by his desperate prison-poems that Mas'ūd-i Sa'd will always live.

Ever since I was born, O wonder! I am a captive;
see, till the day of my death I am dedicated to prison.
As soon as I first put on my back the shirt of labour
evil fate seized hold of me by the collar.
How long, O heaven, will you continue every hour
hammering on my brain? Why, I am not an anvil!

Why do you bathe my body in blood? I am not a spear;
why do you scrape away at my heart? I am not an arrow.
Why do you charge against me? My sword is blunt enough;
why do you gallop at me? My arena is very narrow. . . .
Enchained, not my body but my soul also wastes away;
I rain from my eyes not tears, but my very brain.
I am not mad, yet I am exactly like the mad;
I have no epilepsy, yet I resemble epileptics.
In my weakness and affliction I have become as a shadow;
I go in fear and trembling because of my own shadow.
When I look at myself shut up here in prison
it is as though I were groping alone in a wilderness.
The threshold of my cell is as pitch-black as the tomb,
the face of my jailor is that of a revolting pig.
Now I surrender my soul's grief to utter despair,
anon I assuage the fire within my heart with my tears.
I see my body is very weak, but my heart is strong:
I put my hope in the goodness and grace of God.
I have spoken a little part of my sorry story,
though I command words multitudinous enough.
I am weeping all the time like a cloud or a candle,
and intone this verse as a spell and a litany:
'Come now to my succour, all you good Moslems,
for the sake of God, if I myself am a good Moslem!'

Contemporary with Mas'ūd, and like him a native of Lahore, Abu 'l-Faraj Rūnī also earned his living by the gift of words; Mas'ūd once engaged with him in an artful exchange of compliments. Rūnī had inscribed over the door of a new house which Mas'ūd built for himself:

Bu 'l-Faraj, on the subject of this edifice whereon
such a multitude of words has flowed back and forth,
has so many admiring words to say, that the mind
has come to a stop, and owned itself utterly defeated.

Mas'ūd replied:

> Truly, the mind of Master Bu 'l-Faraj has become
> a mine brimful with gems, alike of verse and prose;
> intelligence, the fine-piercing and far-thinking,
> saw his words, and owned itself utterly defeated.

This remark, the sincerest flattery which one panegyrist could pay another, might well have been applied to another practitioner of the royal art, Abū Bakr Azraqī, who courted and enjoyed the favour of the Saljūq Amīr Ṭughānshāh of Nīshāpūr (d. 1186); concerning his highly-mannered productions E. G. Browne observes that 'these are very difficult to translate, and, as a rule, unreadable when translated.' A fair example of his poetry is this formalized description of a garden in Ṭughānshāh's palace.

> In the springtime the face of the tulip is there seen,
> in the autumn season the eye of the anemone peeps;
> the trees are of frankincense, the leaves of emerald,
> the herbs all of bluestone, the earth of ambergris.
> A great pool stands in the forecourt of the garden
> deep as a philosopher's soul, profound as a poet's wit;
> its nature is neither of the sea, nor of celestial Kausar—
> deep it is as the sea, of Kausar its purity,
> pure even as the soul, beautiful even as learning,
> serene even as the air, refined even as fire;
> darting about in it are fishes with silver faces
> like the new moon bright in the radiant heavens.

It is a relief to turn for a while from these artificers of applause to the unforced and ironic wit of a man who lived in those same times, but for whom poetry was an amusement and not a profession. 'Umar Khaiyām needs no elaborate introduction to the western world in this twentieth century; FitzGerald having promoted him from semi-obscurity to world fame, versions of his *Rubā'īyāt* have appeared in almost every literary language. The story of how European scholars, led by the Russian Zhukovski, gradually whittled down the total of poems, more than a thousand, attributed to 'Umar until almost nothing was left, and how the discovery of two ancient manuscripts in the 1940's restored beyond serious question his claim to authorship —all this is told in my book *Omar Khayyám: a New Version*. There I have also discussed at some length the 'philosophy' of 'Umar and his poetic style and method; having nothing to add on these topics, I will instead refer to his other writings—the metaphysical essays and *Algebra* in Arabic, and the *Naurūz-nāma* in Persian. The former lie outside the range of this book; the latter, a treatise on the history of the Persian New Year festival with an assortment of tenuously-related appendices, has been held to be of doubtful authenticity, though certainly very ancient. One of the numerous asides relates how wine was first discovered.

'In the histories it is written that there once reigned in Harāt a powerful and absolute monarch, having much treasure and property and a countless army; Khurāsān was also under his sway. He was of the family of Jamshīd, and his name was Shamīrān; the village of Shamīrān by Harāt which is still extant was founded by him. He had a son called Bādhām who was very brave, manly and strong; in those times there was no archer like him.

'Now one day King Shamīrān was seated on his veranda in company with his nobles, his son Bādhām also being in attendance on him, when by chance a phoenix came upon the scene; it uttered a loud cry, fluttered down and landed in front of the throne, a little way off. King Shamīrān looked and saw a snake coiled around the neck of the phoenix; its head thrust down, it was set upon biting the phoenix.

' "Heroes!" the king cried out. "Which of you will rescue this phoenix from this snake and shoot an arrow straight at it?"

' "It is your servant's task," Bādhām replied, and he shot an arrow in such wise that he fastened the snake's head to the ground, no harm befalling the phoenix. The phoenix escaped, fluttered around there for a while, and then flew off.

'By chance the next year on the same day King Shamīrān was seated on his veranda, when that phoenix came again, fluttered over their heads, and landed on the very spot where the snake had been shot. He placed something on the ground with his beak, uttered a few cries, and flew off. The king looked, and saw the phoenix.

' "What do you think?" he addressed the company. "Is that the same phoenix as the one we rescued from the snake, and now it's returned this year and brought us a present by way of repayment? Look, it's hitting the ground with its beak. Go and see, and bring me what you find."

'Two or three of his courtiers went, and saw two or three seeds in all placed there. They picked them up, and brought them before King Shamīrān's throne. The king looked, and saw that the seeds were very hard. He summoned the scholars and viziers and showed them the seeds.

' "The phoenix has brought us these seeds as a present," he said. "What do you think? What ought we to do with these seeds?"

'They all agreed that the seeds should be sown and carefully tended, to see what would appear by the end of the year. So the king gave the seeds to his gardener.

' "Sow them in a corner of the garden," he told him. "And put a fence round them, so that no animals may get at them. Look out for birds too, and report progress from time to time."

'The gardener did as he was ordered. That was in the month of Naurūz. After some while a shoot sprang up from the seeds. The gardener informed the king, and the king and the learned men came and stood over the seedling.

' "We've never seen such a shoot or such a leaf," they stated. Then they went back.

'In the course of time the shoots multiplied, the eyes became swollen, and clusters hung down from them resembling millet. The gardener came to the king and told him that there was no tree in the garden that looked more cheerful. The king went again with the scholars to look at the tree. He saw that the shoot had become a tree, and the clusters were all hanging down from it. He stood marvelling.

' "We must be patient," he said. "We must wait till all the trees are in fruit, to see what sort of a tree this is."

'The clusters grew large, and the unripe grapes matured. Still they did not dare to touch them until autumn came, and the other fruits such as apples, pears, peaches and pomegranates were ripe. Then the king came into the garden and saw the grape-tree looking like a bride adorned. The clusters had grown huge and turned from green to black; they shone like agate, and one by one the grapes poured from them.

'The scholars were all unanimous that these were the fruit of the tree. The tree was fully mature, and the grapes had begun to pour from the clusters. That was a sure sign that the virtue of the fruit lay in its juice. The juice must be gathered and put in a vat, to see what the result would be. No one dared put a grape into his mouth; they were afraid it might be poison and they would all be dead. So they put a vat in the garden and collected the grape-juice until the vat was full.

' "Whatever you see happen, you're to let me know," the king ordered the gardener. Then they went back.

'When the grape-juice in the vat fermented, the gardener came and told the king.

' "This is what's come from that tree. But I don't know whether it's poison or antidote."

'So they decided to take a murderer out of prison and give him some of that liquor to see what would happen. They acted accordingly; they gave some of the liquor to the murderer, and when he had drunk a little he made a wry face.

' "Would you like some more?" they asked him.

' "Yes," he answered.

'They gave him another drink, and he began to make merry and sing and dance about. He wasn't at all overawed by the king's presence.

' "Give me one more drink," he shouted. "Then you can do what you like with me. Men are born to die."

'So they gave him a third drink. He swallowed it down, and his head became heavy. He dropped off to sleep, and did not come to his senses until the next day. When he had recovered consciousness they brought him before the king.

' "What was that you drank yesterday, and how did you feel?" they asked him.

' "I don't know what it was I drank, but it was delicious," he replied. "I wish I could have three more glasses of it to-day. The first glass I had some trouble swallowing, because it tasted acid, but when it had settled in my stomach I found I wanted to have another. When I drank the second glass I felt lively and merry. All my shyness disappeared, and the world seemed a wonderful place to live in."

'So King Shamīrān learned what drinking was. He made a great feast, and instituted the noble custom of wine-bibbing.'

It would be pleasant to be sure that the author of this lively story was FitzGerald's Omar. But frivolity and the courting of kings were not the only occupations of twelfth-century poets. Bābā Ṭāhir, and perhaps Abū Sa'īd, had led the way in writing mystical verse; now the first great Ṣūfī epic was composed. Abu 'l-Majd Majdūd ibn Ādam Sanā'ī was born at Ghazna, according to one authority in 1046 when Maudūd was on the throne; this date, however, seems incredibly early, for he did not begin composing poetry until the reign of Mas'ūd III (1099–1115), and it was to Bahrām Shāh (1117–51) that he dedicated much of his work including his greatest piece, the *Ḥadīqat al-ḥaqīqa*, completed in 1131. After travelling widely in Khurāsān he made the pilgrimage to Mecca; he returned in his last years to Ghazna, where he died. Widely different dates for his death are given, ranging from 1131 to 1194; the Persian scholar Mudarris Riḍavī, who edited Sanā'ī's *Dīvān*, after a careful sifting of the available evidence concluded that the date 1141 is likeliest to be correct. Sanā'ī's output was vast, if we are to accept as genuine all the poems credited to him. His *Dīvān* of odes, lyrics and quatrains makes 872 pages in Riḍavi's edition, the *Ḥadīqat al-ḥaqīqa*, also edited by Riḍavī, occupies 748 pages; his *Sair al-'ibād*, brought out by Kūhī Kirmānī, is a mere trifle of some 770 verses, but no fewer than five other didactic pieces are attributed to him.

In his odes Sanā'ī comes stylistically nearest to Nāṣir-i Khusrau; while discoursing nobly on the majesty of God and the dedicated life, he rails incessantly against the evil times in which it was his misfortune to live and urges the wicked to repent of their sins before the wrath to come.

Moslems, the mansion of life in this world possesses two doors:
noble and commoner, good and wicked, all pass through them both.
Two doors there are to the being of man, for first and last
the one is bolted by destiny, the other is barred by fate.
When the time to exist comes, destiny unlocks the former door;
when the hour of destruction strikes, fate lifts the latter's latch.
Yes, you are ever a prisoner; yet you are fettered to hope;
hope is intent on its course, but doom purposes another end.
Every learned man in this world who ponders this solemn truth
sees that the world is full of peril, and his soul is full of fear.

In 1124 Sanā'ī found himself in the company of many poets and scholars of Khurāsān and Iraq; when they had recited their verses, one of their number invited him to reply. He responded with the following lines:

You have listened enough to talk of China and Rome,
rise now, and come, see the kingdom of Sanā'ī.
There you will see hearts empty of lust and greed,
there you will see souls free of pride and hatred.
Gold there is none, yet a kingdom to mine at will,
corn none, yet heaven's steed to saddle and ride,
foot none, yet all the spheres freely to tread,
hand none, yet a whole empire within your grasp.
No royal traps are his, yet spirit-wise
he has lifted up his throne to the highest heaven;
escaped from the strict order of space and time,
delivered out of the series of months and years,
he takes his solace in secret privacy
claiming his own an empire in ambuscade.
Like Joseph once in the pit, he has gone aloft
even to the skies, drawn by a rope secure,
spurned underfoot the seven regions of doubt
now to inhabit the secret palace of faith.
Contentment has hid the treasure of all the world
deep in the oyster-shell of his inmost soul;
empty of every care, he is free and gay,
gay as the rose, the lily, the jessamine,
harbours no wrath against his adversaries,
never a frown wrinkles his brow serene.

Sanā'ī's lyrics show him a forerunner of the great masters yet to come; he uses the imagery of love and wine to express his spiritual raptures.

Since my heart was caught in the snare of love,
since my soul became wine in the cup of love,
ah, the pains I have known through loverhood
since like a hawk I fell in the snare of love!
Trapped in time, I am turned to a drunken sot
by the exciting, dreg-draining cup of love.

Dreading the fierce affliction of loverhood,
I dare not utter the very name of love;
and the more amazing is this, since I see
every creature on earth is at peace with love.
'Yield up your soul, your faith, your heart to me'—
so I hear in my soul the message of love:
my soul, my faith, my heart—I surrender all,
so at last to attain my desire of love.

In another poem Sanā'ī describes love, like many other mystics, as a sea.

Moslems all! I love that idol
With a true and jealous zeal;
Not for dalliance, but bewildered
In amazement here I kneel.

What is love? A mighty ocean,
And of flame its waters are,
Waters that are very mountains,
Black as night, and swarming far.

Dragons fierce and full of terror
Crouch upon its waveswept rim,
And a myriad sharks of judgment
In its swelling billows swim.

Grief the barque that sails those waters,
Fortitude its anchor is,
And its mast is bent and tossing
To the gale's catastrophes.

Me they cast in sudden transport
Into that unfathomed sea,
Like the man of noble spirit
Garmented in sanctity.

I was dead; the waters drowned me;
Lo, the marvel, now I live,
And have found a gem more precious
Than the treasured worlds can give.

Passing over the remarkable *Sair al-'ibād*, a pilgrim's progress which moved R. A. Nicholson to hail in Sanā'ī a Persian forerunner of Dante, it is necessary to give some account, however brief, of the *Ḥadīqat al-ḥaqīqa*, his longest and most ambitious poem. The first mystical epic in Persian, and as such the prototype to which 'Aṭṭār and Rūmī turned when they came to develop this genre, it is divided into ten chapters, each chapter being subdivided into sections with illustrative stories; it thus gives the superficial impression of a learned treatise in verse. E. G. Browne entertained no great love for the poem, giving it as his opinion that it is 'one of the dullest books in Persian, seldom rising to the level of Martin Tupper's *Proverbial Philosophy*, filled with fatuous truisms and pointless anecdotes, and as far inferior to the *Mathnawí* of Jalálu'd-Dín Rúmí as is Robert Montgomery's *Satan* to Milton's *Paradise Lost*.' Henri Massé is not quite so devastating, but even so he remarks, 'On peut regretter que, dans son oeuvre, l'expression ne soit pas toujours à la hauteur de l'idée.' As against these verdicts, Mudarris Riḍavī speaks of the *Ḥadīqat al-ḥaqīqa* as 'one of the masterpieces of Persian poetry; few books equal it in smoothness and fluency of language, coupled with subtlety and loftiness of ideas. The *Ḥadīqa*,' he adds with pardonable enthusiasm, 'has left its influence on the whole civilized world and has secured a high and honoured place in international literature.' Clearly there is room to mediate between these widely conflicting judgments; Rūmī at least was in no doubt of Sanā'ī's stature.

'Aṭṭār was the spirit,
Sanā'ī his eyes twain,
And in time thereafter
Came we in their train.

What was Sanā'ī seeking to achieve when he wrote the *Ḥadīqa*? He claimed boldly enough to be an innovator, and challenged any who might dispute the fact to produce his evidence.

> No one in the world has ever uttered such speech:
> if anyone has so spoken, say, 'Bring, and read!'

He is also complacently sure of his own immortality.

> Henceforward, so long as men have speech at all,
> the philosophers of the world will read this book:
> till the day I built up so fine a city,
> nobody had ever beheld a city like this.
> None will speak ever finer words than these:
> till the resurrection this must content the world.
> When you leave aside the Koran and the Traditions,
> nobody has matched the manner of my speech:
> men of refinement are unanimously agreed
> this is the unique and only choice discourse;
> anyone who knows what words are and is wise
> pays reverence to it as he would to the Koran.

Such boasts make an unfortunate impression, until they are considered in relation to the conventions ruling in Sanā'ī's time. A poet, however humble and holy he might be in his spiritual life, had to shout his own wares if he wished to secure a hearing; and Sanā'ī was passionately eager to be heard, because he believed he had a vital message for an age given over to ignorance and ungodliness. His style in the *Ḥadīqa* is proof of this revivalist fervour; whereas in his odes he will match in mannerisms the most accomplished euphuists of his generation, the language he employs in his religious epic is simple and direct, reminiscent of the clear and rapid Persian which Ghazālī wrote in his *Kīmiyā-yi sa'ādat*. The *Ḥadīqa* often betrays itself as a product of old age; there is much repetition, and the subject-matter is set out in a fairly chaotic fashion. Yet Sanā'ī's achievement in this book is far from negligible, and not all of his stories are insipid.

In a book I once read that the Spirit of God
went forth one night into the wilderness.
A watch had passed when, suddenly seized by sleep,
he made haste to find himself a slumbering-place.
Seeing a stone cast down, he took it for his pillow,
fared on no further, and soon was fast asleep.
A while he slept; then hastily he awoke
to see the Devil standing above his bed.
'You outcast, you accursed dog,' he cried,
'upon what business do you come slinkingly here?
The place that is the sanctuary of Jesus,
how do you think to find yourself a shelter there?'
'Well, you have given me much trouble,' replied
the Devil, 'meddling about in my domain.
Why do you want to interfere with me?
Why do you meddle about in my domain?
The kingdom of this world is all my domain;
you haven't any place there; it's all my place.
First you plunder me of what's mine by right,
then you abuse me in your sanctuary.'
'How have I given you trouble?' Jesus asked.
'When did I make assault on your property?'
'That stone you have as your pillow,' the Devil replied,
'isn't it of this world? Then how did you filch it?'
Jesus in all haste flung the stone from him;
the Devil's phantom thereupon melted away
saying, 'You've saved yourself, and driven me off;
you've set the both of us free from captivity.
Henceforward I shall not interfere with you;
you for your part leave my property to me!'

It was to Bahrām Shāh the Ghaznavid also that Abu 'l-Ma'ālī Naṣr Allāh ibn Muḥammad, later vizier to Khusrau Malik, dedicated his Persian version of *Kalīla wa-Dimna*, that famous collection of animal fables of Indian origin which Ibn al-Muqaffa' had translated out of Pahlavi into Arabic. Naṣr Allāh is alternatively stated to have been born in Shīrāz and Ghazna; he made his version of Ibn al-Muqaffa' about 1144; Khusrau Malik rewarded his ministerial services by having him executed. The Persian style of his translation was long applauded for its chasteness and elegance; but his modern editor 'Abd al-'Aẓīm Garakānī, followed by Bahār, has pointed out the difficulty of forming an entirely dependable judgment of it today, since no really ancient manuscript has yet been discovered and the text is thought to have been considerably tampered with by medieval copyists. In this respect Naṣr Allāh has suffered the same fate as Ibn al-Muqaffa', whose Arabic is notoriously hard to reconstruct for identical reasons. Despite this handicap, it is possible to form some impression of the spirit in which Naṣr Allāh approached his task, by setting side by side the story of the Ascetic and the Pot as given in the two texts. Naṣr Allāh is seen sometimes to expand, sometimes to contract, seemingly as his fancy took him.

Ibn al-Muqaffa'

They assert that a certain ascetic once lived in the land of Jurjān, and he had a good woman who kept him company. They remained for some time without being granted a child. Then, after despairing, she became pregnant and the woman rejoiced, and the ascetic rejoiced likewise; he praised God and prayed to Him that the child might be a boy. He said to his wife, 'Rejoice, for I have hope that he shall be a lad who will be a great comfort and joy to us. I will choose for him the fairest of names, and I

Naṣr Allāh

They state that there was once an ascetic, and he had a wife chaste of body, the reflection of whose face reinforced the rearguard of dawn, and the colour of whose tresses gave succour to the vanguard of night.

Slender of waist, she adorned her
necklaces
more fairly than her necklaces
adorned her.

Her he took under his control, and he was very eager that he should have a son. When some time had passed and the event had not will bring him all the instructors.' The woman said, 'What induces you, O man, to speak of a thing of which you know not whether it will come to pass or not? Whoever does that will be visited with what visited the ascetic who poured on his head fat and honey.' He said to her, 'How did that come about?' She said, 'They assert that there was once an ascetic who every day received from the house of a merchant a portion of fat and honey; of this he would eat enough for his sustenance and need, and the rest he set aside and put in a jar which he hung up on a peg on the side of the house until it was full. One day while the ascetic was stretched out on his back with his stick in his hand and the jar hung over his head, he thought about how dear fat and honey were. So he said, "I will sell what is in this jar for a dinar, and buy with it ten goats, and they will become pregnant and give birth once every five months. It will not be long before there are many goats, when the young of these beget others." He calculated in this fashion over a number of years, and found the total came to more than four hundred goats. So he said, "I will buy for these a hundred cattle, one cow or one bull for every four goats, and I will buy some land and some steeds, and I will hire some ploughmen, and breed with the bulls, and profit of the milk and offspring of the cows, and by the time five years are gone I shall have acquired much wealth out of the farm. Then I will occurred, he gave up hope; then, after despair, God had compassion on him and his wife became pregnant. The elder rejoiced, and resolved every day to give thanks to God anew. One day he said to his wife, 'Soon you will have a son. I will give him a fine name, and teach him the manners of the Way, and I will exert myself to train and educate him, so that in a short time he will be ready to undertake the works of religion, and be worthy to receive heavenly graces. Our name will live through him, and he will beget children, and we shall be glad and rejoice in him.

> The days make promises thereof, and I pray
> to God for the fulfilment of those promises.'

The woman said, 'How do you know that I shall have a boy? It is possible that I may not have a child, and even if I do it may not be a boy. And supposing the Creator does bestow this blessing, it could be that we shall not live to an old age. In short, this is a long business, and you like an ignoramus sit on the steed of desire and prance about in the arena of boastfulness. These words fit exactly the case of the holy man who uselessly poured honey and fat over his face and hair.' The ascetic asked, 'How was that?' She said, 'They relate that once there was a holy man, and a merchant who sold sheep-fat was his neighbour. Every day he sent a quantity of his merchandise for the sustenance of the ascetic. The ascetic build a fine house and buy slaves male and female, and marry a good woman, and she will become pregnant, then she will produce a fine and noble boy, and I will choose for him the fairest of names, and when he is old enough I will give him a fine education, and I will be severe with him and if he obeys me, well; if not, I will beat him with this stick." And he waved his hand at the jar and broke it, and all its contents ran down over his face.'

used some and put the rest in a jar and set it aside. One day he looked at it and thought, "If I can sell this honey and fat for ten dirhams and buy five sheep with it, all five will give birth, and of their offspring whole flocks will be produced, and they will be a support for me, and I shall marry a wife from a great family, and undoubtedly a boy will come. I'll give him a fine name, and I'll teach him knowledge and manners, and if he's stubborn I'll punish him with this stick." This idea got such a hold of him that he suddenly seized the stick and heedlessly struck the suspended jar. It broke at once, and the honey and fat ran down over his face.'

Naṣr Allāh's *Kalīla ū Dimna* continued in fashion until the changed taste of post-Mongol Persia found its style too simple; it was then ousted from public favour by Ḥusain Vā'iẓ Kāshifī's *Anvār-i Suhailī*. The esteem in which Naṣr Allāh was held in his own day of power is shown by a poem addressed to him by Saiyid Ḥasan of Ghazna, another of Bahrām Shāh's circle.

O ease of my spirit and joy of my body,
your company gladdens the heart of sorrow;
reason, seeking your lip, becomes a drunkard,
the thorn, brushing your cheek, becomes a rose-bower.
Your pen at the time of word-embroidering,
your hand at the time of bounty-giving
pours balm on the wounded body of virtue,
lays salve on the throbbing brow of passion.
Had I the hundred notes of the bulbul,
did I possess ten tongues like the lily,
let me be repeating for ever and ever,
still I could not say how much I thank you.

The first half of the twelfth century produced a rich crop of prose-works, of which only the most important will be mentioned here. The fame of Aḥmad Ghazālī (d. 1126) has been overshadowed by that of his illustrious brother, but he wrote a number of notable books in Arabic, and to Persian literature he contributed a treatise which, though slender in bulk, is remarkable both for the beauty and subtlety of its contents, and for the influence it exerted on later writers. The *Savāniḥ* is a meditation in seventy-five short sections on the divine mystery of love, lover and beloved; the discussion, as in Anṣārī's *Munājāt*, is frequently interrupted by brief poems. In the following extract the story of Maḥmūd of Ghazna's love for his handsome slave Ayāz is taken as a parable of mystical passion.

'One day Maḥmūd was seated with Ayāz. He said, "O Ayāz, the more I suffer on your account and the more perfect my love for you becomes, the more you are estranged from me. Why is this?

Daily my heart's distress the more rejoices thee,
More masterful thou art in showing cruelty;
Though I am ever more thy slave in loverhood,
Thou all the while more freely disregardest me.

O Ayāz, would that there existed between us that familiarity and boldness which obtained before love came, when there was no veil. Now everything is veil upon veil. How is that?" Ayāz answered:

"While thou art with thyself, though thou be seated nigh
Myself, how many weary leagues between us lie!
Thou canst not come to me till thou becomest one:
Upon love's road is room for only 'thou' or 'I.'

In that time my part was the subjection of slavery, and yours the authority and grandeur of masterhood. Then love's outrider came and loosed the knot of slavery. In the loosing of that knot the free and easy status of possessor and possessed vanished. Then the true relationship of lover and beloved became established. To be a lover is to be a prisoner; to be beloved is to be a prince. How can boldness exist between prince and prisoner?" '

Virtuosity of a different kind is displayed in the *Maqāmāt* of Ḥamīdī. It was the Persian Badī' al-Zamān al-Hamadhānī (d. at Harāt in 1007) who first composed in Arabic a book of entertaining dialogues on such varying themes as theological discussion and thieves' roguery. This, along with the more celebrated *Maqāmāt* of al-Ḥarīrī (d. 1122), was the model taken by Ḥamīd al-Dīn Abū Bakr of Balkh for his book, begun in the summer of 1156, so much admired by the poet Anvarī that he declared:

Every speech, apart from the Koran and the Traditions of
 Muhammad,
beside the *Maqāmāt* of Ḥamīd al-Dīn has now become
 gibberish.
Know for a blind man's tears the *Maqāmāt* of Badī' and Ḥarīrī
compared with that ocean overflowing with the water of life.

Ḥamīdī perfected the popular fashion of rhymed prose, and set a standard which later writers eagerly sought to emulate. He wrote twenty-four of these essays; E. G. Browne's imitation of the description of Balkh before and after the Ghuzz raid of 1153 is a clever reflection of the original.

'But when to the confines of that country I at length drew

near—and to those journeying from Balkh did lend my ear—far otherwise did things appear.

"Who news of absent friends doth seek to know
Must needs hear tidings both of joy and woe."

Thus spake informants credible: "Haste thee not, for thy goal and aim—is no more the same—as that of days which are past—and a season which did not last:—those fragrant breezes now are changed to the desert's deadly gale—and that sugar-sweetness is transformed to draughts of lethal bale;—of those sweet beds of basil only thorns remain—and of those cups of pleasure naught save an aching pain.—What boots it to behold thy fair-faced fere—in weeds of woe and garments dark and drear—or to witness the spring-land of thy mays—a prey to dispraise—withered and sere?

Can these dumb remnants mark Umm Awfá's home?"

Said I: "What overlooker's evil eye did light—on those fair gardens bright?—And what dread poisoned desert-blast—of desolation drear hath past—to wreck their order, and their beauty to the winds to cast?" Then they, "O youth!—such evil change, in sooth—awaking in us boundless grief and ruth—too often hath accrued—from Fortune rude—and fickle Fate's undreamed vicissitude.—Heaven is harsh, I ween—yet is not what is heard as what is seen.—Haste thee, and onwards go—that thou may'st see and know;—for to attempt to picture the unseen—is vain, I ween." '

It may well have been in the same year 1156 that Niẓāmī the Prosodist (Aḥmad ibn 'Umar ibn 'Alī Niẓāmī 'Arūḍī) composed his *Chahār maqāla* for 'the King of this time, that learned, just, divinely-favoured, victorious, and heaven-aided monarch, *Ḥusámu'd-Dawla wa'd-Dín*, Helper of Islám and the Muslims,

Exterminator of the infidels and polytheists, Subduer of the heretical and froward, Supporter of hosts in the worlds, Pride of Kings and Emperors, Succourer of mankind, Protector of these days, Fore-arm of the Caliphate, Beauty of the Faith and Glory of the Nation, Order of the Arabs and the Persians, noblest of mankind, *Shamsu'l-Ma'álí*, *Maliku'l-Umará*, Abu'l-Ḥasan 'Alí b. Mas'úd'—a somewhat obscure prince of the Bāmiyān line of the Ghūrid dynasty. This valuable and attractive book discusses in four discourses, enlivened with many anecdotes, the four influential professions of medieval Persia: the civil service, poetry, astrology and medicine. It is in this work that we find the famous prescription for a successful career in literature.

'Now the poet must be of tender temperament, profound in thought, sound in genius, clear of vision, quick of insight. He must be well versed in many divers sciences, and quick to extract what is best from his environment; for as poetry is of advantage in every science, so is every science of advantage in poetry. And the poet must be of pleasing conversation in social gatherings, of cheerful countenance on festive occasions; and his verse must have attained to such a level that it is written on the page of Time and celebrated on the lips and tongues of the noble, and be such that they transcribe it in books and recite it in cities. For the richest portion and most excellent part of poetry is immortal fame, and until it be thus confirmed and published it is ineffectual to this end, and this result cannot accrue from it; it will not survive its author, and, being ineffectual for the immortalizing of his name, how can it confer immortality on another? But to this rank a poet cannot attain unless in the prime of his life and the season of his youth he commits to memory 20,000 couplets of poetry of the Ancients and 10,000 verses of the works of the Moderns, and continually reads and marks the *díwáns* of the masters of his art, observing how they have acquitted themselves in the strait passes and delicate places of song, in order that thus the fashion and varieties of verse may become ingrained in his nature, and the defects and beauties of poetry may be inscribed on the tablet of his understanding.'

Bahār rates the *Chahār maqāla* as one of the four masterpieces of early Persian prose, placing it on the same level as the *Tārīkh-i Baihaqī*, the *Qābūs-nāma* and the *Siyāsat-nāma*. Applauding its easy fluency, exact concision and conversational tone, he remarks that by the criterion of style it might well have been assigned to the preceding century, had not its approximate date of composition been firmly established. 'Its freedom from verbal synonyms, the absence of consecutive clauses, frigid rhyme, rhythmical congruity and all the other rhetorical devices employed in that epoch—all this informs us that its author did not wish to compose his book in the manner of his own age, having a greater liking for the style of the old masters.' A comparison of the specimen from Ḥamīdī and the following passage—both translations are the work of E. G. Browne—amply confirms Bahār's analysis.

'Another of the House of Sámán, Amír Manṣúr b. Núḥ b. Naṣr, became afflicted with an ailment which grew chronic, and remained established, and the physicians were unable to cure it. So the Amír Manṣúr sent messengers to summon Muḥammad b. Zakariyyá of Ray to treat him. Muḥammad b. Zakariyyá came as far as the Oxus, but when he saw it he said: "I will not embark in the boat: God Most High saith, 'Do not cast yourselves into peril with your own hands'; and, again, it is surely a thing remote from wisdom voluntarily to place one's self in so hazardous a position." Ere the Amír's messenger had gone to Bukhárá and returned, he had composed the treatise entitled *Manṣúrí*. So when a notable arrived with a special led-horse, bringing a message intermingled with promises of reward, he handed this *Manṣúrí* to him, saying: "I am this book, and by this book thou canst attain thine object, so that there is no need of me." When the book reached the Amír he was in grievous suffering, wherefore he sent a thousand dínárs and one of his own private horses, saying: "Strive to move him by all these kind attentions, but, if they prove fruitless, bind his hands and feet, place him in the boat, and fetch him across." So, just as the Amír had commanded, they urgently entreated Muḥammad b. Zakariyyá, but to no purpose. Then they bound his hands and feet, placed him in the boat, and, when they had ferried him across the river, released him. Then they brought the led-horse, fully caparisoned, before him, and he mounted in the best of humours, and set out for Bukhárá. And when they enquired of him, saying, "We feared to bring thee across the water lest thou shouldst cherish enmity against us, but thou didst not so, nor do we see thee vexed in heart," he replied: "I know that every year several thousand persons cross the Oxus without being drowned, and that I too should probably not be drowned; still, it was possible that I might perish, and if this had happened they would have continued till the Resurrection to say, 'A foolish fellow was Muḥammad b. Zakariyyá, in that, of his own free will, he embarked in a boat and so was drowned.' But when they bound me, I escaped all danger of censure; for then they would say, 'They bound the poor fellow's hands and feet, so that he was drowned.' Thus should I have been excused, not blamed, in case of my being drowned." '

Much history was being made by the rival dynasties of the twelfth century, whose internecine struggles were fatally undermining the house of Islam and preparing the way for the devastating invasions from the east shortly to begin. To keep abreast of events, and to relate them to the past, ambitious authors were busily engaged upon their general and special, their extended and epitomized histories. Ibn al-Balkhī composed his *Fārs-nāma* for Ghiyāth al-Dīn Muḥammad the Saljūq (1104–17), a brief and simple account of the pre-Islamic and post-Islamic vicissitudes of Persia. An anonymous author wrote the *Mujmal al-tawārīkh*, a concise and lively history of the world down to the year 1126. At the other end of the century Abū Bakr Muḥammad Rāvandī was compiling his *Rāḥat al-ṣudūr* on the Saljūqs, Ibn Isfandiyār his local *Tārīkh-i Ṭabaristān*. Before that, however, Abu 'l-Ḥasan 'Alī ibn Zaid Baihaqī had brought out, two years before his death in 1170, a 'full account of the geography of the Baihaḳ district, of its taxation, of various princes and governors, of men born in Baihaḳ, who had distinguished themselves by religious or political activity, etc.' Such is W. Barthold's description of the *Tārīkh-i Baihaq*, to be strictly distinguished from the *Tārīkh-i Baihaqī*.

The *Tārīkh-i Baihaq*, which conforms more or less to the pattern of numerous Arabic local histories with the stress it lays on biography, has now been published. Bahār characterizes it as 'one of those very interesting and useful Persian books whose equals do not exceed two or three, both as regards style and reliability, and in being full of much useful historical, literary and scientific material that makes it unrivalled in its own field.' The style is a compromise between ancient and modern, and mediates between the fashions of the eleventh and the twelfth century; it shows a higher proportion of Arabic words than the *Chahār maqāla*, and introduces more freely quotations from the Arabic and Persian poets; at the same time it has not abandoned the simplicity and concision of the early models.

'Once upon a time a Kurd, a goldsmith, a schoolmaster, a Dailamite and a lover were seated together in the desert. The sky was wrapped in a pitch-black mantle. Suddenly the moon came up over the eastern horizon, and poured molten gold upon the ground. They gazed at one another with delight and said, "Each of us must invent in turn a simile to describe this moon, according to the range of his understanding and imagination."

'The goldsmith was the first to speak, since the precious quality of gold stimulates the desire to outstrip others.

' "This moon," he said, "is like an ingot of pure gold emerging from the crucible."

'The Kurd said, "It is like a summer cheese coming out of the mould."

'The lover said, "It is like the face of my beloved: it has borrowed her charm and beauty, and mimics her radiant loveliness."

'The schoolmaster said, "It is like the white flour sent on Thursdays to the schoolmaster from the house of a rich and generous man."

'The Dailamī said, "It is like a gold-incrusted shield which is carried before a king when he goes abroad."

' "Every man to his taste," says the Arabic proverb.'

'The *Ḥadā'iq al-siḥr fī daqā'iq al-shi'r* of Amīr Rashīd al-Dīn Muḥammad 'Umarī Balkhī, known as Rashīd-i Vaṭvāṭ, is one of the masterpieces of Persian prose, and one of the most important literary works so far written in this language.' With these words, 'Abbās Iqbāl introduces his edition of the best-loved Persian treatise on poetics. Born in Balkh towards the end of the eleventh century, Vaṭvāṭ served as secretary and court-poet to Atsīz the Khvārizmshāh (d. 1156); he died well over ninety years old in 1182. The *Ḥadā'iq al-siḥr* was written, as its author declares, at the instance of Atsīz. The king showed him a book called the *Tarjumān al-balāgha* (of which a brief account has been given above); on glancing through it he found it to be 'pretty unsatisfactory and by no means free of faults,' and he therefore resolved to improve upon it. The treatise is of no great size—only eighty-seven pages in Iqbāl's edition—but it is packed with definitions and examples of all the varieties of rhetorical embellishment. E. G. Browne gives a detailed account of its contents in the second volume of his *Literary History of Persia*. It is certainly not a book to read for pleasure or at leisure, though of undoubted technical value; its anecdotes are few and far between.

'It is related that Avicenna was one day seated in the bazaar when a peasant passed by carrying a valuable lamb on his shoulders.

'"How much is your lamb?" Avicenna asked.

'"One dinar," the peasant replied.

'"Leave the lamb here," Avicenna said. "Come back in an hour and I'll give you the money."

'"What!" the peasant exclaimed, recognizing who he was. "You a learned philosopher, how can you be so ignorant? The lamb is opposite the balance; until you have weighed it, surely you won't take it home."

'Avicenna was delighted, and gave the peasant twice what he had asked for the lamb. In order to appreciate the subtlety of the peasant's remark, it is necessary to reflect that the first thing that occurs to anyone when the word "lamb" is mentioned is that it is an animal, while a "balance" is the thing gold is weighed in. But the peasant was referring to Aries and Libra, the signs of the zodiac, which are opposite one another. The pleasantry he uttered had a learned flavour, and was quite worthy of Avicenna himself.'

This survey of twelfth-century prose closes with a glance at the Persian writings of an eminent Ṣūfī. Shihāb al-Dīn Suhravardī Maqtūl, of very considerable account as an Arabic author, has in recent times been rediscovered as a brilliant inventor of Persian allegories. He was only thirty-seven when Saladin's son al-Malik al-Ẓāhir ordered him to be executed for blasphemy at Aleppo in 1191, yet into his short life he crowded much deep thinking and good writing. Striving to reconcile Aristotelian logic with Ṣūfī mysticism, he was working towards a metaphysic that would take account of Zoroastrian ideas and do justice to the Neoplatonic doctrine of illumination. His Arabic books are more in the nature of technical dissertations; when he turned to Persian he found fulfilment for his artistic impulse in composing fables that are in true line of succession to Plato's myths. The parable here translated symbolizes the descent of the soul into the material world: Greek philosophy and Islamic dogma are brought together by the skilful use of Koranic quotations, and Arabic verses are cited to heighten the discourse.

'A certain king possessed a garden which through all the four seasons never lacked for fragrant herbs, verdant grasses and joyous pleasances; great waters therein flowed, and all manner of birds sitting in the branches poured forth songs of every kind. Indeed, every melody that could enter the mind and every beauty that imagination might conceive, all was to be found in that garden. Moreover a company of peacocks, exceedingly graceful, elegant and fair, had there made their abode and dwelling-place.

'One day the king laid hold of one of the peacocks and gave orders that he should be sewn up in a leather jacket, in such wise that naught of the colours of his wings remained visible, and however much he tried he could not look upon his own beauty. He also commanded that over his head a basket should be placed having only one aperture, through which a few grains of millet might be dropped, sufficient to keep him alive.

'Some time passed, and the peacock forgot himself, the garden-kingdom and the other peacocks. Whenever he looked at himself he saw nothing but a filthy, ugly sack of leather and a very dark and disagreeable dwelling-place. To that he reconciled himself, and it became fixed in his mind that no land could exist larger than the basket in which he was. He firmly believed that if anyone should pretend that there was a pleasurable life or an abode of perfection beyond it, it would be rank heresy and utter nonsense and stupidity. For all that, whenever a breeze blew and the scent of the flowers and trees, the roses and violets and jasmine and fragrant herbs was wafted to him through the hole, he experienced a strange delight and was curiously moved, so that the joy of flight filled his heart. He felt a mighty yearning within him, but knew not the source of that yearning, for he had no idea that he was anything but a piece of leather, having forgotten everything beyond his basket-world and fare of millet. Again, if ever he heard the modulations of the peacocks and the songs of the other birds he was likewise transported with yearning and longing; yet he was not wakened out of his trance by the voices of the birds and the breath of the zephyr.

'One day he was enjoying these sounds and scents—

> The zephyr wafted o'er me, as if to say
> "I bring you news of your love, so far away."

For a long while he meditated upon whence this fragrant wind and these sweet voices might be coming—

> O lightning-flash, illumining the sky,
> From what remote enclosure do you fly?

He could not understand; yet at such moments an involuntary happiness possessed him—

> If Laila the Amirite should whisper to me
> Greetings, when I am laid in the stony tomb,
> I would answer her with joy, even though it be
> But the screech of an owl issuing out of the gloom.

This ignorance was because he had forgotten himself and his original homeland—

> as those who forgot God, and so He
> caused them to forget their souls.

'Every time a breeze or a sound reached him from the garden he was moved with longing, yet he did not realize the reason or know the cause—

> The lightning sped from Ma'arra deep in the night
> And tarried at Rama, weary of so long flight,
> Stirring the camels, the horses, the cavalry
> Till the very saddles wellnigh leapt for glee.

'For many a long day his bewilderment continued. Then one day the king commanded his servants to bring the bird and release it from the leather jacket and the basket—

For it is only a single scaring—

then behold, they are sliding down
from their tombs unto their Lord—

when that which is in the tombs is overthrown
and that which is in the breasts is brought out—

surely on that day their Lord shall be aware of them!

'When the peacock came forth out of the veil he saw himself in the midst of the garden. He beheld the hues of his wings, the garden, the flowers, the various forms, the world's expanse, the wide arena to wander and fly in; he heard the voices and songs of every species; and he was seized with wonder at his own estate, and overcome by vain regrets—

"Alas for me
in that I neglected my duty to God"—

"We have now removed
from thee thy covering, and so thy sight today is piercing"—

Why, but when the soul leaps to the throat of the dying
and that hour you are watching,
and We are nigher him than you, but you do not see Us—

No, indeed: but soon you shall know.
Again, no indeed: but soon you shall know.'

FIVE

Five Saljūq Poets

In this chapter some account, necessarily inadequate—for each section might well be expanded into a full-length monograph—will be given of five great poets whose active lives spanned the middle century of the Saljūq period. Three were panegyrists, two writers of epic; all were masters of their craft, all possessed a high degree of originality. In an age rich in fine literature, these five men undoubtedly dominated the scene; two of them figure in Muḥammad Qazvīnī's list of the seven immortals. Their names are Mu'izzī, Anvarī, Khāqānī, Niẓāmī and 'Aṭṭār.

The first of these, Amīr al-Shu'arā' Muḥammad ibn 'Abd al-Malik Mu'izzī of Nīshāpūr, passed half of his long life, which according to some authorities stretched from 1049 to 1148, in the eleventh century. His father 'Abd al-Malik Burhānī, who died in 1073, bore the title 'Prince of Poets' before him; it was on his death-bed recommendation that Mu'izzī gained the attention of his first and his father's last patron, Malik Shāh.

> A while under your auspices, O world-conquering king,
> I scraped the dust of tyranny from the cheek of time;
> now I carry to the Lord of the Throne, endorsed by you,
> the sign-manual of good-doing, the charter of happiness.
> Fate accorded me a six and forty years' span of life
> that in your royal service I have reckoned a century.
> Now I have passed on this long service to my son
> and, after a ten-days' sickness, now end my journey.

I depart; but my son comes, my own true successor—
him now I commend to God and to my Sovereign.

Mu'izzī, being a young and untried man, was not immediately promoted by Malik Shāh to the highest rank. The story told of his advancement is picturesque. The Sulṭān one year had gone out to look for the new moon which would signal the beginning of the fast of Ramaḍān. As soon as the crescent appeared, Mu'izzī exclaimed impromptu:

O moon, you are like the beloved's eyebrow, one might say,
or no, you are like the prince's bow, one might say;
you are a horseshoe wrought of pure gold, one might say,
an ear-ring suspended from the sky's ear, one might say.

The Sulṭān was so pleased by this poem that he gave its author a horse.

Mu'izzī at once recited:

When the king saw the fire within my heart
he raised me from the earth to above the moon;
when he heard me speak a verse like water
he bestowed on me a noble horse like air.

The poet had contrived the highly appreciated trick of mentioning the four elements in a single quatrain, and was rewarded with a regular allowance and a title. Finally, as Muḥammad 'Aufī puts it, 'three poets under three dynasties enjoyed success and favour and attained unrivalled rank: Rūdakī under the Sāmānids, 'Unṣurī under the Ghaznavids and Mu'izzī under Malik Shāh.' After Malik Shāh's death in 1092 his favourite poet was obliged to wander in the wilderness for a while, seeking patrons wherever they might be found. In December 1096, however, Malik Shāh's grandson Sanjar was made governor of

Khurāsān by his elder brother Barkiyārūq, and from that time Mu'izzī's fortune prospered. It was not until 1117 that Sanjar succeeded to the throne, but Mu'izzī reaped the reward of long courtship by receiving the coveted laureateship like his father before him. It is often said that he was accidentally killed by an arrow shot by his royal master, but this legend has been decisively disproved; the poet died of extreme old age.

Mu'izzī's *Dīvān* has been edited by 'Abbās Iqbāl in 829 pages, showing a total of 18,623 couplets. The learned editor in defence of his author felt obliged to protest against the contemporary fashion of 'only considering as poetry what is full of wisdom and learning, counsel and good advice.' Poetry, he argued, was an art, not a science, and should be judged by its aesthetic and emotive qualities. 'Mu'izzī is a poet in the full meaning of the term, and his words have a most powerful effect on every man of taste who loves elegance and eloquence. As holder of the post of Prince of Poets he carried out to the utmost his obligation and occupation as a panegyrist. It is unjust to demand of such a poet anything more than the discharge of his office. What we have to see is whether he acquitted himself well or ill in relation to the requirements of his own epoch. One should never apply the criteria of one's own days to a man who lived centuries ago and in very different times. From the standpoint of poetry —that is, in regard to style, sweetness of speech, elegance of expression and eloquence of ideas, considered against the background of the requirements of his own time—Mu'izzī stands out as one of the artistic virtuosi of the Persian language. For fluency of expression and control of words perhaps no equal to his *Dīvān* can be found in all our poetry, with the exception of the *Dīvān* of Ẓahīr al-Dīn Fāryābī and the *Kullīyāt* of Shaikh Sa'dī. . . . The editor is no fanatical admirer of Mu'izzī's personality. His only object, in these days when the Persian language is passing through a devastating crisis and every illiterate upstart is inventing words out of his own fancy and striking at the very roots of our nationhood, is to invite men of sound minds to peruse one of the most perfect examples of the Persian language. It may be that by the application of such antidotes those soul-destroying poisons will be neutralized, and the healthy body of our beautiful language not perish utterly at the hands of these amateur physicians.'

This is not the place to expand upon the battle of styles raging in modern Persia which provoked 'Abbās Iqbāl to this outburst. Panegyric to long-dead princes, as we have observed before, is not apt to make very interesting reading for foreigners who depend for their enjoyment on translations; and even E. G. Browne felt obliged to remark that 'to us, who are sufficiently familiar with Ḥáfidh and other comparatively modern poets, Mu'izzí, unless we keep constantly in mind the epoch at which he flourished, does not appear as a poet of striking power or originality.' This doubtless explains why so few versions from Mu'izzī have as yet been made. E. G. Browne offered two, one of them as follows:

Since that sugar-raining ruby made my heart its thrall,
Hath mine eye become a shell to harbour pearls withal.
Yea, as oysters filled with pearls must surely be the eyes
Of each lover who for those sweet sugar-liplets sighs.
Yet the shafts of thy narcissus-eye blood-drinking fail
To transfix my heart protected by thy tresses' mail.
Picture fair, by whose belovéd presence by me here
Seems my chamber now like Farkhár, now like far Cashmere,
If thy darkling tresses have not sinned against thy face
Wherefore hang they, head-dependent, downward in disgrace?
Yet, if sin be theirs, then why do they in heaven dwell,
Since the sinner's portion is not Paradise, but Hell?

R. A. Nicholson also translated two odes, of which one is here quoted:

If my Belov'd—fair picture!— deigned but to look upon me,
My passion's grief and sorrow were not so sore a burden;
And if her glance tale-telling had not revealed her secret,
From all the world my secret would have been hidden always.
'Twould seem as though I dwelt in a Paradise of gladness,
If now and then my Sweetheart along the road were passing.
O that my food were made of her lips' twin rubies only,
That o'er her in requital mine eye might shed its rubies!
And O that she would never my banquet leave behind her,
That with her cheeks my banquet might glow like beds of tulips!

The artificiality of Mu'izzī's poetry is well demonstrated by this little lyric. The same characteristic commands our notice when we turn to his famous elegy lamenting the deaths in quick succession of Niẓām al-Mulk and Malik Shāh. The tropes and figures which abound in this poem make an unfortunate impression of insincerity to modern taste; they were accepted by the age for which Mu'izzī wrote as proof of high artistry and deep feeling. The lament runs to considerable length, and only a few verses are given below:

Shughl-i daulat bī-khaṭar shud, kār-i millat bā-khaṭar
tā tahī shud daulat ū millat zi shāh-i dād°gar:
mushkilast andāza-yi īn ḥāditha dar sharq u gharb,
hā'ilast āvāza-yi īn vāqi'a dar baḥr u bar.

The empire has lost its grandeur, the people stand exposed to peril
since empire and people were bereft of their just sovereign:
hard it is to measure the impact of this event on east and west,
terrible is the echo of this happening through land and sea.
Men say Shauwāl means frantic: what an astonishing thing!
Certainly the etymologists were well-informed on this meaning;
the secret of this meaning is known now since the king's death—
kingdom and empire were turned upside down in the month of Shauwāl.

In one month the aged minister departed to paradise sublime,
the youthful king followed after him in another month;
the world is full of commotion at the going of minister and king,
no man knows how far this commotion is going to reach. . . .
O king, if you are drunk, return from drunkenness to sobriety,
or if you are in sweet sleep, raise your head out of sweet sleep,
that you may see a nation wounded by the arrow of fortune,
that you may see a world held in the bonds of destiny,
that you may see the garden of the kingdom hueless and scentless,
that you may see the tree of the empire barren of leaf and fruit,
that you may see the realm overturned by various wonders,
that you may see the age shaken by various portents. . . .
You did unlimited good while in the world of mortality;
in the world of immortality may you rise again with good men!

In poetry persons three are prophets:
all men are agreed on this pronouncement.
Firdausī, and Anvarī, and Sa'dī—
though true, 'After me there is no prophet.'

These famous verses, quoting in the last line a Tradition of Muḥammad, sum up the esteem in which Auḥad al-Dīn 'Alī Anvarī is held by the Persians. Born in Abīvard to the west of Marv, he studied at Ṭūs where he acquired that all-round education of which he was able later to boast.

Of music, logic and philosophy I have a little acquaintance—
I speak the honest truth, I don't say I know them profoundly.
In theology, too, as much as a clear brain can believe,
if you will believe me, I'm quite clever at exposition;
I am no stranger either to astronomy and astrology—
if you don't credit me, trouble to test me: I'm quite ready.

These were qualities which, when allied to a sweet diction, a nimble wit and a genius for flattery, recommended him to the notice of Sulṭān Sanjar. Anvarī succeeded at court, for he candidly recognized that 'beggary is the poet's law'; but inwardly he resented the circumstances which made talent dependent for reward upon the whim of the powerful. He therefore maintained through long years spent in the shadow of princes the integrity of the true artist. This was to prove a consolation and a bulwark, for after Sanjar's death in 1157 his luck deserted him; the Saljūq empire declined towards its dissolution, and patrons became progressively harder to find. His fall from grace is said to have come about in the following way: relying on his competence in reading the stars, he predicted a storm for a day which proved to be cloudless from dawn to sunset, and as he had always taken pride in being a learned poet, his learning being discredited, his poetry also fell under suspicion. His last years were passed in scholarly retirement; he died about 1190.

Anvarī was a prolific writer; the Lucknow lithograph of his *Kullīyāt* contains 770 pages. His poetry is marked not merely by a rich variety of rhetorical figures; literary taste by his time had become so accustomed to such verbal gymnastics that some further proof of poetic skill was looked for, and the answer found was ever-deeper erudition and obscurity more profound. These qualifications for greatness Anvarī mastered early; of the first poems with which he won Sanjar's approval Daulatshāh remarks that they 'are difficult and require a commentary.' The very attributes which commended Anvarī to the rulers of his day, and to all succeeding scholiasts and schoolmasters, render him almost incommunicable in another language. Yet under the impact of deep emotion he could compose poems which have successfully stood the searching test of translation. When Sanjar was held captive by invading Ghuzz tribesmen who devastated the fair cities of north-eastern Persia, his laureate lamented his predicament in lines which were to attract the interest of Captain William Kirkpatrick, serving British interests in eighteenth-century India. Writing in the first volume of the *Asiatick Miscellany*, published at Calcutta in 1785, he commented: 'The poem is one of the most beautiful in the Persian language. The sentiments are throughout natural, and not unfrequently sublime; the images are for the most part striking and just; the diction is at once nervous and elegant, animated and chaste; and the versification, although not everywhere equally smooth and flowing, seems, notwithstanding, to be happily adapted to the subject, the measure being, as I believe, the most slow and solemn that is used in Persian poetry.' So an English officer was able to savour and pronounce upon Anvarī's work a century and three-quarters ago, and to make this lament into a famous paraphrase which he entitled 'The Tears of Khorassan.'

I

Waft, gentle gale, oh waft to Samarcand,
When next thou visitest that blissful land,
  The plaint of Khorassania plunged in woe:
Bear to Turania's King our piteous scroll,
Whose opening breathes forth all the anguished soul,
  And close denotes what all the tortur'd know.

II

Whose red-tinged folds rich patriot blood enclose,
The mortal fine impos'd by ruthless foes,
  And misshap'd letters prove our trembling fears:
Whose every word reveals a pungent grief,
Whose every line implores a prompt relief,
  While every page is moistened with our tears.

III

Soon as loud Fame our wretched fate shall sound,
The ear of Pity shall receive a wound,
  And feel th'extreme of intellectual pain:
Soon as our dismal tale shall meet the view,
The melting orbs shall catch a purple hue,
  And sanguine drops the mournful verse distain.

The original poem runs to seventy-three couplets; Kirkpatrick's version is a remarkable display of virtuosity. Ninety years later E. H. Palmer of Cambridge made a fresh translation which is not so inflated as his predecessor's, and is in its own way quite as admirable. Palmer also paraphrased cleverly and amusingly one of Anvarī's later poems, a bitter satire composed in his disillusioned old age; the ode is again of great length, and only three stanzas from the English imitation are here quoted.

There's a tale of a daw and an eagle—
But I needn't allude to the verse,
For a duck may dress up like a sea-gull
And no one be twopence the worse.
Because I'm admired as a singer,
With envy you're ready to die.
Are you to put *your* dirty finger
In every one's pie?

Get out! for though Gog, *redivivus*
As Calumny, batter and storm,
He won't of our rampart deprive us,
If Sikander's alive and in form.
Now in case you are tempted too greatly
To tread on such delicate ground,
I'll tell you a story that's lately
Been going the round.

A fop that I won't waste a curse on
To make me look stupid and small,
Says, 'Who is that strange-looking person?
I can't recollect him at all.'
Says Balkh, 'Well he is as you've reckoned,
But I can the matter arrange,
As *I'm* a new world every second
No wonder *he's* strange.'

So the fallen idol of Sanjar consoled himself when snapped at by younger rivals eager to drive him further into the wilderness; he even retained enough resilience to court the favour of new princes.

> Than the present my rhymes could have been at
> No brighter or luckier date,
> With a Nasir and Togral Takin at
> The head of the state.

Away in north-western Persia another famous poet of even greater obscurity than Anvarī was serving another but less eminent prince. Afḍal al-Dīn Badīl ibn ʿAlī Khāqānī, born at Shirvān on the west coast of the Caspian Sea (the report that his birthplace was Ganja is unsubstantiated) in the early years of the twelfth century, learned early the vital importance of invective to the aspiring poet; he proved an apt enough pupil. His career at court very nearly ended as soon as it was begun. He composed a panegyric, full of the usual and expected hyperbole, and concluded by begging the ruler, Akhtisān ibn Minūchihr the Shirvānshāh, for a modest gift.

> Give me a robe to warm me in its fold,
> Or a young slave to nestle in my hold.

'When the Khāqān perused this verse, he ordered Khāqānī to be slain,' Daulatshāh informs us. 'On hearing of this decree, Khāqānī immediately divined what was amiss. He caught a fly, pulled out its wings and sent it to the Khāqān. "The crime was not mine but this fly's," he wrote. "He changed my '*and* a young slave' into '*or* a young slave'." The Khāqān appreciated the point and was very pleased with Khāqānī.' In Persian 'or' differs from 'and' ('with') by a single dot: the fly was accused of having smudged Khāqānī's writing and so made it appear that he entertained doubts of his patron's capacity for munificence.

Some years later the poet, perhaps tiring of the petty intrigues of a provincial court and ambitious to swim in wider, albeit deeper waters, sought permission to leave his employment: he wished to make the pilgrimage to Mecca. His request was finally granted; the long journey inspired Khāqānī to compose his *Tuḥfat al-'Irāqain*, a long poem in rhyming couplets in which he described conventionally the lands and cities through which he had passed. In this work he lavishes fulsome compliments upon the various grandees who flattered him with their attention and hospitality *en route*; he immortalizes his family relations including his grandfather, his father, his mother 'who was a cook' and his uncle 'who was a physician'; and in boastful strain he expatiates upon his own attainments.

I have no equal on the face of the earth,
no one in the world possesses words like mine;
henceforth let all ask the Word for words, but
ask me for the secrets of word-spinning.
I was but a mote of the substance of Reason;
I became a sun in the shadow of Reason.
I am the world-ruling sun of Speech
and all these poetasters are like moons;
they are my inferiors by three degrees
and have augmented their capital from me.
Though they show some talent when I'm not there,
they are nothing when they come near me—
though the moon sheds light when the sun is hidden,
in the presence of the sun it flees away.

On his return from Mecca in 1157 Khāqānī found the conspiracy of poetasters much more dangerous than he had imagined. Akhtisān disliked his boastful record of successes in other courts, and confined him to the fortress of Shābirān. Thus Khāqānī had time enough to practise the genre for which Mas'ūd-i Sa'd had been famous; his *ḥabsīya* is thought to be a masterpiece of prison-poetry. Even in such narrow straits and dire discomfort he forgot none of the tricks of his trade; his doleful verses are crowded with brilliant ornament and far-fetched conceits.

When at dawn my smoke-like sigh billows up as a canopy,
my night-measuring eyes sit bathed in blood like sunrise.
The party of grief is prepared, myself a burning willow-twig,
so that my wine-straining eyelids may thus act as a filter.
The orange-hued dome of heaven is a very kaleidoscope:
how long must I boil, for my yellow bile all to flow out?
My morning sighs rain like arrows; why doesn't that old wolf
in shepherd's clothing throw down his shield before my clamour?
Since this iron-grey vat has scoured and fired my iron-dross
it is wrapped in smokeblack expressed from my bewildered heart.

The commentators explain that the 'old wolf in shepherd's clothing' is the nine-layered heaven, the controller of human destinies; the 'iron-grey vat' is Khāqānī's cell. As for 'myself a burning willow-twig,' it is pointed out that burnt willow was employed in the process of clarifying wine.

Khāqānī was eventually released, but suffered the double bereavement of his wife and his young son; the elegies which he composed on their deaths are remarkable for sincerity and comparative freedom from artifice. The strenuous efforts which he made to find a new patron who would be both rich and unfickle fill many pages of his extremely voluminous *Dīvān*. He even went so far in his wide search as to approach the 'Caesar' of Byzantium, for whose sake he declared himself ready to become a Christian; wearing the robes appropriate to his new profession, he would dispute on Christian dogmatics so subtly before the theologians of Constantinople that they would gape in wonder at his erudition, and hail him as a welcome defender of their faith. Alternatively, if that pleased the emperor better, he was prepared and able to 'revive the laws of the *Zend-Avesta*' in his native Persia. All this proved, however, to no purpose; Khāqānī died at Tabrīz in 1185 or some years after, and was buried a Muslim.

While the writings of Mu'izzī, Anvarī and Khāqānī, for all their ingenious inventiveness and technical virtuosity, seem to the western critic to possess but a limited, almost a parochial appeal, in Niẓāmī we encounter a genius of universal significance, the first in Persian literature worthy to take place beside Firdausī. Niẓām al-Dīn Ilyās ibn Yūsuf called Niẓāmī was born at Ganja (now within the Soviet Caucasus) in 1140. Orphaned of father and mother at an early age, and soon bereft of the uncle who had been his guardian, he turned for consolation to the comforts of religion, and enjoyed a deserved reputation for piety all his life. Discovering the gift of poetry, and admiring the mystical compositions of Sanā'ī who had found in Bahrām Shāh a purchaser for that kind of verse, he wrote his *Makhzan al-asrār* in emulation of the *Ḥadīqat al-ḥaqīqa*; it was to another Bahrām Shāh, the son of Dāwud, that the poem was dedicated. There is dispute regarding the chronology of this and Niẓāmī's other works, but the likeliest date for the completion of the *Makhzan al-asrār* is 1176.

The poem begins with an elaborate series of exordia: first in praise and worship of God, followed by veneration of the Prophet Muḥammad, then a hopeful tribute to Bahrām Shāh, and finally an explanation of how the work came to be attempted. Thereafter the matter is organized into twenty discourses, each illustrated by anecdote. Niẓāmī's style has been well described by C. E. Wilson: 'Niẓāmī uses a mode of expression which is rare, though not unique, among Persian poets, who, though often obscure, are generally what may be called conventionally obscure. Niẓāmī, on the other hand, like many European poets, is unconventionally obscure. He employs images and metaphors to which there is no key save in the possession of the poetic sense and of sound judgment. In a poet like Jāmī, a great admirer and imitator of Niẓāmī, the style, in spite of its frequent quaint conceits, is so lucid that we can almost anticipate the sense. In Niẓāmī we cannot do so, but have to use our best judgment and imagination.' The following anecdote from the tenth discourse of the *Makhzan al-asrār* indicates how much more mannered Niẓāmī's writing is compared with Sanā'ī's.

The Messiah's foot, which ever described the world,
one day adventured into a little bazaar;
he saw a dog-wolf fallen upon the pathway,
its Joseph having emerged out of the well,
and over that carcase a throng of sightseers
hovering like a carrion-eating vulture.
One said, 'The disgustingness of this to the brain
brings darkness, like a puff to a lantern.'
Another said, 'That isn't all it produces;
it's a blindness to the eyes, a pain to the heart.'
Each man played a variation upon that theme,
cruelly abusing the wretched carcase.
When the time for speaking came to Jesus
he let go the faults, and went straight to the substance.
He said, 'Of all the engravings within His palace
no pearl is there so white as that dog's teeth;
yet these two or three men, out of fear and hope,
whitened their teeth with that burnt oyster-shell.'

By 'Joseph emerged from the well' is intended, we are told, the departure of the dog's spirit out of its body. The phrase 'whitened their teeth with that burnt oyster-shell' is explained as follows. Burnt oyster-shell was used in those times as a dentifrice; the 'burnt oyster-shell' is here a symbol for the dog's decaying carcase, the pearl (soul) within which has been plucked forth; the critics 'whitened their teeth' by grinning at the revolting spectacle, and men grin both when they are afraid (as of their own inevitable death) and hopeful (as for the merciful forgiveness of God).

Niẓāmī's final theme in the *Makhzan al-asrār*, like Sanā'ī's in his *Ḥadīqat al-ḥaqīqa*, is a lament over the wickedness triumphant in his days. Disappointed at the poor reception accorded to his essay in religious verse but resolved still to earn his living by poetry, he turned from his first model Sanā'ī and decided to take up the heroic and romantic themes which had conferred immortality, though not wealth, on Firdausī.

> Having a treasure like my 'Treasury of Secrets'
> why should I trouble myself about mere passion?
> However, there is no one in the world today
> who hasn't a passion for poems on passion.

That was his justification for writing his next work, the *Khusrau u Shīrīn*, probably completed in 1180. This poem recounts in some 7,000 couplets the love-story of the Sāsānian emperor Khusrau Parvīz and his beloved Shīrīn, and the tragedy of Khusrau's rival Farhād who, on receiving false tidings of the death of his lady, hurled himself down from the mountain through which (as a Herculean labour) he had wellnigh tunnelled. From ancient Persia Niẓāmī next moved to ancient Arabia; the *Lailā u Majnūn*, begun in 1188 and dedicated to Khāqānī's old patron Akhtisān, has as its theme the melancholy infatuation of the desert-poet Qais for the lovely Lailā and the disastrous fate which overtook them both. James Atkinson, who made such a successful presentation of the *Shāh-nāma*, published in 1836 a skilful version of this poem from which the following extract is quoted; the lovers are dead, and their friend Zaid realizes in a dream the mystical import of their immortal love.

> The minstrel's legend chronicle
> Which on their woes delights to dwell,
> Their matchless purity and faith,

And how their dust was mixed in death,
Tells how the sorrow-stricken Zyd
Saw, in a dream, the beauteous bride,
With Majnun, seated side by side.
In meditation deep, one night,
The other world flashed on his sight
With endless vistas of delight—
The world of spirits;—as he lay
Angels appeared in bright array,
Circles of glory round them gleaming,
Their eyes with holy rapture beaming;
He saw the ever verdant bowers,
With golden fruit and blooming flowers;
The bulbul heard, their sweets among,
Warbling his rich mellifluous song;
The ring-dove's murmuring, and the swell
Of melody from harp and shell:
He saw within a rosy glade,
Beneath a palm's extensive shade,
A throne, amazing to behold,
Studded with glittering gems and gold;
Celestial carpets near it spread
Close where a lucid streamlet strayed;
Upon that throne, in blissful state,
The long-divided lovers sate,
Resplendent with seraphic light:—
They held a cup, with diamonds bright;
Their lips, by turns, with nectar wet,
In pure ambrosial kisses met;
Sometimes to each their thoughts revealing,
Each clasping each with tenderest feeling.
—The dreamer who this vision saw
Demanded, with becoming awe,
What sacred names the happy pair
In Irem-bowers were wont to bear.

A voice replied: 'That sparkling moon
Is Laili still—her friend, Majnun;
Deprived in your frail world of bliss,
They reap their great reward in this!'
Zyd, wakening from his wondrous dream,
Now dwelt upon the mystic theme,
And told to all how faithful love
Receives its recompense above.

The fourth of Niẓāmī's quintette of short epics (though 'short' is perhaps not a very apt description for a poem of more than 10,000 verses) is the *Iskandar-nāma*, a superb treatment of the medieval legend of Alexander the Great and his quest for the Fountain of Life. This poem was written in two parts having the separate titles *Iqbāl-nāma* and *Khirad-nāma*, and was published in two editions, the first in 1191 and the second about 1200. One of its chief topics is the role of philosopher-minister assigned to Aristotle; in treating this motive Niẓāmī underlines, as throughout his writings, the need of the just ruler for sound advisers. This was a point to be made again and again by Persian poets, who tended increasingly to regard themselves as, in this respect, successors to Plato; we are also reminded of the part played in the royal circle by the vizier, and the control of imperial patronage that he exercised, so that no poet aspiring to the ruler's favour dared neglect to win the sympathy of his chosen minister. The story of Alexander had of course featured among the many episodes depicted by Firdausī; Niẓāmī was glad to acknowledge his indebtedness to the great master, not only by composing this work (alone among his five) in the heroic *mutaqārib* metre but also in direct confession. Firdausī was the pioneer, himself the eager follower.

That ancient orator, the wizard of Ṭūs,
he who adorned the face of Speech like a bride,
in that poem, composed like jewels pierced,
left unspoken many things well worth saying.

Meanwhile in 1198, about four years before his death, Niẓāmī completed his last and in many ways his greatest work, the *Haft paikar*. The hero of this poem is the emperor Bahrām Gūr, whose whole life-history is recounted. The chief interest, however, concerns his discovery as a young man of seven portraits in the palace of Khavarnaq, each representing a beautiful princess —of India, China, Khvārizm, Russia, Persia, Byzantium and Morocco. Bahrām falls in love with all seven and, having recently succeeded to the throne, makes them all his brides; he builds a separate dome for each, fashioning it in the style and colour appropriate to the clime from which each hails. There he visits them on seven successive days of the week, to be entertained with stories illustrating the astrological aspect and inner symbolism of the seven colours—black, yellow, green, red, blue, sandal-wood and white. The theme afforded Niẓāmī full scope for the exercise of his varied gifts; by later artists illustrating manuscripts of his works it was gratefully welcomed as a challenge to their skill and inventiveness. Here is Niẓāmī's picture of 'that great Hunter' at the chase; the version is C. E. Wilson's.

Upon a day, on Yaman's hunting-ground,
In company with brave men of that land,
The prince whose name had Bahrām Gūr become,
Whose Bahrām bore the ball off from the sky,
Was breathing in the pleasure of the chase—
Munẓir preceding, and Nu'mān behind.
Lost in amazement at the majesty
His form from head to foot displayed were all.
A cloud of dust rose suddenly afar,
Such that the sky united with the earth.
The monarch of the world urged on his steed,
Like flowing water towards that dust he rode.
A lion, with aggressive claws stretched out,
On a wild ass's back and neck he saw.

So from above to bring it to the ground
The prince took out his bow and lay in wait,
Sought from the quiver a sharp-pointed shaft,
Then put it to the string and drew it back.
The sharp point struck the shoulders of the two,
And having pierced them passed through both the holes;
Then to its notch 'twas buried in the ground—
What profits mail or shield before such shaft?
When from the thumbstall he had sent the shaft,
The prince stood holding in his hand the bow.
The onager and lion fell and died;
The shaft lay in the ground's heart to its plumes.
The Arabs seeing such a shot approved
The ruler of the Persians he should be.
Whoever cast his eyes upon that prey
Kissed with all reverence the prince's hand.
From that time forth they called him Lion-strong;
Thenceforth entitled him King Bahrām Gūr.
When they had reached the town they told the tale
In full of onager and lion slain.
Munẓir gave orders to his ministers
That painters should with their materials come,
That they should in Khavarnaq paint in gold
The lion crouching on the onager;
The prince in pose, the arrow to its notch
In the earth when he'd shot and pierced the two.
The picture by the painter painted, all
Who saw it thought the animals were real.
They praised the Almighty Maker of the world
Upon the hand so mighty of its king.

In addition to these five idylls, affectionately known as the *Khamsa* or *Panj Ganj* ('Five Treasures') and emulated by many later poets, Niẓāmī composed a considerable number of odes, of which, however, comparatively few have survived. These exhibit his characteristic style, a richness of palette reinforced by new compound-words and original conceits. His lament for old age follows the familiar pattern, but is marked by a sincerity not always found in such compositions.

In this meadow where I stand, my loins doubled up with old
    age,
what portion can I hope to pluck henceforth from the bough
    of life?
My palm-tree offers no longer shade or fruit for anyone
since the swift wind of vicissitude stripped bare my branches.
Heaven, with its back bent over me, is making my grave;
the whiteness of my hairs proclaims the camphor of the tomb.
Once there was a double string of pearls in my mouth,
but the cruel sky loosed and scattered all my pearls.
My day has come to a close, and like an owl I would fly
forth from this desolation to the habitation of death.

Niẓāmī had turned away from religious poetry when his *Makhzan al-asrār* failed to achieve its author's purpose. His contemporary 'Aṭṭār, on the other hand, persevered in Sanā'ī's footsteps all through his long life, pouring out sequence after sequence on mystical themes of astonishing variety and richness. This writer, a man of most remarkable originality, presents the modern researcher with many difficult problems. The ancient sources show variants in his name and genealogy, but this much is reasonably certain, that he was called Farīd al-Dīn 'Aṭṭār, Muḥammad son of Ibrāhīm. As for the dates of his birth and death, regarding these there exists the widest difference of opinion; the old authorities offer 1117 or 1118 for the former, but anything between 1193 and 1234 for the latter event. Professor Sa'īd Nafīsī, who has written a valuable monograph on 'Aṭṭār's life and works, reaches the conclusion that he was born in 1136 and died in 1230—a fine old nonagenarian, but not an exceptional centenarian. However, all this confusion over vital statistics is as nothing compared with the bewilderment investing the poet's bibliography. The medieval biographers like to say that 'Aṭṭār wrote 114 books, one for each Sūra of the Koran. Nafīsī has listed sixty-six titles actually ascribed; he accepts as genuine only twelve, of which three are no longer extant. Even this drastically reduced total leaves 'Aṭṭār the author of no less than 45,000 couplets, besides a prose book which has been printed in two sizeable volumes.

'Aṭṭār's most celebrated book is the *Manṭiq al-ṭair*, the 'Bird-Parliament' as FitzGerald called his brief but masterly epitome. This poem displays the author in his characteristic role of allegorist, introducing to Persian verse the mystical parable which Suhravardī at about the same time was acclimatizing to Persian prose. The plot, profoundly elaborated out of a thin legend attributed to Abū Ḥāmid al-Ghazālī, relates how all the birds, under the leadership of the Hoopoe, went upon a long pilgrimage in search of the mythical Sīmurgh, whom they desired to make their king: the story symbolizes the quest of human souls after union with God. The following extract from FitzGerald's version depicts the final scene of full realization:

And so with these poor Thirty: who, abasht
In Memory all laid bare and Conscience lasht,
By full Confession and Self-loathing flung
The Rags of carnal Self that round them clung;
And, their old selves self-knowledged and self-loathed,
And in the Soul's Integrity re-clothed,
Once more they ventured from the Dust to raise
Their Eyes—up to the Throne—into the Blaze,
And in the Centre of the Glory there
Beheld the Figure of—*Themselves*—as 'twere
Transfigured—looking to Themselves, beheld
The Figure on the Throne en-miracled,
Until their Eyes themselves and *That* between
Did hesitate which *Sëer* was, which *Seen*;

They That, That They: Another, yet the Same;
Dividual, yet One: from whom there came
A Voice of awful Answer, scarce discern'd
From *which* to Aspiration *whose* return'd
They scarcely knew; as when some Man apart
Answers aloud the Question in his Heart—
'The Sun of my Perfection is a Glass
Wherein from *Seeing* into *Being* pass
All who, reflecting as reflected see
Themselves in Me, and Me in Them: not *Me*,
But all of Me that a contracted Eye
Is comprehensive of Infinity:
Nor yet *Themselves*: no Selves, but of The All
Fractions, from which they split and whither fall.
As Water lifted from the Deep, again
Falls back in individual Drops of Rain
Then melts into the Universal Main.
All you have been, and seen, and done, and thought,
Not *You* but *I*, have seen and been and wrought:
I was the Sin that from Myself rebell'd:
I the Remorse that tow'rd Myself compell'd:
I was the Tajidar who led the Track:
I was the little Briar that pull'd you back:
Sin and Contrition—Retribution owed,
And cancell'd—Pilgrim, Pilgrimage, and Road,
Was but Myself toward Myself: and Your
Arrival but *Myself* at my own Door:
Who in your Fraction of Myself behold
Myself within the Mirror Myself hold
To see Myself in, and each part of Me
That sees himself, though drown'd, shall ever see.
Come you lost Atoms to your Centre draw,
And *be* the Eternal Mirror that you saw:
Rays that have wander'd into Darkness wide
Return, and back into your Sun subside.'

The *Ilāhī-nāma* tells the story of a king who had six sons, whom he invited to reveal to him their dearest wishes: the theme conjures up an *Arabian Nights* atmosphere. Each son confesses in turn his heart's ambition. The first prince dreams of marrying the daughter of the King of the Fairies; the second wishes to possess all magical science; the third would own Jamshīd's world-revealing cup; the fourth craves to discover the Water of Life; the fifth is ambitious for the Ring of Solomon; the sixth longs to know the alchemist's secret of converting dross into gold. The king's reply to all his sons is the same, though worked out with a variety of well-recounted anecdotes: their hearts are fixed on material and transient things, whereas true happiness is only to be attained by pursuing the spiritual and the eternal. The *Muṣībat-nāma* follows again a different pattern, while exposing the identical doctrine. The framework is provided by the famous story of the 'Ascent' of Muḥammad, that miraculous night-journey in which he passed through the seven heavens and held converse with previous prophets on his way to the near presence of God. Earlier mystics, notably the Persian Abū Yazīd of Bisṭām, had experienced spiritual 'ascensions' in imitation of the Prophet; now 'Aṭṭār constructs a poem of some 7,000 couplets on this theme. The aspiring soul passes through forty 'stations' on its celestial ascent; among the persons and personifications encountered are Gabriel, Michael, the Throne, the Footstool, the Heavenly Tablet, Paradise, Hell, the Sun, the Moon, the Four Elements, the Mountains, the Seas, the Mineral, Vegetable and Animal Kingdoms, Satan, the Spirits, Mankind, Adam, Noah, Abraham, Moses, David, Jesus and Muḥammad; the last two 'stations' are the Heart and the Soul. That concludes the journey *to* God; there yet remains to be accomplished the journey *in* God, but of that the poet refrains from speaking, hoping to describe this final stage of spiritual union in another work.

The three poems summarized above have the common feature of an underlying 'plot' around which the many incidents and illustrations are scattered. They are mystical romances after the fashion of Suhravardī's prose-myths, or Sanā'ī's *Sair al-'ibād*; they recall in this respect the famous *Ḥaiy ibn Yaqẓān*, Ibn Ṭufail's philosophical allegory which Simon Ockley popularized in eighteenth-century England. In his *Asrār-nāma* 'Aṭṭār approximates to the *Ḥadīqat al-ḥaqīqa* of Sanā'ī, and foreshadows the *Mathnavī-yi ma'navī* of Jalāl al-Dīn Rūmī. Indeed, we are informed that Rūmī as a young man received a copy of the *Asrār-nāma* from the hands of the aged 'Aṭṭār; certainly Rūmī admits his indebtedness to this work, from which he borrows a number of stories told in his own *Mathnavī*. Here is the parable of the Parrot and the Mirror, first as recounted by 'Aṭṭār.

I have heard tell how, to begin with, men
will place a looking-glass before a parrot,
and when the parrot in that mirror peers
he sees forsooth a thing most like himself;
then someone speaks in a melodious voice,
the sound contriving from behind the glass,
and the delightful parrot therefore deems
the voice he hears comes from another parrot.
Listening word by word, his heart is glad
and very gently he repeats the sounds.
Your mirror Being is, a glass concealed;
not-being is the frame that holds the glass,
and every form, deficient or complete,
within that mirror as an image shows.
Since you see nothing else but the reflexion
and stand and sit as the reflexion does,
you come to think that every sound and act
belongs to the reflexion, which you know;
but when you sit within the mirror's mirror
you see no more the mirror, but the Face.

Rūmī develops 'Aṭṭār's idea by making the 'mirror' the

mystic's spiritual instructor, while the unseen speaker and teacher is God.

A parrot peers into the looking-glass
and there beholds the image of itself.
The well-instructed teacher, hid behind
the mirror, then melodiously speaks;
the little parrot thinks the muttered words
are uttered by the parrot in the glass
and so learns human speech from its own kind,
for it is ignorant of that old wolf's cunning.
The sage is teaching from behind the mirror,
for parrots only learn from other parrots;
the parrot learns to speak from that wise man,
but gathers naught of his mysterious meaning.
So it acquires speech, word by word, from Man:
what should the parrot know of Man but this?
Thus, too, the puffed-up pupil sees himself
within the mirror of the teacher's body;
how should he glimpse the Universal Reason
behind that glass, what time the words are spoken?
He fondly thinks it is a man who speaks;
of Universal Reason he knows nothing.
He learns the words, the mystery he ignores—
he is a parrot, not an intimate.

In addition to the foregoing poems 'Aṭṭār is established by Nafīsī as the author of the *Khusrau-nāma*, composed shortly after the death of his mother; the *Mukhtār-nāma*, a collection of over two thousand quatrains arranged under fifty headings; the *Pand-nāma*, a mere trifle of 850 couplets of ghostly counsel; and a *Dīvān* of odes and lyrics, which in Nafīsī's edition amounts to some 10,000 verses. Many of the poems in the *Dīvān* show great originality, and it is clear that 'Aṭṭār's influence on Rūmī as a composer of this style of verse was very considerable. In the following extract 'Aṭṭār pictures himself upon a spiritual voyage:

> When in the night of dryness
>   I call on Thee,
> The vessel of my spirit
>   Goes riding free.
>
> And where the mighty ocean
>   Before me lies
> A hundred salty torrents
>   Flood from mine eyes.
>
> I make for me a vessel
>   Out of Thy name,
> And into distant waters
>   I sail the same.
>
> And by that mighty motion
>   Upon each breath
> My spirit everlasting
>   Far ventureth.

'Aṭṭār also compiled biographies and sayings of Muslim saints and mystics in his prose *Tadhkirat al-auliyā'*, a source-book of great value for the study of early Ṣūfism. He writes a clear, antique Persian, unaffected by the euphuistic mannerisms affected by many of his contemporaries, having a quiet dignity and an unpretentious beauty of diction most in keeping with his subject. The quality of the material contained in this large work, which has yet to be translated into English (Baron Erik Haermelin has put it into Swedish), is exemplified by the story of how Dhu 'l-Nūn the Egyptian experienced the call to God. The version is by R. A. Nicholson, editor of the original text.

'The cause of his conversion was as follows. He received a sign from Heaven that he should go to visit such and such an ascetic at such and such a place. He found that this man, having suspended himself from the branch of a tree, was saying, "O body! help me to obey God, or I will keep thee like this until thou diest of hunger." Dhu 'l-Nún began to weep. The ascetic heard him sobbing and cried, "Who is this that pities one whose shame is little and whose sins are great?" Dhu 'l-Nún approached and greeted him and asked what he was doing. He replied that his body would not consent to obey God but desired to mix with mankind. "I thought," said Dhu 'l-Nún, "it must have shed the blood of a Moslem or committed a mortal sin." The ascetic said, "Do not you know that when once you have mixed with mankind, every evil thing will ensue?" "Thou art a fearful ascetic." "If you wish to see one who is more ascetic than I, climb this mountain." Dhu 'l-Nún went up the mountain and saw a young man seated in a cell; one of his feet, which he had cut off, was lying outside and worms were eating it. "One day," he said in answer to Dhu 'l-Nún's question, "I was sitting in this cell, when a woman passed by. My heart inclined to her and my body urged me to follow her. I put one foot outside. I heard a voice saying, 'After having served and obeyed God for thirty years, art not thou ashamed to obey the Devil now?' Thereupon I cut off the foot which I had set outside, and I am waiting here to see what will happen to me. Why have you come to a sinner like me? If you wish to see a man of God, go to the top of the mountain." The mountain was so high that Dhu 'l-Nún could not reach the top, but he inquired about that ascetic and was told that he had long been living in a cell on the highest peak of the mountain; that one day a man disputed with him and declared that daily bread is gained by means of human effort; that he then vowed he would never eat anything gained by this means, and that after he had remained without food for some time, God sent bees which flew around him and gave him honey. Dhu 'l-Nún said, "My heart was deeply moved by what I had seen and heard, and I perceived that God takes in hand the affairs of them that put their trust in Him and does not let their tribulation come to naught. Afterwards, as I was going on my way, I saw a little blind bird perched on a tree. It alighted on the ground. I said to myself, 'How does the poor creature get food and drink?' It dug a hole in the earth with its beak, and two basins appeared, one of gold containing sesame and one of silver containing rosewater. The bird ate and drank its fill and flew back to the tree, and the two basins vanished. On seeing this Dhu 'l-Nún became altogether beside himself. He resolved to trust in God and was truly converted. Having gone some distance further, at nightfall he entered a ruined building, where he found a jar of gold and jewels covered by a board on which was inscribed the name of God. His friends divided the gold and jewels, but Dhu 'l-Nún said, "Give me this board, my Beloved's name is upon it"; and he did not cease kissing it all day. Through the blessing thereof he attained to such a degree that one night he dreamed and heard a voice saying to him, "O Dhu 'l-Nún! the others were pleased with gold and precious jewels, but thou wert pleased only with My name: therefore have I opened unto thee the gate of knowledge and wisdom." '

It is to this same work that we owe the preservation of the beautiful prayer of Rābi'a the woman-saint: 'O God! if I worship Thee in fear of Hell, burn me in Hell; and if I worship Thee in hope of Paradise, exclude me from Paradise; but if I worship Thee for Thine own sake, withhold not Thine everlasting beauty!'

Daulatshāh states that 'Aṭṭār was murdered in Nīshāpūr on April 26, 1230, by the Mongol invaders. E. G. Browne, followed by Sa'īd Nafīsī, rejected this assertion after a scrutiny of the evidence; Nafīsī, however, who (as noted above) agrees to fix the poet's death in the year 1230, concedes that ' 'Aṭṭār did not die a natural death.' The legend that after his murder the poet took his head into his hand and walked half a league to the place where he now lies buried makes fanciful reading; even more remarkable is the story that it was during this final journey that 'Aṭṭār composed the obviously unauthentic *Bīsar-nāma* ('The

Poem of the Headless Man'). However, Nīshāpūr was sacked by Chingiz Khān in 1221, and thus 'Aṭṭār's long life spans the turbulent years, which did not shake his spiritual serenity, when Persian rule collapsed before the bloodthirsty legions from the East. His works form a bridge between the Saljūq and the Mongol periods.

SIX

Some Historians of the Thirteenth Century

Of the writing of history in Persian there is no end. In a general survey of Persian literature it is not possible to attempt more than a glance at the most significant authors—significant, that is, from the literary standpoint—and many otherwise important names must be passed over in silence. Thus it is regrettably necessary to neglect such interesting works as the *Fārs-nāma* of Ibn al-Balkhī, the *Rāḥat al-ṣudūr* of Rāvandī, the *Tāj al-ma'āthir* of Ḥasan Niẓāmī, that valuable collection of official correspondence entitled *al-Tawassul ilā 'l-tarassul*, the *Niẓām al-tawārīkh* of the famous exegete and theologian al-Baiḍāwī, and many others duly listed in C. A. Storey's admirable and exhaustive *Persian Literature: a Bio-Bibliographical Survey*. The thirteenth century, with its crowded years of falling and rising empires, produced a rich crop of historical writings, and some account will now be given of the most noteworthy of these.

The first book to be mentioned happens not to have been originally composed in Persian, or in this century; it is the translation, made by Abu 'l-Sharaf Nāṣiḥ ibn Ẓafar Jarbādhaqānī, of the Arabic *al-Kitāb al-Yamīnī*, a 'very ornate and verbose' biography of Sulṭān Maḥmūd of Ghazna completed in 1021 by Abū Naṣr al-'Utbī. The Persian interpreter, as Theodor Nöldeke demonstrated long ago in an erudite monograph, took a fairly cavalier view of his functions, his 'object being not so much to produce an accurate rendering as a rhetorical imitation of his original; hence he considers himself at liberty to change, omit and add as much as he pleases.' Some impression of the relationship between the original and the version may be gained by comparing Sir Henry Elliot's translation from al-'Utbī ('he was alarmed at first at the declared difficulty of the text, but found it to vanish after a little examination') with what the Rev. James Reynolds, albeit inadequately qualified, made of Jarbādhaqānī. The incident selected for comparison is Maḥmūd's conquest of Multān.

Elliot after al-'Utbī:—

'Intelligence reached the Sultán of the acts committed by the ruler of Múltán, Abí-l futúh, namely, respecting the impurity of his religion, the seditious designs of his heart, and the evidence of his evil doings, and his endeavours to make proselytes of the inhabitants of his country. The Sultán, zealous for the Muhammadan religion, thought it a shame to allow him to retain his government while he practised such wickedness and disobedience, and he beseeched the assistance of a gracious God in bringing him to repentance, and attacking him with that design in view. He then issued orders for the assembling of armies from among the Musulmáns for the purpose of joining him in this holy expedition,—those on whom God had set his seal and selected for the performance of good deeds, and obtaining either victory or martyrdom. He departed with them towards Múltán in the spring, when the rivers were swollen with the rain, and the Indus and other rivers prevented the passage of the cavalry, and offered difficulties to his companions. The Sultán desired of Andpál, the chief of Hind, that he would allow him to march through his territory, but Andpál would not consent, and offered opposition, which resulted in his discomfiture. The Sultán, consequently, thought it expedient to attack Rái Andpál first, notwithstanding his power, in his jungles, to bow down his broad neck, to cut down the trees of his jungles, to destroy every single thing he possessed, and thus to obtain the fruit of two paradises by this double conquest. So he stretched out upon him the hand of slaughter, imprisonment, pillage, depopulation, and fire, and hunted him from ambush to ambush, into which he was followed by his subjects, like "merchants of Hazramaut, who are never without their sheets." The spears were tired of penetrating the rings of the coats of mail, the swords became blunt by the blows on the sides, and the Sultán pursued the Rái over hill and dale, over the soft and hard ground of his territory, and his followers either became a feast to the rapacious wild beasts of the passes and plains, or fled in distraction to the neighbourhood of Kashmír. When Abí-l futúh, the ruler of Múltán, heard what had happened to the chief of Hind, notwithstanding all his power and the lofty walls of his fort, and his shining sword, and when he began to measure their relative strength, and considered how Andpál, a much greater potentate than himself, had been subdued, he looked upon himself, as compared with the Sultán, as a ravine in comparison with the top of a mountain. He, therefore, determined with all expedition to load all his property on elephants, and carry it off to Sarandíp, and he left Múltán empty for the Sultán to do with it as he chose. The Sultán marched towards Múltán, beseeching God's aid against those who had introduced their neologies into religion and had disparaged it. The inhabitants of the place were blind in their errors, and desirous of extinguishing the light of God with their breath, so the Sultán invested Múltán, took it by assault, treated the people with severity, and levied from them twenty thousand thousand dirams with which to respite their sins. Then the reports of the Sultán's conquests spread over distant countries, and over the salt sea as far even as Egypt; Sind and her sister (Hind) trembled at his power and vengeance; his celebrity exceeded that of Alexander the Great, and heresy (*ilhád*), rebellion, and enmity, were suppressed.'

Reynolds after Jabādhaqānī:—

'Abúl Futáh, Prince of Multán, was notoriously characterized as one of malignant craftiness, deceitful treachery, dubious fidelity, and detestable inclination. He set up a claim over the people of the Khutbah (i.e. the chief sovereignty) of Multán, to deal with them according to his will and pleasure, and cast the people into the lubricity of his error, and the ruin of his folly. They signified the case to the Sultán, whose reverence for Islám and jealousy for the faith stirred up and excited him to a sufficient examination into this crime, and into the subject matter of this error. And in this point he sought God's direction, and consigned all his thoughts to this religious consideration, and prepared for the affair. And he assembled a numerous company and brave army of the first men of the faith and obedience of Islám. And when that artist Spring had delineated her paintings upon the tracts of mountain and plain, and the emperor Sun had clothed all the districts of the earth with precious dresses and embroidered robes, taken from the treasury of his glorious palace, he raised the cry, "To Múltán!" And because the river torrents and superfluous rains had filled the ferrying places of the Jíhún with divers full channels and overflowing torrents, and the road was thus obstructed and affording room for excuses, he sent to Andbal, who was King of India, a person to request of him that he would permit a passage through the midst of his kingdom that the army of Islám might pass. He, however, placed the hand of repulse upon the face of the Sultán's request, and took the road of stubbornness and obstinacy. For this cause the Sultán was enraged, and began to assign two voices to sing one theme, and was resolved that before he concluded his first intentions he would by the shout of victory give to the winds the substance of that King's kingdom and the nest of his empire. So he commanded that they should extend the hand of plunder, and levelling, and destruction, and burning unto his villages and cities. And they cast Jaibal or Andbal forth from one strait unto another, and from one path to another; and they stripped all the provinces of his country, and cut off the roads and resources of his kingdom, until they expelled him to the province of Kashmír. And when Abúl Futáh, Prince of Multán, witnessed that with Jaibál, who was his high mountain and blocking pass, that hope had departed, he learnt that he had entered a well* (*whence he could not extricate himself*), and that it was impossible for flying hares to compete as travellers with foxes, and that he ought not to frame an imagination of the possibility of resistance (Verse).

' "The experienced knows when the moonlight flashes upon the sword striking hand, that the sword is not distant from his breast more than the measure of a cubit."

'He therefore packed up his treasures and his hoards, and transported them on the back of camels to Sarandib, and relinquished Multán. The Sultán, when he had arrived at those provinces, and had made a full discovery of the articles and attributes of the point, seeing that all were involved in this mad error and vain folly, confined those citizens who were inhabitants and natives, in the fort, and treated them with rigour, and pinched and corrected them with the food of punishment, (fining) them twenty thousand loads of a thousand direms, and placed upon their neck the redemption money of foes, and the tax of the rebellious. The account of his stand for religion and for the illustration of the knowledge of the (orthodox) demonstrations passed to all cities, and even arrived at Egypt. And the dread of his sword was of effectual advantage in the land of Hind and Sind, and the main source of heresy, and infidelity, and perversity in those parts was intercepted and cut off.'

It is a far cry from the austere simplicity of the tenth century version of Ṭabarī, to this fanciful refurbishing of the prolix 'Utbī. Yet Persian prose, having embarked upon this course, its sails swollen with the spice-laden breezes of Arabia, would not put back into its home-port for many long years to come. Princely appetites (and it is appropriate always to remember that these books were written in the first place to capture royal favour) greatly relished the rich sauces of far-fetched metaphor and

* Conjectural reading, MS. illegible.

intricate rhyme, and would have turned in disgust from plainer and more honest fare. The morbid fancy of medieval kings became the duty, and presently the pride and pleasure of their complaisant subjects; the fashion authorized by the Saljūqs commended itself very well to their Mongol supplanters; the giddy slope of tortuous and grandiloquent rhetoric runs true from Jarbādhaqānī to Juvainī and Vaṣṣāf. It is therefore a welcome relief to turn to the provincial and less sophisticated style of Ibn Isfandiyār, author of the *Tārīkh-i Ṭabaristān* which he began in 1210 when 'overwhelmed with grief at the news of the murder of Rustam b. Ardashír b. Ḥasan b. Rustam, the ruler of Ṭabaristán.' Turning to ancient books for consolation, he happened upon a number of rare manuscripts including an Arabic translation made by Ibn al-Muqaffa' of the Pahlavi treatise addressed by Tansar, chief *herbad* of Ardashīr Pāpakān the first of the Sāsānians, to Jasnafshāh the Prince of Ṭabaristān. Ibn Isfandiyār rendered this precious document into Persian—the original Pahlavi has perished along with the Arabic version—and used it as the introduction to his description and history of his native province. The narrative is lively and well supplied with anecdotes; there is a liberal sprinkling of quotations from the poets. The text is available to scholars in the edition of 'Abbās Iqbāl; the general reader may conveniently sample its contents in E. G. Browne's abridged translation. Here is a brief character-sketch of Shāh Ghāzī Rustam (d. 1163).

'When the Ispahbad used to sit late drinking wine, none of his servants dared go to his home, for, if he wanted one of them, and did not find him, he would on such occasions punish him with death. So only when he fell asleep towards morning did they dare to depart to their homes to rest. One night three hundred of these servants conspired together to kill him, and those who were on duty, watching their opportunity, fell upon him, and so plied their swords and maces that, when they left him dead, not one of his limbs was whole. Then they went out, saying that the

Ispahbad desired to be left alone, and bade all disperse, which they did. Sháh Ardashír, learning what had happened, desired to pursue the murderers, but was dissuaded; but such as were recognized were arrested wherever they were found and sent to him, singly or in batches, and he caused them to be hung up and shot with arrows, until in the course of a year, all had been taken and killed. The Ispahbad had four sons and one daughter. Two of the sons, Yazdigird and 'Alí, died before their father, while Ḥusámu'd-Dawla Sháh Ardashír and Fakhru'l-Mulúk Rustam survived him. His daughter was noted for her piety, devoutness and virtue. Náṣiru'd Dín Rúz-Bihán composed the following verses on the death of the Ispahbad:

O you whose coming and going was like a torrent,
like fire you consumed precipitately a whole world.
Like the wind there was never rest in you or slumber;
now you are sunk into the earth like quicksilver.'

The artful poet had been inspired by his grief to perform in his quatrain the much-appreciated trick of referring to the four elements.

The name of Muḥammad 'Aufī has already appeared several times in these pages, on account of his literary history which is still our chief source of information on the early Persian poets. Born about 1175 in Transoxiana, he found preferment at the Indian court of Nāṣir al-Dīn Qubācha, ruler of Sind; it was to his vizier 'Ain al-Mulk that he dedicated the *Lubāb al-albāb*, in which the poets are arranged according to profession. In 1228 Sind was seized by Shams al-Dīn Īltutmish, once slave and later son-in-law to Quṭb al-Dīn Aibeg, King of Delhi; to him 'Aufī quickly transferred the allegiance which he had been pleased to show to the slain Qubācha, and as proof of his new loyalty he inscribed Īltutmish's name on the dedication page of his new work. The *Jawāmi' al-ḥikāyāt*, a massive encyclopaedia of above two thousand anecdotes, is admittedly not a history in the strict sense of the term; yet intermingled with many curiosities and puerilities are fragments of historical information which invest it with extreme importance. When he compiled his first book 'Aufī had exhibited all the fashionable preciosity of his age; in his second enterprise he generally writes a clear and simple Persian; Bahār however has called attention to the inconsistency of his style in this work, shrewdly speculating that 'Aufī was influenced by the various sources on which he drew. Two extracts from different sections lend verisimilitude to this conjecture; first here is part of a description of a sea-battle.

'Fifty vessels loaded with men and armaments moved forward upon the lake, so that the stars marvelled at their configuration, and the glowing fire of the natural spirit was extinguished by their awful majesty. The ships proceeded over the water as though they were water-fowl in flight, with paddles for wings, or fleet Arab steeds whose bridles, contrary to habit, were fastened to their cruppers, or elephants urged on over the watery arena by their rider the wind, the curve of their gigantic oars plashing like an elephant's writhing trunk as they strode easily onwards.'

An effective contrast is provided by the graphic account of the assassination of the Ghaznavid usurper Ṭughril (d. 1052).

Ṭughril the Rebel, slave of Sulṭān Mas'ūd ibn Maḥmūd, seized power in the reign of Sulṭān 'Abd al-Rashīd. Stimulated and encouraged by the Sulṭān's weakness and his own strength, he took the kingdom; 'Abd al-Rashīd retired perforce to the citadel. Ṭughril then seated himself upon the throne, and ordered 'Abd al-Rashīd to be exterminated. He laid hands on Maḥmūd's properties and set about wasting his treasures. As vizier he appointed Abū Sahl Zauzanī, who though a competent and accomplished man was so enamoured of wealth and rank that he was blinded to the baneful result of those proceedings. This Ṭughril occupied all his time with drinking, and his vizier Abū

Sahl Zauzanī managed the affairs of state, disregarding the consequences of the king's conduct and careless of his own salvation. Now there was at that time a clerk in the Ministry of Correspondence called Messenger Abū 'Umar, who has reported as follows.

'There was a friendship between me and Nūshtagīn, one of the sword-bearers who paraded in full equipment on court days. One day he said to me, "Do you see what a fool he is? To think that such a scoundrelly dog should be sitting in the place of our kings!

A cloud's in the place of the moon,
a poison in the place of sugar,
a stone in the place of a jewel,
a thorn in the place of jasmine.

All hearts are pained by his stupidity, all breasts wounded by this anguish, and I have resolved to sacrifice myself for the empire and discharge my duty to the House of Maḥmūd. I shall strike him down; if he dies, my object will be achieved, and if after that they kill me, I shall not mind."

' "Brother," I warned him, "this is no easy task you've taken in hand. It calls for plenty of thought."

' "There's no need for any thought," he replied. "Seeing I'm quite ready to die, the affair will be quite easy for me to arrange."

'So he applied himself to this task, enrolling a number of conspirators to assist him. All the time I enquired what he was doing, and urged him to proceed with the utmost secrecy. In due course Ṭughril the Rebel celebrated New Year's Day; he distributed robes of honour to sundry persons, and bestowed titles and sums of money. Then on Wednesday, 6 Dhu 'l-Qa'da, Ṭughril the Rebel decided to come to court and to sit on the throne.'

Nūshtagīn now takes up the story.

'I and three colleagues made up our minds to kill him. I told my fellow-conspirators, "I'll start first, weighing in with a mace. If that does the job, well and good; if not, then you lay about him with halberts and finish him off. If we get killed, our fame will be broadcast throughout the world and we'll become proverbial for loyalty and dutifulness."

'We armed ourselves after this manner and stood before the royal dais. When Ṭughril entered a trembling seized my body, so that my companions could even hear my teeth rattling. I stuck a piece of wood between my teeth so that the noise of their chattering might be drowned; then I put my trust in God. As soon as Ṭughril stepped on to the dais I smote him under the breast with my mace, so hard that I fell over. My three companions then set about him with halberts and short swords and finished him off. One of my colleagues got killed, but I and the other two remained unscathed. Confusion seized the court. Then I got up and cut off his head, while the rabble came and tore him to pieces, sticking his head on the top of a stake.'

The biography of the saintly Abū Sa'īd ibn Abi 'l-Khair which Muḥammad ibn al-Munauwar composed, by the latest reckoning at the turn of the thirteenth century, has been very fully described by R. A. Nicholson in his *Studies in Islamic Mysticism*, to which those may turn who wish to know more of the *Asrār al-tauḥīd*. It was a very different kind of hero, Jalāl al-Dīn Mangubarti the Khvārizmshāh, the last Persian ruler to resist the Mongols, miserably murdered by a Kurd in 1231, that Shihāb al-Dīn Muḥammad ibn Aḥmad Nasavī mourned in his *Nafthat al-maṣdūr* ('The Consumptive's Cough'), in its own way a little masterpiece of decorative rhetoric.

'He was a sun that lighted up a darkened world, and then was veiled in setting; nay rather, he was a cloud that drenched the earth's drought-year of trouble, and then rolled up its carpet. He was the candle of the assembly of the Sultanate, that blazed brightly and was then consumed; he was the rose of the garden of kingship, that laughed gaily and then withered. He was a

Messiah who restored to life a dead world, and then ascended to the skies; he was a Kai-Khusrau who took vengeance on the Chinese, and then sank into the pit. What shall I say, what seek by this meandering? He was the light of the eye of the Sultanate; like a lantern he finally flared up and was extinguished—no, no, he was the builder of Islam, that "began a stranger and a stranger returned".'

A picture of an earlier scene in Jalāl al-Dīn's stormy career, when he was fleeing into India before Chingiz Khān's legions, is given in Elliot's extract from the *Tārīkh-i Jahān-gushāy* of Juvainī.

'When the Sultán had survived the double danger of water and fire, namely, the whirlpools of the Sind and the flame of Changíz Khán's persecution, he was joined by six or seven of his followers, who had escaped from drowning, and whom the fiery blast of evil had not sent to the dust of corruption; but, as no other course except retreat and concealment among the forests was left to him, he remained two or three days longer in his covert, until he was joined by fifty more men. The spies whom he had sent out to watch the proceedings of Changíz Khán returned, and brought him intelligence that a body of Hindú rascals, horse and foot, were lying only two parasangs distance from the Sultán, occupied in rioting and debauchery. The Sultán ordered his followers to arm themselves each with a club, and then making a night attack upon this party, he slew most of them, capturing their animals and arms. He was then joined by other parties, mounted on horses and mules, and soon after certain intelligence was brought to him that two or three thousand men of the armies of Hind were encamped in the neighbourhood. The Sultán attacked them with a hundred and twenty men, and slew many of those Hindús with the Hindí sword, and set up his own troops with the plunder he obtained.

Arabic Verse

Whoever requires anything from me, let him live by his sword,
Whoever requires anything from other men, let him solicit them.

'When the news spread throughout Hindustán of the Sultán's fame and courage, five or six thousand mounted men assembled from the hills of Balála and Mankála, for the purpose of attacking him. On his gaining intelligence of this movement, he set upon them with five hundred cavalry which he had under him, and routed and slew the Hindú armies. The effect of this success was that he was joined by several more adherents from all quarters, so that his force amounted to three thousand men. When the world-conquering Changíz Khán, who was then in the neighbourhood of Ghazní, heard of these new levies, he despatched a Mughal army, under Túrtáí, to expel him, and as the Sultan was not able to oppose him, he went towards Dehli, when Túrtáí crossed the river. The Mughals, when they heard of his flight, returned and pillaged the country round Malikpúr.'

'Alā' al-Dīn 'Aṭā Malik Juvainī, born of a good family in Khurāsān in 1225, never knew what it was to live under Persian rule; he made his career in the service of the Mongol conquerors, and was with Hūlāgū Khān's expedition of 1256 which destroyed the headquarters of the Assassins at Alamūt. In 1259 he was promoted Governor of Baghdad, captured and sacked the previous year by his foreign masters; in 1260 he completed the book which has secured him immortality. The *Tārīkh-i Jahān-gushāy* records in three volumes of ornate prose the history of Chingiz Khān, his ancestors and successors; the dynasty of the Khvārizm-Shāhs, who vainly attempted to stem the onslaught from the East; and the Ismā'īlīs and Assassins, whose overthrow Juvainī had personally witnessed. The learned and accomplished author, who did much for the revival of Islamic culture after the catastrophes of the first half of the century, eventually—one might add inevitably, for was he not a 'collaborator'?—fell into disgrace, and died miserably in 1283.

Of the factual value of Juvainī's book W. Barthold has remarked that 'it is for us an historical authority of the first rank. The author is probably the only Persian historian who had travelled in Mongolia and described the countries of Eastern Asia from his own experiences. The accounts of Čingiz-Khān's conquests are given nowhere else in such detail; many episodes, such as the battles on the Sir-Daryā above and below Otrār and the celebrated siege of Khodjand are known to us only from the *Ta'rīkh-i Djihān-Kushāi.*' Bahār, who has analysed Juvainī's style and pointed out its grammatical eccentricities and linguistic innovations, remarks that in his diagnosis of the causes of the collapse of Persian resistance Juvainī anticipates, alone among Persian writers, the philosophy of history later so famously developed by Ibn Khaldūn. He also calls attention to a feature which Juvainī shares with 'Aufī, that alternation of comparatively straightforward narrative with highly-ornamented rhetoric. The following extract from the preface of the first part (Juvainī has had the good fortune to be edited by that splendid scholar Mīrzā Muḥammad of Qazvīn, encouraged by his old friend E. G. Browne) illustrates the verbal tricks of this professor of artifice in his most magisterial mood.

Ba-sabab-i taghyīr-i rūzgār u ta'thīr-i falak-i davvār** u gardish-i gardūn-i dūn* u ikhtilāf-i 'ālam-i bū-qalamūn** madāris-i dars mundaris* u ma'ālim-i 'ilm munṭamis** gashta, u ṭabaqa-yi ṭalaba-yi ān dar dast-i lagad-kūb-i ḥavādith pāy-māl-i zamāna-yi ghaddār* u rūzgār-i makkār** shudand, u ba-ṣunūf-i ṣurūf-i fitan u miḥan giriftār* u dar ma'raḍ-i tafriqa u bavār** mu'arraḍ-i suyūf-i ābdār*** shudand u dar ḥijāb-i turāb mutavārī māndand... kidhb u tazvīr*-rā va'z u tadhkīr** dānand; taḥarmuz u namīmat-rā ṣarāmat u shahāmat nām*kunand u zabān u khaṭṭ-i uyghūrī-rā faḍl u hunar-i tamām** shināsand; har yak az abnā'u s-sūq* dar zīy-i* *ahl-i fusūq*** amīrī* gashta a har mazdūrī* dastūrī** u har muzavvirī vazīrī* u har mudabbirī dabīrī** u har musrifī* mushrifī** u har shaiṭānī* nā'ib-i dīvānī** . . . dar chunīn zamānī ki qaḥṭ-sāl-i muruvvat* u futuvvat** bāshad u rūz-i bāzār-i ḍalālat* u jahālat**, akhyār* mumtaḥan* u khvār** u ashrār*** mumakkan** u dar kār****; karīm*-i fāḍil* tāfta-yi* dām-i* miḥnat* u la'īm**-i jāhil** yāfta-yi** kām-i** ni'mat**; har āzādī* bī-zādī** u har rādī*** mardūdī; har nasībī* bī-naṣībī** u har ḥasībī*** na dar ḥisābī, u har dāhī-yi qarīn-i* dāhiya-yī* u har muḥaddithī rahīn-i** ḥāditha-yī** u har 'āqilī* asīr-i 'aqīla-yī* u har kāmilī** mubtalā ba-nāzila-yī** u har 'azīzī*tābi'-i har dhalīlī ba-iḍṭirār* u har bā-tamyīzī** dar dast-i har firūmāya-yī giriftār.** . . .*

It is quite impossible in translation to reproduce even the faintest semblance of the intricate word-play of the original, the meaning of which, with its endless repetitions, can be summed up briefly: 'Thanks to the countless vicissitudes of fate* that treacherous heaven has wrought of late** the learned man* is now despised*, the charlatan** most highly prized**, the virtuous* is oppressed*, the vicious** cherished and caressed**, etc.'

Juvainī was a most accomplished exponent of the prized art of verbal arabesque, at a time when that art had reached its full maturity. A less ambitious style was affected by his elder contemporary Abū 'Umar Minhāj al-Dīn ibn Sirāj al-Dīn Jūzjānī, author of the *Ṭabaqāt-ī Nāṣirī* which is our most important source-book for the early history of Muslim India. Jūzjānī's father had been appointed advocate-general to the forces by Muḥammad Ghūrī in 1186, and so the son grew up in the entourage of a powerful Afghan court. But Sirāj al-Dīn was murdered on an embassy to Baghdad; and presently Minhāj al-Dīn, who aspired to become a scholar, fled from the Mongols into India. Sulṭān Īltutmish promoted him 'law-officer, and director of the preaching, and of all religious, moral and judicial affairs,' a surely onerous but well-paid post which he held from 1232 to 1238. Dynastic squabbles following the death of this famous ruler compelled Jūzjānī to run to Bengal, but the accession of Nāṣir al-Dīn Maḥmūd in 1246 ensured the safety of Delhi and restored and even augmented Jūzjānī's fortunes. In gratitude he named his universal history, completed in 1260, the *Ṭabaqāt-ī Nāṣirī* after his new patron.

'The *Tabakát-i Násirí* is held in high esteem both in India and Europe,' wrote John Dowson in 1869. 'Firishta and others refer to it as an excellent work of high authority; Anquetil du Perron calls it a "precious work," and Elphinstone mentions it as a work of the highest celebrity. Stewart in his History of Bengal follows it very closely, and considers it "a very valuable book." These encomiums are not altogether undeserved; it is written in a plain, unaffected style, and the language is considered very correct. The author but rarely indulges in high-flown eulogy, but narrates his facts in a plain, straightforward manner, which induces a confidence in the sincerity of his statements, and the accuracy of his knowledge. He appears to have been industrious in collecting information from trustworthy persons, and he often mentions his authority for the facts he records. Still he is very meagre in his details, and Mr. Morley justly observes, "many portions of the history are too concise to be of much use." He is also particularly disappointing occasionally in the brevity with which he records important matters about which he might have obtained full information, such, for instance, as the irruption of the "infidels of Changíz Khán" into Bengal.' The Indian sections of this massive history in twenty-three books were edited long ago by W. Nassau Lees and translated by H. Raverty; fragments of a still earlier version made by an anonymous munshi and revised by Dowson are printed in the second volume of *The History of India as Told by its own Historians*, from which the following illustration is taken.

'Sultán Zahíru-d daula wa Nasíru-l Millat Razíu-d dín Ibráhím, son of Mas'úd, was a great king—wise, just, good, God-fearing, and kind, a patron of letters, a supporter of religion, and a pious man. When Farrukh-zád became king, Ibráhím was taken out of the fort of Barghand, and brought to that of Nai, and on the death of Farrukh-zád all men concurred in recognizing his succession. An officer named Hasan went to wait upon him, and with the approbation of the people of the kingdom he was brought out from the fort, and on Monday he auspiciously ascended the throne. The next day he spent in mourning for his late brother, and paid a visit to his tomb, and to the tombs of his ancestors. All the nobles and great men walked on foot in attendance upon him. He bestowed no favours upon any one, and hence apprehensions about his rule took possession of the hearts of the people. When the intelligence of his accession reached Dáúd, the Saljúkí, he sent some nobles into Khurásán, and made peace with him. After the death of Dáúd, his son, Alp Arslán, confirmed this treaty of peace. Ibráhím strengthened himself in the possession of his ancestors; the disorders which had arisen in the country from the late extraordinary events he rectified, and the Mahmúdí kingdom began once again to flourish. Ruined places were built afresh, and several fortified places and towns were founded, as Khaírábád, Ímanábád, and other places. Many wonders and marvels appeared in his reign, and Dáúd, the Saljúkí, died, who in havoc, war, slaughter, and conquest, passed like a flash of lightning. Ibráhím was born at Hirát, in the year of the conquest of Gurgán, 424 H. (A.D. 1033). He had thirty-six sons and forty daughters. All the daughters he married to illustrious nobles or learned men of repute. One of these princesses was ancestress in the third degree of Minháj Siráj. The cause of the emigration of the author's ancestors from Júzján, was that Imám 'Abdu-l Khálik, who is buried at Táhirábád, in Ghazní, saw in a dream while he lived in Júzján, an angel who told him to rise, go to Ghazní, and take a wife. Upon his awaking it struck him that this might be some work of the devil, but as he dreamed the same thing three times successively, he acted in compliance with his dream, and came to Ghazní. There he married one of the daughters of Ibráhím, and by that princess he had a son named Ibráhím. This Ibráhím was father of Mauláná Minhájú-d dín 'Usman, who was father of Mauláná Sirájú-d dín, the wonder of his time, and father of Minhájú-s Siráj. Sultán Ibráhím reigned happily for forty-two years, and died in the year 492 H. (A.D. 1098), at the age of sixty.'

It must have been regretted by many students of Indian history that Jūzjānī's economy of speech, an inheritance from the older school of Persian writing, should not have been maintained by the later annalists of Muslim India. But the future belonged rather to the 'diplomatic' verbiage of Nasavī and Juvainī. Jūzjānī, though living through and a victim of the Mongol invasions, had written his history of the world almost without reference to the conquerors, whose story occupies only the last section of his last book. Juvainī had pinpointed a rather different focus of interest when he took as his first subject the ancestors of Chingiz Khān. When Rashīd al-Dīn Faḍl Allāh came to compose his universal history, he assigned his first volume to 'the Turkish and Mongol tribes, their divisions, genealogy and legends.' This was indeed natural; born in Hamadhān about 1247, Rashīd al-Dīn 'began his career in the reign of the Mongol ruler Abāg̲h̲ā K̲h̲ān (1265–82) as a practising physician.' So writes E. Berthels, who adds: 'But as in addition to a remarkable knowledge of medicine he was an exceedingly talented and far-seeing statesman, he rose under G̲h̲āzān K̲h̲ān (1295–1304) from his earlier position to the rank of a *ṣadr* (and also court historian) which was given him after the execution of Ṣadr-i D̲j̲ihan Ṣadr al-Dīn Zand̲j̲ānī (May 4, 1298). In 1303 he accompanied his sovereign in this capacity on a campaign against Syria. Under Ūld̲j̲āitū (1304–16) Ras̲h̲īd attained the zenith of his career.' The death of his Mongol master was immediately followed by intrigue and disaster; Rashīd al-Dīn was accused by his political enemies of having poisoned Ūljāitū; he was of course found guilty (with or without the extraction of a 'confession'), and executed on July 18, 1318. His body was exposed and insulted before being given a Muslim burial; even then his bones were not allowed to rest, for in 1399 Tīmūr's mad son Mīrān-Shāh ordered them to be dug up and reinterred among the Jews.

It was in 1306 that Rashīd al-Dīn completed and presented to Ūljāitū the first volume of his *Jāmi' al-tawārīkh*; the rest of his gigantic task occupied him a further five years. 'The most remarkable feature of this great work is the conscientiousness with which Rashīd went to work and endeavoured to find the best and most reliable sources. Although the Mongol chronicles, the celebrated *Altan däptär*, could hardly be accessible to him as a Persian, he obtained the necessary facts from them through his friend Pūlād-čink-sānk and partly from Ghāzān himself who had a remarkable knowledge of his people's history. The information about India was furnished him by an Indian *bhikshu*, about China by two Chinese scholars. The many-sidedness of Rashīd al-Dīn's learning is simply astounding in a medieval scholar of the time. He knows of the struggles between Pope and Emperor, even knows that Scotland pays tribute to England and that there are no snakes in Ireland.' Berthels' estimate of the value of this stupendous book is not exaggerated; it is a sufficient tribute to Rashīd al-Dīn's erudition that to this day no scholar has come forward with the wide variety of equipment necessary to attempt a satisfactory edition of his whole writings.

Rashīd al-Dīn's theory of historiography is set forth in the section on the Jews. 'The essential condition for a historian is that he should write the history of each people according to their own claims and should express no opinion of his own concerning them, either in exaggeration or palliation. Whether they be true or false he must set them down exactly in accordance with the intention and claim of each people, so that responsibility for exaggeration or palliation, for truth or falsehood, may rest upon their intentions and not upon the historian. This theory is repeated here so that if anything be found incomprehensible or unaccountable, the humble historian be not taken to task therefor, nor have the tongue of blame lengthened against him, but rather his intention shall be held blameless by reason of these principles; if it please God Almighty.' The version given is that by Professor R. Levy, who observes that Rashīd al-Dīn's story of the Creation is based upon a Midrashic account rather than the Book of Genesis.

'The first things which God Almighty created were the heavens and the earths and what exists between the two, such as the heavenly hosts and the armies of the earths—thus, speaking generally. The details are, that on Sunday light and darkness and the four elements came into existence; light became particular to the heavens and darkness to the finite world. On that day also time was divided into night and day, and the holy angels and spiritual beings were created. On Monday the elements were composed, temperament was revealed, and hell was created. On Tuesday vegetable growths in all their various states were created, namely ground herbage, grass, and trees. Also heaven was created on that day, after God had at dawn gathered all the waters into one place and called them "sea." Also he drove some of the waters into river courses, so that the surface of the earth appeared and parts of it were dried and became capable of cultivation. On Wednesday he created the sun, moon, and other heavenly bodies, and endowed them with light. And he made the sun the agent of day and the conqueror of darkness, and the moon the agent of night. To each of them he gave special qualities of different kinds in the physical world. On Thursday he created two families in the animal world—birds and fishes; that is, the animals of the air and of the water such as fowl, fish, and so forth. On Friday, at the first hour he created all animals that exist on the surface of land, at the second hour he created Adam, upon whom be peace, the human being perfect in form and in essence, distinguished from the rest in his creation and his quality, wise, understanding, righteous, reasonable, having the power of deep thought and of administration and able to conceive the true values of beings by means of divine inspiration. At that hour too a great bird descended from heaven and settled on the shore of the sea and cried out: "O ye birds and fishes, be warned, for God hath now with his own might created upon this earth an animal strange and wonderful, having majesty and grandeur. He hath set upon him the name 'man' and hath planted in him overwhelming power whereby he may bring down fowl from the air or bring up fish from the depth of the sea, by command of God, Most High. Also he hath put his blessing upon his children, offspring and kindred, and in the whole race of them whose name is 'man' he hath established the power to propagate and generate, by his own command, may he be aggrandized and exalted, that their children may be many and without number and their existence may be the cause of the endurance and continuation of the world's prosperity".'

Rashīd al-Dīn's description of the British Isles occurs in the third chapter of the second section of his work, 'On the history of the Franks and what is known of the land of the Franks, its seas and islands.' The geographical situation is defined with reference to Portugal, between whose Rey and the Rey of Spain war breaks out from time to time. 'Opposite this land, in the midst of the Ocean, are two islands. One is Ibarniyā (Ireland), and one of the properties of the soil of that land is that poisonous reptiles die there. In that land also mice do not propagate. The men there are long-lived, red-complexioned, tall, strong-bodied and brave. There a spring of water flows such that if a piece of wood is placed in it, after a week its surface turns into stone. The name of the larger island is Ānglatar (England), where are mountains having many special properties and innumerable minerals, such as gold, silver, copper, tin and iron, besides all manner of fruits. One of the marvels of that land is a tree that produces bird-fruit. At the time of flowering, a sort of bag like an apple comes out containing the shape of a bird. When this gets large it comes to life and hops out. They look after this and feed it with grain, until it grows to the size of a duck. The meat of the inhabitants of that land consists for the most part of that bird. They report that there is a difference of opinion among the Christians, who during their fasts do not eat any living thing, whether to eat this bird; some consider that it belongs to the vegetable kingdom because it is the fruit of a tree, while others hold it to be animal since it bleeds. In both of the islands are sheep of whose fleece excellent broadcloth and very fine scarlet are produced. The name of the king of both islands is Suqūṭlāndiya (Scotland!), and they pay tribute to the Rey of Ānglatar.' It is interesting to find the old legend of the barnacle-goose turning up here; it reappears in the geography of Ḥamd Allāh Mustaufī, who was writing a quarter of a century later. Rashīd al-Dīn has much information about the reign of William of Holland, Holy Roman Emperor.

'History of Gulmus Caesar. He was prince of Hūlandiya, and they elected him and enthroned him as Caesar. In his reign Lūduvīkūs (Louis) who was Rey dā Farans (roi de France) went to Egypt with a complete army and launched an attack; he seized Damietta, and busied himself with preparing the conquest of Egypt. The Sulṭān of Egypt came and defeated him, and he became captive in the hands of a prince called Manfarid (Manfred). He ransomed himself with much money, and the Sulṭān sent Manfarid to recapture the island of Sicily. The Pope of the time sent the Rey dā Farans to kill Manfarid and to recover Sicily. In those days the Mongol army marched into Majaristān (Hungary) and Pūlūniya (Poland) by way of the Qipchāq steppes, killing many people and plundering. In that land such famine and hardship befell that men ate the flesh of children. Almighty God had compassion on them, and something like flour rained out of heaven of which they baked bread, so that it became their food. In that reign a mountain was split open and moved to another place, burying five thousand men. In the reign of the Rey dā Farans a Jew in Toledo made a garden. A stone appeared having no fissure; they broke it open, and inside found a book with pages of wood inscribed in Hebrew, Greek and Latin. Its words were like the Psalms, and there was written in it among other things: "This book will come to light in the reign of the Rey dā Farans," and "The Messiah, the Son of God, shall be born of the Virgin Mary to save men from Hell, and He shall be tortured at the hands of God's worst creatures." The Jew showed the book to the people, and himself turned Christian with all his household. After that Luṭuvīkūs the Rey dā Farans set out for Syria with an infinite and innumerable army, but when he reached Tunis he was defeated and obliged to pay tribute; and he had imagined from the multitude of his army that he would seize all the lands of Islam and overthrow the Muslims. He died suddenly. The length of his (sc. William's) reign as Caesar was 10 years, 11 months and 18 days.'

The concluding entry in Rashīd al-Dīn's sketch of European history is dated 705 (1305–6), and names Banaṭiktūs of Tarafīs (Benedict XI of Trévise) as the reigning Pope; actually he had just been succeeded by Clement V. Seven years later Rashīd al-Dīn presented to Ūljāitū the man born to write a continuation of Juvainī. 'Abd Allāh ibn Faḍl Allāh of Shīrāz, better known as Vaṣṣāf (short for Vaṣṣāf-i Ḥaḍrat, 'Panegyrist of the Presence'), had been a tax-collector before turning author of the *Tajziyat al-amṣār*, a survey of Persian history from 1257 to 1328. Vaṣṣāf may have owed his advancement to Rashīd al-Dīn, a writer of small rhetorical pretensions, but he modelled his style on Juvainī at his most intricate and verbose. C. Rieu remarks of his work that it 'contains an authentic contemporary record of an important period, but its undoubted value is in some degree diminished by the want of method in its arrangement, and still more by the highly artificial character and tedious redundance of its style. It was unfortunately set up as a model, and has exercised a baneful influence on the later historical compositions in Persia.' E. G. Browne, who quotes this comment with undisguised approval, adds that 'we could forgive the author more readily if his book were less valuable as an original authority on the period of which it treats, but in fact it is as important as it is unreadable.' R. Levy has instituted a telling comparison between Rashīd al-Dīn's account of the Mongol capture of Baghdad and Vaṣṣāf's treatment of the same event. Rashīd al-Dīn writes:

'On the 9th of Ẕú 'l Ḥijja in the year 655 . . . having crossed the Tigris they came to the edge of the 'Ísá canal. Súnjak Núyán begged Manjú for the command of the advanced troops that were to operate to the west of Baghdad, and when permission was given he marched away and reached Ḥurmat. Mujáhidu 'l Dín Dawátdár, who was in command of the Caliph's army, and Ibn Karz had encamped between Ya'ḳúbiya and Bájisra. When they heard that the Mongols had reached the west bank they crossed the Tigris . . . and joined battle with the Mongol army. . . . In that district [of Dujayl] there was a great sheet of water. The Mongols cut the dykes surrounding it so that the whole of the near forces of the Baghdad army were overwhelmed by the water. Buḳá Tímúr at sunrise on Thursday, the 10th of Muḥarram, attacked Dawátdár and Ibn Karz and victoriously put the Baghdad army to flight.'

Vaṣṣāf's version of these historic happenings is as follows.

'They that examine the records of the incidents of all ages and they that are acquainted with the contents of the pages of events, the unveilers of the countenance of the virgins of novelty, and they that show forth the changes of the months and centuries (may Alláh encompass them all in his wide mercy!) have testified thus: The City of Peace in the time of the 'Abbásid Caliphs was ever guarded from the hardships and ills of fortune in the sanctuary of safety and security. It was the envy of all the emperors of the world, and its palaces and mansions shared secrets with the aether of the skies. Its surrounding districts and adjacent lands were equal with the Garden of Blessings in pleasantness and freshness. In its air and in its open spaces the bird of security and peace was for ever flying, and in it were blessings and delights of every kind, comforts and luxuries of every variety, so that the mind in wonderment is incapable of enumerating them.

> Khiz̲r's draught is Baghdad's water,
> Moses' fire is there at Baghdad,
> Egypt's capital naught becomes,
> When Baghdad's prime encounters it.

Its schools and colleges are filled with champions of the rarest learning. In those days discord went with tied hands and broken feet. The masters of the various crafts and arts, in the greatness of their skill, were such that they could limn sparks of fire upon running water, and in its zeal for true portraiture the pen of slander broke from shame when it touched water. . . .'

But only a German could do full justice to Vaṣṣāf's turgidity, and Joseph von Hammer's specimen published in 1818 is a masterpiece of cunning emulation.

'Nachdem der Länder erobernde Padischah Hulaguchan die Geschäfte Bagdad's, Mossul's und Diarbekir's durch den cathegorischen Ausspruch des Schwertes entschieden, diese Districte gereinigt und die Gränzen romanischer Lande mit äusserstem Bestreben und kaiserlichen Muthe bewahrt hatte—

> Mit Rath und Schwert umfasst und schützet Er das Land,
> Umfassende und Schirmer stehn in Gottes Hand—

nachdem er alles Land und jeden Rand furchtbaren Wächtern und strengen Richtern übergeben, jedes Schloss mit Truppen besetzt, und sich endlich von diesem Geschäft geletzt hatte, stellte der Mewlana der Genauforschenden, der Sultan der Wahreit-Bestimmenden, der Helfer des Volkes und des Glaubens, Mohammed von Tus (Gott woll' ihn erhöhen von Gnaden zu Gnaden, und am Tage des Gerichts seine Rechenschaft erledigen in Gnaden) dem Herrscherthrone (es stehen wie der Pol die Säulen desselben hoch) unterthänigst vor, dass wenn die geheimnisskundige Ilchanische Gesinnung für gut befände, so wolle er zur Erneuerung astronomischer Gesetze und Berichtigung voriger Beobachtungen eine Sternwarte errichten, und Tafeln verfertigen, dem vorhersehenden durchprüfenden Scharfsinn Seiner Ilchanischen Majestät die künstigen Vorfälle der Monathe und Jahre und allgemeine und insbesondere Umwandlungen anzeigen, durch das Aufzeichen der Constellationen und der Eintheilung der Aufgänge die Wendungen der Jahre von einander unterscheiden, und nach genommener Einsicht der Cardinalpuncte, welche im Verhältnisse der grossen, mittleren und kleinen Gaben stehen, nach Erforschung des grossen Hauses, des Herren, des Adels, der Dreyecke, der Gränzen und Linien, und aller Planeten, dem Padischah die Beschaffenheit seines Lebens und Seelenzustandes, die Lage und Dauer des Reichs, die Fortpflanzung des Stammes und Geschlechtes, wahrhaft eröffnen.'

SEVEN

Medieval Persian Fiction

THE discussion of the origins of that famous collection of tales known as the *Arabian Nights* has been in progress now for a century and a half, and much learned literature on the subject has accumulated during that time. This is not the place to enter upon a consideration of that great topic, and the reader interested to have a concise and authoritative summary of the present state of knowledge and speculation is recommended to peruse the article 'Alf Layla wa-Layla' contributed by Professor Enno Littmann to the new edition (Fasc. 6, Leiden and London, 1956) of *The Encyclopaedia of Islam*. The *Nights* are mentioned here simply because it is impossible to appreciate the function and scope of fiction in medieval Persian literature without bearing in mind the Persian source of many of the stories put into the mouth of the beautiful Scheherezade. In this chapter three works of fiction will be described that belong more or less closely to the *Arabian Nights* genre, and acquired literary form in approximately the same era. It should however be remembered that many hundreds of the stories occurring not only in the self-confessed collections of anecdotes—of which the most comprehensive is Muḥammad 'Aufī's *Jawāmi' al-ḥikāyāt*—but also in the works of many epic and didactic poets have been fished out of the same abounding ocean.

The *Sindbād-nāma*, the hero of which has nothing but his name in common with Sindbad the Sailor, has attracted the attention of scholars since the early years of the eighteenth century, when Pétis de la Croix brought this cycle of stories to the notice of a public whose curiosity had so lately and powerfully been stirred by Galland's *Mille et Une Nuits*. In 1884 W. H. Clouston, that talented *vulgarisateur* of orientalia, published a version of *The Book of Sindibād*. B. Carra de Vaux, who noted that the historian al-Mas'ūdī, writing in 947, had mentioned the 'Book of Sindibād' in the same context as the 'Thousand Nights,' summarized the framework of the collection as follows: 'A king entrusts the education of his son to the sage Sindibād. The prince is ordered by his tutor to keep silence for seven days; during this time he is calumniated by the favourite queen and the king is on the point of putting him to death. Seven viziers, by each telling one or two stories succeed in postponing his execution and on the eighth day the prince, who has recovered the use of his speech, is proved innocent.' The family resemblance to the *Nights* is obvious.

In 1949 Ahmed Ateş published the Persian text of the *Sindbād-nāma* compiled by Muḥammad ibn 'Alī ibn al-Ḥasan Samarqandī called Ẓahīrī. This book was written in 1160–1 and dedicated to Qilij Ṭamghāj Khāqān Rukn al-Dīn Mas'ūd, who was ruler of Samarqand from 1160 to 1178. Early in his work after the usual flattering preliminaries, Ẓahīrī gives us an account of the transmission of the story. 'It must be realized that this book was originally in Pahlavi. Down to the time of the mighty, learned and just prince Nāṣir al-Dīn Abū Muḥammad Nūḥ ibn Manṣūr the Sāmānid—may God illumine his proof—no person had translated it. The just prince Nūḥ ibn Manṣūr commanded Master 'Amīd Abu 'l-Fawāris Fanārūzī to translate it into Persian, to remove the inconsistency and confusion which had found their way into it, and to amend and correct it. In the year 339 (950–1) Master 'Amīd Abu 'l-Fawāris undertook the task and applied his mind to it, and rendered this book into the Durrī idiom. But the style was very poor, being barren of ornament and void of decoration. Though there was ample room for rhetoric and abundant scope for artful elegance, no tire woman had adorned this bride, none had driven the steed of expressiveness into the field of eloquence, none had fashioned a garment and furnished jewels for these maiden words of virgin wisdom, so that it was near to being completely effaced from the pages of the days and altogether obliterated from the margins of time.'

Of 'Amīd Fanārūzī's 'Durrī' version, made for the Sāmānid Nūḥ I (Ẓahīrī slipped in calling his father Manṣūr, the father of Nūḥ II, instead of Naṣr), nothing has survived. Though Ẓahīrī does not mention the fact, of which he may well have been ignorant, the Saljūq poet Azraqī, who probably died before 1072, made a rhymed paraphrase of the *Sindbād-nāma* which has equally perished. Ẓahīrī's intention, as the passage quoted above indicates, was to give 'literary' flesh to the bare bones of a tale told; in this he succeeded brilliantly, according to the conventions ruling in Khurāsān during his time, for he writes an intricately rhymed and balanced prose and frequently adorns his leisurely narrative with passages from the Arabian and Persian poets—Ahmed Ateş has identified extracts from no fewer than forty-eight separate authors. It is not without interest to consider which poets Ẓahīrī quotes most frequently: al-Mutanabbī is easily first with fifty-six citations, followed by Anvarī with nineteen; 'Umar Khaiyām is quoted five times, Firdausī thrice. Here is the story of the Soldier, the Boy, the Cat and the Snake.

'The third vizier, who had heard stories of the vicissitudes of the days and tales of the wonders of time, said: May the life of the learned and just king continue for many years! The masters of history have so related that in the past ages and bygone centuries there was a certain man who was a soldier, and he had a wife so beautiful, that she was unexampled in the loveliness of her form and unparalleled in the grace of her figure. Her fashioning and disposition were the frontispiece of charm, her attributes and features were the exordium of the volume of elegance; the rose took its hue from the bloom of her cheek, the moon mounted into the sky from the horizon of her unrivalled beauty—

> A moon in the sky of loveliness, whose lustre
> never eclipse or obscuration dimmed.

By chance she became pregnant, and when the time for depositing her burden came, on quaffing the pains of parturition she yielded up her life, leaving behind her a boy of moonlike aspect and sunlike countenance, an orphan solitary as a solitaire. Her husband entered the chamber of sorrow, where he panted with anguish and sighed with grief, chanting to himself these verses:

Fate drew its bow contemptuously against me
until my heart was entirely ringed by arrows,
so that thereafter, as the shafts assailed me,
their points were shattered upon other points.

Heaven has altogether cut off affection from me,
heaven has sold its very soul to torment me;
or this is the first of my trial, or the last of my life,
so tight is the noose into which heaven has drawn me.

But he laid a salve on the wound of separation from his beloved in the contemplation of his child, saying: If it were not for the fact that this orphan would remain without anyone to tend and spend on him, and would become like a myrtle-seed crushed by the mill-stone of vicissitudes, I would have preferred extinction to survival, death to life; I would have put an end to these tribulations and treacheries of separation, that are bitterer than poison and more unpalatable than death itself, and slaughtered my precious soul upon the grave of my slender-waisted darling, who now like a tall young cypress sleeps in the dust of the tomb, and like the moon is hidden in darkness. For it would seem easier to endure death, than life passed in separation from those one loves; therefore it has been said that lovers live but a short span, since the agony of banishment and the anguish of separation dissolve their tender spirits, whereof some issue forth like water through the ducts of their tears, some are exhaled like vapour upon the breath of their sighs, and so by slow degrees are annihilated. Every true Arab who ever became a lover, in the very springtime of his years and the prime of his life yielded up his soul to the young cavalcade of love; as Majnūn parted from Lailā, Kuthaiyir passionate for 'Azza, Wāmiq enamoured of 'Adhrā. A certain man of the Banū Tamīm tribe was once asked, How is it that in your tribe every man who falls in love dies? He replied, Because our hearts are tender, and our women chaste.

> Whoever dies of love, so let him die—
> no good is there in love immune to death.
>
> He said, When lovely ones remove their veil
> after this fashion lovers die before them.

That man, parted from his wife, survived through the weary days and nights. He had brought an affectionate nurse and skilful midwife to cherish like the zephyr and nourish like the northern breeze that nursling child who was the envy of the flowers of spring. He found comfort and consolation in the company of the son for the loss of the mother, for "he who is denied the original is contented with the copy." Bereft of all his hopes, broken-hearted at life's bitterness, he ever said:

> Without you, O my soul, I go on living;
> having no stock-in-trade, I yet play merchant.
> Shame be upon me for what I am doing! Why
> do I go on living so long without you?
> You are not, and I am in the land of the living:
> let the truth be told, I am making a dear bargain.
> Without your face there is no life; and yet
> I am contriving somehow to live, as you know how.

Now this soldier had a cat, that had for many moons made his sleeve its pillow. All its life it had passed in his service, and established its rights both immediate and long past. Since the death of the child's mother it had not departed a single moment from the neighbourhood of his cradle, watching over his life and guarding his property. Whenever the nurse was busy, it was he who rocked the cradle. Now one day both the father of the infant and the nurse were absent from the house, and the cat in accordance with its usual custom was stretched asleep in front of the cradle. A black snake came out of a hole and attacked the child. The cat, anxious for the child's safety, by natural habit faced the snake and stood to do battle against it. Now with its claws, anon with its teeth it tore at the snake's throat and gnawed its head and neck, until the snake perished. The child was preserved from danger, while the cat steeped its fur in the snake's blood. When the father returned the cat ran forward to greet him, and because it had brought low such an adversary and averted such a disaster and exposed its life to such danger, it purred and mewed and made a great fuss, hoping for a titbit as a reward, a bone perhaps or a piece of bread. As soon as the man set eyes on the cat and saw its mouth stained with blood, a great fear and terror overcame his heart because of his extreme love and affection for the child; for "children make their fathers niggardly, cowardly and sorrowful." The thought struck him that the cat had killed the child; and because it is the nature of men to be hasty, suspicious and easily swayed, this idea got such a firm hold of his mind that he took a stick and beat the cat on the head, bringing it low. When he passed from the portico to the porch, and from the porch to the parlour, he saw a black snake lying there dead, its blood all flowing out, while the child was safely sleeping in his cot. Then he beat his hands and rent his robes, exclaiming in sorrow and regret (Koran 39: 56):

Alas for me,
in that I neglected my duty to God!

And he let flow the tears of penitence over the expanse of his cheeks from the fountain of his eyes, repining bitterly for that haste to which Satan had prompted him, and the slanderous suspicions in which he had indulged. He reproached himself over and over again, saying: What extravagance this was, that resulted from my hasty nature and my afflicted and unjust soul! What inhumanity and want of compassion, that my avaricious spirit visited upon this animal, and that such an unpraiseworthy temper and excessive injustice manifested in me!

> Injustice is a fire: despise it not when it is small,
> for many a billet of fire has consumed a whole land.

This was a hurtful wrong, this was a mighty injustice that befell this animal, and I cannot feel secure that no calamity will not descend upon me and my child in recompense for this unpraiseworthy deed. The creature protected my child against the attack of the enemy, and preserved it from the malice of the adversary, and I requited its actions with iniquity; and in the law of humanity and the code of chivalry there will be no averting the shame that has resulted from this precipitateness.'

The *Sindbād-nāma* as narrated by Ẓahīrī is a highly sophisticated version of a string of simple tales. Not unlike in character, though with less literary pretensions, is the *Bakhtiyār-nāma*, also allegedly based on a Pahlavi source, of which the oldest extant version was made early in the thirteenth century by Shams al-Dīn Muḥammad Daqā'iqī of Marv who is in addition credited with a *Sindbād-nāma*. 'The story is briefly told,' in the words of J. Horowitz. 'The son of King Āzādbak͟ht is abandoned by his parents on their flight, soon after his birth, and brought up by robbers and with them ultimately taken prisoner by the king. The latter, being pleased with him, takes him, under the name of Bak͟htiyār, into his service. When he has attained a high position, the jealousy of the viziers is aroused, who, taking advantage of an accident, cause him to lose the king's favour and he and the queen are thrown into prison. To save herself the queen declares that Bak͟htiyār has tried to seduce her. For ten days, the ten viziers, one after the other, try to persuade the king to condemn Bak͟htiyār to death; the latter however always manages to have the execution put off by telling a story suiting his predicament. When finally on the eleventh day the execution is definitely to take place, the robber captain, who brought him up, appears and proves to the king that Bakhtiyār is his son. The viziers are thereupon executed while Bakhtiyār becomes king in place of his father, who abdicates in his favour.' Versions of the tale are also found in Arabic (as in the Breslau edition of the *Arabian Nights*), Uigur, Malay and Fellihi.

It was Sir William Ouseley who introduced the *Bakhtiyār-nāma* to Europe when in 1801 he published 'The Bakhtyar Nameh, or Story of Prince Bakhtyar and the Ten Viziers; a Series of Persian Tales.' In his 'Advertisement' he wrote: 'Whatever opinion may be formed of these Tales by the European Reader, it appears that they are popular favourites among the Asiaticks, from the number of copies which have been transcribed: Besides three in my own possession, I have seen five or six in the collections of various friends. From all these manuscripts (as this work is chiefly designed for the use of those who begin to study the Persian language) I selected that which seemed written in the most pure and simple style; for several copies, in passing through the hands of ignorant or conceited transcribers, have suffered a considerable depravation of the original text; and one, in particular, is so disguised by the alterations, and augmented by the additions of some Indian Moonshee, that it appears almost a different work. These additions, however, are only turgid amplifications and florid exuberancies, according to the modern corrupt style of Hindoostan, which distinguishes the compositions of that country from the chaste and classical productions of IRAN.' In addition to the Persian text, printed in the old Dutch types at Wilson & Co.'s Oriental Press in Wild Court, Lincoln's Inn Fields, Sir William Ouseley provided a plain version. 'This Work is so easy, that it has not seemed necessary to augment its bulk by notes: nor, although the translation will be found sufficiently literal, have I retained those idioms which would be not only uncouth, but perhaps unintelligible in English.'

In the spring of 1854 Edward FitzGerald, newly embarked upon his exciting exploration of Persian, wrote from Bath to his young teacher Edward Cowell: 'I was at Bristol last week & bought for s6 Ouseley's *Bakhtyar Nameh*—a legible type & a free Translation—I dare say a stupid Book enough.' The poet's hasty verdict has not been entirely endorsed by scholars, who however have not tended to exaggerate the value and importance of the book. A French version by Baron Lescallier was published at Paris in 1805; G. Knoes latined the legend in 1807; W. A. Clouston republished Ouseley in 1883; R. Basset produced a new French translation in 1893; in 1926 E. Berthels brought out a new edition of the Persian original at Leningrad in which he offered the conjecture that the *Bakhtiyār-nāma* as now extant is an abridgment of Daqā'iqī, his text having been shorn of much of its literary excrescences. Berthels' text is considerably more austere than that of Ouseley, but this does not mean that Ouseley is closer to Daqā'iqī; on the contrary, his recension despite all his reluctance reflects the activities of the later Indian embellishers, whose ornament is the vapid and tawdry commonplace of decadence. The relationship between the two editions may be glimpsed by comparing the opening paragraph of Ouseley's translation with a literal interpretation of Berthels' corresponding text. Ouseley offers:

'Thus it is recorded by the authors of remarkable histories, and the narrators of delightful tales, that there was once in the country of Seiestan a certain king, possessing a crown and a throne, whose name was *Azadbakht*; and he had a vizier entitled *Sipehsalar*, a person of such bravery and skill that the moon concealed herself among the clouds from fear of his scymitar. This vizier had a daughter endowed with such exquisite beauty that the rose of the garden and the moon of the heavenly spheres were confounded at the superior lustre of her cheeks. Sipehsalar loved this daughter with excessive fondness, so that he could scarcely exist an hour without her. Having gone on an expedition to inspect the state of the country, it happened that he found himself under a necessity of passing some time from home. He immediately dispatched confidential persons with orders to bring his daughter to him from the capital. These persons, having arrived at the vizier's palace, paid their obeisance to the damsel, who ordered her attendants to prepare for the journey to her father. The horses were instantly caparisoned, and a litter provided with magnificence suitable to a princely traveller. The damsel, seated in this, commenced her journey, and went forth from the city.'

Berthels' text gives the following:—

'They have related that there was a king in the kingdom of Persia, master of a crown, a throne and a banner, whose name was Āzādbakht. He had ten viziers and a commander-in-chief (*sipahsālār*). The latter had a beautiful daughter, and every day until he had played the backgammon of companionship with her he did not place himself at the disposal of any other person. By chance one day he went out to inspect his province, to inform himself of the condition of the weak. When he had passed some time in those regions, a yearning for his daughter tugged at the collar of his heart and he sent a trusty subordinate to bring his daughter to him, so that he might pass some days with his daughter's beauty. When the messenger reached the city, he gave an account of the father's desire to the daughter, and the daughter was also longing to see her father; she therefore ordered her servants to make all preparations for the journey. They brought a litter to the door of the palace and seated the daughter in the litter, and coming out of the city in perfect order they set forth on the road.'

Whether the modern reader will concur with FitzGerald's diagnosis of the *Bakhtiyār-nāma* can best be determined by offering to reprint *in toto* one of the Prince's tales as translated by Ouseley.

'It is related that Abyssinia was once governed by a certain monarch, whose armies were very numerous, and his treasuries well filled; but not having any enemy to engage him in war, he neglected his troops, and withheld their pay, so that they were reduced to great distress, and began to murmur, and at last made their complaints to the vizier. He, pitying their situation, promised that he would take measures for their relief, and desired them to be patient for a little while. He then considered within himself what steps he should take; and at length, knowing the king's inclination to women, and understanding that the princess of Irak was uncommonly beautiful, he resolved to praise her charms in such extravagant language before the king, as to induce him to demand her from her father, who, from his excessive fondness, would not probably consent to bestow her on him, and thus a war would ensue, in which case the troops should be employed, and their arrears paid off.

'Pleased with the ingenuity of this stratagem, the vizier hastened to the king, and after conversing, for some time, on various subjects, contrived to mention the king of Irak, and immediately described the beauty of his daughter in such glowing colours that the king became enamoured, and consulted the vizier on the means whereby he might hope to obtain possession of that lovely princess. The vizier replied, that the first step was to send ambassadors to the king of Irak, soliciting his daughter in marriage. In consequence of this advice, some able and discreet persons were dispatched as ambassadors to Irak. On their arrival in that country, the king received them courteously; but when they disclosed the object of their mission, he became angry, and declared that he would not comply with their demand.

'The ambassadors returned to Abyssinia, and having reported to the king the unsuccessful result of their negotiation, he vowed that he would send an army into Irak, and lay that country waste, unless his demands were complied with.

'In consequence of this resolution, he ordered the doors of his treasuries to be thrown open, and caused so much money to be distributed among the soldiers, that they were satisfied. From all quarters the troops assembled, and zealously prepared for war. On the other hand the king of Irak levied his forces, and sent them to oppose the Abyssinians, who invaded his dominions; but he did not lead them to the field himself, and they were defeated and put to flight. When the account of this disaster reached the king of Irak, he consulted his vizier, and asked what was next to be done. The vizier candidly declared that he did not think it necessary to prolong the war on account of a female, and advised his majesty to send ambassadors with overtures of peace, and an offer of giving the princess to the king of Abyssinia. This advice, although reluctantly, the king of Irak followed: ambassadors were dispatched to the enemy with offers of peace, and a declaration of the king's consent to the marriage of his daughter.

'These terms being accepted, the princess was sent with confidential attendants to the king of Abyssinia, who retired with her to his own dominions, where he espoused her; and some time passed away in festivity and pleasure. But it happened that the king of Irak had, some years before, given his daughter in marriage to another man, by whom she had a son; and this boy was now grown up, and accomplished in all sciences, and such a favourite with the king of Irak, that he would never permit him to be one hour absent from him. The princess, when obliged to leave him, felt all the anxiety of a mother, and resolved to devise some strategem whereby she might enjoy his society in Abyssinia.

'One day the king of Abyssinia, on some occasion, behaved harshly to the queen, and spoke disrespectfully of her father. She in return said, "Your dominions, it is true, are most fertile and abundant; but my father possesses such a treasure as no other monarch can boast of; a youth, sent to him by the kindness of Heaven, skilled in every profound science, and accomplished in every manly exercise; so that he rather seems to be one of the inhabitants of paradise than of this earth." These praises so excited the curiosity of the king, that he vowed he would bring this boy to his court, were he even obliged to go himself for him. The queen replied, "My father would be like a distracted person were he deprived even for an hour of this boy's society; but some intelligent person must be sent to Irak in the character of a merchant, and endeavour by every means to steal him away." The king approved of this advice, and chose a person well skilled in business, who had experienced many reverses of fortune, and seen much of the world. To this man he promised a reward of an hundred male slaves, and an hundred beautiful damsels, if he should succeed in bringing away this boy from the king of Irak's court. The man inquired the name of the boy, which was Firokhzad, and, disguised as a merchant, set out immediately for Irak. Having arrived there, he presented various offerings to the king; and one day found an opportunity of conversing with the boy. At last he said, "With such accomplishments as you possess, were you in Abyssinia for one day, you would be rendered master of slaves and damsels, and riches of every kind." He then described the delights of that country, which made such an impression on Firokhzad, that he became disgusted with Irak, and attached himself to the merchant, and said, "I have often heard of Abyssinia, and have long wished to enjoy the pleasures which it yields. The king's daughter is now in that country, and if I could contrive to go there, my happiness would be complete: but I know not how to escape from this place, as the king will not permit me to be one hour absent from him." The merchant gladly undertook to devise some means for the escape of Firokhzad; and at last having put him into a chest, and placed him upon a camel, he contrived one evening to carry him off unnoticed. The next day the king of Irak sent messengers in all directions to seek him. They inquired of all the caravans and travellers, but could not obtain any intelligence concerning him. At last the merchant brought him to Abyssinia, and the king, finding that his accomplishments and talents had not been over-rated, was much delighted with his society; and as he had not any child, he bestowed on him a royal robe and crown, a horse, and sword and shield, and adopted him as his son, and brought him into the haram. When the queen beheld Firokhzad, she wept for joy, embraced him, and kissed him with all the fondness of a mother. It happened that one of the servants was a witness, unperceived, of this interview. He immediately hastened to the king, and represented the transaction in such a manner as to excite all his jealousy and rage. However, he resolved to inquire into the matter; but Firokhzad did not acknowledge that the queen was his mother; and when he sent for her, she answered his questions only by her tears. From these circumstances, he concluded that they were guilty; and accordingly he ordered one of his attendants to take away the young man to a burying-ground without the city, and there to cut off his head. The attendant led Firokhzad away, and was preparing to put the king's sentence into execution; but when he looked in the youth's face, his heart was moved with compassion, and he said, "It must have been the woman's fault, and not his crime;" and he resolved to save him.

'When he told Firokhzad that he would conceal him in his own house, the boy was delighted, and promised, that if ever it was in his power he would reward him for his kindness. Having taken him to his house, the man waited on the king, and told him that he had, in obedience to his orders, put Firokhzad to death. After this the king treated his wife with the utmost coldness; and she sat melancholy, lamenting the absence of her son. It happened that an old woman beheld the queen as she sat alone, weeping, in her chamber. Pitying her situation, she approached, and humbly inquired the occasion of her grief. The queen made no reply; but when the old woman promised not only to observe the utmost secrecy, if entrusted with the story of her misfortunes, but to find a remedy for them, she related at length all that had happened, and disclosed the mystery of Firokhzad's birth.

'The old woman desired the queen to comfort herself, and said, "This night, before the king retires to bed, you must lay yourself down, and close your eyes as if asleep; he will then place something, which I shall give him, on your bosom, and will command you, by the power of the writing contained in that, to reveal the truth. You must then begin to speak, and, without any apprehension, repeat all that you have now told me."

'The old woman having then found that the king was alone in his summer-house, presented herself before him, and said, "O king! this solitary life occasions melancholy and sadness." The king replied that it was not solitude which rendered him melancholy, but vexation, on account of the queen's infidelity, and the ingratitude of Firokhzad, on whom he had heaped so many favours, and whom he had adopted as his own son. "Yet," added he, "I am not convinced of his guilt; and since the day that I caused him to be killed, I have not enjoyed repose, nor am I certain whether the fault was his or the queen's." The old woman replied, "Let not the king be longer in suspense on this subject. I have a certain talisman, one of the talismans of Solomon, written in Grecian characters, and in the Syrian language; if your majesty will watch an opportunity when the queen shall be asleep, and lay it on her breast, and say, 'O thou that sleepest! by virtue of the talisman, and of the name of God which it contains, I conjure thee to speak to me, and to reveal all the secrets of thy heart.' On this," said the old woman, "she will immediately begin to speak, and will declare every thing that she knows, both true and false."

'The king, delighted at the hopes of discovering the truth by means of this talisman, desired the old woman to fetch it. She accordingly went home, and taking a piece of paper, scrawled on it some unmeaning characters, folded it up, and tied it with a cord, and sealed it with wax; then hastened to the king, and desired him to preserve it carefully till night should afford an opportunity of trying its efficacy. When it was night, the king watched until he found that the queen was in bed; then gently approaching, and believing her to be asleep, he laid the talisman on her breast, and repeated the words which the old woman had taught him. The queen, who had also received her lesson, still affecting the appearance of one asleep, immediately began to speak, and related all the circumstances of her story.

'On hearing this, the king was much affected, and tenderly embraced the queen, who started from her bed as if perfectly unconscious of having revealed the secrets of her breast. He then blamed her for not having candidly acknowledged the circumstance of Firokhzad's birth, who, he said, should have been considered as his own son. All that night they passed in mutual condolence, and on the next morning the king sent for the person to whom he had delivered Firokhzad, and desired him to point out the spot where his body lay, that he might perform the last duty to that unfortunate youth, and ask forgiveness from his departed spirit. The man replied, "It appears that your majesty is ignorant of Firokhzad's situation: he is at present in a place of safety; for although you ordered me to kill him, I ventured to disobey, and have concealed him in my house, from whence, if you permit, I shall immediately bring him." At this information the king was so delighted, that he rewarded the man with a splendid robe, and sent with him several attendants to bring Firokhzad to the palace.

'On arriving in his presence, Firokhzad threw himself at the king's feet; but he raised him in his arms, and asked his forgiveness, and thus the affair ended in rejoicing and festivity.'

In an earlier chapter some account was given of the *Mirror of Princes*, composed by the grandson of Qābūs ibn Washmgīr, ruler of Ṭabaristān at intervals from 976 to 1012. To this monarch a certain Marzubān ibn Rustam, a prince descended from Kā'ūs the brother of the Sāsānian Anūshirvān the Just, dedicated a collection of fables composed in the local dialect. Early in the thirteenth century Sa'd al-Dīn Varāvīnī, of whom nothing further is known, presented to Abu 'l-Qāsim Rabīb al-Dīn Hārūn ibn 'Alī, vizier to the Atābeg Uzbek ibn Muḥammad ibn Īldigiz, ruler of Azerbaijan from 1210 to 1225, the *Marzubān-nāma*, advertised as a translation into classical Persian of Marzubān's book. (A quite different version of the same 'original' was published by Varāvīnī's contemporary Muḥammad ibn Ghāzī of Malaṭya under the title *Rauḍat al-'uqūl.*) Before describing further the contents of this remarkable book, it is not without interest to recall the circumstances under which it came to be edited and printed.

In 1906 Muẓaffar al-Dīn Shāh, yielding at last to prolonged popular clamour, granted a constitution to the Persian nation, and in October of that year the first National Assembly was inaugurated. Muẓaffar al-Dīn died early in 1907, and from his accession his son Muḥammad 'Alī plotted to wipe out the democratic gains of the previous year; after much oppression and confusion, during which Cossack troops bombarded the Persian parliament, he was obliged in 1909 to abdicate. Among the leaders of the young liberals was Mīrzā Muḥammad of Qazvīn, soon to establish himself as the greatest scholar Persia had produced for centuries. He, like others working for the same political goal, found that the only means for furthering the common object was to go into exile. On November 20, 1908, he wrote, 'It is now nearly four years that I have been living in Europe, in the shadow of the wing of bounty and as a guest at the table of munificence of that great man'— Professor Edward Granville Browne. These words are taken from the preface of Mīrzā Muḥammad's edition of the *Marzubān-nāma*, published in the E. J. W. Gibb Memorial Series. 'It is obvious,' he added, 'that the literary and political history of Persia will never forget the infinite debt owed to that great man, and will perpetuate his lofty name for ever, so long as night and day endure, upon the pages of the daily newspapers which are a mirror to the good and evil wrought by the sons of time.'

In his introduction to the *Marzubān-nāma* Sa'd al-Dīn Varāvīnī claims: 'From the beginning of my working life, which coincided with the first years of my youth, down to the present day when I am old and grey, I have been engaged in gathering the jewels of poetry as a necklace for the appraisal of eminent gentlemen, and submitting the precious coins of prose to the mint of the approval of kings and nobles. . . . Having studied the words uttered alike by contemporary authors and those of the recent past, and having probed with the lancet of meticulous inquiry to expose the merits and the defects of them all, I rejected the bad from the good and separated the original from the second-hand.' Among the books which Varāvīnī mentions as having occupied him are the *Kalīla wa-Dimna* ('a crown on the brow of those who glory in pre-eminence, studded with shining gems and glittering jewels'), the *Sindbād-nāma* ('in my view unprofitable, though some have thought very highly of it'), and the *Maqāmāt* of Ḥamīdī ('the ring-dove of whose genius cooed incessantly'); other titles selected for special notice include the *Risālāt-i Bahā'ī* (that is, *al-Tawassul ilā 'l-tarassul*), the *Tarjuma-yi Yamīnī* (Jarbādhaqānī's translation of 'Utbī), and Nasavī's *Nafthat al-maṣdūr*. Wishing to leave behind him some memorial of his own literary attainments, after long study and careful deliberation 'one day the precursor of the good tidings of the dawn of this felicity showed its face above the horizon of my thoughts, and an inspirer from behind the veil of the unseen world poked the finger-tip of awakening into the ribs of my desire.' In other words, Varāvīnī settled upon turning into modern idiom the *Marzubān-nāma*, rivalled only by the *Kalīla wa-Dimna* for the 'rarities of wisdom and compelling counsel' with which it was stuffed.

The *Marzubān-nāma* is divided, as the 'original' had been, into nine lengthy chapters. In the first chapter the story is told of how Marzubān ibn Rustam came to write his book; it includes a long conversation between the prince and the minister, enlivened by sundry anecdotes and fables. The second chapter is concerned with the death-bed counsel offered by 'the Fortunate King' to his six sons. The third is devoted to King Ardashīr and the wise and virtuous Dānā-yi Mihrān-bih. The rest of the book is taken up with a succession of animal fables, much after the pattern of the *Kalīla wa-Dimna*. Varāvīnī writes in a high-flown style not without a certain perhaps unconscious humour, as in the excellent story of the Thief and the Flea.

'Once upon a time a thief resolved to cast his noose over the battlements of the palace of the Chosroes and nimbly to creep into his treasury. For some while the tumult of this melancholy passion had besieged the door and roof of the thief's brain, and the vessel of his thoughts was filled with this idea, so that at last he could conceal it no longer; for "unless a man with bronchitis coughs, he soon becomes a consumptive." In all the world he could not descry any suitable intimate or congenial confederate with whom to share his secret, apart from a flea that he discovered in the midst of his garments.

' "This feeble creature has no tongue to speak with," he observed. "And even if it could, seeing it is aware that I nurture it with my own blood, how could it ever approve of disclosing my secret?"

'The soul in his body, like a flea in the drawers or a pebble in the shoe, so tormented the hapless fellow with the importunity of its nagging that he told his secret to the flea. Then one night fate made assault against him and incited him to embark upon that perilous emprise. By a variety of cunning devices he hurled himself into the Chosroes' palace. By chance he found the bedchamber void of the presence of any servants, and he secreted himself underneath the couch. The Chosroes entered and went to bed. No sooner had he laid his head on the pillow with the intention of sleeping, than the flea transferred itself from the thief's garments to the royal bedclothes, and there created such a disturbance that the Chosroes became extremely vexed. He ordered lights to be brought and a good search made in the folds of the bedclothes. The flea jumped out and hopped under the bed. As a result of the flea's leap the thief was discovered and duly punished.'

Many of the stories, put into the mouths of animal protagonists, describe similarly the relations between the animal world and man.

What was the motive behind this convention? Bahār offers an explanation: 'It was the rule in ancient times that advisers and counsellors never spoke directly and straightforwardly in offering counsel and advice to their lords and masters. That they deemed would have been ineffective; they considered it was better to deliver every advice and counsel either in the garb of metaphor, simile and parable or as if spoken by others, particularly animals. This usage was established and agreed among the wise men of India and Iran; after Islam the wise men of Persia did not abandon this custom and procedure.' What began (if this diagnosis is correct) as a courtly subterfuge ended by becoming a popular institution; animal fables have been immensely popular throughout Persian literary history, and have by no means lost their appeal even today. Here is another example from Varāvīnī in which no humans are featured; La Fontaine has something very similar.

'There was once a cock that had been about the world and rent the skirts of duplicity, seen many stratagems of foxes and heard tales of their tricks. One day he sallied forth in the surroundings of a village to take a walk in a garden. He fared further, and presently stood at the head of a road. The roses and anemones had loosed ringlets of musky curls from their brows and crowns over their shoulders and necks, fastened ruby buttons on the fringes of their caps and arrayed in embroidered gowns and variegated robes, like brides in the bridal-chamber or peacocks on parade trailed over their feet the skirts of delicate charm. The cock, surveying the scene, crowed loudly. A fox that was in the neighbourhood heard the cry and conceived an appetite for the cock; full of hopeful greed, he raced towards the cock which leaped upon a wall in terror.

' "Why are you afraid of me?" the fox asked. "I was just now wandering in the neighbourhood when suddenly the sound of your call to prayer came to my ears. Listening to the sweet strains of your gullet, my heart began to flutter in the cage of my breast.

Though you are a man of Rūmī stock, the words 'Give us joy' that the Prophet spoke to the Abyssinian Bilāl penetrated to my hearing through the veil of pleasurable ecstasy and moved the chains of passion within me; like Bilāl from Abyssinia and Suhail from Rūm, the call of love and the tug of yearning drew me to you.

> It is for your sake that I wander about the head of your street;
> the nightingale comes to the meadow's edge in quest of the rose.

See, I have come seeking a blessing, that I may enjoy the benedictions of your sweet words and society, and for a brief moment repose in your conversation and company. I would also inform you that the king of this time has ordered it to be proclaimed, that none shall commit injustice against any person or suffer the fear of tyranny or oppression to enter any heart, so that the hand of insolence may not be outstretched by the strong against the weak, and that all may live together in a spirit of simple benevolence and charity. The dove may henceforth share the same nest as the eagle, the lamb lie down on the same couch with the wolf; the lion in the thicket shall no more be occupied with lying in wait for the jackal, the panther shall withdraw the teeth of gluttony from the slaughter of the deer, the dog shall not fall upon the hide of the fox, and the falcon shall not pounce upon the crest of the cock. Now all aversion and repugnance must cease between us, and bound in perfect compact we must henceforward mutually and increasingly succour one another."

'While the fox was still speaking, the cock stretched out his neck and stared down the road.

' "What are you looking at?" enquired the fox.

' "I see some animal coming from yonder plain," the cock replied. "It has the body of a wolf, with a tail and long ears, and it is coming in our direction so fast that the wind cannot catch its dust."

'At these words the stone of despair struck the teeth of the fox, and a feverish ague of fear fell upon his limbs. He gave up his designs on the cock and in a state of confusion and stupefaction sought a place of refuge, some fortified spot to go to.

' "Come, let us see what sort of animal this actually is," the cock said.

' "The signs and tokens which you have described indicate clearly that it is a saluki," the fox answered. "I would have no pleasure in looking at it."

' "But," the cock objected, "were you not saying that a herald has proclaimed throughout the world, in the name of the king's justice, that no one shall commit enmity or oppression against another, and that this day all who seek the lie and make tyranny their trade have given up molesting God's creatures for fear of his might and chastisement?"

' "That is true," the fox replied. "But it is possible that that dog may not have heard the herald. This is no occasion for further delay."

'So saying, he fled and dived down a hole.'

EIGHT

Sa'dī of Shīrāz

SHĪRĀZ, capital of the southern province of Fārs which supplied the west with that name Persia by which Iran is commonly designated, escaped the devastations of the Mongol incursion and under the Salghurid Atābegs enjoyed comparative peace and prosperity through the tumultuous years of the thirteenth century, a tranquillity purchased by voluntary surrender in 1256 to the Scourge of Islam. The city, which had already produced a goodly crop of scholars and divines, was now to become the centre of a brilliant literary movement that would give to Persia two of her greatest poets. The writing of literary history imposes an obligation, all too often irksome, to observe a strict economy of words and frequently to dismiss in three or four paragraphs authors whose achievements entitle them to less cavalier treatment. It is proposed now to relax this harsh rule and to devote separate chapters to a chosen few of Persia's most outstanding writers; it is just that the first to claim this indulgence should be Sa'dī of Shīrāz.

It is confidently asserted by many Persian biographers that Sa'dī was born in 1184; those who entertain a different opinion agree nevertheless upon 1185. European scholars have until very recently accepted these alternatives as fixing a date *circa* 1184 for Sa'dī's birth. There appear to be reasonably good grounds for believing the widespread report that he died in 1292; but it is not only on account of the implication of unusual longevity that modern investigators have looked again into the traditional nativity. It was 'Abd al-'Aẓīm Khān Garakānī who first argued cogently for the rejection of the established view; his representations have been conceded as convincing by a number of later authorities including ʻAbbās Iqbāl, Bahār and Shafaq. Two internal reasons have always been offered in defence of the old chronology. In chapter IX of the *Būstān* Saʻdī writes:

> O you whose life has now reached to seventy,
> perhaps you were asleep while it went with the wind.

Now it is certain that the *Būstān* was completed in 1257; therefore the poet, allowing for lunar reckoning, must have been born not later than 1189. But this is to assume that Saʻdī is here soliloquizing, whereas it is his practice throughout the *Būstān* to address in the second person the reader to whom the particular section is thought apposite; and as the theme of chapter IX is penitence, what is more natural than that the poet should here direct his appeal to the elderly sinner? The second internal piece of evidence alleged is that in anecdote 20 of Book II of the *Gulistān* Saʻdī claims to have received certain instruction from Abu ’l-Faraj Ibn al-Jauzī, and the person generally known by that name is the famous polygraph who died in 1200. Garakānī however suggests that Sibṭ Ibn al-Jauzī was here intended, and his death occurred in 1257; while ʻAbbas Iqbāl puts forward another Abu ’l-Faraj Ibn al-Jauzī, a son of Sibṭ Ibn al-Jauzī, who perished with his father and brothers during the Mongol massacre of Baghdad.

In any case it has long been recognized that Saʻdī’s writings afford a very insecure basis for the reconstruction of his biography. ‘In the short stories of *Gulistān* and *Būstān*,’ writes J. H. Kramers, ‘there occur many personal recollections of the author. In his monograph on Saʻdī, Massé has tried to restore a biography based on those informations. But he seems to have trusted Saʻdī’s veracity too much. The truth of many of these stories has been doubted before (Barbier de Meynard, Rückert) and Saʻdī himself declares that whoever has been much about in the world, may lie a great deal.’ There is also the stubborn fact that in his preface to the *Gulistān*, undoubtedly completed in 1258, Saʻdī (as translated by R. A. Nicholson) writes: 'One evening I was thinking over bygone days and regretting a life wasted in foolish ways, piercing the stone of my heart with the diamond of tears, and reciting these verses which the occasion commanded to mine ears:

Each moment steals a breath of life once more,
And few, I see, are now remaining o'er.
What! Fifty years by lethargy possessed!—
Yet mayst thou realize the fleeting rest . . .'

If Sa'dī is here intending to imply—and the context appears to point in this direction—that his own age at the time of writing was about fifty, then his birth must have taken place about the year 1208.

The equally vexed problem of Sa'dī's nomenclature is not unconnected with the problem of his nativity. Even his personal names create difficulty, but it must suffice here to quote the opinion of Bahār, which others share, that he was called Abū 'Abd Allāh Musharrif (or Musharrif al-Dīn) ibn Muṣliḥ. How did he acquire the poetical soubriquet Sa'dī? The accepted version states that he was so called after the famous Atābeg of Fārs, Abū Shujā' Sa'd ibn Zangī, who died in 1226. It would not be impossible, though most unlikely, that a stripling in his teens should have so far advanced in royal favour as to be permitted to style himself by his name. 'Abbās Iqbāl however, pointing out that the *Gulistān* is dedicated to Sa'd ibn Zangī's grandson, also named Sa'd, suggests that it was from him that the poet derived his *nom de plume*. This conjecture is reinforced by the striking fact that in all his writings Sa'dī never composed a single verse in honour of Sa'd ibn Zangī.

Sa'dī tells us in the *Būstān* that he was orphaned at an early age:

Full well I know the pains that orphans bear,
For as a child I lost my father's care.

There seems to be no reason to doubt this statement. It may also be presumed true that after receiving his early education in Shīrāz he went to Baghdad, perhaps to escape from the political turmoil which followed the death of Sa'd ibn Zangī, and there studied at the Niẓāmīya Academy. To accept that he became a disciple of 'Abd al-Qādir al-Jīlānī the Ṣūfī, 'with whom,' says T. W. Haig, 'he made the pilgrimage to Mecca,' would be to allow an extraordinary anachronism, for 'Abd al-Qādir died in 1166. Less inherent improbability attaches to Sa'dī's claim to have met the equally eminent mystic Shihāb al-Dīn al-Suhrawardī (d. 1234), and it has been suggested that he may also have encountered Jalāl al-Dīn Rūmī some time during his extensive travels. For after completing his studies Sa'dī fared very far indeed afield, to judge by the statements of an autobiographical character which punctuate his discourse. Tale 31 of Book II of the *Gulistān* makes out that he was for a time prisoner of the Crusaders: Massé dates this episode in the year 1221, but Garakānī puts it eight years later.

'I had grown weary of the society of my Damascus friends, and therefore made my way into the Jerusalem desert, where I enjoyed the companionship of the beasts; until the time came when the Franks made me their prisoner, and kept me with Jews in a trench at Tripoli digging clay. One of the leading citizens of Aleppo, with whom I had been formerly acquainted, chancing to pass by, recognized me and said, "Sirrah, what manner of life is this?" I said, "What can I say?

I fled from men to mountain and to plain,
For I had nothing from mankind to gain;
How is my case? Regard me in this den,
Where I must sweat with men that are not men.

Better to hang in chains, when friends are there,
Than dwell with strangers in a garden fair."

'He had compassion on my condition, and with ten dinars procured my release from bondage. He took me along with him to Aleppo, and there made me marry his daughter, adding a dowry of a hundred dinars. Some time passed. She was a woman always scowling, disobedient and growling; she began to give me plenty of her shrewish tongue, and made life wholly miserable for me.

A bad wife comes with a good man to dwell:
She soon converts his present world to hell.
Beware of evil partnership, beware:
From hellish torment, Lord, thy servants spare!

'Once in a torrent of abuse she said, "Are you not that man whom my father bought back from the Franks?" I said, "Yes, I am that man whom he bought back from the Frankish chains for ten dinars, and delivered into your bondage for a hundred dinars." '

Other countries visited by Sa'dī, according to his own accounts, included Arabia, Egypt, Morocco, Abyssinia, Central Asia and India. His story in the *Būstān* (here quoted in R. A. Nicholson's version) of how he killed the temple-priest at Somnath (Gujerat) is very celebrated, but hardly convincing.

I saw an idol in the town Somnát,
Bejewelled, as in heathen days Manát,
And wrought of ivory with art extreme:
No fairer beauty couldst thou ever dream.
From every land come pilgrims to behold
And venerate that effigy unsouled;
From China and Chigil the rajahs flock,
Hoping true kindness from that heart of rock;
Before that image mute, and dumb withal,
The world's most eloquent, beseeching, fall.
In vain I asked myself, in vain explored,
Why living men a lifeless shape adored.

There was a Brahman who of me spoke well,
My friend and comrade, sharer of my cell.
Him softly I approached and sought his ear—
'Great is my wonder at the doings here:
How can a helpless idol so entrance
And hold them fast in bonds of ignorance?
No strength its hands, its feet no movement own,
It cannot rise up if you hurl it prone.
Its eyes are made of amber: 'tis unwise
To seek fidelity in stony eyes.'
At this, my friend became my foe entire,
And he with anger blazed, and I caught fire.
He told the priests—in all the multitude
I did not see a face that promised good:
The pack of Guebres who Pá-Zand intone
Set on me for the sake of that old bone.
Because the crook'd way straight and sure they deem,
The straight way crook'd accordingly must seem;
For though a man be wise and keen of wit,
He is a dunce where fools in judgment sit.
Lost as the drowning wretch, I saw no course
But to dissemble —'twas my one resource.
With savage enemy on vengeance bent,
The path to safety lies in soft consent.
Loud I extolled the Brahman archimage:
'O deep interpreter and master sage,
Me too this idol pleases with its grace
Of form and beauteous heart-bewitching face;
I find it marvellous in outward show,
But of the inward sense I nothing know.
I come to these parts late and have less skill,
A stranger, to distinguish good from ill.
But thou, who art as queen on this chessboard
And chief adviser of thy country's lord,

Thou know'st what meaning in this form may lie,
Of whose glad votaries the first am I.
To worship blindly is to go astray,
Happy the traveller that knows the way!'
The Brahman's visage gleamed with joy: on me
He looked approval. 'Noble sir,' said he,
'Thou hast done right to ask, and none dare chide:
They reach the journey's end who seek a guide.
Like thee, I have wandered much abroad; and ne'er
I saw an idol of itself aware,
Save this, which every morning from its stand
To God Almighty doth uplift a hand.
If here thou wilt remain till night is gone,
Thou'lt see the mystery at to-morrow's dawn.'
Here at the old man's bidding I remained,
Like Bízhan in the pit where he was chained.
Long as the Last Day seemed the night I stayed
Amidst the Guebres who unwashen prayed,
And priests unused to water: every one
Reeked as a carcase rotting in the sun.
Methought, I had committed some great sin,
The grievous torment so to linger in.
All night I lay with bosom sorrow-riven,
One hand pressed on my heart, one raised to heaven,
Till, hark, the drum's reveille in mine ear,
And voice of Brahman shrill as chanticleer!
Night, as a black-robed preacher risen to pray,
From willing scabbard drew the sword of Day;
The fire of Morning fell on cindery Night,
And in a moment all the world was bright.
As though mid negro swarms in Zanzibar
Stepped sudden forth a blue-eyed fair Tatár,
So eagerly, with unwashed faces, poured
From gate and court and street the miscreant horde.

Nor man nor woman in the town was left:
Not even a needle would have found a cleft
In that pagoda's throng. And there I stand,
Choking with grief, by slumber half unmanned—
When lo, the idol lifted up its hand!

At once from all a mighty shout arose,
Like to a raging sea when tempest blows.
Soon as the fane was emptied of its folk,
The Brahman, smiling, glanced at me and spoke:
'No longer, I perceive, art thou in doubt;
Falsehood is vanished, Truth shines clearly out.'
Seeing him firm in ignorance and blind
To monstrous fancies rooted in his mind,
I durst not utter any word of sooth:
From falsehood's champions one must hide the truth.
When thou behold'st an iron-fisted man,
To break thy fingers were a foolish plan.
I made pretence to weep, expressed my sore
Contrition for the words I spake before.
Tears moved their miscreant hearts, and at the shock
They yielded, as the torrent moves the rock;
Toward me with low obeisance then they sped
And took my arm and to the idol led.
I sued for pardon to that ivory form
In chair of gold on ebon throne enorm;
I kissed the despicable idol's hand—
Accurst be it, accurst the adoring band!
For some while I the infidels did ape
And learned the priestly doctrine's every shape.
At length they trusted me within the fane;
So glad was I, scarce Earth could me contain.
I bolted fast the temple-door one night,
And darting like a scorpion left and right,

Looked up and down, the ebon throne beside,
Until a gold-embroidered screen I spied:
Behind it sat the attendant devotee,
And in his hand an end of cord had he!
The riddle was resolved, and plain the tracks
As when for David iron grew as wax.
At once I saw that when he pulls the cord,
The idol's hand is lifted to its Lord.
Ashamed to meet mine eye, the priest devout—
His foul disgrace thus turned all inside out—
Started to run, and after him I flew:
The rascal headlong down a well I threw;
For 'twas most certain he would ever strive
To murder me, if he remained alive,
And fearing lest his secret I betray,
Would not be loth to strike my life away.
I slew the villain with a stone outright,
For dead men tell no tales; then took to flight.

Sa'dī reappeared at Shīrāz some time towards the end of the reign of Abū Bakr ibn Sa'd ibn Zangī (1231–60), and must have made quick strides in winning the Atābeg's patronage. He gives us a picture of his former departure from his native town, and of his joyous homecoming, in the preface to the *Gulistān*. In E. G. Browne's words:

O knowest thou not why, an outcast and exile,
In lands of the stranger a refuge I sought?
Disarranged was the world like the hair of a negro
When I fled from the Turks and the terror they
 brought.
Though outwardly human, no wolf could surpass them
In bloodthirsty rage or in sharpness of claw;
Though within was a man with the mien of an angel,
Without was a host of the lions of war.

At peace was the land when again I beheld it;
E'en lions and leopards were wild but in name.
Like that was my country what time I forsook it,
Fulfilled with confusion and terror and shame:
Like this in the time of 'Bú Bakr the Atàbek
I found it when back from my exile I came.

Sa'dī will have taken the usual road of panegyric into his ruler's heart, though strangely few poems in this style can be assigned with certainty to this period of his life. The *Būstān*, sometimes called the *Sa'dī-nāma*, is his first dated composition, and this, as has already been stated, was finished and presented to Abū Bakr ibn Sa'd in 1257. This poem 'contains within its ten sections of facile and often beautiful verse, dissertations on justice, good government, beneficence, earthly and mystic love, humility, submissiveness, contentment, and other excellences.' Such is Professor R. Levy's brief description of a work which quickly attained and has ever since enjoyed a popularity almost unexampled in Persian literature. Not a few before Sa'dī had composed didactic poetry; Nāṣir-i Khusrau and Sanā'i were the most eminent of his forerunners, and it would be interesting if we could know more about the lost *Āfarīn-nāma* of Abū Shakūr, for this may well have been Sa'dī's model. Gnomic verses had been liberally sprinkled by Firdausī through the pages of his *Shāh-nāma*, and no writer of idyll, ode or quatrain neglected the national pastime of tricking out homely adages in rhetoric and rhyme. Sa'dī entered into a rich inheritance; but he is felt to have excelled all his predecessors, and all his successors too, by the fluent affability and seemingly (but only seemingly) artless simplicity of his diction. Many verses from the *Būstān* have achieved the status of proverbs, the surest proof of epigrammatic brilliance. The interweaving of popular wisdom with appropriate anecdote is done with great skill, and Sa'dī also shows himself a master at telling a simple story; the inclusion of numerous incidents from his own adventurous life, whether true or false, or a mixture of truth and falsehood, lends an authority and a verisimilitude to the lessons inculcated.

> Crush not yon ant, who stores the golden grain:
> He lives with pleasure, and will die with pain:
> Learn from him rather to secure the spoil
> Of patient cares and persevering toil.

Sir William Jones's celebrated quatrain encouraged the hope that the *Būstān* in a suitably elegant version would place Sa'dī beside Pope and Dryden in the esteem of English readers. That hope has unhappily not been realized; the *Būstān* defies successful transplantation, and all attempts so far made suggest that only an eighteenth-century poet could have done the thirteenth-century Persian adequate justice. The poem meanwhile continues to cast its magic spell over Sa'dī's countrymen, and it was appropriate that the best edition should have been prepared, on the occasion of the septemcentenary (lunar reckoning) of its composition, by that distinguished scholar and statesman Muḥammad 'Alī Furūghī. 'Perhaps one can say,' writes Furūghī in his short introduction, 'that this book has no like or parallel, either in Persian or in any other language, as regards elegance, eloquence, fluency, delicacy, charm, wisdom and insight. It is not my intention here to wear out my pen praising the immortal works of the great master, for I suppose that in order to discharge this duty a power of expression such as that of the master himself would be required, and no one who does not possess such a capacity ought to attempt the task.' He adds that 'in the history of Persian literature, with the exception of the composition of Firdausī's *Shāh-nāma* and the *Mathnavī* of Maulānā Jalāl al-Dīn no event has rivalled in importance' the appearance of the *Būstān* and the *Gulistān*.

Sa'dī quickly followed up the *Būstān*, his first offering on coming home from exile, by producing in the next year the *Gulistān*. His reasons for writing the *Būstān* had been succinctly if poetically explained:

Much have I wandered through the realms of earth
and passed full many days with many men,
from every corner rich advantage reaped,
and gathered grain at every harvest-home.
Not having viewed the chaste inhabitants
of dear Shiraz—God's mercy on that land!—
for many moons, affection for my friends
urged me be gone from Syria and Rúm.
It irked me from that garden to return
to those I loved so well with empty hands,
and I recalled how men from Egypt bring
candy as presents for the ones at home;
though of that candy I had none to give,
yet I had words than candy sweeter far.

Now Sa'dī had an equally romantic story to tell of how his new book came to be composed; the version quoted is that dedicated by Francis Gladwin to Marquis Wellesley at Patna in 1806.

'It was the season of spring; the air was temperate, and the rose in full bloom. The vestments of the trees resembled the festive garments of the fortunate. It was mid-spring, when the nightingales were chanting from the pulpits of the branches; the rose decked with pearly dew, like blushes on the cheek of a chiding mistress. It happened once, that I was benighted in a garden, in company with one of my friends. The spot was delightful, the trees intertwined; you would have said that the earth was bedecked with glass spangles, and that the knot of the Pleiades was suspended from the branch of the vine. A garden with a running stream, and trees from whence birds were warbling melodious strains: that filled with tulips of various hues; these loaded with fruits of several kinds. Under the shade of its trees the zephyr had spread the variegated carpet. In the morning, when the desire to return home overcame our inclination for remaining, I saw in his lap a collection of roses, odoriferous herbs, and hyacinths, which he had intended to carry to town. I said, "You are not ignorant that the flower of the garden soon fadeth, and that the enjoyment of the rose-bush is but of a short continuance; and the sages have declared, that the heart ought not to be set upon anything that is transitory." He asked, "What course is then to be pursued?" I replied, "I am able to form a book of roses, which will delight the beholders, and gratify those who are present; whose leaves the tyrannic arm of the autumnal blasts can never affect, nor injure the blossoms of its spring. What benefit will you derive from a basket of flowers? Carry a leaf from my garden: a rose may continue in bloom for five or six days; but this rose-garden will flourish forever." As soon as I had uttered these words, he flung the flowers from his lap, and, laying hold on the skirt of my garment, exclaimed, "When the beneficent promise, they faithfully discharge their engagements." In the course of a few days, two chapters (one on the comforts of society, and the other containing rules for conversation) were written out in my note-book, in a style that may be useful to orators, and improve the skill of letter-writers. In short, whilst the rose was yet in bloom, the book entitled the Rose Garden was finished: but it will be truly perfected on gaining a favorable reception at court, and when it obtains an indulgent perusal from that prince who is the asylum of the world, the shadow of the Most High, the ray of providential beneficence, the treasury of the age, the refuge of religion, the favorite of Heaven, the mighty arm of the victorious empire, the lamp of the resplendent religion, the most splendid of mankind, the aggrandizer of the faith, Sad, son of Atabuk the great; that potent monarch to whom nations bend the neck; lord paramount of the kings of Arabia and Persia; sovereign of land and sea; inheritor of the throne of Solomon, Mozuffuruddeen, may God perpetuate the good fortune of both, and prosper all their righteous undertakings!'

Gladwin's version is not free from error, but it conveys remarkably well, within certain limits, the glittering rhetoric of the original. In this tender evocation of a Persian spring Saʿdī compares his *Gulistān* with a Persian garden, and the comparison is very apt. The eight partitions into which it is divided are planted each with its own cluster of gay and sombre stories, in that seductive intermixture of rhymed prose and verse which had by now come to be regarded as the prerequisite of elegant composition. In my *Kings and Beggars* (a translation of the first two chapters) I have at some length gone into the contents and arrangement of the *Gulistān*, and sketched its bibliography; the book is very famous, and has enjoyed a vogue in Europe for over three centuries, since André du Ryer brought out in 1634 a garbled French paraphrase of about one half, and in 1651 George Gentz published at Amsterdam a creditable edition with a Latin translation of the whole. 'The first book that I would recommend,' Sir William Jones advised the readers of his *Grammar of the Persian Language*, 'is the Gulistān or *Bed of Roses*, a work which is highly recommended in the East, and of which there are several translations in Europe.' Edward FitzGerald took Jones's counsel when he began the study of Persian, and on January 24, 1854, he wrote to his old friend Elizabeth Cowell: 'Tell Cowell I get on famously (as I think) with Sadi, whom I like much: he is just one of the Writers who *can't* be seen in a Translation: his merits are not strong enough to bear decanting I think—Certainly Eastwick is *wretched* in the Verse: and both he and Ross (I know both versions) seem to me on a wrong tack wholly in their *Style* of rendering the Prose.'

Ten years later Ralph Waldo Emerson penned in Concord a preface to the first American edition of Francis Gladwin's translation. Viewed even through the distorting glass of that imperfect version, the *Gulistān* made a lively impression on the mind of the great essayist. 'At first sight,' he remarks, 'the Oriental rhetoric does not please our Western taste,' and he continues:

'Life in the East wants the complexity of European and

American existence; and in their writing a certain monotony betrays the poverty of the landscape, and of social conditions. We fancy we are soon familiar with all their images: Medschnun and Leila, rose and nightingale, parrots and tulips; mosques and dervishes; desert, caravan, and robbers, peeps at the harem; bags of gold dinars; slaves, horses, camels, sabres, shawls, pearls, amber, cohol, and henna; insane compliments to the Sultan, borrowed from the language of prayer; Hebrew and Gueber legends molten into Arabesque;—'t is a short inventory of topics and tropes, which incessantly return in Persian poetry. I do not know but, at the first encounter, many readers take also an impression of tawdry rhetoric, an exaggeration, and a taste for scarlet, running to the borders of the negrofine,—or, if not, yet a pushing of the luxury of ear and eye where it does not belong, as the Chinese in their mathematics employ the colors blue and red for algebraic signs, instead of our pitiless *x* and *y*.'

Yet Emerson concedes that this is only a superficial verdict.

'These blemishes disappear or diminish on better acquaintance. Where there is real merit, we are soon reconciled to differences of taste. The charge of monotony lies more against the numerous Western imitations than against the Persians themselves, and though the torrid, like the arctic zone, puts some limit to variety, it is least felt in the masters. It is the privilege of genius to play its game indifferently with few as with many pieces, as Nature draws all her opulence out of a few elements. Saadi exhibits perpetual variety of situation and incident, and an equal depth of experience with Cardinal de Retz in Paris, or Doctor Johnson in London. He finds room on his narrow canvas for the extremes of lot, the play of motives, the rule of destiny, the lessons of morals, and the portraits of great men. He has furnished the originals of a multitude of tales and proverbs which are current in our mouths, and attributed by us to recent writers.'

So the eminent critic warms up to his encomium on Sa'dī.

'When once the works of these poets are made accessible, they must draw the curiosity of good readers. It is provincial to ignore them. . . . In these songs and elegies breaks into light the national mind of the Persians and Arabians. The monotonies which we accuse, accuse our own. We pass into a new landscape, new costume, new religion, new manners and customs under which humanity nestles very comfortably at Shiraz and Mecca, with good appetite, and with moral and intellectual results that correspond, point for point, with ours at New York and London. It needs in every sense a free translation, just as, from geographical position, the Persians attribute to the east wind what we say of the west. Saadi, though he has not the lyric flights of Hafiz, has wit, practical sense, and just moral sentiments. He has the instinct to teach, and from every occurrence must draw the moral, like Franklin. He is the poet of friendship, love, self-devotion, and serenity. There is a uniform force in his page, and, conspicuously, a tone of cheerfulness, which has almost made his name a synonyme for this grace. The word *Saadi* means *fortunate*. In him the trait is no result of levity, much less of convivial habit, but first of a happy nature, to which victory is habitual, easily shedding mishaps, with sensibility to pleasure, and with resources against pain. But it also results from the habitual perception of the beneficent laws that control the world. He inspires in the reader a good hope. What a contrast between the cynical tone of Byron and the benevolent wisdom of Saadi! . . . I find in him a pure theism. He asserts the universality of moral laws, and the perpetual retributions. He celebrates the omnipotence of a virtuous soul. A certain intimate and avowed piety, obviously in sympathy with the feeling of his nation, is habitual to him. All the forms of courtesy and of business in daily life take a religious tinge, as did those of Europe in the Middle Age. . . . The Persians have been called "the French of Asia"; and their superior intelligence, their esteem for men of learning, their welcome to Western travellers, and their tolerance of Christian sects in their territory, as contrasted with Turkish fanaticism, would seem to derive from the rich culture of this great choir of poets, perpetually reinforced through five hundred years, which again and again has enabled the Persians to refine and civilize their conquerors, and to preserve a national identity. To the expansion of this influence there is no limit; and we wish that the present republication may add to the genius of Saadi a new audience in America.'

Such are the comments of a wise American of the nineteenth century; let us now turn to a penetrating analysis of Sa'dī's prose style conducted by a twentieth-century Persian, for it assists us much to understand the very high esteem in which the *Gulistān* is still held after seven hundred years of copying and recopying, commentary and supercommentary. Muḥammad Taqī Bahār has examined all Sa'dī's prose writings, the six *Epistles* as well as the *Gulistān*, and has demonstrated the variety of styles employed by their author to match the diversity of his themes. The first *Risāla*, composed for a commonplace book, is in the simple Persian of the old historians though flavoured with learning by the use of many Arabic words. The second *Risāla* consists of five sermons, the first two in even more straightforward prose enlivened with verse extracts; the third is closely modelled on Anṣārī, the fourth resembles Hujvīrī; the fifth is considered a 'masterpiece' and the artistic equal of the *Gulistān*. The third *Risāla* contains an exchange of letters between Sa'dī and the 'Ṣāḥib-Dīvān' Shams al-Dīn Juvainī, Prime Minister to Hūlāgū Khān and Abāqā Khān and brother of Juvainī the historian; here the poet writes with great elegance but much exaggeration and artificiality. The fourth *Risāla*, an answer to an enquiry from a certain Sa'd al-Dīn, is a subtle discussion of intellect and emotion as means to the knowledge of God, and Bahār compares it with Rūmī's prose in the *Fīhi mā fīhi*; while the fifth, a 'Mirror of Princes,' returns to the unambitious simplicity of the first. The sixth *Risāla* is a collection of three separate tracts describing Sa'dī's encounters with Abāqā Khān and other famous persons.

But 'it is in the *Gulistān* that one must look to discover Sa'dī's art, mastery and personality. Had this book, small in size but large in substance, not existed two thirds of the master's personality and sublime rank would vanish, and it may well be that Persian prose would have been deprived for ever of such a splendid and valuable treasure.' Bahār declares that in this work Sa'dī invented a wholly new style of prose, different alike from the rugged models of antiquity and the artificial extravagances of his own time. He defines the *Gulistān* as belonging to the *maqāma* type of composition and in that sense comparable with the *Maqāmāt* of Ḥamīdī; but 'whereas the latter is a pure and arid imitation of Badī' al-Zamān and Ḥarīrī, into the former no element of imitation enters; the *Gulistān* is entirely original and abounds in new invention.' Bahār enumerates fourteen features characterizing the style of the *Gulistān*; he calls attention to the careful balance observed in the construction of the eight chapters, the consideration always given to holding the reader's interest, the nice alternation of prose and verse, the brevity and succinctness of the anecdotes, the avoidance of difficult and outlandish words, the strict regard for polite proprieties. But it is the discussion of the element of rhythm within the patterned prose that constitutes the most striking section of this brilliant diagnosis. Referring to the presence of rhythm to a varying extent in all ancient prose, including the Koran itself, Bahār claims that with Sa'dī this feature becomes deliberate and all-pervasive while remaining natural and unforced. He cites in evidence, as a random but typical example, Tale 35 of Book I:

Bā ṭā'ifa-yi buzurgān ba-kashtī dar nishasta būdam: zauraqī dar pay-i mā gharq shud: dū barādar ba-girdābī dar uftādand: yakī az buzurgān guft mallāḥ-rā ki 'bi-gīr īn har duvān-rā ki ba-har yakī panjāh dīnārat diham': mallāḥ dar āb uftād: tā yakī-rā bi-rahānīd ān digar halāk shud: guftam 'baqīyat-i 'umrash na-mānda būd az īn sabab dar giriftan-i ū ta'khīr kard u dar ān digar ta'jīl': mallāḥ bi-khandīd u guft 'ānchi tū guftī yaqīn ast u digar mail-i khāṭir ba-rahānīdan-i īn bīshtar būd ki vaqtī dar biyābānī mānda būdam u ū marā bar shuturī nishānda u zi dast-i ān digar tāziyāna-yi khvurda am dar ṭiflī': guftam 'ṣadaqa llāhu man 'amila ṣāliḥan fa-li-nafsihi wa-man asā'a fa-'alaihā.'

I was seated on shipboard with a party of notables, when a skiff following us foundered, and two brothers fell into a whirlpool. One of my companions said to the mariner, 'Save these two, and for each one I will give you fifty dinars.' The mariner dived overboard, but by the time he had brought out one of the pair, the other had perished. I said, 'The other had not longer to live, and therefore he delayed saving him, and hastened to rescue the other.' The mariner laughed, and said, 'What you said is true. Furthermore, my mind was more inclined to bring this one out, because once when I was fordone in the desert, he put me on a camel; as for the other, all I ever had at his hands was a whipping when I was a child.' I said, 'God's words are surely true, that *whoso doeth good, doeth it unto himself, and whoso doeth evil, against himself he doeth it.*'

In this passage rhythmical phrases occur very frequently, and in some instances a group of words can, by a very slight manipulation, be converted into a complete line of poetry. Bahār cites these examples.

For *zauraqī dar pay-i mā gharq shud* read *zauraqi andar pay-i mā gharq° shud*, and you get a hemistich of the *sarī'* metre: –oo–|–oo–|–o–.

For *ba-girdābī dar uftādand* read *ba-girdābī dar uftādand° bā-ham*, and you get a hemistich of the *hazaj* metre: o–––|o–––|o––.

For *tā yakī-rā bi-rahānīd* read *tā yakī-rā bi-rahānīd° ba-jahd*, and you get a hemistich of the *ramal* metre: –o––|oo––|oo–.

For *guftam baqīyat-i 'umrash na-mānda būd* read *guftam magar baqīyat-i 'umrash na-mānda būd*, and you get a hemistich of the *muḍāri'* metre: ––o|–o–o|o––o|–o–.

But these instances can be multiplied almost indefinitely;

following Bahār's analysis, it becomes clear that the whole of the *Gulistān* is a most intricate weave of subtly varied rhythms, an astonishing exercise in perfectly controlled virtuosity.

A third work on popular ethics is commonly attributed to Sa'dī, the *Pand-nāma* (sometimes known as the *Karīmā*) in 201 *mutaqārib* couplets. 'Of the "Pund Namuh," a work which has long enjoyed a deserved celebrity in the east, and which, from the excellent maxims it inculcates, is often used as a favourite text-book in the seminaries of the Orientals, there was an excellent version published about the year 1795, by that accomplished Persian scholar, Francis Gladwin, Esq., in his "Moonshee"; a work calculated for the student; still more recently, an elegant paraphrase, with an Hindee translation of the original, was composed by that eminent Hindoostanee philologist, Dr. J. Gilchrist; which, however, is not adapted to the general reader, being confined to one of his valuable text-books. Besides these, the author is not acquainted with any other version of the original.' So wrote Ebenezer Pocock in his *Flowers of the East*, published at London in 1833; he followed up these remarks with a polished verse-translation, and added as a postscript: 'Such are the Ethics of one of the best writers that Persia has ever produced. Such generous feeling for the afflicted—such noble daring in the cause of truth and unbiassed justice, would almost exalt him to be the guardian penman of a free state: and we cannot help regretting, that such a man had not been favoured with a purer creed, and more dignified ritual, than those of Mahomet.' Yet the ascription of the *Pand-nāma* to Sa'dī is very debatable, though the sentiments expressed in its simple verses are entirely in conformity with his teaching.

To advocate virtue and truth in a time of red terror, and to preach justice to princes cowering before Mongol tyranny, certainly called for courage of a rare order, and an unwavering devotion to the high principles of Islam. Sa'dī composed his quota of panegyrics, and was qualified to flatter kings as bombastically as the most servile encomiasts of his people; it is characteristic of his boldness that he did not hesitate to tell his royal patrons bluntly how they ought to conduct themselves, and why. In the very opening of an ode addressed to the Atābeg Abū Bakr ibn Sa'd he declares:

Kings rule by turns in this transient abode:
now it is your turn, see you rule with justice.

To the Atābeg Saljūq-Shāh, cousin of Sa'd II of the twelve days' reign, who ruled Fārs for two years before being killed by the Mongols, Sa'dī remarked:

The world abides not; only the marks of justice abide:
labour for good and righteousness, strive for nobility.
Take not amiss your slave's slip: the mightiest kings
have given ear to the counsel of their humblest servants.
Happy is he whom men speak well of, when he is dead,
for the sons of Adam leave naught behind them but a tale.

And it was in the same admonitory spirit that Sa'dī spoke to Inkiyānū, appointed Governor of Shīrāz by Hūlāgū Khān in 1270:

Fortune has turned enough, and turns again:
the prudent man binds not his heart to the world.
You who have now the means, work to some end
ere the time comes that you can work no more.
Rustam, Isfandiyar that man of steel—
such heroes as the Book of Kings records
that those who lord it in the land may know
what others left to be remembered by,
all these are gone, and we, O bold of eye,
from their example never a warning take.
You, who were once a sperm within the womb
and then a child sucking his mother's breast,
then soared in stature for a certain space
to be a full-grown cypress, silver-cheeked,

so that at last you were a famous man,
knight of the tourney, hero in the field:
what you have seen abode not as it was,
and what you see shall likewise not abide.
This delicate body, whether soon or late,
must turn to earth, and in the earth shall lie.
Throne, fortune, high command, dominion—all
these things are nothing, since they pass away:
far better than some palace daubed in gold
is the memorial of a goodly name.

Besides all this, Sa'dī was above all a very great lyric poet; indeed it was he who, in the judgment of eminent Persian critics, first established the superiority of the lyric over the formal ode. 'Before Sa'dī's time,' Garakānī writes, 'not so much attention had been paid by poets to the writing of lyrics, and it may be said that this genre first acquired importance in the master's own age, and through his genius reached the pinnacle of advancement and esteem.' Shafaq echoes these remarks: 'Certainly, famous poets before him composed some lyrics: but the ode was the official and admired form of verse, while the lyric played only a minor role. Sa'dī however preferred the lyric, which primarily expresses the feelings, over the ode with its general pursuit of ulterior purposes. It was he who popularized the lyric.' The transition from ode to lyric clearly took place during the thirteenth century, though Sanā'ī a hundred years earlier had composed freely in both forms. But his treatment of the lyric was mystical, whereas with Sa'dī the lyric is firmly established as a medium for conveying human, carnal passion; there is also evidence that he practised and perhaps invented the convention of employing the lyric as a concealed panegyric. At first sight his love-poems appear to be addressed to the customary object of affection, the handsome youth or the wayward mistress; but it is possible to read into many of his declarations a petition to the ruling prince or his powerful minister. For the rest, he introduces into his poems that familiar repertory of themes and conceits so characteristic of the classical Persian lyric, degenerating in later times into a lifeless mannerism. It is perhaps his greatest glory that he pioneered the way for Ḥāfiẓ, his only superior as a lyrical poet.

Sa'dī's use of the lyric is marked by perfect technical control, ease and fluency of diction, a pleasing formality, and an occasional true touch of the sublime. Its general qualities are well reflected in the following version by E. G. Browne; the main theme is *carpe diem*, with the subsidiary and related topic that love demands a reckless disregard of all consequences.

Precious are these heart-burning sighs, for lo,
This way or that, they help the days to go.
All night I wait for one whose dawn-like face
Lendeth fresh radiance to the morning's grace.
My Friend's sweet face if I again might see
I'd thank my lucky star eternally.
Shall I then fear man's blame? The brave man's heart
Serves as his shield to counter slander's dart.
Who wins success hath many a failure tholed.
The New Year's Day is reached through Winter's cold.
For Laylá many a prudent lover yearns,
But Majnún wins her, who his harvest burns.
I am thy slave: pursue some wilder game:
No tether's needed for the bird that's tame.
A strength is his who casts both worlds aside
Which is to worldly anchorites denied.
Tomorrow is not: yesterday is spent:
To-day, O Sa'dí, take thy heart's content!

To those who like comparative translation, R. A. Nicholson's version of the same poem presents an interesting contrast.

Dear to me this lamentation, though it melt my soul with fire,
For it passes the day somehow: surely else I should expire.

Not so beautiful is Morning, setting earth and heaven alight,
As the face for which I waited, waited all this weary night.
Ah, if I may see again that love-enkindling face, now far,
Thanks I'll say till Resurrection unto my victorious star.
If I shrink when blame is cast on me, I play the woman's part:
Howsoe'er the arrow pierce thee, meet it with a manly heart!
They that hunger after pleasure needs must know the taste of pain:
He that hopes for New Year's springtide, let him freeze and not complain.
Prudent harvester of reason love's deep bliss did never learn:
'Tis Majnún reads Lailà's secret—he whose wits in frenzy burn.
Fling thy noose about another! Self-devoted here I stand:
Who would tie the foot of falcon long familiar with his hand?
Lovers gambling all the goods away of that world and of this
Are endowed with something precious that our sleek ascetics miss.
Yesterday is gone, To-morrow not yet come. Do thou waylay
Opportunity, O Sa'dí! Make the utmost of To-day!

For an evocation of the metaphysical, seventeenth-century atmosphere of some of Sa'dī's lyrics, let us turn to another of R. A. Nicholson's versions.

Lovers' souls 'gin dance with glee
When the zephyr fans thy roses.
Ne'er melts thy stony heart for me,
Mine as a sunk stone heavily
In thy dimple's well reposes.

Life were an offering too small,
Else 'tis easy to surrender
Unto thee, who need'st not call
Painter's art to deck thy wall:
Thou alone dost give it splendour.

Better sicken, better die
At thy feet than live to lose thee.
Pilgrim to Love's sanctuary,
What car'st thou, 'neath desert sky,
How the thorns of Absence bruise thee?

For a combination of all the characteristics of Sa'dī's lyrical style, including the use of this form in panegyric, consider the following poem obviously (though not explicitly) addressed to the Crown Prince.

Soul of mine, may my soul
Thy ransom be,
Thou who hast not a friend
In memory!

Thou art gone, and to none
Payest thou heed;
Never fir moved so freely
In the mead.

Grace of God rest on him
Whose loving care
Nurtured thee, and on her
Who did thee bear.

May good chance all thy fondest
Hopes fulfil,
And protect thee from malice
And ill will.

What did He, who thy face
So sweetly drew,
That a world into tumult
Wild He threw?

Once shall I seize my monarch's
Reins, and say
'From the fair, cruel charmers
Justice, pray!'

With those eyes slumbrous dark,
That lily brow,
Nevermore my lost heart
Returnest thou.

Intellect doth with love
But ill agree,
Where the slave slays the lord
Implacably.

He, that had on love's threshold
Never yet
Laid his foot, there at last
His brow has set.

Face to dust went; and now
Not strange it were
If the head, blown by passion,
Goes to air.

The wild fowl, that did burst
And break his chain,
In the trap, though so crafty,
Falls again.

Others weep, whom an alien
Hand assails;
For the hand of his own love
Saʿdi wails.

'Now,' I said, 'through the world
I'll wander free,
Break my slave's chains, and go
In liberty.

Are there not out of Fars
Homes to be had?
Not in Rúm, Shám, or Basra,
Or Bagdad?'

Yet these still hold my garment
By the hem—
Earth of Shíráz, and Rukna's
Silver stream.

Lastly, one more example of Sa'dī's magically simple yet sophisticated diction ends with a curious but charming note of self-applause, condoned in the Persian poet who has many competitors at court, which suggests that this poem was composed for recitation by a professional minstrel.

When the enemy doth throw
His lasso,
As his will determines, so
We must do.

None has earned, till he has loved,
Manly fame,
E'en as silver pure is proved
By the flame.

Never did reformer take
Passion's way,
But that he both worlds did stake
In the play.

To his memory I am so
Wholly turned
That with self my mind is no
More concerned.

Thanks to love sincere and whole
I confess;
Love, that burned my heart, my soul
Doth caress.

Sa'di! poet sweeter page
Never writ
For a present to an age
Great with wit.

May thy sugar tongue remain
Ever blest
That hath taught the world such pain
And unrest.

NINE

Rūmī

JALĀL AL-DĪN MUḤAMMAD IBN MUḤAMMAD called Rūmī was born at Balkh in 1207, son of Bahā' al-Dīn Muḥammad ibn Ḥusain called Bahā' al-Dīn Valad; according to certain authorities he was a great-grandson through his grandmother of Sulṭān Muḥammad Khvārizmshāh, but this assertion involves a historical impossibility and his royal descent, if true, must have been from another line. Less doubt is entertained concerning his claim to the caliph Abū Bakr as a remote ancestor. His father was a noted preacher and Ṣūfī who never lost any opportunity of emulating the great Ghazālī in expressing his detestation of philosophy and scholasticism, and this is said to have excited against him the anger of that doughty theologian Fakhr al-Dīn al-Rāzī who enjoyed the protection of the ruling house. Whether on account of this quarrel (which seems unlikely, for al-Rāzī died in 1209) or for some other cause, such as the onset of the Mongol invasions, Bahā' al-Dīn Valad presently found himself obliged to flee from Balkh. Jalāl al-Dīn was still a boy when his father set out on his forced wanderings through Persia, Iraq, Arabia and Syria; it is related, and there is nothing inherently improbable in the story, that at Nīshāpūr he met Farīd al-Dīn 'Aṭṭār, then an aged and greatly revered figure; 'Aṭṭār divined the spiritual aptitude of the lad and presented him with a copy of his *Asrār-nāma*, telling Bahā' al-Dīn that 'soon his son would set on fire the consumed ones of the world.' The refugees came to rest finally in Qonia; there Bahā' al-Dīn died in 1230, and there with certain intervals Rūmī resided to the end of his life. He had married and begotten a son named Sulṭān Valad while the family were temporarily halted at Zarinda, forty miles to the south-east of Qonia.

Rūmī received his early education from his father, a good scholar, who recorded his meditations in a book entitled *Ma'ārif*; the influence of his instruction and writings is apparent in Rūmī's own work. Shortly after Bahā' al-Dīn's death his old friend from Balkh, Burhān al-Dīn Muḥaqqiq of Tirmidh arrived in Qonia, and found Rūmī established in the favour of the Saljūq Sulṭān 'Alā' al-Dīn Kai-Qubād, preaching in public in succession to his father. Burhān al-Dīn at once undertook to initiate the young zealot into the inner mysteries of Ṣūfī discipline and doctrine; when he died in 1240, Rūmī 'in turn assumed the rank of Shaykh and thus took the first, though probably unpremeditated, step towards forming a fraternity of the disciples whom his ardent personality attracted in ever-increasing numbers.' We are told that during his discipleship to Burhān al-Dīn, and on his advice, Rūmī went to study further in Aleppo, whence he proceeded to Damascus for perhaps four years (the eminent Murcian theosophist Ibn 'Arabī died there in 1240) before returning to Qonia to attend his teacher in his last days.

'Suddenly the sun of love and truth cast its rays on that pure soul, and so fired and inflamed him that his eyes were dazzled by its light.' With these words Rūmī's modern Persian biographer and interpreter Badī' al-Zamān Furūzānfar introduces the most remarkable and influential episode in the poet's life, his encounter with the wild mystic Shams al-Dīn of Tabrīz. The meeting took place in 1244 when Shams al-Dīn, a wandering dervish of some sixty years, arrived in Qonia. 'Jalālu'l-Dīn found in the stranger that perfect image of the Divine Beloved which he had long been seeking,' writes R. A. Nicholson. 'He took him away to his house, and for a year or two they remained inseparable.' What passed between the older and the younger mystic during their close association is not recorded, but all ancient sources agree that thenceforward Rūmī was a changed man. 'Meanwhile,' Nicholson continues, 'the Maulawī disciples of Rūmī, entirely cut off from their Master's teaching and conversation and bitterly resenting his continued devotion to Shamsu'l-Dīn alone, assailed the intruder with abuse and threats of violence. At last Shamsu'l-Dīn fled to Damascus, but was brought back in triumph by Sulṭān Walad, whom Jalālu'l-Dīn, deeply agitated by the loss of his bosom friend, had sent in search of him. Thereupon the disciples "repented" and were forgiven. Soon, however, a renewed outburst of jealousy on their part caused Shamsu'l-Dīn to take refuge in Damascus for the second time, and again Sulṭān Walad was called upon to restore the situation. Finally, perhaps in 1247, the man of mystery vanished without leaving a trace behind.' Following this final disappearance it was rumoured in Qonia that Shams al-Dīn was dead, murdered, said some, at the hands of certain jealous disciples of Rūmī. The poet received the reports with incredulity and exclaimed:

Who was he that said
The immortal spirit is dead,
Or how dared he say
Hope's sun hath passed away?

An enemy of the sun,
Standing his roof upon,
Bound up both his eyes
And cried: 'Lo, the sun dies!'

Rūmī is said himself to have made a prolonged journey to Damascus in quest of his beloved friend, and it has been suggested that the whirling dance of his Order, to the accompaniment of plaintive music from the reed-pipe, commemorates this desperate and fruitless search.

But it is not quite correct to say that 'the man of mystery vanished without leaving a trace behind.' His teachings have survived in a book, as yet unpublished, entitled *Maqālāt*, an examination of which proves beyond doubt that this was the source of a number of the mystical apologues and ideas that occur in Rūmī's writings. However, presently the poet found consolation in the affection of his pupil and deputy Ṣalāḥ al-Dīn Zarkūb; when he died, in about 1261, Rūmī transferred his passionate attachment to Ḥusām al-Dīn Ḥasan, destined to succeed him as head of the Order on his death in 1273. Rūmī was laid to rest beside his father, and over his remains a splendid shrine was erected which continues to this day to draw pilgrims from all parts of the Muslim world.

These are the bare facts of a life rich in mystical experience, a life of saintly and ecstatic devotion which quickly gave rise to a wealth of pious legends. Rūmī's son Sulṭān Valad composed a spiritual biography of his father in verse, the *Valad-nāma* which takes rank as a document of the first importance. Later in time, and of more questionable authority, comes the long life of the saint included by Aflākī, disciple of Rūmī's grandson Chelebī 'Ārif, in his *Manāqib al-'ārifīn*. The historicity of this account may be judged from the following extracts, quoted in the translation of Sir James Redhouse.

'One beautiful moonlight night, Jelāl and Shems were together on the terraced roof of the college, and all the inhabitants of Qonya were sleeping on their housetops. Shems remarked: "See all these poor creatures! They are dead to every sense of their Creator on this beautiful night of God's decree. Wilt thou not, Jelāl, of thy infinite compassion, wake them up, and let them gain a share in the shower of blessings of this night?" Thus appealed to, Jelāl faced toward Mekka, and offered up this prayer to God: "O Thou Lord of heaven, and of earth, for the love of Thy servant Shemsu-'d-Dīn, vouchsafe wakefulness to this people." Immediately a black cloud gathered from the unseen world. Thunders and lightnings burst forth; and so heavy a rain fell, that all the sleepers, catching up what clothing they could find, quickly took refuge in their houses below. Shems smiled at the saintly joke, and was greatly amused.'

'At Damascus, when a young student, Jelāl was frequently seen by others to walk several arrow-flights' distance in the air, tranquilly returning to the terraced roof on which they were standing. Those fellow-pupils were among his earliest believers and disciples.'

'In the days of Jelāl there was in Qonya a lady-saint, named Fakhru-'n-Nisā (the Glory of Women). She was known to all the holy men of the time, who were all aware of her sanctity. Miracles were wrought by her in countless numbers. She constantly attended the meetings at Jelāl's home, and he occasionally paid her a visit at her house. Her friends suggested to her that she ought to go and perform the pilgrimage at Mekka; but she would not undertake this duty unless she should first consult with Jelāl about it. Accordingly she went to see him. As she entered his presence, before she spoke, he called out to her: "Oh, most happy idea! May thy journey be prosperous! God willing, we shall be together." She bowed, but said nothing. The disciples present were puzzled. That night she remained a guest at Jelāl's house, conversing with him till past midnight. At that hour he went up to the terraced roof of the college to perform the divine service of the vigil. When he had completed that service of worship, he fell into an ecstasy, shouting and exclaiming. Then he lifted the skylight of the room below, where the lady was, and invited her to come up on to the roof also. When she was come, he told her to look upwards, saying that her wish would come to pass. On looking up, she beheld the Cubical House of Mekka in the air, circumambulating round Jelāl's head above him, and spinning round like a dervish in his waltz, plainly and distinctly, so as to leave no room for doubt or uncertainty. She screamed out with astonishment and fright, swooning away. On coming to herself, she felt the conviction that the journey to

Mekka was not one for her to perform; so she totally relinquished the idea.'

'A friend of Jelāl's once took leave of him at Qonya, and went to Damascus. On his arrival there, he found Jelāl seated in a corner of his room. Asking for an explanation of this surprising phenomenon, Jelāl replied: "The men of God are like fishes in the ocean; they pop into view on the surface here and there and everywhere, as they please."'

'It is related that, after his death, when laid on his bier, and while he was being washed by the hands of a loving and beloved disciple, while others poured the water for the ablution of Jelāl's body, not one drop was allowed to fall to the earth. All was caught by the fond ones around, as had been the case with the Prophet at his death. Every drop was drunk by them as the holiest and purest of waters. As the washer folded Jelāl's arms over his breast, a tremor appeared to pass over the corpse, and the washer fell with his face on the lifeless breast, weeping. He felt his ear pulled by the dead saint's hand, as an admonition. On this, he fainted away, and in his swoon he heard a cry from heaven, which said to him: "Ho there! Verily the saints of the Lord have nothing to fear, neither shall they sorrow. Believers die not; they merely depart from one habitation to another abode."'

It is permissible to look askance at such stories as these, typical products, one might say, of the medieval imagination. Yet hints at the supernatural phenomena described can be found in Rūmī's own poems, and these may indeed have given rise to the stories. Thus, levitation may have been thought to be referred to in the quatrain:

My dusty body
Is heaven's light;
Angels are jealous
To watch my flight.

Cherubim envy
My purity;
Before my valour
All demons flee.

The miracle of the shower may have been inspired by these verses:

Rain fell on the head
Of a man of passion,
Fell in such a fashion
To his house he fled.

Clapping wings, the swan:
'Pour on me Thy shower
Whose immortal power
I was fashioned on.'

The incident of the friend who left Rūmī in Qonia and found him in his room in Damascus recalls the poem in which a similar idea is expressed:

O blessed hour, when thou and I
Together sit within this hall:
Two forms, two shapes then, thou and I—
Two bodies, and a single soul.

The garden's lustre and the trill
Of deathless birds such life bestow,
The hour when thou and I at will
Into that flower-garden go!

The stars that wheel upon their way
Lean down to look upon us then,
And like some moon we shed our ray
To lighten them and other men.

And thou and I no more remain,
But rapt in ecstasy sublime
Soar far beyond the tale inane
Of 'Thou' and 'I' and selfhood's clime.

The sky's brave birds that fly so free
On me and thee all envious gaze
That we should laugh so merrily
Together, in such wondrous ways.

But not so wonderful is it
As that ourselves, who separate grace
Iraq and Khorasan, should sit
Together in this secret place.

Before passing to a consideration of Rūmī's writings, it is interesting to glance at the portrait of the saint as envisaged by Furūzānfar on the basis of contemporary reports and internal evidence. 'Maulānā was a man of a sallow complexion. His body was thin and lean, while his eyes flashed with a hypnotic brightness daunting to those who looked upon him. In his earlier years he wore a scholar's turban and a wide-sleeved gown, but after his encounter with Shams al-Dīn he changed these habits for a blue robe and a smoke-coloured turban, which he never altered to the end of his days. In his conduct he was peaceful and tolerant towards men of all sects and creeds, looking with the same eye on Muslim, Jew and Christian alike and urging his disciples to comport themselves similarly. This state of peace and unity, which came as the result of love and full realization of truth, bestowed on Maulānā a patience and a forbearance such that throughout his life, despite the attacks and unworthy misrepresentations levelled against him by blind-hearted enemies, he was never heard to utter one bitter reply, but with gentleness and charity he strove to bring them to the right path. Though he was looked upon with favour by the kings and princes of Rūm, and though this class eagerly sought his company, he passed all his time with the poor and needy and most of his disciples were of the lower orders. He was a man of infinite modesty and shyness, never approving that his acts of benevolence should be noised abroad. For all his learning, of which we have abundant evidence in his writings, he was entirely free of scholarly arrogance and pride. In all his characteristics and in his true philanthropy he resembles the greatest of the prophets, saints, men of God and servants of humanity, and it can be properly said that he stands in the ranks of the greatest guides of mankind.'

Rūmī is thus seen to have been primarily a mystic of extraordinary devotion and self-dedication; doubtless he would have regarded himself, if he thought of himself, first and foremost as a lover of God seeking by every means union with the Divine, and secondly as a teacher striving by his words and his example to lead others towards the same goal. His poetry was a by-product of his great spiritual fervour, the authentic outpouring of the enraptured soul, with little or no mental premeditation, and this accounts for the technical blemishes which have been remarked in Rūmī's style. As R. A. Nicholson observes, 'Naturally an improvisateur, pouring forth his thoughts as fast as they come to his lips and wrought by sphere-music to a pitch of transport where all conscious sense of polish and style has long ago been annihilated—naturally such a one will offend in this point more conspicuously than self-contained and soberer spirits.' Daulatshāh tells us that 'there was a pillar in the Maulawī's house, and when he was drowned in the ocean of love he used to take hold of that pillar and set himself turning round it. Meanwhile he versified and dictated and people wrote down the verses.' An examination of his odes and quatrains, gathered together in the vast collection known as the *Dīvān-i Shams-i Tabrīz*, discovers abundant evidence of extemporaneous and trancelike composition. As for the circumstances under which his mystical epic, the *Mathnavī-yi ma'navī*, was composed, Aflākī gives the following circumstantial account as Redhouse translates him.

'The reason why the Mesnevī was written is related to have been the following:—Husāmu-'d-Dīn learnt that several of the followers of Jelāl were fond of studying the Ilāhī-nāma of Senā'ī, the Hakīm, and the Mantiqu't-Tayr of 'Attār, as also the Nasīb-nāma of the latter. He therefore sought and found an opportunity to propose that Jelāl should indite something in the style of the Ilāhi-nāma, but in the metre of the Mantiqu-'t-Tayr; saying that the circle of friends would then willingly give up all other poetry, and study that alone. Jelāl immediately produced a portion of the Mesnevī, saying that God had forewarned him of the wishes of the brethren, in consequence of which he had already begun to compose the work. That fragment consisted of the first eighteen couplets of the introductory verses' (the version here quoted is that of Sir William Jones):

Hear, how yon reed in sadly pleasing tales
Departed bliss and present woe bewails!
'With me, from native banks untimely torn,
Love-warbling youths and soft-ey'd virgins mourn.
O! let the heart, by fatal absence rent,
Feel what I sing, and bleed when I lament:
Who roams in exile from his parent bow'r,
Pants to return, and chides each ling'ring hour.
My notes, in circles of the grave and gay,
Have hail'd the rising, cheer'd the closing day:
Each in my fond affections claim'd a part,
But none discern'd the secret of my heart.
What though my strains and sorrows flow combin'd!
Yet ears are slow, and carnal eyes are blind.
Free through each mortal form the spirits roll,
But sight avails not. Can we see the soul?'
Such notes breath'd gently from yon vocal frame:
Breath'd said I? no; 'twas all enliv'ning flame.
'Tis love, that fills the reed with warmth divine;
'Tis love, that sparkles in the racy wine.

Me, plaintive wand'rer from my peerless maid,
The reed has fir'd, and all my soul betray'd.
He gives the bane, and he with balsam cures;
Afflicts, yet soothes; impassions, yet allures.
Delightful pangs his am'rous tales prolong;
And LAILI's frantick lover lives in song.
Not he, who reasons best, this wisdom knows:
Ears only drink what rapt'rous tongues disclose.
Nor fruitless deem the reed's heart-piercing pain:
See sweetness dropping from the parted cane.
Alternate hope and fear my days divide:
I courted Grief, and Anguish was my bride.
Flow on, sad stream of life! I smile secure:
THOU livest! THOU, the purest of the pure!
Rise, vig'rous youth! be free; be nobly bold:
Shall chains confine you, though they blaze with gold?

'Jelāl frequently mentions Husām as the cause of the work's having been begun and continued. In the fourth book he addresses him in the opening couplet:

Of Truth, the light; of Faith, the sword; Husāmu'd-Dīn aye be;
Above the lunar orb has clomb my Mesnevī, through thee.

'And again the sixth book has for its opening verse the following apostrophe:

O thou, Husāmu'd-Dīn, my heart's true life! Zeal, for thy sake,
I feel springs up in me sixth book hereby to undertake.

'Often they spent whole nights at the task, Jelāl inditing, and Husām writing down his inspirations, chanting it aloud, as he wrote it, with his beautiful voice. Just as the first book was completed, Husām's wife died, and an interval ensued. Two years thus passed without progress. Husām married again; and in that year, A.H. 662 (A.D. 1263), the second book was commenced.

No other interval occurred until the work was brought to a conclusion.'

Three books have been published containing the prose utterances of Rūmī. First we have the *Majālis-i sab'a*, seven sermons delivered at unspecified dates but presumably before his meeting with Shams al-Dīn of Tabrīz; for we are informed that after this event the poet only mounted the pulpit once, and then at the urgent request of his disciples. The *Majālis* follow the usual pattern of Muslim preaching; after an elaborate doxology a Tradition of the Prophet is cited, and the rest of the address consists of an exposition of the text, illustrated by quotations from the Koran, pious anecdotes and snatches of poetry. The style of composition is also in keeping with tradition, an involved and artificial prose that makes hard reading and must have been even more difficult to follow when delivered. Secondly, the private letters of Rūmī were anciently collected by an anonymous disciple; these, like the *Majālis*, have been published in Istanbul by the Mevlevī Muḥammad Farīdūn Nāfidh. In his letters, some 144 in number, addressed to relatives and friends and dealing with personal as well as spiritual matters, the poet writes with considerably more ease and fluency though by no means without mannerisms. While the two foregoing books furnish the researcher with much valuable and important material, in general interest they cannot compare with the *Fīhi mā fīhi* of which three editions have now appeared, the third (and most reliable) being the work of Badī' al-Zamān Furūzānfar.

The *Fīhi mā fīhi* comprises what may be loosely described as the table-talk of the saint. Certainly it was not Rūmī himself who made this compilation, but rather a disciple or perhaps his son Sulṭān Valad; it is a posthumous production, and its title seems to be drawn from a line of a poem occurring in Ibn 'Arabī's *al-Futūḥāt al-Makkīya*. Here we find Rūmī discoursing on a wide variety of religious and mystical topics, pointing his observations as usual with stories and quotations. R. A. Nicholson cites two passages in his *Rumi, Poet and Mystic.*

'Jalālu'l-Dīn was asked, "Is there any way to God nearer than the ritual prayer?" "No," he replied; "but prayer does not consist in forms alone. Formal prayer has a beginning and an end, like all forms and bodies and everything that partakes of speech and sound; but the soul is unconditioned and infinite: it has neither beginning nor end. The prophets have shown the true nature of prayer. . . . Prayer is the drowning and unconsciousness of the soul, so that all these forms remain without. At that time there is no room even for Gabriel, who is pure spirit. One may say that the man who prays in this fashion is exempt from all religious obligations, since he is deprived of his reason. Absorption in the Divine Unity is the soul of prayer."'

'When a fly is plunged in honey, all the members of its body are reduced to the same condition, and it does not move. Similarly the term *istighrāq* (absorption in God) is applied to one who has no conscious existence or initiative or movement. Any action that proceeds from him is not his own. If he is still struggling in the water, or if he cries out, "Oh, I am drowning," he is not said to be in the state of absorption. This is what is signified by the words *Ana 'l-Ḥaqq* "I am God." People imagine that it is a presumptuous claim, whereas it is really a presumptuous claim to say *Ana 'l-'abd* "I am the slave of God"; and *Ana 'l-Ḥaqq* "I am God" is an expression of great humility. The man who says *Ana 'l-'abd* "I am the slave of God" affirms two existences, his own and God's, but he that says *Ana 'l-Ḥaqq* "I am God" has made himself non-existent and has given himself up and says "I am God," i.e. "I am naught, He is all: there is no being but God's." This is the extreme of humility and self-abasement.'

In the following extract, in which the conversational tone comes out well, we find Rūmī discussing what must have been a burning topic in the thirteenth century, and expressing a characteristically paradoxical view of the Mongol invaders.

'Someone remarked: "The Mongols seize property, and from time to time they give property to us. That is a strange situation. What is your ruling?" He replied: "Whatever the Mongols seize has come as it were into the grasp and treasury of God. In the same way when you fill a jug or a barrel from the river and carry it away, that becomes your property so long as it is in the jug or barrel and nobody has the right to interfere. Anyone who takes from the jug without your permission is guilty of theft by violence. But once the water is poured back into the river, it passes out of your ownership and is lawful for all to take. So our property is unlawful to them, whereas their property is lawful to us."

'*There is no monkhood in Islam: the congregation is a mercy.* The Prophet, God's blessings be upon him, laboured for solidarity, since the gathering of spirits has a great and momentous effect on unity, whereas with solitariness it is not achieved. That is the secret of why mosques were erected, so that the inhabitants of the parish might gather there and greater mercy and profit ensue. Houses are separate for the purpose of dispersion and the concealment of private relations: that is their use. Cathedral mosques were erected so that the whole city might be assembled there; the Kaaba was instituted in order that the greater part of mankind might gather there out of all cities and climes.

'When the Mongols first came to these parts they were naked and bare, they rode on bullocks and their weapons were of wood; now they are sleek and well-filled, they have splendid Arab horses and carry fine arms. In that time when they were desperate and weak and had no strength, God helped them and answered their prayer; in this time when they are so powerful and mighty, God is destroying them at the hands of the feeblest of men, so that they may know that it was through God's bounty and succour that they captured the world, and not by their own force and power. In the first place they were in a wilderness, far from men, without means, poor, naked and in need. By chance certain of them came as merchants into the territory of the Khvārizmshāh and began to buy and sell, purchasing muslin to clothe their bodies. The Khvārizmshāh prevented them, ordering that their merchants should be slain and taking tribute from them; he did not allow their traders to go there. The Tartars went humbly before their king saying, "We are destroyed." Their king asked them to give him ten days' grace, and entered a deep cave; there he fasted for ten days, humbling and abasing himself. A proclamation came from Almighty God: "I have accepted your supplication. Come forth: wherever you go, you shall be victorious." So it befell: when they came forth, by God's command they won the victory and captured the world.

'Someone said, "The Tartars also believe in the resurrection, and say that there will be a *yarghū* (judgment)." He replied: "They lie, desiring to associate themselves with the Muslims. 'We also know, and believe,' they say. A camel was once asked, 'Where are you coming from?' It replied, 'From the baths.' 'That is evident from your pads,' came the retort. If they really believe in the resurrection, what evidence is there to prove it? The sins and wrongs and evils that they have committed are like snow and ice piled together heap on heap. When there comes the sun of penitence and contrition, tidings of the other world and the fear of God, it will melt those snows of sinfulness as the sun in heaven melts the snow and ice. If some snow and ice should say, 'I have seen the sun, and the sun of summer has shone upon me,' and it still remained snow and ice, no intelligent man would believe it. It is impossible that the summer sun should come and leave the snow and ice intact. Though Almighty God has promised that good and evil shall be recompensed at the resurrection, yet an ensample of that comes to pass every moment and at every instant. If happiness enters into a man's heart, that is his reward for making another happy; if he becomes sorrowful, it is because he has brought sorrow upon a fellow-man. These are presents from the other world and tokens of the day of recompense, so that by these little things men may come to understand those great matters, even as a grain of corn is offered as a token of the whole stack." '

But it is in his poetry that Rūmī's universal genius stands fully revealed—the *Dīvān* and the *Mathnavī*. The *Dīvān* is called after Shams al-Dīn of Tabrīz, and most of the odes contained in it have his name in the concluding 'signature' couplet. 'In calling his lyrics the *Dīwān* of Shams-i Tabrīz,' writes R. A. Nicholson, 'Rūmī of course uses the name Shams as though Shams and himself had become identical and were the same person.' In this fathering of his poems on to his spiritual *alter ego* Rūmī had no intention whatever to deceive, and no one familiar with the situation would have been in the least misled; nevertheless it is the only instance in Persian literature of a poet so acting, and the fact bears eloquent testimony to the strength of Rūmī's conviction that his inspiration as a poet sprang from Shams al-Dīn. It was evidently with reference to this genesis of his muse that he composed the quatrain:

When in my breast
The flame of love was lit,
Whate'er but love my heart possest
Love's fire consumèd it.

The subtle brain,
The school, the book I spurned;
The poet's craft I strove to gain,
And rhyming verse I learned.

Believing Shams al-Dīn to be the Perfect Man, God's image incarnate, in loving him Rūmī loved God, and could sincerely declare:

Dost thou suppose
I do as I command,
Or, as the moment goes,
I am in my own hand?

As a pen I lie
Before my scrivener,
Or like a ball am I,
My mallet's prisoner.

Yet Rūmī did not disclaim authorship of his odes altogether; as Aqā-yi Ulfat of Iṣfahān first pointed out, and Furūzānfar confirmed, very many of his poems carry additionally the pen-name Khāmūsh, which Rūmī clearly adopted as his personal soubriquet.

A problem of authenticity has inevitably arisen in connexion with the *Dīvān* on account of its extraordinary bulk, at all events in some copies. The Lucknow lithograph of 1885, a folio volume written in four columns, extends to 1,036 pages; this was presumably based on the Moti Maḥall manuscript, described by A. Sprenger as containing 'ghazals, 1200 pp. of 34 beyts, tarjī'-bands, 46 pp., and about 4000 rubā'īs (nearly 60,000 beyts in all).' The nineteenth-century Persian scholar Riḍā Qulī Khān credited Rūmī with 50,000 couplets in the *Dīvān*. At the other extreme, some manuscripts of the *Dīvān* comprise only 5,000 verses. When Furūzānfar in 1936 wrote his excellent biography of the poet, he was inclined to the view that the original core of the *Dīvān*, though certainly of considerable size, had been grossly inflated in the course of the centuries by deliberate or accidental false attributions. He presented a well-reasoned argument for the pruning of these excrescences, but reserved judgment on the problem as a whole 'while awaiting the discovery of a really ancient manuscript.' Such a copy has now been found, and is preserved in the library of Sir Chester Beatty in Dublin. Though undated, it can with confidence (on palaeographical grounds) be placed at not later than the early years of the fourteenth century, within a generation of the poet's death. This volume, which has the quatrains as well as the odes, is written in 374 folios, in four columns, 27 lines to the page; the total of couplets thus amounts to approximately 40,000. This evidence is of course not wholly decisive; false ascription may have already taken place by the time the copy was compiled *ad majorem auctoris gloriam*, and in any case the original amanuenses, who recorded many of the poems direct from Rūmī's lips, may not have been able always to distinguish between original composition and quotation. With all reserve, however, it seems clear that we must allow to Rūmī the distinction of being among the world's most abundant poets.

The inequalities of his lyrical outbursts have long been recognized. Of him it may well be literally true that he never blotted a single line; composing as he did spontaneously, he could not be expected to have a meticulous regard for niceties of style, nor to be always alive to the desirability of not repeating himself. It must also be conceded that his range of topics is somewhat circumscribed; he sang as a Ṣūfī, and 'Ṣūfīism,' as R. A. Nicholson wrote in 1898, 'has few ideas, but an inexhaustible wealth and variety of illustration. Among a thousand fluttering masks the interpreter is required to identify each old familiar face.' This poverty of themes is naturally not confined to mystical poetry; profane verse in the languages of Islam was also condemned from the start, because of a strict classical canon of recognized subjects, to an endless repetition of threadbare tropes and worn-out conceits. But it is precisely in this context that Rūmī's genius may be most clearly discerned. Whereas other Persian poets were content to resign themselves to convention, and to restrict their creative impulse to elaborating fresh (but not always so very fresh) variations on given themes, Rūmī seemingly originated an extensive range of new subjects and new illustrations. The stock-in-trade of Ṣūfī quietism, piety, austerity, passion, theosophy had already been exploited by Anṣārī, Sanā'ī, 'Aṭṭār; Rūmī invented the whirling dance to the song of the reed-pipe, and with it set the entire universe of emotion, thought and language spinning to a fresh and exhilarating rhythm. New similes, new metaphors, new images poured from his enraptured soul, as he struggled to give expression to ecstatic experiences of unquestionable power and authenticity.

Doctors we of ancient time
And philosophers sublime,
Roasted flesh and syrup rare,
Face of earth and Sirius star.

For such bones as aching be
Saving liniment are we;
To the sick and breaking heart
Healing comfort we impart.

Hasten then from this abode,
For we take the open road;
Earthly pleasures scarce suffice,
We are folk of Paradise.

Men have argued (but they lied)
That the image does not bide;
One declared, we are a tree,
Said another, grass are we.

Yet the rustling of the bough
Proves the breeze is stirring now;
Silent then, O silent be—
That we are, and this are we.

The challenge of the music resurrected long-buried responses.

Death's Angel cries
When the lute is played;
Our hearts arise
Living from the dead.

These passions deep
That were drowned and died
Like fishes leap
From the boiling tide.

In the transformation of the dance, the mystic feels himself to be one with the circling stars.

Each atom dancing in the plain
Or on the air,
Behold it well, like us, insane
It spinneth there.

Each atom, whether glad it be
Or sorrowful,
Circleth the sun in ecstasy
Ineffable.

The tumult and following tranquillity of a storm at sea symbolize the spirit's experience in its journey out of and back to God.

Happy was I
In the pearl's heart to lie;
Till, lashed by life's hurricane,
Like a tossed wave I ran.

The secret of the sea
I uttered thunderously;
Like a spent cloud on the shore
I slept, and stirred no more.

The poet in ecstasy describes the advent of the Divine Beloved whom he has sought so long; the beautiful version is R. A. Nicholson's.

He comes, a Moon whose like the sky ne'er saw, awake or dreaming,
Crowned with eternal flame no flood can lay.
Lo, from the flagon of Thy love, O Lord, my soul is swimming,
And ruined all my body's house of clay.

When first the Giver of the grape my lonely heart befriended,
Wine fired my bosom and my veins filled up;
But when His image all my eye possessed, a voice descended:
'Well done, O sovereign Wine and peerless Cup!'

Love's mighty arm from roof to base each dark abode is hewing
Where chinks reluctant catch a golden ray.
My heart, when Love's sea of a sudden burst into its viewing,
Leaped headlong in, with 'Find me now who may!'

As, the sun moving, clouds behind him run,
All hearts attend thee, O Tabrīz's Sun!

But in a quieter and more reflective mood Rūmī is inspired to compose a neo-Platonic hymn of greater beauty and deeper insight than any Greek follower of Plotinus had the power to write: R. A. Nicholson is again the masterly translator.

Poor copies out of Heaven's original,
Pale earthly pictures mouldering to decay,
What care although your beauties break and fall,
When that which gave them life endures for aye?

Oh, never vex thine heart with idle woes:
All high discourse enchanting the rapt ear,
All gilded landscapes and brave glistering shows
Fade—perish, but it is not as we fear.

Whilst far away the living fountains ply,
Each petty brook goes brimful to the main.
Since brook nor fountain can for ever die,
Thy fears how foolish, thy lament how vain!

What is this fountain, wouldst thou rightly know?
The Soul whence issue all created things.
Doubtless the rivers shall not cease to flow
Till silenced are the everlasting springs.

Farewell to sorrow, and with quiet mind
Drink long and deep: let others fondly deem
The channel empty they perchance may find,
Or fathom that unfathomable stream.

The moment thou to this low world wast given,
A ladder stood whereby thou mightest aspire;
And first thy steps, which upward still have striven,
From mineral mounted to the plant; then higher

To animal existence; next, the Man
With knowledge, reason, faith. O wondrous goal!
This body, which a crumb of dust began—
How fairly fashioned the consummate whole!

Yet stay not here thy journey: thou shalt grow
An angel bright and have thine home in Heaven.
Plod on, plunge last in the great Sea, that so
Thy little drop make oceans seven times seven.

'The Son of God!' Nay, leave that word unsaid;
Say, 'God is One, the pure, the single Truth.'
What though thy frame be withered, old, and dead,
If the soul keep her fresh immortal youth?

These few examples only touch the surface of a deep and rich mine, whose abundance of pure gold still awaits full discovery and exploitation. Fortunately, thanks to the devoted labours of that superb scholar, my teacher R. A. Nicholson, the contents and meaning of Rūmī's other great poetic creation, the *Mathnavī-yi ma'navī*, are now perfectly disclosed for all to study and appraise. This epic, divided into six books with a total of over 25,000 couplets, in Rūmī's own words 'contains the roots of the roots of Religion, and treats of the discovery of the mysteries of reunion and sure knowledge. It is the Grand Jurisprudence of God, the most glorious Law of the Deity, the most manifest Evidence of the Divine Being.' Begun at the instance of Ḥusām al-Dīn shortly after 1258, the *Mathnavī* was left incomplete (the last book breaks off in the middle of a story) at Rūmī's death; it is likely that he ceased dictation some years before 1273. At first sight the poet appears to ramble on without any definite scheme in mind, taking up topics and illustrating them with anecdotes more or less as the fancy takes him; but Gustav Richter in his *Persiens Mystiker Dschelál-eddin Rumi: eine Stildeutung in drei Vortragen* has disclosed a very different picture. In R. A. Nicholson's words, 'Any one who reads the poem attentively will observe that its structure is far from being so casual as it looks. To say that "the stories follow each other in no order" is entirely wrong: they are bound together by subtle links and transitions arising from the poet's development of his theme; and each Book forms an artistic whole.'

'The *Mathnawī* is a grand Story-book,' wrote Nicholson in 1931. 'There are several hundreds of stories, comprising specimens in almost every *genre*, and no one can accuse the author of lacking invention or fail to admire the easy power with which he moulds his raw material into whatever shape he will. As might be expected, the largest class consists of legends from the *Qur'ān* and its Commentaries, the Traditions of the Prophet, and the Lives of pre-Mohammedan prophets and Muslim saints. *Kalīla and Dimna*, the Arabic version of the Sanskrit *Pancha-tantra*, supplies numerous Beast Fables, where the animals play the allegorical parts assigned to them. Jalālu'ddīn borrows much but owes little: he makes his own everything that comes to hand. The First Story in the poem is taken from Ibn Sīnā (Avicenna); others can be traced back to Sanā'ī, Nizāmī, and 'Attār; and probably a large number were contributed by popular collections of anecdotes like the *Jawāmi'u 'l-Hikāyāt* of 'Awfī. What precisely these literary sources were, and how far they cover the whole ground, is a question that has yet to be investigated. It is likely, I think, that some, perhaps many, of the Tales belong to the miscellaneous store of "wandering" stories carried to and fro by dervishes and other travellers, in which case the author may have put them into verse from memory.' Recently Furūzānfar, whose long and patient researches have done so much to throw light on the biography and personality of Rūmī, has published a monograph establishing the sources of many of the stories told in the *Mathnavī*; this essay proves the poet's wide reading, but the use made by him of the material at his disposal has yet to be systematically investigated. The following examination of a single anecdote suggests lines on which further exploration might be conducted. The Egyptian mystic Dhu 'l-Nūn, who died in 861 and is buried at Giza, once witnessed a remarkable miracle, if we are to believe the reports of the hagiographers. Abū Nu'aim al-Iṣfahānī (d. 1038) recounts the incident as follows, allegedly in Dhu 'l-Nūn's own words.

'We were once at sea making for Jedda, and had on board with us a youth of twenty years or so, who was clothed in the garment of reverential fear. I was longing to speak to him, but could not; we would always see him either reciting the Koran, or fasting, or at his lauds. Then one day, while he was sleeping, a suspicion ran through the ship; the passengers were all examining each other, until they came to the sleeping youth. The owner of the missing purse said, "Nobody was nearer to me than this youth asleep here." When I heard this, I went up to the youth and wakened him. As soon as he had washed himself and prayed four *rak'as*, he said, "Young man, what do you want?" I said, "A suspicion has run through the ship; all the people have examined one another, and now they have come to you." Then the youth lifted up his hands in prayer, and I feared for the passengers on account of his imprecation; when lo, it seemed to us as if every fish in the sea had come to the surface, holding in its mouth a pearl. The youth took a jewel from the mouth of one of the fishes and threw it to the owner of the purse, saying, "Here is a compensation for what you have lost. Now you are quits." '

Some years later, the famous Ṣūfī author al-Qushairī reported Dhu 'l-Nūn somewhat more briefly.

'I was once on board a ship when a villous wrap was stolen. They suspected a certain man, but I said, "Leave him alone, and I will speak gently to him." Now the youth was sleeping in a cloak; he put his head out of the cloak, and I spoke to him about the matter. The youth replied, "Do you speak thus to me? I adjure Thee, Lord, leave not a single fish but it shall bring a jewel!" We saw the surface of the water full of fishes, with jewels in their mouths. Then the young man threw himself into the sea, and passed to the shore.'

The Persian eleventh-century Ṣūfī author Hujvīrī quotes Dhu 'l-Nūn thus.

'Once I embarked in a ship voyaging from Egypt to Jidda. Among the passengers was a youth wearing a patched frock. I was eager to be his companion, but he inspired me with such awe that I did not venture to address him, for his spiritual state was very exalted and he was constantly engaged in devotion. One day a certain man lost a purse of jewels, and suspicion fell on this youth. They were about to maltreat him, but I said, "Let me question him courteously." I told him that he was suspected of theft and that I had saved him from maltreatment. "And now," I said, "what is to be done?" He looked towards Heaven, and spoke a few words. The fishes came to the surface of the sea, each with a jewel in its mouth. He took a jewel and gave it to his accuser; then he set his foot on the water and walked away. Thereupon the real thief dropped the purse, and the people in the ship repented.'

Rūmī introduces this anecdote in the middle of a discourse on the wickedness of attributing evil to holy men; he makes no mention of Dhu 'l-Nūn as the original source of the story, and has the saintly youth quote in conclusion the well-known passage in the Koran where God administers a rebuke to the Prophet for disregarding the appeal of a blind man for instruction.

A dervish, that with saintly fortitude
was full provisioned, journeyed on a ship
wherein it chanced that, as he lay asleep,
a purse of gold was missed. The hue and cry
ran through the vessel; all were strictly searched,
and all to no avail. At last the quest
ended in him: 'Come, let us search as well
the sleeping mendicant,' the call went up.
The owner of the gold, possessed by grief,
awakened him. 'A bag of precious things,'
said he, 'is missing; the whole company
have been examined; you cannot escape
the inquisition. Strip your dervish-cloak,
that their suspicions may be cleared from you!'
'O Lord!' the dervish cried, 'these wicked men
have charged a crime against Thy servant true;
command, and let it be!' Since that his heart
was sorely pained by their suspicions,
forthwith on every side out of the deep
myriads of fishes, each a wondrous pearl,
the ransom of a realm, having in mouth,
put up their heads; pearls from the hand of God
that never man had touched or brought to view.
The dervish took a handful of the pearls
and, casting them upon the boards, sprang up
and sate him high-suspended in the air
and rested there, cross-legged and at his ease,
as monarchs do enthroned—he lifted high
above the zenith, and the ship below.
'Begone!' he cried. 'Take, if ye will, your ship;
I will have God, that so ye may not sail
with a mean thief to keep you company!
Then let us see who shall have greater loss
in this our separation. I am glad
to be with God united, and apart

from His creation; He will ne'er cry thief
against me, He will ne'er deliver me
to the informer.' Then the voyagers
exclaimed, 'Great master, wherefore wast thou raised
to so high station?' Thus he made reply:
'Because I cast suspicion on the poor,
and, for a thing so mean, offended God!
Nay, God forbid; it was not on this wise,
but that I never nourished evil thoughts
of dervishes, but showed true reverence
unto those kings, so gracious and so pure,
whom God Himself exalted, in the time
His Prophet turned his back, and did reveal
on their behalf the holy words, *He frowned.*'

Nicholson has remarked on the 'direct semi-colloquial style' of the tales in the *Mathnavī*, 'rising to dignity where the subject requires it,' and observes that this 'contrasts favourably with the artificial diction of most Persian verse.' Indeed, one of the most remarkable characteristics of Rūmī's diction, not only in these rapid narratives but throughout his poetry and in his prose discourses as well, is his readiness to use words and constructions from common speech which otherwise scarcely appeared in Persian literature until the modernists, in the teeth of indignant opposition from the learned traditionalists, introduced them in their fiction. His combination of demotic with literary language gives an extraordinary vigour to everything he says, and confirms strikingly the old reports of spontaneous and oral composition.

This summary survey of the works of a supremely original genius cannot be better concluded than by quoting again the man who penetrated more deeply into the heart and soul of Rūmī than any scholar of east or west in all these seven centuries, and whose writings on the poet-mystic will live so long as poetry and mysticism engage the attention of enquiring students. 'His *Odes* reach the utmost heights of which a poetry inspired by vision and rapture is capable, and these alone would have made him the unchallenged laureate of Mysticism.' That was Nicholson's final estimate, delivered more than thirty years after the publication of his first book, *Selected Poems from the Dīvāni Shamsi Tabrīz*. When he had completed his edition and translation of the *Mathnavī*, he added: 'Familiarity does not always breed disillusion. To-day the words I applied to the author of the *Mathnawí* thirty-five years ago, "the greatest mystical poet of any age," seem to me no more than just. Where else shall we find such a panorama of universal existence unrolling itself through Time into Eternity? And, apart from the supreme mystical quality of the poem, what a wealth of satire, humour and pathos! What masterly pictures drawn by a hand that touches nothing without revealing its essential character! In the *Díwán* Jalálu'ddín soars higher; yet we must read the *Mathnawí* in order to appreciate all the range and variety of his genius.' And Nicholson recognized as the grand climax of the *Mathnavī* those lines in the third book where Rūmī appears (but only superficially, for the doctrine he enunciates stems direct from Greek philosophy) to anticipate the Darwinian theory, and envisages a consummation of all things in which the God-descended soul of Man returns at last to its original and eternal Home.

I died as mineral and became a plant,
I died as plant and rose to animal,
I died as animal and I was Man.
Why should I fear? When was I less by dying?
Yet once more I shall die as Man, to soar
With angels blest; but even from angelhood
I must pass on: *all except God doth perish.*
When I have sacrificed my angel-soul,
I shall become what no mind e'er conceived.
Oh, let me not exist! for Non-existence
Proclaims in organ tones, 'To Him we shall return.'

TEN

Minor Thirteenth-Century Authors

'THE seventh century of the Hijra, despite the fact that it was an age of the greatest hardship as a result of the Mongol onslaught on the lands of Islam, especially Persia, is nevertheless reckoned as one of the great scientific and literary epochs of Islam.' This is the opening sentence of Jalāl Humā'ī's introduction to his edition of extracts from the *Akhlāq-i Nāṣirī*, of which more will be said later in this chapter. His remarks are perfectly just; the century of Mongol devastation, the century which witnessed the end of the 'Abbāsid caliphate, most of Persia laid waste, the sack of Baghdad, was also a period of intense intellectual and artistic activity. Some of the most prominent authors of these times have been discussed in the preceding three chapters; it is now proposed to examine briefly the writings of five more who, in this context, must be presented as minor figures but in any other century might well have held the centre of the stage.

When the origins of the quatrain were being reviewed, reference was made to the thirteenth-century prosodist Shams-i Qais and his romantic account of the invention of this literary form. The *Tarjumān al-balāgha* of Rādūyānī and the *Ḥadā'iq al-siḥr* of Vaṭvāṭ had already laid the foundations of Persian rhetoric when Shams al-Dīn Muḥammad ibn Qais of Raiy addressed himself to the enterprise of advancing this difficult and specialized study. It was in Marv, and in the year 1217, that he began to write, in Arabic and not in Persian. Rumours of the Mongol attacks on north-eastern Persia sent him scurrying for safety, along with many of his countrymen sufficiently prudent and provisioned to flee the avalanche. He was at the fortress of Farrazīn, between Hamadhān and Iṣfahān, when the invaders caught up with him; in the general confusion he lost the rough draft of his book, but afterwards recovered some portions from a fellow-refugee. Shams-i Qais finally found rest with the Atābeg Sa'd ibn Zangī and his son and successor Abū Bakr, and it was in Shīrāz that he took up once more his project of authorship; he now allowed himself to be persuaded to write in Persian. His book, which he named *al-Mu'jam fī ma'āyīr ash'ār al-'Ajam*, was completed about 1233 and, as its title indicates, discusses Persian poetics only; the parts of the original draft dealing with Arabic poetics were separated off into another book, the lost *al-Mu'rab fī ma'āyīr ash'ār al-'Arab*. After centuries of neglect, Shams-i Qais's valuable work came once more before the public in 1909, in an edition prepared for the Gibb Memorial Series by E. G. Browne and Mīrzā Muḥammad of Qazvīn; a revised edition by Mudarris Riḍavī was published at Teheran in 1935.

In *al-Mu'jam* (which is the correct spelling; E. G. Browne read erroneously *al-Mu'ajjam*) we have a fuller treatment of the science of poetics than in the works of Rādūyānī and Vaṭvāṭ. Not only are the metres and rhetorical figures analysed in greater detail, but the illustrations are far more copious and are often given at length. One section discusses with explanatory drawings such poetic eccentricities as odes composed in the shape of a tree or a bird. The scientific value of the book is therefore very considerable, and no future investigator of Persian poetic technique can afford to disregard it. As a contribution to elegant writing it also deserves more consideration than it has hitherto attracted. On this point, Bahār's observation is well worth pondering: 'According to my taste, Shams-i Qais's prose is one of the best examples of his time. If this man, endowed with such a powerful pen, fine intelligence, sharpness of appreciation and clarity of judgment had written a book rather freer than scientific compilations, such as history or narrative, it would have been a precious treasure. I cannot trace after his time any prose style in Persian so reminiscent of the vigorous prose of his predecessors such as Abu 'l-Ma'ālī, the *Chahār maqāla*, the *Qābūs-nāma*, and the *Siyāsat-nāma* of Niẓām al-Mulk. I think that the *Gulistān* of Sa'dī too is a kind of poetic prose; and certainly I believe that classical prose after Shams-i Qais and Sa'dī descended into the dust, may God have them in His wide mercy!' Bahār comments on Shams-i Qais's freedom from the frigid artifices and rhetorical tricks so dear to his contemporaries, but remarks that words of Arabic origin make up between forty and fifty per cent of his vocabulary.

The court of Sa'd ibn Zangī and Abū Bakr ibn Sa'd gathered to Shīrāz many who had served the princes of northern and eastern Persia before the Mongol storm broke. Among the poets to whose royal panegyrics Sa'dī may well have listened as a boy was Kamāl al-Dīn Ismā'īl of Iṣfahān, nicknamed *Khallāq al-Ma'ānī* or 'Creator of Ideas.' (It is to be remembered that according to the theorists, poetry was made up of two elements—*alfāẓ* or 'words' and *ma'ānī* or 'ideas'; Kamāl al-Dīn Ismā'īl was thus considered to be what, in modern jargon, would be termed a creative artist.) His father Jamāl al-Dīn 'Abd al-Razzāq had been a panegyrist before him, and is chiefly famous for the scurrilous poem which he composed in reply to a satire of Khāqānī's pupil Mujīr al-Dīn, an effusion which drew from Khāqānī a handsome tribute to Iṣfahān by way of amends. Kamāl al-Dīn learned the art of flattering kings from a good master; but he appears to have been disappointed at the reception accorded to his efforts, and he returned from his long tour of the courts to his native city in time to witness and perish in Ogotāy's massacre. The disillusioned poet must have been a familiar figure in those troubled times, and Shams-i Qais devoted a pointed section of *al-Mu'jam* to the well-worn theme that 'no man of intelligence and virtue ought to leave his panegyrist who hopefully presents a poem to him without some prize.'

There is a certain boldness in Kamāl al-Dīn's addresses to the princes whose favour he sought, a moralizing note that anticipates Sa'dī; he may have been a pioneer in this startlingly new approach, and he certainly suffered the fate commonly reserved for pioneers. Thus, a poem dedicated to Rukn al-Dīn Ṣā'id ibn Mas'ūd begins uncompromisingly:

> You make boast of having a heart that's in love with God:
> all good attend you, if your tongue's in accord with your heart!

It is therefore not so very surprising that he should have been moved later to remark:

> I've looked about me to right and left with the eye of reason:
> no worse craft in the world have I seen than the poet's trade.

Kamāl al-Dīn abandoned his literary ambitions on his return to Iṣfahān, and affected the dervish habit and way of life. At this stage of his development he declared (and his new devotion to religion seems to have made little impression on his natural conceit):

> A thousand thanks and praises I sing to Almighty God,
> that not out of greed or covetousness I follow this way;
> I don't earn my living by making up poetry,
> though to be sure poets like me don't happen very often.
> Night and day I sit in my nook of complete content
> caring for no one, and certainly nobody cares for me.

But even then he could not altogether conceal his disappointment with the world. Daulatshāh relates that Kamāl al-Dīn had been very generous to many of his townsfolk, who requited his liberality with ingratitude; he therefore cursed them.

Lord of the Seven Planets, send forth some bloodthirsty infidel
to make Dar-i Dasht a bare plain, Jūpāra a river of blood!

His prayer was soon enough answered. Ogotāy entered Iṣfahān about 1237 and gave the city over to massacre and plunder. E. G. Browne quotes Daulatshāh for the sequel. 'At this time Kamálu'd-Dín Isma'íl had adopted the ascetic life and habit of the Ṣúfís, and had retired to an hermitage situated outside the town, in consequence of which he was not for some time molested. The Iṣfahánís took advantage of this to deposit in his custody some of their treasures and valuables, which he concealed in a well in the courtyard of his hermitage. One day, however, a Mongol boy armed with a crossbow fired at a bird in this courtyard, and in doing so dropped his "drawing-ring," which rolled into the well wherein the treasure was hidden. Search for the ring led to the discovery of the treasure; the Mongol greed was aroused, and poor Kamál was put to the torture to make him reveal other hoards of treasure which they supposed him to possess. In his death-agony he is said to have written with his life-blood the following quatrain.'

My bleeding heart obeys thy will, O Lord!
Is this the rest my years of homage earn?
Be patient, O my soul; now shalt thou learn
In what strange ways God doth man's love reward.

The version of Kamāl al-Dīn Ismā'īl's last poem here quoted was made by Louis H. Gray and Ethel Watts Mumford, American authors of *The Hundred Love Songs of Kamal ad-Din of Isfahan*, published in a limited edition of 200 copies (of which 150 were offered for sale) by David Nutt 'at the Sign of the Phoenix, Long Acre: London: 1903.' It might not have been anticipated that this particular poet would be singled out for acclaim as a prime romantic; but let his translators tell their own story.

'For us Kamal's chief interest lies not in his ghazals and kassidas, with their fulsome eulogies of petty kings long passed away, but in his rubaiyat of love. If Omar, like Koheleth, sings ever of life's vanity, if Abu Said in his quatrains speaks only of the mystic unity of God and man, Kamal of Isfahan knows no theme but the sadness and the passion of love, whose end is the Triumph of Death. All we know of Kamal's heart-history is gleaned from his poetry. His biographers are silent here, and rightly so. Only Occidental 'culture' stoops shamelessly to reveal and print the love-lives of the great. Yet, although the veil may not be raised, we may, now and again, catch stray glimpses of the figures which move behind. We know from the Rubaiyat that his love was unhappy, and that the Beloved was cruel to him and false. Nor can we reproach her justly, for however much we idealize the Beloved and worship her above all else, she is but woman, *varium et mutabile semper*. Of one thing at least we may be sure, if the Rubaiyat speaks truth—Kamal's Beloved was of the daughters of joy, twining her hair, like Lilith, about the hearts of men. ... For an instant, even unto him, longing was reality, as woman gives that she may take away. And thus at last, despairing and broken, mocked by the men he had helped and the woman he had loved, he went forth from Isfahan, nor came again.'

Any comment would be superfluous, and it only remains to rescue from oblivion some extracts from this remarkable New York paraphrase.

LXVI
O Cypress! Rose! Light of the world! beware!
Somewhere the Archer draws the bending bow;
Silent and swift the fatal arrows go—
And one shall find thy marble bosom bare.

LXVII
There is a Gate men call 'Eternity,'
Whereunto lead the paths of Dread and Fear.
Each light-spent day brings thee more surely near
Where dimly gleams the Sword of Destiny.

LXVIII

O arrogant! stake not thy beauty frail
Against the magic of the Moon and Stars;
And mock me not because my silence mars
Thy senseless mirth and talk of no avail.

LXIX

Plays the dawn wind with violet and rose,
And dimples o'er with smiles the river's face;
Unto the cypress lends a subtler grace,
And brings the fevered sick divine repose.

LXX

But oh, forget not—insolent with glory—
The wind that opes the rose, the tulip breaks,
From off the bough the almond blossom shakes;
And Death the ending of Love's sweetest story.

The ardent bibliographer may like to know of Mrs. Theodosia Garrison's version of one quatrain from Kamāl al-Dīn published in *Lippincott's Magazine* for 1900, at page 783.

From a bogus anchorite we now turn to a true mystic, also a victim of Mongol aggression, author of an important but disregarded treatise on Ṣūfism. Najm al-Dīn 'Abd Allāh ibn Muḥammad Rāzī, called Najm al-Dīn Dāya, born in the once flourishing city of Raiy, was initiated into the spiritual life by Majd al-Dīn of Baghdad, disciple of the famous Najm al-Dīn Kubrā. Dāya also studied under Kubrā before the latter was killed in 1221 resisting the Mongol massacre of Khvārizm. He tells us that even before these catastrophic events sent him fleeing westwards, a number of his pupils had requested him to compile a book on mysticism in Persian: 'they desired a compendium small in size but great in meaning, which would give information on the beginning and end of creation, the commencement of the path and the conclusion of the journey, the purpose and quest of the lover and the beloved, to be a world-displaying cup and a beauty-reflecting mirror, of service alike to the immature neophyte and the perfect initiate.' Of the numerous treatises on this subject already composed most were in Arabic, and therefore useless to those whose mother-tongue was Persian; and the Prophet had said, 'Speak to people according to the degree of their understanding.'

But then Dāya's wanderings had immediately ensued. 'It was in the year 617 (1220) that the God-forsaken army of the Tartar infidels, may God forsake and destroy them, gained the mastery over those territories. The confusion and slaughter, the devastation and leading into captivity, the destruction and conflagration that followed at the hands of those accursed creatures were such as had never before been witnessed in any age, whether in the lands of heathendom or Islam.' The Prophet had indeed foretold, more than six hundred years previously, the great slayings that must precede the Last Day; 'and how could slaughter ever be vaster than this that they wrought from the gate of Turkistān to the gate of Syria and Rūm, wherein they laid waste so many cities and provinces, so that in one city alone—Raiy, where I myself was born and brought up—it has been estimated that some 700,000 mortals were slain or made captive.' In a company of friends and dervishes Dāya set forth one night in the year 618 (1221) from Hamadhān where he was then dwelling, 'in a situation fraught with the utmost peril,' and took the road to Ardabīl. News soon overtook them that the infidels had reached and set siege to Hamadhān, slain a huge number of its inhabitants, and then taken the city, martyring many men and making captive many women and children. Most of his own dependants in Raiy had met a martyr's end.

> Hail rained heavy upon my garden;
> of my rose-bush not a leaf remained.

Where was any country to be found in which true believers still dwelt, uncontaminated by the blight of heresy and fanaticism, under the protection of a just and religious king? In every place Dāya asked this question, and always he was given the same answer—in Rūm. There the Saljūqs still reigned, winning glorious victories over the atheists, building 'schools, monasteries, mosques, pulpits, stairways, convents, hospitals and other places of charity, honouring scholars, paying reverence to ascetics and lavishing compassion on all their subjects.' Remembering how his ancestors had always prayed for the welfare of that royal house, and being conscious of the debt owed by him and by all Muslims on account of their benefactions, he forthwith turned his face towards 'that blessed region.' So he made for Caesarea; and at Malaṭya 'by a thousand happy chances' he met 'that world-scholar and pillar of the age' Shihāb al-Dīn Suhrawardī. The latter received him joyously, assuring him that he could not discover a better country in which to settle, or a more kindly and generous monarch to protect him. This he subsequently proved to be a strictly true statement; the Saljūq Kai-Qubād I welcomed Dāya at Caesarea with the utmost warmth and liberality, and thus enabled him at last to devote himself in ease and tranquility to the task of writing his book, the date of commencement being Ramaḍān 618 (October 1221).

The *Mirṣād al-'ibād* is made up of five chapters, subdivided into numerous sections. The first chapter is introductory and describes the plan of the book and the circumstances of its composition. Chapter II reviews the whole order of creation, the gradations of the spirits, the origin of man according to Ṣūfī theory, and the story of Adam and Eve. In the third chapter we follow the course of human history from the first junction of spirit with body, the part played by the prophets in calling mankind back to God, the final revelation vouchsafed to Muḥammad, and the eternal validity of Islam; Dāya elaborates the mystical purification of the human heart and spirit, the Ṣūfī discipline and teaching, the relationship between instructor and disciple, and the exercises necessary to spiritual regeneration. Chapter IV carries the story into the other world, exposing the future that awaits the saved and the damned on the Day of Judgment. The fifth chapter is an enumeration of the duties particularly prescribed for the various classes of men—kings and those in supreme authority, ministers and governors, judges and jurisconsults, possessors of wealth and property, landed proprietors and agriculturalists, traders, artisans and craftsmen.

The author concluded his writing on 1 Rajab 620 (July 31, 1223) in Sīvās, and presented his work to Kai-Qubād in these words: 'In completing this service, this feeble person requests of that heaven-exalted presence not wealth or worldly rank, though because of such a frightful calamity and universal catastrophe—God forbid that it should touch the presence of the Sultan—he has fallen into exile from his native land, exchanging for joy sorrow, for abundance paucity, for composure dispersion; I do not say, for glory humiliation, since poverty never sees the face of humiliation, poverty and pride being blood-brothers. "Poverty is my pride" (said the Prophet).

> God knows well, and the days are acquainted with us:
> we are men of noble blood, but we are very needy.

Rather is it my request and hope that in the times of withdrawal and the hours of leisure he may with the hand of supplication and the key of true belief open the door of this treasure-house of divine secrets, full as it is of the coins of infinite godly gifts.' Having 'examined these gems and jewels with the eye of intuitive vision in pure faith,' the Sulṭān may then 'instruct his agent and factor to distribute the charity thus attracted to those deserving in spirit and body.'

Dāya decorates his elegant discourse, after the contemporary fashion, with many quotations from the Koran and the Traditions and many poetic interludes; it is particularly noteworthy that he introduces a very large number of quatrains, much of them presumably original. The contents of his book are extremely varied, as has been indicated; perhaps its greatest value resides in the detailed account of the mystical commemoration (*dhikr*), and the curious discussion of the kinds of 'light' seen in ecstasy. Here is a summary of the prescription for meditation.

'The foundations of meditation rest upon sincere penitence for all acts of disobedience. At the time of *dhikr* one should first take a bath; if that is not possible, then at least the ritual washing should be performed. Clean clothes must be put on, and an empty and darkened apartment made ready; it is preferable to burn a little perfume. The performer should sit cross-legged with his hands resting on his thighs. With heart attentive and eyes closed, he will begin with all reverence to say the words *lā ilāha illā 'llāh* (there is no god but God). This he will do in such manner as to draw *lā ilāha* up from his navel and bring *illā 'llāh* down to his heart, making utterance in a low voice. In pronouncing *lā ilāha* he will expel every thought that comes into his heart as if to say, "I want nothing and I have no object or beloved *illā 'llāh* (but God)." He will continue to repeat this exercise until the very being of the recollector is annihilated in the light of recollection. When the beadle of *lā ilāha* has cleared the heart of the impact of all extraneous things, then the recollector must await expectantly the advent of the revelation of the power of *illā 'llāh*.

> Sweep the place clean, for the king comes suddenly;
> when it is clear, the king will come to the tabernacle.'

The variety of lights seen is described, though in greater detail, as follows.

'As the mirror of the heart is progressively more burnished, the lights become stronger and more abundant. Sometimes these will take on the likeness of a chandelier, a niche, coloured lamps, variegated candles and multifarious flaming torches. Then celestial lights will appear in the form of small and large stars, then in the likeness of moons, and after that of suns. Finally immaterial lights will be seen. Each light has its own source and significance. Lightning-flashes originate out of ritual washing and prayer; these flicker briefly however, whereas the more sustained gleams spring from the Koran. The lights that take the form of a chandelier, a lamp, a niche and a glass are borrowed from the saintliness of the instructor or the light of the Prophetic presence. The variegated candles and flaming torches are the effect of various acts of recollection, the Koran, morning devotion, silence, litanies and weeping; that is the light of gnosis manifesting in the heart. If heavenly bodies are seen, these are spiritual lights appearing in the sky of the heart according to the degree to which it is burnished. In the final stage of illumination the mystic will see neither this world nor the next, he will neither know nor perceive aught but his Lord, and that without the veil even of the spirit. Then his heart will be light, his body will be light, his hearing, sight, hands, mouth, tongue—all his outward and inward parts will be light.'

The advent of the Mongols brought a different fortune to a very different type of man. We shall now look at the life and some of the achievements of Naṣīr al-Dīn Abū Ja'far Muḥammad ibn Muḥammad of Ṭūs, philosopher, theologian and scientist, known as Naṣīr al-Dīn Ṭūsī, on whom Professor Levy remarks that 'the verdict of history is a most unfavourable one. It might have been expected that the conduct of a man of his undoubted mental qualities would have been regulated by some standard higher than that of personal advantage. Yet he appears not only to have betrayed his Isma'ílí master to Húlágú, but to have been instrumental in bringing the last Caliph treacherously to his death at the hands of the Mongols.' Born at or near Ṭūs (Ghazālī's birthplace) in 1201 of a Shī'ite family, Ṭūsī entered early the service of Nāṣir al-Dīn 'Abd al-Raḥīm ibn Abī Manṣūr, the generous and enlightened Ismā'īlī governor of Quhistān.

'The nature of his relations with the Ismailis still remains hopelessly obscure,' writes W. Ivanow, the eminent authority on the history and literature of that remarkable sect. 'References to it are so confusing and contradictory that not much sense can be made out of them. What is certain and indisputable is the fact that his connection was long, on a more or less permanent basis.' The problem is equally regarded as insoluble by Professor Jalāl al-Dīn Humā'ī of Teheran, who in 1956 published the text of the first preface to Ṭūsī's *Akhlāq-i Nāṣirī*. This scholar observes: 'As for whether the Master in fact detested the Ismā'īlī way of life and association with that sect, and those days really had the character of imprisonment for him, and whether anything that he wrote in conformity with their beliefs was simply under compulsion and by way of dissimulation or was dictated by the expediency of time and circumstance as the case arose—the truth of this is entirely unknown to us.' The plain record is, that Ṭūsī is credited with having written during this period a number of semi-philosophical, semi-theological treatises setting forth the Ismā'īlī doctrine, the most ambitious of these being the *Taṣavvurāt* which Ivanow has edited and translated; the original draft of the *Akhlāq-i Nāṣirī*, his most famous Persian book, was also made while he enjoyed Ismā'īlī patronage, if that is the correct term to use. Ivanow indeed goes so far as to state: 'Personally, I would be inclined to think that the present work (the *Taṣavvurāt*) was really compiled by him at a comparatively early period of his association with the Ismailis, and it was probably with it serving as a fore-study that the *Akhlāq-i Nāṣirī* was later on composed. That latter work shows more maturity in the treatment of the ethical problems, although, as it may appear, Ṭūsī was a poor stylist and writer, though possibly not as hopeless as a poet, if the verses which go under his name are really his.'

It is not without interest to compare passages from these two works dealing with the same topic, the superiority of man over the animal creation. In the *Taṣavvurāt* we read, in Ivanow's version:

'The animal is superior to all plants owing to its stronger power (expressed) in its senses and ability of free movement.

And if animals, taken from the first, are systematically arranged, from gnats, flies and worms which come into existence from the putridity of the air and of various substances, to the birds which come into being from eggs, and to the animals which are strongly built, and are born from male and female, then the last (in the row) will join the human power (*quwwat-i insānī*), although its traces may be still weak, as in the ape which in face, intelligence and comprehension approximates to man and can learn some actions and movements of human beings, if so trained. Man is superior to all animals by his greater force, by ability of speech and clear reasoning which he has. If (various kinds of) men are taken, from the first, and one placed after another, like the Negro from Zanzibar, in the Southern-most countries, the Negro does not differ from an animal in anything except the fact that his hands have been lifted from the earth—in no other peculiarity or property—except for what God wishes. Many have seen that the ape is more capable of being trained than the Negro, and more intelligent. To end (the series) are men of the proper type (*ṣūrat*), of balanced nature, helpful in their decisions, well built, handsome, dignified in their relations with other men in social life, contented and peaceful, excelling and distinguished in ingenuity and cleverness, skilful and perfect in the different varieties of arts and crafts, on which depend the well-being, beauty and flourishing condition of this world of becoming and decaying, and the sources of sustainance of the people. They are rare and wonderful examples of the noble qualities of character, if we consider notables and aristocrats and high-ranking officials. And up to the kings whose decision and plans, might and victorious arms can seize whole continents of the world. (If we arrange them) amongst the people of the world, in a systematical series, up to the learned, who are the last (highest) degree of them, it will become linked up with the first (lowest) degree of the angels. The angel is superior to every man, i.e. excels men in the proximity and (closer) relation to the principle of its own origin (*kull*). And the last degree of the angels is connected with the first degree of the Holy Principles (*ḥudūd-i qudsī*). The degree of the latter may be defined as the "ultimate limit in what is behind them can never be reached by the inquirer".'

In the *Akhlāq-i Nāṣirī* (the translation is 'as dictated by Professor S. A. F. Moulvi, B.A., of the Deccan College to B.A. students': Poona, 1902) Ṭūsī writes:

'The diversity of kinds of animals is greater than the disparity of grades of plants, owing to the nearness of the former to the elementary matter and distance of the latter from it. The noblest of the species (of animals) is that in whom shrewdness and perception may have reached to such an extent that the individual becomes capable of receiving training and instruction, so as to acquire that excellence which was not inherent in his nature, as, for instance, a horse who has been broken in, and a trained falcon. And greater the degree of excellence, greater is his superiority in rank, so much so, that mere observation of actions is sufficient for their training, so that whatever gestures or acts that they mark in others, they mimic them or imitate them exactly; and this is the highest stage in animal life, and the first stage of humanity is united with it. They are men who inhabit the lands situated around populated countries, such as Soudan, Morocco, and others. The conduct and action of these classes of men are similar to those of beasts and brutes. Up to this point all proportion and disproportion arise through the propensity of nature, and after this, all grades of perfection and imperfection are determined by will and judgment. Then a man in whom these powers are perfectly realized, and who can in the best way carry them from imperfection to perfection, by the (judicious) use of organs and eliciting pre-requisites, he will command excellence over him, who possesses the said qualities in a low degree. The first stages are occupied by those who by means of wisdom and acuteness of perception invent excellent arts and devise subtle crafts and delicate and fine tools. They are followed by a class of men, who are deeply engaged in knowledge, sciences and acquisition of excellencies, with great thought, reflection and consideration. Surpassing them are those who glean the knowledge of realities, and precepts of law from the members of divine court without (any corporeal) medium, but only through revelation and inspiration, and, by perfection of morality and arrangement of the affairs of the present and future life, become the means of tranquillity and cause of happiness of humanity in all countries and throughout all ages. And this is the foremost rank of humanity, and the difference of grades is greater than that in animals, in the same ratio as it is between animals and plants, as stated in the foregoing pages. When man reaches this station, he begins to communicate with the sublime world, to enjoy the rank of holy angels and to associate with simple intelligences and souls until he reaches the end—the supreme unity, where the two extremities of the circle of unity meet, like that of a circumference which begins from and ends in the same point. Here the intermedii depart, gradation and discord vanish, beginning and end unite, and nothing but the reality of realities and the end of ends, which is the absolute truth, outlives them all.'

The train of thought and mode of expression in both passages run closely together; the ultimate source is of course Aristotle, as modified by al-Fārābī and Ibn Sīnā. On the other hand, in the *Taṣavvurāt* there are many traces of characteristic Ismā'īlī doctrine, whereas the *Akhlāq-i Nāṣirī* is wholly free of it; but Humā'ī states that in the first recension of the latter work, which has not yet been printed but is extant in at least four ancient manuscripts, certain Ismā'īlī ideas are explicitly set forth. Publication of the original text must be awaited before the problem of Ṭūsī's Ismā'īlī exposition and its subsequent modification can be fruitfully discussed; and critical publication of the *Akhlāq-i Nāṣirī* is certainly most desirable, for this book is surely the most important Persian contribution to academic, as distinct from popular, ethics.

But it is time to resume Ṭūsī's biography. It is reported that at some unspecified date he entered into secret correspondence with Mu'aiyid al-Dīn Muḥammad, vizier to al-Musta'ṣim the last caliph of Baghdad, with a view to transferring his allegiance from the heretics to orthodoxy; he even composed a panegyric in honour of the Commander of the Faithful. The vizier however for whatever reason betrayed Ṭūsī's manœuvre to Nāṣir al-Dīn 'Abd al-Raḥīm, who handed over the recalcitrant scholar to 'Alā' al-Dīn Muḥammad, master of Alamūt. There he remained until Hūlāgū Khān laid siege to the Assassin stronghold, now under the command of 'Alā' al-Dīn's son Rukn al-Dīn Khūrshāh. Ṭūsī is stated to have chosen this moment to take his revenge on his gaolers, by betraying Khūrshāh into Hūlāgū's hands. The year 1256 marked the turning-point in his fortunes. The Mongol rewarded Ṭūsī handsomely for his obliging treachery, and advanced him to high rank in his court; he took him along with him in his onslaught on Baghdad, and Ṭūsī now settled another personal score by assisting his new master to overthrow the capital of Islam and dethrone and murder the Vicar of God. He was pleased to accept appointment by Hūlāgū as vizier in charge of charitable foundations, and thenceforward commanded ample resources to gratify his scientific ambitions.

It was as an astrologer that Hūlāgū appreciated Ṭūsī most highly, for the Mongol conqueror had a lively regard for the messages of the stars. Ṭūsī for his part aspired to academic pre-eminence; eager to outshine Ibn Sīnā himself, he devoted his energies to improving the old Arabic translations of Euclid, Ptolemy, Apollonius, Theodosius, Autolycus and the rest. His devotion to learning must have seemed well rewarded when Hūlāgū commissioned him to erect a splendid observatory at Marāgha. After twelve years' seclusion in this ivory tower he compiled his *Zīj-i Īlkhānī*, of which 'the first *Maḳāla* deals with the eras, the second with the movements of the planets; the third and fourth are devoted to astrological observations.' Hūlāgū was no longer there to receive this learned offering, which Ṭūsī presented instead to his successor Abāqā Khān with the following introduction.

'Almighty God gave power to Chingīz Khān and entrusted to him the kingship of the whole earth. Those who were friendly he entreated kindly; those who were hostile—such as the Khāns of Turkistān and Khiṭā and the Sulṭān of Khvārizm—all them he destroyed. He likewise instituted good laws. Thereafter, when Almighty God took him to His presence, of his sons Ogotāy Qāān sat in his father's place as emperor of the world. He too instituted good laws, and kept the people in tranquillity and peace; he also sent forth an army and converted to friends certain ones who had been enemies. After some years he in turn departed to the presence of Almighty God, and his son Kuyūk Khān, grandson of Chingīz Khān, sat in his father's place as emperor. He desired to look into the affairs of his kingdom, but found no respite to do so, and his days were not many. When his reign came to an end and he departed, by the unanimous consent of their mighty clan Mangū Qāān sat on the throne of the whole world; he was the son of Tūlī Khān, son of Chingīz Khān. When he succeeded he instituted good laws, and repaired the disorder into which affairs had fallen. He devised many good and subtle plans of every variety, and among the good arrangements he made was that he sent his brother Hūlāgū Khān across the Oxus and assigned to him all the lands from Hindustān to the setting sun. When by God's blessing he reached those parts, he first conquered the heretics, seized their dominions and fortresses and annihilated their warriors. After that he took Baghdad and removed the Caliph; then he proceeded to Syria and went as far as the frontiers of Damascus and Egypt. Those who were hostile he destroyed, while those who were friendly he favoured; he entreated kindly scholars of all disciplines, and ordered them to display their skills. He instituted good regulations. At the time that he seized the dominions of the heretics, I Naṣīr al-Dīn who am of Ṭūs and had fallen into the power of the heretics—me he brought forth from that place and ordered to observe the stars. He sought philosophers having knowledge of observation, such as Mu'aiyid al-Dīn 'Urḍi who was in Damascus, Fakhr al-Dīn Khilāṭī of Tiflīs, Fakhr al-Dīn Marāghī of Mauṣil and Najm al-Dīn Dabīrān of Qazvīn. They chose Marāgha as the place for the observations to be made, and applied themselves to this task, making instruments and erecting buildings suitable for the purpose. He also ordered them to bring books from Baghdad, Syria, Mauṣil and Khurāsān and to put them in the place where they would make observations, so that the whole affair went forward in excellent order. The fame of this great work spread throughout the world. Then Almighty God so decreed that Mangū Qāān should depart from our midst, and Qūbilāy Qāān who was younger than he in years sat in his place as emperor. He despatched mandates and good laws to all the world. Then three or four years later Hūlāgū Khān also departed to the presence of God. After that, by the power and blessing of Almighty God his son Abāqā Khān became king of these dominions in his father's place and adorned the world with justice and equity, instituting good rules. So it was in his mighty reign, in accordance with the instructions of that king, that the observation of the stars was completed. On the basis of these observations I, the least of slaves Naṣīr al-Dīn, made this *Zīj-i Īlkhānī* which I now submit to the service of the Prince of the World Abāqā Qāān, hoping that it may meet with his approval, so that by his auspices astronomers hereafter may deduce their almanachs and ascendants from this *Zīj*, and his name remain in the world for thousands of years.'

The foregoing passage is written in very simple Persian with a considerable flavouring of Mongol words. Ṭūsī's style in this late work—he died in 1274, three years after its completion—contrasts strongly with the prose of his earlier life, particularly as displayed in the *Akhlāq-i Nāṣirī*. This treatise on ethics and politics, composed in the first instance (as commissioned by

Nāṣir al-Dīn 'Abd al-Raḥīm) upon the framework of the *Tahdhīb al-akhlāq* of Ibn Miskawaih (d. 1030) but incorporating the ideas of al-Kindī, al-Fārābī and Ibn Sīnā, in its revised edition was dedicated to his Mongol sovereign. Ivanow's opinion that 'Ṭūsī was a poor stylist' will not be shared by all who have read the *Akhlāq-i Nāṣirī*. Though the Persian technical terms invented by Ibn Sīnā and Nāṣir-i Khusrau have been disregarded and the vocabulary is almost oppressively Arabic, the prose is dignified, vigorous and artistic and well suits the author's philosophical purpose. Ṭūsī was a prodigiously productive scholar; his writings in Arabic exceed a hundred titles, and he made important contributions to many branches of knowledge. Dislike of his personal character should not be allowed to cloud our judgment in estimating the value of his literary and scientific achievements. In his second preface to the *Akhlāq-i Nāṣirī* he cites a verse of Arabic which sums up admirably that Shī'ite genius for dissimulation which saved his life in times when the more unyielding orthodox were perishing in their tens of thousands.

Wa-dārihim mā dumta fī dārihim,
wa-arḍihim ma kunta fī arḍihim.

And blandish them, so long as you remain in their house,
and seek to please them, while you are in their territory.

It was a policy which served Ṭūsī's private interests well, even though it made him a traitor to his country and his religion. The Mongols, like their twentieth-century disciples, knew how to handle and exploit to their own ends men of that calibre; and in the end, whether out of conviction or statecraft, the Īl-Khāns accepted Islam and Muslim civilization revived in Persia and Iraq. That such a renaissance could take place at all, after the chaos and slaughter of the preceding years, was in large measure due to the collaboration of such as Naṣīr al-Dīn Ṭūsī and Shams al-Dīn Juvainī, brother of the historian and 'head of the administration of Persia under Mongol rule in the reigns of Hūlāgū (to 1265), Aḅāḳā (1265–82) and Aḥmad (1282–4).'

It was to this Juvainī that Ṭūsī dedicated his small but highly esteemed treatise on Ṣūfism, the *Auṣāf al-ashrāf*, of which a beautiful edition prepared by Naṣr Allāh Taqavī, in the calligraphy of Mīrzā Ḥusain Khān Saifī 'Imād al-Kuttāb, was published at Teheran in 1927. Ṭūsī's final pretension, or perhaps his ultimate aspiration, was to be a mystic; trimming his sails to the new wind that was blowing across the burnt-out lands of western Asia, he abandoned Ibn Sīnā's philosophical quest for union with the Active Intellect in favour of Ghazālī's doctrine of the intuitive knowledge of God. The tract is divided into six chapters, each (except the last) partitioned into six sections; the sixth chapter, which is very brief, stands on its own and is devoted to *fanā*, that 'passing-away' into God which is the goal of the Muslim mystic.

'God Most High has said:

All things perish, except His Face.

In unity there is neither journeyer nor journey, path nor purpose, quest nor quester nor quested. *All things perish, except His Face:* one may neither affirm this statement and declaration, nor deny this statement and declaration; for affirmation and denial are opposites, and duality is the beginning of multiplicity. There, there is neither affirmation nor denial; there is neither denial of denial, nor affirmation of affirmation, nor denial of affirmation, nor affirmation of denial. This they call *fanā*; for creatures ultimately return to *fanā*, even as they primarily originated out of nonentity.

As He originated you, so you will return.

The meaning of *fanā* is singularity with multiplicity.

All that dwells upon the earth is perishing, yet still
abides the Face of thy Lord, majestic, splendid.

In this sense even *fanā* does not exist; whatever enters into speech, whatever enters into the imagination, whatever the intellect attains—all that is naughted.

To Him the whole matter shall be returned.'

Our final vignette from the thirteenth century is the portrait of a man of great poetical gifts and an undoubted devotion to the mystical life, whose career spanned the most troubled years of that turbulent epoch and who yet passed freely from one end of eastern Islam to the other: Fakhr al-Dīn Ibrāhīm ibn Shahriyār, called 'Irāqī. For the details of his biography we can fortunately rely upon an anonymous but early source, the full text and translation of which has been printed in my *Song of Lovers* (Islamic Research Association Series, No. 8: O.U.P., 1939). Some paragraphs from that document are taken into the present account.

'It is said that the poet was born in the village of Kamajān, in the district of Hamadān. His ancestors were all men of learning and consequence. A month before his birth, his father dreamed that he saw the Caliph 'Alī with a company of the pious assembled in a garden, and himself standing there. A man came forward and placed a child on the ground before the Caliph: the latter picked up the child, and calling the poet's father to him, gave the child into his arms, saying, "Take our 'Irāqī, and tend him well, for he will be world-famous." So overjoyed was the father, that he awoke from his sleep. "When 'Irāqī was born," he used to say, "I looked at his face, and perceived that he appeared to be the very child which the Caliph 'Alī had given me." At the age of five 'Irāqī was sent to school. Within nine months he had committed the Qur'ān to memory: at night he would recite in a plaintive voice the portion which had been his task that day, therein weeping awhile, until all who heard his melodious intonations were unable to control themselves for astonishment. Every night his neighbours waited for him, and would not sleep before they heard his recitation. He was attended day and night by a following of his fellow-pupils: a strong bond of affection was forged between him and them, so that they could not be apart for a moment. By his eighth year, his fame had spread throughout Hamadān, and his evening readings of the Qur'ān were attended by multitudes. . . .

'When he was seventeen, and had acquired an understanding of all the sciences, having studied all things well, and being himself already an instructor to others, it chanced that a company of wandering Kalandars came into the city and began to hold seance, chanting the following ode melodiously and sweetly:

> Now have we quit the temple, and unto taverns turned,
> Yea, we have rent faith's pages, the book of virtue burned;
> Within the rank of lovers in Beauty's street we sit,
> Seizing the cup of drunkards, filling and swilling it.
> Hereafter let us glory, while breath doth yet abide,
> For we have raised to heaven the banner of our pride:
> Of piety and purpose much labour we have known,
> Let piety and purpose alike aside be thrown.

Hearing them recite these lines, 'Irāqī was deeply stirred. His glance fell upon a boy of matchless beauty who stood in the midst of the Kalandars: he at once lost his heart to him, and stripping off his cloak and turban he gave himself up to the Kalandars, reciting the poem which begins:

> How sweet it were, if I might be thy lover
> Thy dear companion, and familiar friend!
> If but thy loving glance on me might hover,
> My joy would fill the world, and have no end.

After some time, the Kalandars left Hamadān for Iṣfahān. As soon as they were gone, the poet was filled with yearning for them. Throwing away his books, and forgetting all his learning, he followed after them on the road. They received him with great joy into their fraternity, and he continued with them on their wanderings, through Persia, and afterwards to India.'

In India 'Irāqī was destined to reside for twenty-five years. Apart from a brief visit to Delhi, all this time was spent in reverent attendance upon Bahā' al-Dīn Zakarīyā' of Multān, favourite and saintly disciple of Shihāb al-Dīn Suhravardī.

'When his time was come, he sent for 'Irāqī, and appointed him his successor in the order: he then passed over to the divine mercy. When the other brethren saw this, they were moved to jealousy and hatred. They chose among themselves messengers to present their case before the Sulṭān. "This person," the messengers said, "whom the saint has chosen for his successor does not preserve his rule, but spends all his time reciting poetry, in the company of young boys." The Sulṭān, who had long hated the order, seized this opportunity for wreaking his vengeance. He at once sent a messenger to find 'Irāqī: the latter forthwith said farewell to the brethren. Heedless of those who sought his life, a few of his friends, men of purity and faithfulness, determined to accompany his flight. So the company set forth, taking the road to the sea, for it was in their minds to come to Mecca.'

After performing the pilgrimage, ' 'Irāqī with two disciples journeyed on to Rūm, passing through all the parts of that country, until they came to the great saint Ṣadru'd-Dīn Qonawī. He was expounding the *Fuṣūṣu'l-ḥikam* to a class of students, and 'Irāqī himself derived great benefit from his instruction, as well as from the study of *al-Futūḥātu'l-Makkīya*. Ṣadru'd-Dīn conceived a great affection for 'Irāqī, and believed in him more and more as the days passed. Each day 'Irāqī, as he heard Qonawī's lectures, on the *Fuṣūṣ*, composed his *Lama'āt*: when the book was completed, he submitted it to his master. Ṣadru'd-Dīn read it: then, kissing the pages, and putting them against his eyes,

" 'Irāqī," he said, "you have published the secret of men's words." Now the *Lama'āt* is really the pith of the *Fuṣūṣ*.'

The *Lama'āt*, which belongs to the same literary genre as Aḥmad Ghazālī's *Savāniḥ*, was 'set down in the manner of' that work, as 'Irāqī himself declares in his exordium. The relationship to Ṣadr al-Dīn Qonavī's commentary (which is extant) on Ibn 'Arabī's abstrusely theosophical *Fuṣūṣ al-ḥikam* is not so obvious, though it is worthy of remark that in the oldest manuscript the *Lama'āt* is composed of 27 (not 28) 'flashes,' just as the *Fuṣūṣ al-ḥikam* is arranged in 27 'bezels.' Numerous commentaries were later composed on the *Lama'āt*, one by the poet Jāmī who wrote his own *Lavā'iḥ* in emulation of it. E. G. Browne has translated some pages from 'Irāqī's 'graceful phrases and charming suggestions, verse and prose combined together and subtleties in Arabic and Persian intermingled,' of which the following is an extract.

'The derivation of both Lover and Beloved is from Love, which, in its Abode of Glory, is exempt from differentiation, and, in the Sanctuary of its own Identity, is sanctified from inwardness and outwardness. Yea, in order to display its perfection, in such way as is identical with its Essence and (equally) identical with its Attributes, it shows itself to itself in the Mirror of Loverhood and Belovedness, and reveals its Beauty to its own Contemplation by means of the Seer and the Vision. Thus the names of Loverhood and Belovedness appeared, and the description of the Seeker and the Quest became manifest. It showed the Outward to the Inmost, and the Voice of Loverhood arose: it showed the Inmost to the Outward, and the name of Belovedness was made plain.

No atom doth exist apart from It, that Essence single:
'Tis when Itself it doth reveal that first those "others" mingle.
O Thou whose outward seeming Lover is, Beloved thine
    Essence,
Who hitherto e'er saw the Object Sought seek its own presence?

Love, by way of Belovedness, became the Mirror of the Beauty of Loverhood, so that therein it might behold its own Essence, and by way of Loverhood the Mirror of Belovedness, so that therein it might contemplate its own Names and Attributes. Although but one object is beheld by the Eye of Contemplation, yet when one face appears in two mirrors, assuredly in each mirror a different face appears.

> The Face is only one, yet multiple
> When thou in many mirrors see'st it.

> O how can "Otherness" appear when whatsoe'er existeth here
> In essence is that Other One becoming to our vision clear?'

To resume the anonymous biography: ''Irāqī captured the minds of all in Rūm, and many became his disciples and believers. Among those who believed in him was Amīr Mu'īnu'd-Dīn, the Parwāna. He had a great affection for the poet, and believed in him completely, and often requested him to choose a place for him to make a dwelling where he might lodge. 'Irāqī however refused, being engaged with his own devotions: but finally the Parwāna built a hospice at Dūqāt. It is said that the Parwāna would not add to the score of his life any day on which he did not visit 'Irāqī.' But the time came when Mu'īn al-Dīn, the powerful Saljūq minister who had also patronized Rūmī, fell from royal favour; he was executed in 1276. Before his arrest he entrusted a bag of gold to 'Irāqī, requesting him to go to Cairo and deliver out of prison his son there. The poet obeyed his wishes, and by his boldness and unusual honesty made such a powerful impression on the Mamlūk Sulṭān that he ordered the release of Mu'īn al-Dīn's son, appointed 'Irāqī Chief Shaikh of Cairo, and directed all the Ṣūfīs and ulema to pay him homage.

'The following day, a thousand Ṣūfīs, as well as all the ulema and notables of Cairo, came to court. The Sulṭān gave order that 'Irāqī should be mounted on his own horse, and clothed in robes of honour and a hood. He also decreed that he alone should be mounted, and that the others, notables, ulema and generals alike, should walk at his stirrup. When 'Irāqī perceived the respect paid to him, he thought within himself that no man in that age had ever been treated in that fashion; and pride overcame him. At once, however, he wrestled with his pride, and casting to the ground both hood and head-cloth, stood still for a time: then he put them on his head again. When the assembled company remarked this, they all began to laugh and find fault, saying, "How is such a man deserving of rank?" Others said, "He is mad," and others, "He is a buffoon," all ridiculing him. The vizier said to him, "Why did you do that?" But he replied, "Hold your tongue: what do you know?" News of this was at once carried to the Sulṭān. The next day he sent for 'Irāqī, and asked for an explanation of his conduct. The poet said, "Pride overcame me. If I had not acted in that manner, I should never have escaped from the consequences of my sin." This increased the Sulṭān's faith in him, and he doubled his emolument.'

But 'Irāqī had still one more journey to make: he desired to see Damascus again, where Ibn 'Arabī and many other scholars and saints lay buried.

'His intention was reported to the Sulṭān, who summoned him and forbade him to go. 'Irāqī however spoke with the Sulṭān and won him over: he only stipulated that he should wait long enough to permit him to make all arrangements. 'Irāqī would not delay, and so the Sulṭān ordered a pigeon to be sent, so that at each station the poet might be received with honour. He also wrote to the Maliku'l-umarā' apprising him of 'Irāqī's approach, and saying that all the ulema, Ṣūfīs and notables of Damascus should go out to meet him; that he should be appointed Chief Shaykh of the district; and that a regular allowance should be paid to his servants. 'Irāqī's approach to Damascus was notified to the Maliku'l-umarā', and he made proclamation that all the population should go out to receive him. All gladly complied.

Now the Maliku'l-umarā' had a very beautiful boy. When 'Irāqī arrived, and saw him, he at once lost his heart to him, and before all the people placed his head at the boy's feet. The boy did likewise to him, and the Maliku'l-umarā' consented. The Damascenes criticized the poet's behaviour, but could find no grounds of accusation against him. Six months passed. Then 'Irāqī's son Kabīru'd-Dīn came to visit his father; for although he was sitting in the seat of Bahā'u'd-Dīn Zakarīyā, yet he was drawn by the attraction of parental love, and left the hospice, to the great regret of the brethren, who would have prevented his departure, but for a dream in which it was revealed to them that they must let him go. So for a time Kabīru'd-Dīn enjoyed his father's company. But then 'Irāqī was stricken by a fatal illness, a bloody swelling overcoming his face. Five days he slept, and on the sixth he called for his son and his companions, and with tears in his eyes bade them farewell, reciting the verse, "The day on which a man shall flee from his brother, and his mother, and his father." Then he spoke the quatrain:

When by Decree this world was first begun
Not after man's desire the deed was done;
But of the portion on that Day assigned
None shall win more, nor any less hath won.

So he conversed awhile, until he drank the cup of fate and passed from this perishing realm to the everlasting shore. The Maliku'l-umarā' and the people of Damascus all gathered to pay their last respects to the dead, and with much lamentation buried him in the Ṣāliḥīya cemetery. For three days they mourned him and on the fourth appointed his son Kabīru'd-Dīn as his successor. He also in turn passed over to the divine mercy, and was buried by his father's side. It is said that 'Irāqī died at the age of 78, on the 8th of Dhu 'l-Qa'da, 688 (November 23, 1289).'

In addition to the *Lama'āt* this man, of whom one biographer remarked that 'love was predominant in his nature,' composed a considerable number of melodious and passionate lyrics which have been gathered together into a *Dīvān*, as well as a long poem on mystical love entitled *'Ushshāq-nāma*. The latter work is noteworthy in that the *mathnavī* couplets in which it is for the most part written are interspersed with monorhyme lyrics; 'Irāqī seems to have invented this agreeable form, which was later taken up by Amīr Khusrau. The following sequence illustrates the effect achieved.

That elder of the faith, Imam Ghazzali,
holy of spirit, spiritual of speech,
madly enflamed with every beauteous face
upon love's path the Darling ever sought.
So stirred his soul a sweetheart's loveliness
(his eye was chaste, as was his spirit pure)
that swiftly in a cavalcade he rode
from Ray, a hundred learners at his stirrup.
He saw the darling, like a risen moon,
forth from the bath emerging, with a grace
divinely shaped, and lovely radiance
illumining the world. When he beheld,
forthwith he saw the form of the Beloved,
and standing fast with heart and soul he gazed,
descrying every moment a new face.
So gazed they all that with the elder were,
himself bewildered by that lovely fay,
and all were much affected by the sight,
and suffered him, and passed: save one old man,
by trade a saddler, who unto the saint
exclaimed, 'Enough, pass on! It is not meet
for thee to worship form: art thou not shamed
before this multitude?' The saint replied:
'Say naught: the sight of beauty cheers the eye.

Had I not fallen victim unto form
I might be Gabriel, saddler of the skies.'
All lovers who intoxicated are
drink wine of passion's goblet. Of the soul
he heedeth not, who seeth but outward things:
with Majnun's eye behold the face of Layla.
If thou hast manly strength, behold, a horse,
arms, and the field! When loveliness of form
becomes thy weapon, since thou hast a weapon,
thou canst engage. Behold within the skin
the hidden kernel: see its flashing ray
in the Friend's light. Though thou dost bear the name
of skin, not having kernel, yet to love
thou dost belong, thou hast the Darling's face.
Who seeks of the Beloved but Himself
no attribute his essence can destroy.
His love is my soul's rest, my gain and loss,
my heart's desire His beauty to attain:
the eye hath seen, yet seeks the heart to see.
My heart is held within His snare, and I
am drunk with wine of longing: naught He cares
though I am yearning to behold His face,
and in my passion meditate this lay.

Again my mad heart takes the cup
Of love, upon love's breast reclining:
Again my soul is yielded up,
To love's enfolding might resigning.

The wine hath filled my weary brain
With vapours from love's censer blowing:
Give wine, for sorrow once again
Its melancholy head is showing.

The loveliness of Thy fair face
My mind doth haunt, my heart is stealing,
Else love had never found a place
Within the heart, such joy revealing.

Love's pigeon to my heart doth fly
A message from my Lover giving,
And gladly for His sake I die,
With Him forever to be living.

ELEVEN

The Mongol Aftermath

'IN the year 684 H. (A.D. 1285) the Khán of Multán, the eldest son and heir apparent of the Sultán, and the mainstay of the State, proceeded to Lahor and Deobálpur (Dípálpúr) to oppose the accursed Samar, the bravest dog of all the dogs of Changíz Khán. By the will of fate, the prince with many of his nobles and officers fell in battle, and a grievous disaster thus happened to the throne of Balban. Many veteran horsemen perished in the same battle. The calamity caused great and general mourning in Multán. From that time the deceased prince was called "the Martyr Prince." Amír Khusrú was made prisoner by the Mughals in the same action, and obtained his freedom with great difficulty. He wrote an elegy on the death of the prince.'

Ḍiyā' al-Dīn Baranī, author of the *Tārīkh-ī Fīrūz-Shāhī* from which the above passage is taken, was like Amīr Khusrau (of whom we shall now speak) a disciple of the famous saint Niẓām al-Dīn Auliyā, and a witness of the attempts made by the Mongols to repeat in India their bloody exploits further west. His history of the Delhi Sultanate from the accession of Balban to the sixth year of the reign of Fīrūz-Shāh (1265–1357) is of the greatest value as a contemporary record, and dovetails neatly with the *Ṭabaqāt-ī Nāṣirī* of Jūzjānī. Considerable extracts from this work were translated by John Dowson and included in the third volume of *The History of India as Told by its own Historians*, and the following paragraph from the concluding section illustrates both the straightforward style and the resilient spirit of the author as he looked back on the events of a tumultuous century.

'All men of intelligence in Hind and Sind have seen and remarked the stop which has been put to the inroads of the Mughals of Changíz Khán in this auspicious reign. They have not been able to attack and ravage the frontier territories, nor have they been permitted to come in with professions of friendship and employ their arts to carry off the wealth of the country. They had the presumption to make two attacks. Once they crossed the Sodra and came into the neighbouring country. There they were met by the forces of Islám and were defeated. Many were killed and many were taken prisoners. These latter were placed upon camels, and were paraded in derision round Dehlí, with wooden collars on their necks. Those who escaped from the battle fled in the greatest precipitation and confusion, and many were drowned in the passage of the Sodra. On the other occasion they made a rapid dash into Gujarát. Some perished from thirst, some died by the hands of the soldiers, and some fell in a night attack which the natives of the country made upon them. Not one tenth of these accursed followers of Changíz Khan reached their own country.'

It was the end of a dreadful nightmare; but Baranī naturally could not foresee that Delhi was later to be the splendid capital of a wide dominion to be called the Mughal Empire. The friend whose capture by the invaders in 1285 he had recorded in his chronicle did not live to see the carefree days of a general but deceptive deliverance.

Abu 'l-Ḥasan Yamīn al-Dīn Khusrau, the celebrated Amīr Khusrau, was born at Patigālī on the Ganges in 1253, the second son of Amīr Saif al-Dīn Maḥmūd, a Turk from Khurāsān who had fled into India to become an officer of the Delhi army. He was a precocious boy, if we are to believe his own account: 'I was then eight years old, but in my swift poetic flights I trod upon the celestial spheres. In that tender age when my milk-teeth were falling, I composed verses that dropped from my mouth like bright pearls.' (The translation is by Dr. Mohammad Wahid Mirza of Lucknow, whose *Life and Works of Amir Khusrau* is a most valuable and delightful monograph.) Balban (1265–87) was on the throne to nourish and encourage his natural genius; he took Amīr Khusrau along with him when he marched against Lakhnauti to abate the pretensions of the ex-slave Ṭughril. On his return to Delhi he introduced the youthful poet to his son Muḥammad Khān, Prince of Multān, who had come to the capital to felicitate the Sulṭān on a notable victory; Muḥammad Khān invited Amīr Khusrau to join his own entourage, 'the envy of the garden of Paradise,' and there he made friends with the poet Amīr Ḥasan. 'For five years,' he afterwards recalled, 'I watered the five rivers of Multan with the seas of my delectable verses.' Then, in 1285, the blow fell which led to his patron's death and his own capture by the Mongols.

'Know ye how this year near Multan the right wing of the believers broke before the infidel onslaught. How shall I describe that calamity from which even the Angel of Death sought to flee away? The blood of the martyrs drenched the soil like water, while cords tied the faces of the prisoners like flowers in a wreath. Their heads jostled in the knots of the saddle-straps and their throats choked in the nooses of the reins. Although I escaped alive from this painful calamity, I was taken prisoner and the fear of death left no blood in my thin and feeble body. I had to run headlong like a torrent, while with long tramping a thousand blisters arose on my feet like bubbles, and the skin of my feet was rent. Like an autumn tree, the body was naked, and torn into a thousand shreds by the painful lacerations of thorny bushes. Tears dropped from my eyes as pearls fall from the necks of brides. The despicable wretch who drove me in front of him sat on his horse like a leopard on a hill; a foul stench came from his mouth and filthy moustaches hung on his chin.'

But the poet escaped to tell his tale of woe; he returned home to his widowed mother, and when Kai-Qubād succeeded to the throne of Delhi, Amīr Khusrau once more basked in the sunshine of royal favour. Nāṣir al-Dīn Bughrā Khān, supplanted by his son and sulking at Lakhnauti, moved against the capital with the intention of claiming his rights; Kai-Qubād went out to meet the challenge, but instead of the expected trial of strength a scene of tender reconciliation ensued. Amīr Khusrau was present at this remarkable encounter, and in 1289 he composed his first historical idyll, the *Qirān al-sa'dain*, to immortalize the occasion. E. B. Cowell in 1860 commented that 'the style of the poem (as of all Khusrú's works) is full of exaggeration and metaphorical description, but the facts of the history are generally given with tolerable fidelity. Every now and then, at the end of many of the chapters, there is given a *ghazal*, which is supposed to express the poet's feelings contemporary with that part of the story which has just been described, something like the songs introduced between the parts of Tennyson's *Princess*. These *ghazals* are in various metres, and serve admirably to diversify the poem, while at the same time they form a running commentary, like the choruses of a Greek play, on the progress of the action, and the hopes and fears which it may be supposed to excite in the minds of the spectators. The poet, having actually been present throughout the campaign, is in this way enable to throw himself into the scene, and we have thus an interesting mixture of the epic and lyric elements, each portion of the action being represented from an objective and subjective point of view.'

Kai-Qubād was greatly pleased with this offering, 'perhaps unique,' as Mohammad Wahid Mirza observes, 'not only among the poet's own works but in the whole range of Persian poetry.' It had been at his suggestion, as Amīr Khusrau tells us, that the idyll was written, following his success with a panegyric.

'Two days after, the news of my arrival was conveyed to the king, and the chamberlain came to call me to his presence. I went and placed my face upon the earth, while my heart was in trepidation. I drew out from my waistband the panegyric I had written, and read it out with a loud voice. The king was greatly pleased at my verses, and honoured me in the eyes of my companions. He treated me with great kindness, and gave me a dress of honour of his own wearing, and two bags of *dirhams*, and enrolled me amongst his special attendants. My heart was replete with joy, and my poor house was filled with gold. His majesty said, "Oh, most perfect of poets, whose very crumbs other poets are glad to pick up, if you will, the wish of my heart can be accomplished. I will give you as much as you like, and no desire of yours shall be left ungratified." I bowed to the ground, and replied, "Oh, king, what am I capable of, but writing a few laudatory verses, that I should be treated with such condescension? Your majesty bestows everything upon the needy; what need then can you have of such poor services as mine? My imagination is not lively, and I have no accomplishment, but that of being able to write some indifferent Persian. If the wish of his majesty can be gratified by such poor attainments, I am ready to be honoured with his commands." When I had thus offered my excuses to the king, he thus addressed me: "It is my desire, that you should undertake the trouble of writing in verse an account of the interview between the two kings, namely, my honoured father and myself." When he had said this, he pointed to the treasure before him, and told me to take it away, bestowing upon me at the same time a dress of honour.'

At the age of thirty-six Amīr Khusrau was appointed poet laureate; and though Qai-Kubād did not survive long to enjoy more of his favourite's graceful encomia, thenceforward the 'Parrot of India' (as the poet is fondly called) served Sulṭān after Sulṭān to their satisfaction and his own, until his death in 1325. The long years of almost untroubled ease unloosed a veritable avalanche of verse of every kind. Four more historical idylls were written: the *Miftāḥ al-futūḥ* in honour of victories won by

Fīrūz Khaljī, the *'Ashīqa* on the tragic romance of Khiḍr Khān and Princess Devaldī, the *Nuh sipihr* in celebration of 'the glories of Mubārak Shāh Khaljī's reign,' and the *Tughlaq-nāma* describing the brief kingship of Ghiyāth al-Dīn Tughlaq Shāh. To these five long poems Amīr Khusrau added five (his lucky number) more in emulation of Niẓāmī's *Khamsa*; over the first of these, the *Maṭla' al-anwār* after the fashion of Niẓāmī's *Makhzan al-asrār* and containing 3,310 couplets, he took no more than a fortnight, and the entire series was accomplished between 1299 and 1302. But all this was far from being the sum-total of his poetical output; other writers might be satisfied with a single *Dīvān*, but Amīr Khusrau compiled five—the first he published in 1273, the second in 1285, the third in 1294, the fourth in 1316, and the fifth shortly before his death. Of all this immense production—Daulatshāh quotes Amīr Khusrau as saying that he composed more than 400,000 verses—little has so far been adequately edited, and still less has been translated. In the early days of British orientalism J. H. Hindley (1765–1827) made a pleasing version of one lyric which might have encouraged others to notice the poet, but in fact failed to do so.

> O Thou whose face
> With envied grace,
> The magi's Gods inflames!
> Howe'er my verse
> Thy praise rehearse,
> Still more thy beauty claims.
>
> Sprightly and gay
> As fabled fay,
> Soft as the roseate leaf!
> Say what I will—
> Superior still!
> Wondrous! beyond belief!

My vagrant eye
Did ne'er descry
A fairer form than thine:
Is it of earth?
Or heavenly birth?
Or Fairy's, half divine?

The world I rov'd,
And frequent lov'd
Those charms which all adore:
Maids who excell'd
I oft beheld—
But thou art something more.

Each soul thy prey,
Each heart thy sway
Avows with mad'ning pain;
Thy magic eyes
Of Nergiss dyes
Idolatry maintain.

Khoosro, fair maid,
Intreats thine aid,
A stranger at thy door;
Oh, in God's name,
Regard the claim
Of strangers who implore.

Mohammad Wahid Mirza has offered a few specimens, of which the following is not unrepresentative.

The tipsy rose woke early in the dawn
And filled the poppy's cup with sweetest wine,
Here drowsed the jasmin by the rose's side
There stood alert the cypress straight and fine.

The wind blew soft, the narcissus dozed
Its body swayed, now drooped and now arose,
I in the garden by my friend lay 'wake
My friend—forsooth the moon itself was she,
But soon, alas, my side she left
And grief was all that was left for me.

The foregoing list does not exhaust the catalogue of Amīr Khusrau's writing. Apart from the quantity of Hindi verse of doubtful authenticity with which he has been credited, he compiled at least three books in prose. The *I'jāz-i Khusravī*, completed in 1319 and lithographed in 1876, is a huge collection of model letters thought by the author to be appropriate to all sorts and conditions of men, from saints and mystics to craftsmen and artisans; included in the vast assortment of imaginary epistles are documents allegedly composed for actual occasions, such as the proclamation issued by Sultan Balban after the conquest of Lakhnauti. Amīr Khusrau displays in this work his talent for inelegant as well as elevated composition, as when he execrates a certain huntsman: 'May the crow lay eggs in his fat, may he be attached to the nails of wolves! May he become a hog in his grave!' Still more forthright is his curse upon a clown: 'May Satan wet his moustache with his urine and may the Devil lay eggs in the hair of his chin!' As if to prove his versatility—as if further proof were needed—Amīr Khusrau also edited in his *Afḍal al-fawā'id* the sayings of his spiritual preceptor Niẓām al-Dīn Auliyā; Mohammad Wahid Mirza cites this account of the saint's views on music as an aid to devotion, a controversial topic in Islam.

'On Thursday, the seventh of Shawwāl, I had the good fortune of kissing the Sheikh's feet. Those present were at that time talking of simā' and of those who listen to it, and just then a man came in and related that at a certain place a number of the saint's disciples had gathered together and had with them musical instruments. The Khwāja thereupon said: "I have often forbidden the use of such instruments and other unlawful things. What they have done is not good." And he laid great stress upon this point, even saying that the palm of one hand should not be struck upon the other, nor the back of one hand upon the palm of the other, meaning that clapping was strictly prohibited, and that it was better not to use instruments. He said afterwards: "All great sheikhs have enjoyed simā', and those who know its real worth and have taste and emotion are moved by a single verse heard from a musician, whether there be any instrument or not. But if one lacks the requisite taste it avails him nothing that there be a number of musicians with instruments singing before him." So we know that this affair depends upon emotion and feeling and not on musical instruments.'

Last but not least important, Amīr Khusrau enriched historical literature with his *Tārīkh-i 'Alā'ī*, 'an interesting account of the first years of the reign of Sultán 'Aláu-d dín Khiljí (whom he also styles Muhammad Sháh Sultán), from his accession to the throne in 695 H. (A.D. 1296) to his conquest of Ma'bar at the close of 710 H. (A.D. 1310).' So writes J. Dowson, who adds: 'It will be observed that this small work contains much information on the subject to which it relates. The mode of warfare of that period, especially, receives illustrations such as can be obtained from no other work. The style in which it is composed is for the most part difficult, as the whole is constructed of a series of fanciful analogies.' Sir H. M. Elliot's abstract includes some remarkable bombast, of which Vaṣṣāf himself could have felt proud, in the account of an unsuccessful Mongol incursion.

'When 'Alí Beg, Turták, and Turghí came with drawn swords from the borders of Turkistán to the river Sind, and, after crossing the Jelam, turned their faces in this direction, Turghí, who already saw his head on the spears of the champions of Islám, who, although he had an iron heart, durst not place it in the power of the anvil-breaking warriors of God, was at last slain by an arrow, which penetrated his heart and passed through on the other side. But Turták and 'Alí Beg, as they had never yet come to this country, regarded the swords of the Musulmans as if they were those of mere preachers, and rushed on impetuously with about fifty thousand horsemen. From the mere dread of that army the hills trembled, and the inhabitants of the foot of the hills were confounded—all fled away before the fierce attack of those wretches, and rushed to the fords of the Ganges. The lightning of Mughal fury penetrated even to those parts, and smoke arose from the burning towns of Hindustán, and the people, flying from their flaming houses, threw themselves into the rivers and torrents. At last from those desolated tracts news reached the court of the protector of the world, and a confidential officer, Malik Ákhir Beg, Mubashara, was directed, at the head of a powerful body of thirty thousand horse, to use his best endeavours to attack the accursed enemy, and throw a mighty obstacle in their way. . . . In short, immediately on discerning the dust of the army of Islam, the grovelling Mughals became like particles of sand revolving above and below, and they fled precipitately like a swarm of gnats before a hurricane. . . . Their fire-coloured faces began to fall on the earth, and in the rout, 'Alí Beg and Turták, the commanders, when they saw destruction awaiting them, threw themselves under the shade of the standard of Islám, and exclaimed that the splendour of our swords had cast such fire upon them, that they could gain no repose, until they had arrived under the shadow of God.'

From the greatest Persian poet ever born in India we turn now to a contemporary from the motherland who was also a poet, but is far better known as a historian and a geographer. When Rashīd al-Dīn Faḍl Allāh was vizier to Ghāzān Khān he appointed as financial supervisor of the territories about Qazvīn a native of that city whose great-grandfather had once been

Mustaufī (State Accountant) of Iraq: Ḥamd Allāh ibn Abī Bakr ibn Naṣr Qazvīnī.

'Now during the several times when (as State Accountant) I computed the sum total until the first years of the reign of Ghāzān Khān—whom may God enfold in His forgiveness—the revenue amounted to 17,000,000 and odd (currency dīnārs), but after this early period, by reason of the just government of Ghāzān Khān which brought back such prosperity to the land, it reached the sum of 21,000,000 and odd (currency dīnārs). At the present time it probably does not amount to half this sum, for in most of the provinces usurpation of authority is rampant with the coming and going of armies, so that the people even do withhold their hands from sowing the fields.'

By the year 1340, when Ḥamd Allāh Mustaufī was finishing his *Nuzhat al-qulūb*, thoughtful Persians were already looking back on the period of the great Mongol Īl-Khāns as a golden age. He himself appears to have been born around 1282; his promotion by Rashīd al-Dīn must have taken place in 1311 or thereabouts, and by 1330 he was in the entourage of Rashīd al-Dīn's son Ghiyāth al-Dīn Muḥammad, vizier to Abū Sa'īd and the short-lived Arpa until his execution in 1336. He had by that time already been engaged for over ten years upon the composition of a great epic which was intended as a continuation of the *Shāh-nāma*. This work in some 75,000 couplets—its author had had ample opportunity to study Firdausī's style during the six years in which he revised the text of the *Shāh-nāma*—was ultimately completed in 1335 and has so far not found an editor. 'The author,' wrote C. Rieu in his description of the precious British Museum manuscript, 'is very precise as to facts and dates, and the third book will be found valuable for the history of the Mongol period.' It is in that section of the poem that Ḥamd Allāh gives his account, based on information received from his great-grandfather who was among those present, of the Mongol massacre of Qazvīn; in E. G. Browne's version:

Thence to the town of Qazwín, Subutáy
Like raging tiger came right speedily.
The tale of years at six, one, seven stood
When that fair town became a lake of blood,
And Sha'bán's month had counted seven days
When it was filled with woe and sore amaze. . . .
When came the hosts of war and direful fate
Firm as a rock they closed the city gate.
Upon the wall the warriors took their place,
And each towards the Mongols set his face.
Three days they kept the ruthless foe at bay,
But on the fourth they forced a blood-stained way.
Fiercely the Mongols entered Qazwín Town
And heads held high before were now brought down.
No quarter in that place the Mongols gave:
The days were ended of each chieftain brave.
Nothing could save the townsmen from their doom,
And all were gathered in one common tomb.
Alike of great and small, of old and young,
The lifeless bodies in the dust they flung:
Both men and women shared a common fate:
The luck-forsaken land lay desolate.
Many a fair one in that fearful hour
Sought death to save her from th' invaders' power:
Chaste maidens of the Prophet's progeny
Who shone like asteroids in Virtue's sky,
Fearing the lust of that ferocious host
Did cast them down, and so gave up the ghost. . . .
In terror of the Mongol soldiery
Hither and thither did the people fly,
Some seeking refuge to the Mosque did go,
Hearts filled with anguish, souls surcharged with woe.

From that fierce foe so sore their straits and plight
That climbing forms the arches hid from sight.
The ruthless Mongols burning brands did ply
Till tongues of flame leapt upwards to the sky.
Roof, vault and arch in burning ruin fell,
A heathen holocaust of Death and Hell.

The *Ẓafar-nāma* (such is the title of this poem) was composed in the heroic *mutaqārib* metre, like the *Shāhinshāh-nāma* completed in 1338 by Aḥmad of Tabrīz for Abū Sa'īd. It was Ḥamd Allāh Mustaufī's second essay in authorship; in 1330 he had finished and dedicated to his patron Ghiyāth al-Dīn Muḥammad the *Tārīkh-i guzīda*. 'This work,' in V. F. Büchner's words, 'comprises the history of the Muhammadan world from the creation to 729 (1329) and is written in a very simple, indeed arid style, except for the preface.' The text of this very important book is available in a facsimile edition with an ample synopsis, the work of E. G. Browne, and with a full index compiled by R. A. Nicholson. Some extracts relating to India had already been translated by J. Dowson.

'Sultán Mahmúd, having conquered Bhátiya and Multán as far as the frontiers of Kashmír, made peace with Ílak Khán, who some time after broke faith with him, and advanced to battle against him; but he was defeated, and took to flight. Many beautiful youths fell into the hands of the Záwuliyáns, who were delighted with their prisoners. Ílak Khán then sought the assistance of the Ghuzz and the Turks of Chín, the descendants of Afrásiyáb, but was again defeated in an action at the gates of Balkh, and took a second time to flight. He again made peace with the Sultán, and went to reside in Máwaráu-n-nahr. Sultán Mahmúd then made war with Nawása (the grandson of) the ruler of Multán; conquered that country; converted the people to Islám; put to death the ruler of Multán, and entrusted the government of that country to another chief. Sultán Mahmúd now went to fight with the Ghorians, who were infidels at that time. Súrí, their chief, was killed in this war, and his son was taken prisoner; but dreading the Sultán's vengeance, he killed himself by sucking poison which he had kept under the stone of his ring. The country of Ghor was annexed to that of the Sultán, and the population thereof converted to Islám. He now attacked the fort of Bhím, where was a temple of the Hindus. He was victorious, and obtained much wealth, including about a hundred idols of gold and silver. One of the golden images, which weighed a million *miskáls*, the Sultán appropriated to the decoration of the Mosque of Ghazní, so that the ornaments of the doors were of gold instead of iron.'

Finally in 1340, Ḥamd Allāh published his renowned cosmography, the *Nuzhat al-qulūb*, of which the geographical part was edited and translated by G. Le Strange, and the zoological section by J. Stephenson. The contents of this book, like its style, are for the most part exceedingly austere, as might be expected indeed of a former finance officer; but the author unbent a little towards the close of his careful task and added a concluding section 'describing the wonders of the land and sea throughout the habitable world. Now it will be found,' he continues, 'that some of the following accounts are of a nature that the mind cannot compass, but in view of the omnipotence of God most high, and there being (as it is said) no limit to His power, therefore to these things a full credence should be vouchsafed.' To certain marvels Ḥamd Allāh is able to offer personal testimony.

'At the foot of mount Sablān is found a tree round and about which much grass grows; but no beast or bird dare either taste of the fruit of the tree, or touch the grass: for to eat of either is to die; hence it is believed that for sure this is the dwelling place of demons. In the province of Bākūyah (Bākū), according to the same authority the ground is hot with fire: so much so that both bread and meat can be cooked by being laid on the same. This fire is not extinguished by rain, but rather burns fiercer. I myself have seen this; and a further wonder is this, that in those parts lies a meadow in which if anyone should dig a little ditch, fire will burst forth in a flame through the cutting.'

For other matters the author is content to quote the records of his predecessors.

'Of Wonders by Sea. Now these exceed all reckoning and compute, so that none has knowledge to comprehend them all. Hence it is that they are wont to say—"They tell so and so of the Sea" in relating what is marvellous. Here, therefore, I shall relate only what I have found in the books of such of the learned as are worthy of credence, or have myself heard related by narrators who were to be depended on, and the responsibility is on the narrator. Qazvīnī says that in the Indian Sea there are creatures that come out of the water to pasture on the land, and from their mouths fire issues, which burns up the grass lands round and about. He further states that in the Caspian Sea there is an island on which a spring gushes out from the rock, and in the water of this spring pieces of copper are found of the weight of a scruple or half a scruple. By the same author it is reported that during the reign of the Caliph Wāthiq the Chief of Sarīr made a fishing excursion on the Caspian Sea in honour of Sallām the Interpreter, who was here on his way to investigate the condition of the Wall of Gog and Magog. On this occasion they caught a large fish, inside the belly of which was found a mermaid of surpassing beauty, wearing neither smock nor drawers, but with a skin like that of a human being down to her knees. She began to beat her face and tear her hair, making great lamentations, and after a while she died. The writer of the *History of Maghrib* also vouches for the truth of this story. In the same work it is stated that in the Island of Qayṣūr, which is in India, there is a place where there are certain fish; and as soon as these are taken away from the water they turn to hard stone and lose their animal nature. Ibn Khurdādbih reports that in India there is found a fish that is twenty ells in length. Inside this lives a second fish, and inside this again a third, and so to a fourth, each fish within the last. In the same work it is stated that in those seas lives a turtle that is twenty ells round. It gives milk, and from its tortoise-shell they make weapons of war, also they find inside it more than a thousand eggs. In the same work it is said that in the Red Sea lives a fish that is like a camelopard, and it gives milk. Of its skin they make armour, and bucklers, and javelins are unable to penetrate the same.'

Chaos descended upon Persia once more with the collapse of the central Īl-Khānid government. A century which began with an alien but now believing despotism benevolently striving to rebuild the ruined civilization which Chingīz and Hūlāgū had been powerless to destroy entirely, ended with the emergence out of Transoxiana of a new monster, Tīmūr the Lame, who yielded the palm for terrorism to none of the previous scourges of mankind. In the middle years, as the greatest poet of that age—as many would declare, the greatest of all Persian poets—expressed the matter, men in their bewilderment might well exclaim:

Again the times are out of joint; and again
For wine and the loved one's languid glance I am fain.
The wheel of fortune's sphere is a marvellous thing:
What next proud head to the lowly dust will it bring?
'Tis a famous tale, the deceitfulness of earth;
The night is pregnant; what will dawn bring to birth?
Tumult and bloody battle rage in the plain:
Bring blood-red wine, and fill the goblet again!

Of Ḥāfiẓ and his reaction to the world in which he found himself more will be said in a later chapter. Here some account will be given of the writings of one who has been called Persia's

Voltaire, the greatest satirist of a people with a perennial genius for satire, Niẓām al-Dīn 'Ubaid Allāh Zākānī, the famous 'Ubaid-i Zākānī. E. G. Browne has dedicated a long and entertaining section of his *Literary History of Persia* to this remarkable figure; but the publication at Teheran in recent times (the edition used is dated 1955) of the collected works affords an opportunity for a fresh study.

'Of his life,' writes E. G. Browne, 'as usual, little is known, save that he was originally from Qazwín (for which city he seems to have had little affection, since he is constantly gibing at the stupidity of its inhabitants), lived at Shíráz (to which, on the other hand, as several of his poems show, he was much attached) during the reign of Shaykh Abú Isḥáq Injú (who was killed in 747 (1346–7)), abandoned serious writing for a ribaldry more in accord with the taste of the great men of that time, but none the less (as several of his poems and a well-known anecdote about his death indicate) suffered much from penury and debt, and finally died about 772 (1371).' Zākānī's modern editor, Professor 'Abbās Iqbāl, has added little fresh information to this meagre biography. He quotes Zākānī's contemporary Ḥamd Allāh Mustaufī for the statement that the satirist's family were originally Arabs of the Banū Khafāja tribe who had long before settled in Qazvīn. There they had divided into two branches, one attaining distinction and wealth in the administrative services, while the other devoted itself to learning both religious and secular; it was to the former branch that our hero belonged. From the epithet *ṣāḥib-i mu'aẓẓam* which Mustaufī bestows on him Iqbāl deduces that Zākānī must have been at some time and somewhere a vizier, at all events before the year 1330 in which the *Tārīkh-i guzīda* was completed. By then he had already made a name for himself as a poet and a writer of elegant prose, for Mustaufī states that 'he has fine poems and unrivalled essays.' Iqbāl attaches little value to the anecdotes—some of which are reproduced by E. G. Browne—recounted in Daulatshāh, and is not prepared to accept blindly the traditional date of Zākānī's death. However, he produces interesting evidence that he was certainly alive as late as 1367, for at the beginning of that year Zākānī transcribed (the manuscript is still extant in private hands) a work on astronomy entitled *Ashjār u athmār* by 'Alīshāh ibn Muḥammad Khvārizmī. This volume incidentally bears an endorsement in the writing of Zākānī's son Isḥāq recording that it had passed into his possession 'by inheritance' in the year 772 (1371), so that the traditional *obiit* is after all triumphantly confirmed.

Bearing in mind that Zākānī may at one time have held high office, let us look first at his *Mūsh u gurba*, a very curious ode (not, as Browne alleges, a *mathnavī*) in ninety-four couplets in the *khafīf* metre which, in 'Abbās Iqbāl's words, 'has enjoyed the highest reputation throughout all Persian-speaking lands.' In 1945 the Persian scholar and poet 'mas'uud e farzàad' published privately at London a version of this poem called *Rats against Cats* which he had made at Teheran in 1933, dedicating his work

'to the generation of unbelievably brilliant and sincere Persian individuals
now mostly between thirty and forty years old,
who naturally aimed, not at becoming prime ministers or millionaires,
but rather at producing for humanity, new things—useful or beautiful,
and whose scientific or artistic pursuits and studies
suffered grievously (and in certain cases, alas, fatally)
because of social and domestic conditions that,
so far as these individuals were concerned,
were as appallingly uncongenial,
as those which, centuries ago, made Obeyd write this poem.'

Farzād's version is in fluent and energetic English having a delightful blend of sarcastic humour.

Destiny, heaven-ordained, once so ordained
That there should live in Kerman town
A cat, but no mere cat; a dragon of a cat.
Drum-bellied, shield-chested,
Serpent-tailed, eagle-clawed. . . .

His translation is full of charm and insight, but a little free. A new version is here offered on the basis of the newly-edited text, which differs substantially from previous editions.

If you have reason, learning and intelligence,
hearken to the tale of the Cat and the Mice:
I will now recite for your benefit a tale
the inner meaning of which will surely amaze you.
You who are wise, intelligent and learned,
recite the story of the Mice and the Cat,
the story of the Mice and the Cat in verse—
lend me your ears—smooth as rolling pearls.

By heaven's ordinance a certain Cat
once dwelt in Kerman, mighty like a dragon,
his belly a drum, his breast as it were a shield,
his tail a lion's, a leopard's his claws.
In the time of roaring, the thunder of his voice
smote with terror even the ravening lion,
and when he thrust his paw upon the table
the lion fled incontinently before him.
One day he entered a certain wine-cellar
having in mind to go a-hunting mice;
behind a barrel he established his ambush
just like a highwayman deep in the desert.
All of a sudden a little rustling mouse
jumped nimbly from a wall on to the barrel,
poked his head in the barrel and took a swig,
got promptly drunk, and like a bellowing lion

roared: 'Where's that Cat? I'll tear off his head
and then I'll stuff his skin full of straw.
As far as I'm concerned, he's just a mail-coat
handy for unriveting in the jousting-yard!'
The Cat heard him, but didn't breathe a word;
he just whetted his claws and his teeth,
then suddenly pounced, and seized the mouse
like a panther hunting in the mountains.
The mouse whimpered: 'I am your slave:
please forgive me the sins I've committed.'
'Don't tell so many lies,' the Cat replied.
'I'm not falling for your cunning tricks.
I was listening to every word you said,
you foul cheat, you miserable Mussulman!'
With that the Cat killed and ate the mouse
and then padded delicately off to the mosque,
washed his hands and face, wiped them carefully
and recited a rosary like any Mullah:
'Creator God, behold, I have now repented;
henceforth my teeth shall not rend another mouse.
In expiation of this innocent blood I'll
give two maunds of bread in alms to the poor.'
So submissively and abjectly he prayed that
presently the tears rolled down his cheeks.
A little mouse hiding behind the pulpit
scurried out to tell the news to all the Mice:
'Great tidings! The Cat has turned a penitent,
a true worshipper, a godly Mussulman!
The admirable creature just now in the mosque was
praying, petitioning, contritely bewailing.'
When the Mice heard this remarkable story
gladness possessed them, and they laughed for joy.
Then up sprang seven most select mice,
every one of them a landed gentleman,
and out of the love they bore for the Cat

each carried a cargo of assorted presents—
one in his hand held a flask of wine,
another a dish of roasted lamb,
another a tray loaded with raisins,
another a round plateful of dates,
another a pot brimming with cheese,
another yaghourt with a round of bread,
another on his head a salver of pilau
sprinkled with the juice of best Oman lemons.
So unto the Cat those mice proceeded
uttering salaams and paeans of praise,
then with the utmost politeness made memorial:
'We freely lay our lives down before you.
Here is our oblation, worthy we hope
of your magnificence; pray to accept it.'
When the Cat set eyes on the mice, he exclaimed:
'Surely your provision is laid up in heaven.
A long, long while I have endured hunger;
now this day I have provision abounding.
Many other days I have kept the fast
that I might be pleasing to the All-Merciful.
Whosoever faithfully does the will of God,
his daily bread shall surely be abundant.'
Then he added: 'Pray come forward
a step or two, my darling comrades!'
The little mice all of them moved forward,
their hearts trembling like a linden-tree.
Suddenly the Cat pounced on the mice
like a lone champion of the day of battle;
five most select mice he seized to him,
each one a gentleman, each an aristocrat,
two in one claw, two in the other talon,
one in his mouth, like a rampaging lion.
The other two who escaped with their lives
swiftly bore the tidings to their brother Mice:

'Why do you sit idly here, O Mice?
Dust be on your heads, you fine heroes!
Five chieftain mice he has torn to pieces,
that Cat, with his claws and his teeth.'
The Mice, sorrowing over such calamity,
straightway garmented themselves all in black
and scattering dust on their heads, they cried:
'Alas, alas for you, Chief of the Mice!'
Then with a single accord they resolved:
'We will go to the Sultan's capital
to represent our case to the Shah,
that we are victims of the Cat's aggression.'
The King of the Mice, seated on his throne,
spied from afar the Mice's cavalcade.
All bowed before him in dutiful obeisance:
'O King-Emperor of the world's ages,
the Cat has committed aggression against us:
King of Kings, succour the oppressed!
Formerly he took only one of us each year;
now his greed has become enormous—
these days he seizes five at a time
since he repented, and became a Mussulman.'
When they had uttered their sorrow to the King
the King proclaimed: 'My dear people,
I shall exact such vengeance of the Cat
as will be spoken of down the long centuries.'
Within a week he had equipped an army—
three hundred and thirty thousand mice—
all armed with spears and bows and arrows,
all accoutred with trenchant swords,
columns of infantry drawn up on the wing
and in the middle scimitars leaping.
When the great army was all assembled
out of Khorasan, Resht and Gilan,
a mouse unique, the Minister of War,

one who was clever, courageous and cunning,
cried: 'It is necessary one of us shall go
unto the Cat, to the city of Kerman,
saying: "Come to the capital to make obeisance
or else—prepare yourself for war!" '
A little mouse it was, a former ambassador,
that set forth to the city of Kerman.
Gently, so gently he addressed the Cat:
'I am an ambassador from the King.
I have come bearing tidings to you:
the King of the Mice makes ready for war.
Either go to the capital to make obeisance
or else—prepare yourself for war!'
The Cat replied: 'Straw-nibbling mouse,
never will I step forth from Kerman!'
But in the meantime surreptitiously
he mustered a terrible army of cats—
well-armed cats, fit to hunt lions,
cats of Isfahan, Yezd and Kerman.
When the army of cats was all mobilized
he gave the order to take the field.
The army of Mice by way of the salt-lands,
the army of Cats down from the mountains—
in the desert of Fars the two armies
gave battle together like regular heroes.
The fight raged fiercely in that valley,
every one a Rustam battling in his corner;
such a mass of mice and cats were slain that
their numbers could not easily be reckoned.
Then like a lion the Cat charged impetuously,
striking directly at the heart of the Mice.
A little mouse hamstrung the Cat's steed;
the Cat tumbled out of his saddle.
'Allah, Allah!' the shout went up among
the Mice. 'Seize them, seize the brutes!'

The Mice beat on their drums, rejoicing
over a victory and enormous triumph.
The King of the Mice rode on his elephant,
before and behind him his army shouting.
He bound the Cat's two hands together
with thread and tent-ropes and pieces of string.
The King cried: 'Hang him high on the gallows,
the ignoramus, the black-faced dog!'
When the Cat beheld the King of the Mice
he boiled with rage like a bubbling cauldron;
strong as a lion, kneeling on one knee
he tore the cords asunder with his teeth;
then seizing the mice, he dashed them to the ground
so that they became one with the dust.
The army of Mice scattered in one direction,
the King of the Mice fled in another:
gone was the elephant and the elephant-rider,
gone the treasure, the crown, throne and palace.

This is a story both weird and wonderful,
a souvenir from 'Ubaid-i Zākānī:
dear heart, accept the moral of this story
and you will live happy all your days:
having heard the ballad of the Mice and the Cat
meditate well its meaning, my dear son.

To what purpose was this cautionary tale written? It is to be observed that Zākānī was following an ancient convention when he constructed his poem in the form of an animal fable, and Bahār's political explanation of this subterfuge, which has been quoted in an earlier chapter, certainly needs to be borne in mind. 'One feels almost certain,' Farzād remarks, 'that the story was based partially at least, on fact; and that it glanced at some political event, contemporary or recent. Possibly a governor of no deep religious faith and of non-Persian origin staged a repentance scene in a mosque, and used the greater measure of popularity which thus came to him, for subjecting the innocent people (whom he despised, religion and all) to an exploitation far crueller than ever before. Perhaps he eventually grew too strong to obey even the king, and this led to a punitive expedition against him, which culminated in a victory for the king's army. At the last moment, however, the governor himself may have managed to escape punishment.' It is tempting to see, as 'Abbās Iqbāl has done, some reference to the career of Mubāriz al-Dīn Muḥammad the Muẓaffarid, a prince of Arab ancestry 'who is described' (as K. V. Zettersteen remarks) 'as brave and devout but at the same time cruel, bloodthirsty and treacherous'; the cities of Kirmān, Yazd and Iṣfahān featured very prominently in his campaigns against Abū Isḥāq Injū, defeated and executed in 1356 or 1357. It was to this prince that Zākānī dedicated many of his panegyrical odes; and in 1354 his enemy Mubāriz al-Dīn took the oath of allegiance to the 'Abbāsid 'caliph' in his refuge in Cairo. However, nothing like certainty is possible in these matters; and in any case the *Mūsh u gurba* has a perennial relevancy. It may also be noted that, ironically enough, the fate which overtook his hero Abū Isḥāq did not impede Zākānī from subsequently courting Shāh Shujā', his conqueror's son.

E. G. Browne has given a sufficient account of Zākānī's bitter parody of the conventional and popular manual of ethics, his *Akhlāq al-ashrāf* composed in 1340, with its 'double doctrine' of morality and virtue; the same splendid scholar has presented excellent extracts from the brief and pithy *Ta'rīfāt*, written 'for the guidance of my sons and dear ones,' as well as from the *Risāla-yi Dilgushā* with its repertory of amusing (and in many instances quite shockingly indecent) anecdotes. Less notice has been taken of the lyrics which, though comparatively few, possess great charm and present a pleasant and surprising contrast with the larger bulk of Zākānī's writing. These poems deserve study not only for their own sake, but because they reveal their author as bridging the gap between Sa'dī and Ḥāfiẓ, and introducing into the *ghazal* innovations that must assuredly have exercised influence on his junior contemporary who attended the same court circles. It is especially noteworthy that Zākānī's lyrics are almost without exception very brief, their average length not exceeding seven couplets.

The heart that is not bound in the chain of a beloved's tress
in the eyes of men of true vision is not worthy of any account;
the head that is not a workshop of melancholy passion
has no business at all in the factory of joy.
Break completely with reason, and taste the ecstasy of madness,
for those whose hearts are truly alive reckon reason as naught.
Do not reproach wretched me, for upon the highway of love
no choice whatsoever resides in the hands of the helpless lover.
Repeat not again that every ocean has a shore,
since shore there is none to the ocean of love's grief.
Yearning for the fair ones' tresses, restless and bewildered
I am: no turn of fortune was ever so distracted as I.
If 'Ubaid is dishonoured for drunken dissoluteness,
in those two qualities no disgrace or dishonour are mine.

There we have the characteristic Ḥāfiẓian doctrine of unreason fully set forth. The most famous of Ḥāfiẓ' lyrics (in Sir William Jones's immortal version) has the stanza:

Boy, let yon liquid ruby flow,
And bid thy pensive heart be glad,
Whate'er the frowning zealots say:
Tell them, their Eden cannot show
A stream so clear as Rocnabad,
A bower so sweet as Mosellay.

Zākānī opens one of his finest *ghazals* with a fond reference to those two beauty-spots of Shīrāz.

The scent of the earth of Musalla and the water of Ruknabad
drive out of the mind of the exile the thought of his own dear
home.
O blessed resting-place, O life-augmenting realm,
may your exalted foundations for ever be prosperous!
In every nook you repair to the nightingale is trilling,
whatever meadow you visit, there the box-tree preens itself;
wheresoever you look, there shines a beauty like Shirin,
wheresoever you pass, there sighs a lover like Farhad. . . .
Count for precious good fortune the chance occasion of joy,
for the body is feeble of frame and life's foundations unsure.
Clutch the skirt of a loved one, and do whatever you will;
quaff the pure bright wine, and let be whatever betides.
Turn aside to the wine and the plaintive flute, for men say
the world is set upon water, and man is based upon air.
Sweet is the delicate charm of this world; but like 'Ubaid
I am the slave of that man who has set not his heart thereon.

Ḥāfiẓ himself scarcely expressed the *carpe diem* more charmingly.

Lastly a few words should be added about Zākānī's '*Ushshāq-nāma*, available now at last in 'Abbās Iqbāl's not altogether satisfactory edition. This somewhat ambitious but skilful *mathnavī*, stated in the rubric to have been composed in 1350 for Shāh Abū Isḥāq, was evidently written in emulation of the '*Ushshāq-nāma* of 'Irāqī; it shares not only its title, but also the uncommon feature of introducing occasional *ghazals* to punctuate the general discourse. There however the resemblance ends; for whereas 'Irāqī in his poem celebrates mystical love, the burden of Zākānī's song is a human, perhaps an all too human passion. The tale that is told is common enough; the poet falls in love with a handsome creature of undefined sex, and pursues the object of his affection by letters entrusted to an obliging messenger. At first his advances are spurned; then they are encouraged; there is a delightful meeting; but finally the lovers are parted, and this time no hope seems to remain of a reunion. Zākānī ends with a supplication to God.

Now, by the boundless fortitude of Job,
the blood-besprinkled tears that Jacob shed,
the merit of the travellers on the Way,
the virtue of the goodly men of Truth,
have pity on my miserable soul,
open before me thy compassion's gate.
Grant the desire of my distracted heart
and bring me to the idol of my choice;
let me no more in wretched exile dwell,
by thy own bounty loose my fettered foot.
Visit with mercy my most ruined state
and have compassion on my morning sighs;
show generosity to me, forlorn,
a hapless wanderer about the world;
heap not henceforward pain upon my pain,
point me the way where I may find my love.
Release 'Ubaid's sore-wounded heart from grief,
and in thy grace accord him his desire.

Was Zākānī wooing the Shāh himself, or perhaps some prince or favourite of his court?

TWELVE

Some Fourteenth-Century Poets

In the next following chapter we shall be examining the work of the greatest of the post-Mongol poets, in the view of many the greatest poet of all—Ḥāfiẓ. Here a brief account will be given of five poets of the fourteenth century whose writings illustrate different aspects of the literary activities of that troubled and uncertain period. Our first subject is an author of no very great originality, whose reputation in Europe has surely exceeded his merits; a good example—though not so astounding as 'Umar Khaiyām—of how the wayward interest of occidentals can sometimes prevail over the more informed and balanced judgment of native criticism, though unlike 'Umar Khaiyām he has not wrung from his countrymen a belated confession of genius.

It was the prodigious Austrian scholar Joseph von Hammer-Purgstall who first brought to public notice the name of Maḥmūd Shabistarī, when in 1838 he published his pretty edition, accompanied by a German verse-translation, of the *Rosenflor des Geheimnisses*; European travellers however had known of the poem as early as 1700, and the erudite had been made aware of its contents during the 1820s by that pioneer of Ṣūfī studies F. R. D. Tholuck. Of Shabistarī's life very little is recorded; he was born near Tabrīz, enjoyed a far fame for saintliness and godly learning, and died in his homeland about the year 1320. His only surviving poem, the *Gulshan-i rāz*, is a 'summa theologica of the Ṣūfīs' (to borrow Chardin and Bernier's description) in 1,008 rhyming couplets. Cast in the form of questions and answers on a variety of mystical topics, it was composed according to its author at the instance of Amīr Ḥusainī of Harāt, successor to Bahā' al-Dīn Multānī the pupil and initiate of Shihāb al-Dīn al-Suhrawardī. Von Hammer-Purgstall's initiative was followed up in 1880 by E. H. Whinfield, who produced a critical edition of the Persian text with a prose, indeed a prosaic English version. Whinfield, remembering that Tabrīz was visited during Shabistarī's lifetime by embassies from Pope Nicholas IV and Pope Boniface VIII, as well as by Marco Polo, speculated that 'possibly Mahmud's acquaintance with Christian doctrines may have been derived or improved from intercourse with Halton or some of the other monks attached to these missions'; this however seems most improbable, and the echoes of the Gospels which occur in verses 940–3 could certainly have been reflected from earlier Muslim writers.

For this cause said Jesus at the time of His ascension,
'I go unto my Father which is on high.'
You too, O soul of your Father, turn to your Father,
Your companions are gone, go forth too.
If you desire to take wing as a bird,
Cast the carrion world to the vultures.
Give to the base the treacherous world,
It is not meet to give carrion but to dogs.

A rather less humdrum impression of Shabistarī is to be gathered from a metrical version which was published anonymously in 1887 (along with a few selections from 'Umar Khaiyām), prefaced by the explanation that 'the following translation of the Dialogues of the Gulshan-i-Rāz was begun in the year 1879, and was thrown aside on the appearance of Mr. Whinfield's prose translation of the entire work in the ensuing year. Subsequently the author of the present was induced to complete that portion which sets forth the principles of the Sufi philosophy.' It is added that 'the original from which the present translation was made is a special edition, setting forth at its conclusion that it was printed (lithographed) for H.H. Agha Khan in Bombay, A.H. 1280.' A fair example of this version is the question and answer to the seventh problem, the true meaning of that famous *Ana 'l-Ḥaqq* utterance which cost al-Ḥallāj his life in 922.

QUESTION

What meaneth then 'I am the God of truth,'
If every atom shadow forth the Lord?

ANSWER

Within these words the mighty secret lies
Wholly unveiled, for save the Almighty, who
Shall say unto thee 'Truly I am God'?
To thee, like Mansour, every living thing
Seems drunken, and desire of drunkenness.
Ever in praise they firmly grasp the truth.
Would'st thou the secret learn, then whisper low
'All praise the Lord.' When thou hast carded self
As men card wool, even as a carder thou
Shalt raise this cry. So take thou from thine ears
The cotton-wool of doubt. Hark! ONE ALMIGHTY
GOD!—
Ever this cry from God to thee doth come.
Doth thy bark tarry till the judgment-day?

Shabistarī is also credited with three prose treatises of which two, the *Ḥaqq al-yaqīn* and the *Mir'āt al-muḥaqqiqīn*, appear in a mystical miscellany printed at Shīrāz in 1938. E. G. Browne has given the chapter-headings of the former work, which in its style and contents somewhat resembles, though at a lower poetical level, the *Lama'āt* of 'Irāqī. The *Mir'āt al-muḥaqqiqīn*, the theme of which is the mystical apprehension of God through self-knowledge (in accordance with that apocryphal Tradition beloved of the Ṣūfīs, *man 'arafa nafsahu fa-qad 'arafa Rabbahu*), sets forth in seven chapters a theosophical interpretation of the nature of the universe culminating in the famous proposition that man is a microcosm mirroring within himself the macrocosm without him.

'Just as in the heavens there are twelve signs of the Zodiac, such as Aries, Taurus, Gemini, Cancer, Leo, Virgo, Libra, Scorpio, Sagittarius, Capricorn, Aquarius and Pisces, so in the human body there are twelve exterior and interior orifices, such as the two eyes, the two ears, the two nostrils, the mouth, the two nipples, the navel and the two private parts. Just as in the heavens there are twenty-eight Houses, such as the two horns of Aries and its rump, and so forth, so in the body there are twenty-eight sinews. Just as the heavens have 360 degrees, so in the body there are 360 veins. Just as in the heavens there are seven planets, so in the body there are seven principal members, as has been mentioned. Just as in the heavens there are many fixed stars, so in the body there are many natural faculties, such as the attractive, the retentive, and so forth, as has been stated in the beginning. Just as the heavens comprise four elements, so the body comprises four humours, namely the yellow and black biles, the blood and the phlegm. Besides these there are many other resemblances, too numerous to be listed in this compendium. As for the resemblance of the body to the year, this consists in the fact that the year is made up of twelve months, while the body has twelve orifices; the year has four seasons, while in the body there are four elements; the week is contained in seven days, while the body is contained in seven members as is well known; the year has 360 days, while the veins of the body are also 360.'

All this and much like it can be found in the *Rasā'il Ikhwān al-Ṣafā'*, that celebrated synthesis of authentic science and fantastic speculation which has always appealed to the Ismā'īlīs; and the fact that an Agha Khan interested himself in the publication of the *Gulshan-i rāz* accentuates the problem whether Shabistarī (if he was indeed the author of these tracts) may not himself have had Isma'īlī leanings. At all events it is not easy nowadays to subscribe to E. G. Browne's opinion of the *Gulshan-i rāz*, that it is 'on the whole one of the best manuals of Ṣúfí Theosophy which exist.'

Azerbaijan produced during those times of Īl-Khānid rule a man who was a greater poet and a more original thinker than Shabistarī, though he has attracted little attention in the West. Rukn al-Dīn Auḥadī, born at Marāgha about 1270, became a disciple of the mystical poet Auḥad al-Dīn Kirmānī from whom he derived his literary name; but he also had worldly ambitions, which he sought to realize by composing panegyrics in honour of Abū Sa'īd and his vizier Ghiyāth al-Dīn, son of Rashīd al-Dīn Faḍl Allāh. Another leading personality whom he courted with his pen was Naṣīr al-Dīn Ṭūsī's grandson Wajīh al-Dīn Shāh Yūsuf; it was to him that he dedicated a *mathnavī* entitled *Dih-nāma* (otherwise known as *Manṭiq al-'ushshāq*), completed in 1306. Auḥadī was evidently disappointed, like many Persian poets before him and since, by the reception accorded him in his home-town, to judge by the verses he wrote on setting forth for Iṣfahān where he resided for many years.

Isfahan is the fourth clime, indeed it is the fourth heaven;
thither now I must wend, like Jesus without load or ass.
Here not one of the great lords will cast a glance on me;
henceforth I must betake me to where men of true vision dwell.
How long shall I go on gathering glass beads in Azerbaijan?
I am a diver by instinct, and must seek my ocean of pearls.

Persian critics consider that as a composer of odes Auḥadī stands at ease in the third rank of excellence, though it is conceded that his high moral purpose was beyond question. This quality is thought to be most eminently displayed in his best-known poem, the *Jām-i Jam*, of which Riḍā-zāda Shafaq remarks that 'it is possible to find few *mathnavīs* in the Persian language that deal with social and educational problems on a comparable level.'

This extensive composition, which the author finished in 1332 and offered to Ghiyāth al-Dīn (four years before his execution following the defeat of his royal nominee Arpa), has had the advantage of being edited in 1929 by that industrious scholar Vaḥīd Dastgirdī in 264 pages. The *Jām-i Jam* has thus belatedly recovered in some measure the public esteem which it enjoyed when first issued, for (to quote E. G. Browne) 'Dawlatsháh, followed by the *Haft Iqlím*, states that this poem was so popular that within a month of its production four hundred copies of it were made and sold at a good price, but adds that in his time (892 (1487)) it was seldom met with and little read.'

Auḥadī writes of many things in his somewhat rambling but organized poem, which its modern editor has arranged under no fewer than 116 headings. A glance at some of these titles indicates the nature and intention of the book: 'In praise of Sulṭān Abū Sa'īd Bahādur,' 'In praise of Khvāja Ghiyāth al-Dīn Muḥammad,' 'A description of the Palace,' 'A description of the congregational mosque,' 'On the beginning of Creation,' 'On the origin of Man,' 'On Man's superiority to the animals,' 'Advice to kings to be just,' 'On the etiquette of attending upon kings,' 'On marriage and procreation,' 'On bad women,' 'Some advice to bad women.'

Though to your eyes a woman looks beautiful,
plain ugly she is when she ruins your house.
A modest woman is a candle in a home,
a bold woman is a calamity any time;
a pious woman is a pride to her man,
an ungodly woman undoes him altogether—
having emptied his table and his water-jug
she grabs her veil and puts on her slippers,
drags him off to the cadi and cries, 'My dowry!
Give it back to me, if not willy, then nilly!'
A sober woman agreeable to obey you
is like a kernel nestling in your nut;

a wicked woman is a torment to your heart—
drive her out quick, or she'll make you miserable.
If your wife behaves rawly, scold her thoroughly;
if she won't cover her face, put her in a shroud.
Never put a pen in the hand of a bad woman—
it's better to cut off your own hand than do that,
better for a husband to put on mourning
than for his wife to write him a black book.
God has made the wheel lawful to women:
bid them leave pen and paper to their husbands.

But Auḥadī has other themes than these: 'On repressing lust and birth-control,' 'On the education of children,' 'On miserliness,' 'On the present disrepute and unprofitableness of poetry,' 'On the state of judges and justice,' 'Reproof to wicked lawyers,' 'On the benefits of travel,' 'On seeking a guide and leader,' 'On penitence,' 'On the meaning of retreat,' 'On the virtue of sleeplessness,' 'On silence,' 'On abstinence,' 'On trust in God,' and so forth; for the second half of the poem is largely given over to an account of Ṣūfī discipline and practice. His book is thus a curious combination of worldly and other-worldly wisdom, in some sort an amalgam of the *Qābūs-nāma* with the *Ḥadīqat al-ḥaqīqa*. The level of his versification is not very high, and his occasional anecdotes are generally rather pointless and not well told. Since interest is taken in all references to Christianity that occur in Muslim writings, this summary description of the *Jām-i Jam* is concluded with some extracts from an alleged discourse of Jesus.

One day the Messiah was with his friends,
his disciples and the repositories of his secrets;
he made exposition to them on the subject of love,
declared the matter openly, and then concealed it.
In the midst of his discourse his companions saw
he was weary, the tears raining from his eyes;
so they asked him for a sign and a proof of love.

He said, 'To-morrow is the day of Abraham's
  fire.'
When upon the next day he proceeded to his task
and set his foot upon the plant of the gallows
he said, 'If there be any man present here,
this surely is a sufficient proof of love.
Whosoever turns his countenance to God,
he must press his back against the Cross;
until his body has been tied to the gallows
his soul cannot mount up into heaven.
Four nails have been prescribed for the body;
heaven is the candlestick of the soul's candle.
The claim of the true friend lacks not for proof:
even thus deliver your soul from your body.
How can any man be said to be fatherless?
Is not your Father in heaven sufficient?
He who knows how to bring the dead to life,
how could he ever slay his enemies?'

We now turn to consider a poet who, though not of the very highest rank, nevertheless excels by far all but one who wrote in this fourteenth century. Amīr Fakhr al-Dīn Maḥmūd, called Ibn Yamīn, was born in 1286, probably in Turkistān. His father Amīr Yamīn al-Dīn settled in the village of Faryūmad (near ancient Baihaq and modern Sabzavār), according to Rashīd Yāsimī about the year 1298; he was himself a successful poet and a man of substance who taught his son his craft, and when he died in 1322 he left Ibn Yamīn not only affluent but also established as a court-poet esteemed by the princes of Khurāsān. Most of the products of Ibn Yamīn's earlier career perished, no doubt along with his fortune, when his own copy of his collected poems vanished in 1342 in the battle between Mu'izz al-Dīn Muḥammad of the Kurt dynasty, and the poet's patron at that time, Wajīh al-Dīn Mas'ūd the Sarbadār. Mas'ūd was heavily defeated in this engagement; Ibn Yamīn, being taken captive, prudently transferred his allegiance to the victor to whom he addressed a poem in which the following lines occur.

If by a stratagem Heaven snatched my poems from my hand,
thanks be to God, the one who made them still remains with me;
and if Time has robbed me of my string of royal pearls,
I will not think upon the pain, seeing I have the cure.
If the wind has plucked a bloom from the rose-bush of my genius,
yet I have a garden stocked with tulips, basil, eglantine;
and if one of my oyster-shells is emptied of its gleaming pearl,
still my mind is as full of gems as the Sea of Oman itself.

Ibn Yamīn did not boast falsely; during the last twenty-five years of his life, which ended in 1368, he composed sufficient to enable Sa'īd Nafīsī, when he came to publish the *Dīvān* in 1939, to assemble more than 5,000 verses.

The Austrian tradition of Persian scholarship which von Hammer-Purgstall had so brilliantly begun was continued by one having the impressive and, to all appearances, slightly unpronounceable name of Ottokar Maria Freiherr von Schlechta-Wssehrd, who in 1852 (second edition, 1879) published *Ibn' Jemin's Bruchstücke*, a selection of 159 pieces. (The term *Bruchstücke* gives a rather misleading impression; the original word *Muqaṭṭa'āt* implies not so much 'fragments' as 'occasional pieces,' for each poem is complete in itself, and many are brief epigrams obviously composed under particular circumstances.) This initiative, and the comparative success which attended it, encouraged Brigadier-General E. H. Rodwell, in honourable retirement from the Indian Army, to produce in 1933:

Ibn Yamin | *Persico* | Ibn-i-Yamin | 100 short poems | The Persian text with paraphrase.

Rodwell paid a respectful tribute to the work of his predecessor: 'Both editions are in my humble opinion very attractive. Many pieces are slightly altered in the edition of 1879. The translation is sometimes very free, and Count Schlechta, as for shortness I propose to call him, seems sometimes to have added to his text out of the treasure-house of his own erudition.' It is instructive to compare the methods and merits of the two interpreters by putting side by side their versions of the same poem. The Austrian gave us for instance:

Hast du ein Feld und Ochsen zwei zum Pflug,
Nenn einen 'Schah,' der anderen 'Wesir';
Und scheint dir diess zum Wohlsein nicht genug,
Geh hin und Geld von Juden borge dir.
Noch besser so als dich ins Dienste neigen
Und Sclavenhuld'gung jedem Wicht bezeigen!

The Englishman, who took in an additional opening couplet, put it this way:

If at hope's journey's end things go not well,
On the still threshold of contentment dwell.
If thou hast land, plough oxen, too, a pair
Call one *Amir* the other call *Wazir*.
And if thy livelihood too meagre seems,
Borrow from Jews—and thus augment thy means.
This seems to me one thousand times as good
As early serving for thy livelihood.

The following would be a literal translation:

By traversing the long road of hope you'll never get rich
save only if you tarry on the threshold of contentment.
Go, get yourself a pair of oxen and a field for sowing—
call one of them Prince, the other Prime Minister!
And if this doesn't yield you enough to live on happily,
you can always borrow a loaf of barley-meal from the Jews.

That's surely a thousand times better than at the crack of dawn
to gird your loins and say 'Sir' to one no better than you.

Since Rodwell spent more hours with Ibn Yamīn than any other European in this century, it is interesting to see how he assesses his genius. He first quotes the verdict of Rashīd Yāsimī, himself a poet who published a biography of his fellow-poet in 1924. 'If Ibn Yamin is not a poet of the first rank in the composition of odes (*ghazal*) or longer poems (*qaṣida*), he has a right to a high place amongst the authors of poems dealing with ethical subjects, and we may count his moral poems as outstanding and conspicuous examples of Persian poetry.' Rodwell then proceeds to estimate Ibn Yamīn in comparison with 'Umar Khaiyām, the yardstick for Englishmen of all things Persian.

'Both poets lived in the same district of Khurásán to a good old age; both breathe the literary atmosphere in which they lived; both of them were Arabic scholars, but neither of them is in the first rank of Persian poets; both of them looked with wonder and astonishment on their environment; both of them expressed themselves in language which can easily be understood by common and unlearned people; both of them used as the vehicle of their philosophy short and pithy forms of verse; both of them emphasize the temporary nature of our existence in this passing world: both of them look on speculations with regard to a future state as waste of time and folly—but 'Omar Khayyám as an astronomer is more antinomian than Ibn Yamin and expresses himself more freely, more courageously, and more profoundly. Ibn Yamin has nothing to match Khayyám's *Kúza-náma*. On the other hand, Ibn Yamin, who claims to be the apostle of Wisdom, or perhaps we should say of common sense, has in his armoury a keen sense of humour, and can defend himself with the winged shafts of satire. . . . Moreover, Ibn Yamin is free from the Bacchanalian addresses to the *Sáqi*, many of them probably spurious, which tarnish the lustre of Khayyám's reputation; and whereas the latter, failing in his search for something that would satisfy his spiritual aspirations, falls back on a pretended worship of the wine-cup—Ibn Yamin, taking pleasure in wine and the society of his friends, is by nature Spartan rather than hedonist, and devotes his genius to teaching his fellow-men how to live wisely and happily. . . . If we weigh in the balance the reputation of these two philosophers during their own life-time, we find that Ibn Yamin for his livelihood held on to the skirts of warring chiefs, had frequent periods of disappointment and depression, but lived to enjoy the fruits of his laureateship in popular esteem. On the other hand, 'Omar Khayyám, though much esteemed by a small band of free-thinkers, was anathematized and persecuted by religious zealots, and his poetry remained unhonoured and almost unknown until by a curious chain of accidents it was as it were revealed, glorified in an English dress, and acclaimed by the multitude as expressing in some measure the sentiments of the elusive and shallow individual known as "the man in the street." Moreover, as was to be expected, the Apostle of common sense has never been charged with Sufism or mysticism—a charge made not infrequently against Khayyám and vehemently rebutted by Edward FitzGerald.'

Rodwell's judgment is in the main shrewd and well conceived. It is however a little surprising that he should have found, to his evident satisfaction, that his 'Apostle of common sense' was exempt from the charge of 'Sufism or mysticism,' in view of at least one splendid set of verses which E. G. Browne translated surpassingly well.

From the void of Non-existence to this dwelling-house of clay
I came, and rose from stone to plant; but that hath passed away!
Thereafter, through the working of the Spirit's toil and strife,
I gained, but soon abandoned, some lowly form of life:
That too hath passed away!

In a human breast, no longer a mere unheeding brute,
This tiny drop of Being to a pearl I did transmute:
That too hath passed away!
At the Holy Temple next did I foregather with the throng
Of Angels, compassed it about, and gazed upon it long:
That too hath passed away!
Forsaking Ibn-i-Yamín, and from this too soaring free,
I abandoned all beside Him, so that naught was left but HE:
All else hath passed away!

Ibn Yamīn was second to none of his countrymen in his conceit of his own poetic abilities, and put the blame for his comparative obscurity not on himself but on the times in which he lived.

If only I had someone like Maḥmūd to look after me,
what would 'Unṣurī weigh in the balance against me?
If only I had someone like Sanjar to nurse my art,
I would soon tarnish the lustre of Anvarī's fame.
What was the source of those two poets' greatness?
Why, the munificence of Maḥmūd and Sanjar!
I am as I am because, thanks to the times I live in,
I've no heart for poetry, my thoughts being on my next meal.
But for that, Ibn Yamīn, no one would ever have reckoned
that they had any advantage over you whatsoever.

Another poem of a 'Christian' subject elaborates the favourite comparison of this transient world with an ugly old woman who buries successive husbands.

I have heard tell how Jesus (peace be upon him)
in humble prayer once cried, 'O great Artificer,
reveal to me, as Thou createdst it,
the beauty of this so fascinating world.'

Over this wish a little while elapsed.
One day he was wandering in the wilderness
when far off on the plain he espied a woman
with neither friend nor stranger for company.
Jesus addressed her: 'Woman, who art thou,
sundered so far from all thy kith and kin?'
This was her answer: 'I am that same woman
whom thou hast looked to see so long a time.'
'Why, what have I to do with women's company?'
Jesus replied in great astonishment.
The woman answered: 'Most illustrious master,
pray pardon me—but I am called the World.'
Then the Messiah said: 'Reveal that face
which has ensnared so many human hearts!'
Lifting her hand, she drew her veil aside
disclosing to him her well-hidden secret,
and he beheld an old, foul, black-faced hag
defiled by a hundred blemishes and blotches;
one of her hands was dabbled all with blood,
the other henna'd to the finger-tips.
'Filthy, revolting creature,' the Messiah
exclaimed, 'how came this hand to drip with gore?'
'This very instant,' the old woman explained,
'I slew, alas, a husband with this hand,
and I have daubed the other hand with henna
because another suitor seeks to wed me.
As soon as I remove the one by violence
with gentleness the other I embrace,
yet, what is so amazing, having had
so many husbands, I am still a virgin.'
Then marvelled the Messiah exceedingly.
'Disgusting, hideous harlot,' he exclaimed,
'how has thy maidenhead remained intact
when thou hast taken more than a thousand men?'
The stinking slut replied after this wise:

'O paragon and model of these days,
of all the multitude that have desired me
not one have I discovered a true man,
while of the others who were truly men
not one has courted me, for very shame.
If that is how I have fared with all my husbands,
be not amazed that I am still a virgin.'

But it is in his shortest poems that Ibn Yamīn establishes himself as among the greatest epigrammatists of a people much given to epigram.

The man who knows, and knows he knows,
gallops the steed of joy beyond the skies.
The man who knows not, and knows he knows not,
also saves himself from the shame of folly.
The man who knows not, and knows not he knows not,
abides in compound ignorance to all eternity.

In this world it behoves a man
to look on himself as a chess-player—
taking from his opponent whatever he can
and hanging on grimly to all he's got.

If a foreigner were vizier to the king of the world
his heart would always hanker after his own people;
though the falcon perches on the forearm of kings,
its heart is forever yearning for its familiar nest.

When you find yourself snubbed by people anywhere
quickly depart from that place, and go somewhere else:
if a tree had the means to move from place to place
it wouldn't suffer the ruthless tyranny of the axe.

What did that father say, when he was at his last gasp?
'Soul of your father, listen to one good piece of advice:
though you've a very dear friend, never tell him your secret
or your very dear friend will soon tell his other friends.'

Contentment is the key-note of very many of Ibn Yamīn's best poems, as in the following final example.

Dear heart, since your origin is earth, don't strain for the heights;
doesn't the element earth gravitate towards lowliness?
The sensible man is he who knows his own limitations
and keeps within them, so long as he's in the noose of being.
Somewhere to live, sufficient to eat to keep you alive—
it's just plain greed, to desire beyond these simple things.
Enough wine's in the bowl for everyone to have a glass;
to want more is really the limit of drunkenness.
Hear one word, dear heart, from your old friend Ibn Yamīn:
if you really and truly believe in the good God above,
surely, to seek for more than a bare sufficiency
and to sweat to get it—that's the acme of folly.

It is now more than a hundred years since Franz von Erdmann, having already had to do with Niẓāmī, called the attention of scholars to the extensive writings of Kamāl al-Dīn Maḥmūd ibn 'Alī of Kirmān, known as Khvājū; yet to this day all of his that has been published, apart from occasional citations, is some selected passages brought out by Kūhī Kirmānī in 1929. Yet Khvājū was one of the outstanding and certainly one of the most productive poets of his age. Born at Kirmān early in 1281, he graduated early in life to the courts of kings, and like his senior Auḥadī tried his luck first on Abū Sa'īd and Ghiyāth al-Dīn. Caught up in the general chaos which followed the disintegration of the Īl-Khānid Empire, Khvājū wandered from provincial capital to provincial capital singing now to the Muẓaffarids of Yazd and Shīrāz, now to the Jalā'irids of Baghdad; his principal patrons were Mubāriz al-Dīn Muḥammad and Amīr Abū Isḥāq Injū, and it was in the latter's service that he died at Shīrāz, probably in 1352. He had had time, between his palace appearances, to dabble in mysticism; his spiritual preceptor was 'Alā' al-Daula Samnānī (d. 1336), a retired statesman who composed a number of books including a very extensive Ṣūfī commentary on the Koran.

Khvājū left behind him, first a full *Dīvān*, reckoned by Daulatshāh to contain 20,000 verses but now much reduced, made up of the usual collection of odes, lyrics and quatrains. His odes are for the most part panegyrical, but include some religious pieces considered by Shafaq to be equal to those of Sanā'ī. This scholar also finds touches of Sanā'ī, as well as 'Aṭṭār, Rūmī and Sa'dī in Khvājū's lyrics; the following poem is thought to illustrate his debt to his predecessors.

I have found my true wealth in being without wealth;
a beggar, I can outboast all the kings of the earth.
Stranger to my friends, sick of the world and life itself,
I have found true friendship in the society of the Beloved.
Many years I cried my poverty at the door of men's hearts,
and so of course I have found a kingship above all kings;
many a night I fared through this valley until day,
till at last I have found the dawn of union with Him.
Having emerged from the shadows of this earthly dunghill
I have found both worlds radiant in the light of God.

Some of Khvājū's lyrics on the other hand anticipate the style of Ḥāfiẓ, who did not hesitate to include him among the poets from whom he borrowed.

In the view of men of true vision Solomon's realm is the wind;
no, rather he is a true Solomon who is free of all realms.

Those who say that the world is laid to rest upon water—
do not heed them, good sir: behold, it rests on the wind.
Open your eyes like the narcissus, and see in this earth
how many rose-like faces and fir-like statures lie.
Pitch not the tent of your joy at the door of this ancient inn:
its base is a yawning void, its floor is foundationless.
All the time the sun in heaven shines on another;
what can one do? That is how the mean creature was made.

E. G. Browne however, having read some seventy-five of Khvājū's lyrics, declared himself 'not able to discover any striking beauty or conspicuous merit' in them; V. F. Büchner, who looked again at the collected works, was ready to echo Browne's final verdict that 'his verse, while graceful and pleasing, lacks any conspicuous distinction or excellence.' Into the making of this judgment went a consideration of Khvājū's other and more ambitious compositions, the five *mathnavī* idylls composed in emulation of Niẓāmī's *Khamsa*. The first of these, completed in 1332 and dedicated to Ghiyāth al-Dīn, has for its theme 'the adventures of Humāy, son of Shāh Hūshang, and his love of Humāyūn, princess of China'; it is therefore called *Humāy u Humāyūn*, and runs to 3,203 couplets. The second, the *Naurūz u Gul*, recounts the romance of a prince of Khurāsān and a princess of Rūm in 2,615 verses; it was finished in 1341 and offered to Mubāriz al-Dīn's vizier Tāj al-Dīn Aḥmad. This is considered by Shafaq to be the best of Khvājū's *mathnavīs*.

Khvājū tried a change of subjects and a change of patrons with his next composition. The *Kamāl-nāma*, presented to Abū Isḥāq of Shīrāz in 1343, takes up a serious and religious stand from the very start, with its tribute to the Ṣūfī saint Abū Isḥāq Kāzarūnī.

How pleasant it is to gird up the loins,
to close the eyes and restrict the glance,
to wash the hands of wine and drunkenness,
to lift up the head and become enraptured.

The fourth of Khvājū's five, the *Rauḍat al-anwār*, is also a religious poem, having been written on the lines of Niẓāmī's *Makhzan al-asrār*. This work, dated one year earlier than the *Kamāl-nāma*, was a tribute to Abū Isḥāq's minister Shams al-Dīn Maḥmūd, to be killed in battle in 1345; it is divided into twenty discourses. Khvājū quite boldly challenges comparison with his model.

> Though you are a famous exponent of letters
> and a convinced admirer of Niẓāmī's verse,
> pass now beyond his *Treasury of Secrets*,
> outstep his channel and circumference.

For all that, the *Rauḍat al-anwār* still awaits an editor.

Concerning the fifth of Khvājū's *Khamsa*, which was concluded in 1344, some uncertainty prevails. Büchner seeks to identify it with the very rare *Mafātīḥ al-qulūb*, while Shafaq thinks to find it in the better-known *Gauhar-nāma*. Both are mystical poems; but the latter, written for Bahā' al-Dīn Maḥmūd, a descendant of Niẓām al-Mulk and vizier to the Muẓaffarid Mubāriz al-Dīn, was not completed until 1345 and would therefore seem to exclude itself from the *Khamsa*.

More material is generally accessible for studying the work of the fifth lesser poet of the fourteenth century, for his *Kullīyāt* have been lithographed at Bombay in 236 pages. Jamāl al-Dīn Salmān, son of 'Alā' al-Dīn Muḥammad, called Salmān-i Sāvajī was born at Sāva, 'a fine city midway between Raiy and Hamadhān,' as Yāqūt describes it; adding that whereas Sāva was Sunnī and Shāfi'ī, its neighbour Āva was Shī'ī and Imāmī, and the two communities quarrelled incessantly. The Arab geographer adds that in 1220 the Tartars destroyed both towns and slaughtered all the inhabitants; they also burned the library of Sāva, 'than which there was no greater in the world.' However, the city was rebuilt, and Salmān's father was serving in the administration there when the poet came into the world, about the year 1300.

Salmān at first followed the family tradition by joining the civil service, but discovering a talent for poetry he decided to try the less secure but potentially more lucrative profession of panegyrist. He appears to have scored his first success with Abū Sa'īd and Ghiyāth al-Dīn Muḥammad, whose deaths in 1335 and 1336 he mourned in noble numbers. For most of his career however he was attached to the Jalā'irid court at Baghdad, attending upon Ḥasan-i Buzurg the founder of the dynasty (reigned 1336–56) and his consort Dilshād Khātūn, widow of Abū Sa'īd, and later upon their son Sulṭān Uvais (d. 1376), whom he was able to congratulate in 1352 upon the birth of his elder son Ḥasan.

> A moon out of the station of nobility, offspring of the sun of perfection—
> may Allah increase him in beauty!—has adorned the world in beauty;
> from the meadow of pomp and majesty heaven has caused to spring
> a rose-bush—may Allah cause it to grow into a handsome tree!
> On the day of Friday, the ninth of the second month of Rabī',
> when by Arab reckoning seven hundred and fifty-three years were gone,
> the auspicious-footed Shaikh and Prince came into existence.

This Ḥasan survived his father by only a few hours, for he was assassinated by his barons immediately after Uvais died. Salmān lived on to congratulate Ḥasan's scarcely more fortunate brother Ḥusain on coming to the throne, and even to celebrate with true panegyrist's *sangfroid* the victory in 1375 of Shāh Shujā' the Muẓaffarid who drove Ḥusain out of Tabrīz. This was almost his last public appearance, however, for the poet died the following year.

In a great part of his formal odes Salmān sings the praises of Uvais, 'said by Dawlatsháh to have been of such striking beauty that when he rode out the people of Baghdád used to flock into the streets to gaze upon a countenance which seemed to re-incarnate the legendary comeliness of Joseph.' Uvais included among his accomplishments a considerable gift for verse, and the poem which he composed on the approach of death is much admired.

From the capital of the Spirit one day I departed to the city of the Body;
a stranger I was a few days here, and now have departed to my homeland.
Slave of a mighty Lord I was, and had run away from my Master;
but in the end I departed to Him, shamefast, with sword and winding-sheet.
Dear companions of mine, who am now excluded from this world,
may your joy be long in this house from which I have now departed.

Salmān's elegy on the death of Uvais is not contained in the *Dīvān*, but part of it is preserved elsewhere.

Wheel of heaven, turn gently, for no slight thing you have wrought;
By your slaying of its king, Iran to destruction is brought.
Out of its very zenith a heaven you have pulled down,
Levelled its crest with the earth and cast in the dust its crown.

As a panegyrist Salmān is considered by Persian critics to be of the calibre of Anvarī himself, whose writings (with those of the other great court-poets of the past) he conscientiously studied. His technical skill in handling difficult rhymes is particularly admired, and applause has been bestowed on his mastery of rhetorical figures and elaboration of novel conceits. Shafaq singles out for special mention the erotic prelude from a paean in honour of Uvais.

> Whence does the breeze of Naurūz bring this perfume of
> the soul?
> My spirit hastens swiftly to the street of the beloved.
> The very earth is stirring to the soft caress of the wind
> that seems to give a token of Jesus' life-giving breath.
> I cannot tell what the roses are whispering, that again
> the nightingales break silence and sing a loud lament;
> the rose-bud has pent such delicate emotions in its heart
> which now the bulbul expresses for all the world to hear.

The intricate interplay of conventional themes freshly varied recalls the art of the illuminator or the subtle craft of the carpet-weaver; the soft music of the words induces a languid mood of abandon, and must have been very potent in loosening the purse-strings of an impressionable monarch.

In addition to his odes Salmān also composed two idylls, the *Firāq-nāma* and the *Jamshīd u Khvarshīd*, and a full quota of lyrics and quatrains occupying a hundred pages in the Bombay lithograph. The lyrics, which are of exceptional grace and sweetness, dwell lovingly on the favourite topics of passionate attachment and reckless devotion; the images of wine and tavern are repeatedly exploited, and the double rhyme presents no difficulty.

> Your tress has cast a madness in my head;
> your tress has turned my whole world upside down.
> One drop of blood remained within my heart;
> my eye has poured that too into the sea.
> That lofty stature saw my lifeless frame
> and drew it like a shadow in its wake.
> When the deer sniffed your fragrance on the breeze
> it flung its musk-pod to the wilderness.

He made me faithful promise for to-day;
now to to-morrow he to-day postpones.
The whole world was the quarry of his love,
and out of all he struck down me alone.
Saki, the wine he poured into the cup—
that was a fire he kindled in my heart;
that wine's perfume enticed me from the mosque
and clapped me in the Christian hostelry.
The road to mosque our elder too has left
and turned aside into the Magian lane.
Salmān within the tavern lost his life:
he found it there, and there he flung it back.

The foregoing poem is composed in a short metre and abounds in Ṣūfī imagery. The next poem is also mystical and recalls in its broad sweep and passionate rhythm the odes of Rūmī. As in many of Ḥāfiẓ' lyrics, the prince to whom the verses are addressed (the opening couplet suggests that either he was on a journey, or Salmān felt himself temporarily out of favour) is thought of as an incarnation of the eternal Spirit of God, to whom allegiance was secured by the solemn compact into which mankind was believed to have entered at the dawn of creation, according to the Ṣūfī interpretation of Koran VII 171.

By the right of ancient comradeship, while I am far from your company
I am bereft of my very life, I am cut off from my very soul.
Did you not draw me to yourself like a bow at the first with all your strength?
Then why do you fling me from yourself like an arrow now so contemptuously?
Nay, it is Fate that casts me off from your company, and I know full well
that though I come with a hundred pleas you would not hold me excusable.

If I were damned to dwell in Hell, the memory of you would allay my pains,
and if I were blessed with Paradise, your beauty would still be my desire.
Yearning for wine and my mistress fair drives utterly out of my ardent heart
the image of my celestial bliss, the longing for my sweet, heavenly brides.
How can advice be acceptable to him whom your wanton eyes lay waste?
Go, my counsellor: I am drunk. Saki, come hither: I crave for wine.
Boast not, Salmān, to be temperate in the intoxicating season of her eyes;
I have been drunk since eternity, and who dares to say I am temperate?

The style and mannerisms of Ḥāfiẓ are very apparent in the following poem, especially in its concluding couplet.

Sore smitten be the soul unsmitten by the shaft of his tyranny;
delivered from grief be the heart undelivered from his love's bonds!
If cure is none to be found, say, succour us then with new anguish;
we will make do with the dry thorn, if the rose is denied us.
So long as the water of goodness and grace flows in his river
no page in the volume of beauty's meadow remains unwashed.
The curve of his brow is shaped like the new moon, and alas!
he knows for a certainty that the moon is not always new.
With foxy craft his ringlets lasso the necks of lions;
no game is there that ever escaped from his cunning noose.
The blackness of his tresses enrages the envious musk:
not for nothing is the heart's blood bound in the musk-deer's navel.

Most assuredly, never box-tree grew by margin of river
(as I have seen it) more graceful than your cypress stature.
Venus herself chants to the lute this song of Salmān:
'Sore smitten be the soul unsmitten by the shaft of his tyranny.'

The conceit of Venus chanting in heaven the poet's song is taken up by Ḥāfiẓ, and characteristically given new value.

Dar ās°mān na 'ajab gar ba-gufta-yi Ḥāfiẓ
surūd-i Zuhra ba-raqṣ āvarad Masīḥā-rā

No wonder then, if in heaven to the words invented by Ḥāfiẓ
the song of Venus entices to dance the Messiah himself.

The attentive student of Ḥāfiẓ cannot fail to recognize in the poems of Salmān many features which have always been thought to be most characteristic of the Nightingale of Shīrāz. We shall be considering presently the question of Ḥāfiẓ' originality, and the extent of his debt to those who composed lyrics before him; to conclude this chapter it may be helpful to set down in juxtaposition a few extracts illustrative of that 'plagiarism' which all Persian (and Arab) poets have practised from the beginning, and none more constantly or more discriminately than Ḥāfiẓ. The material for this review is drawn from the masterly monograph on Ḥāfiẓ composed in Urdu by the Indian scholar Shiblī Nu'mānī; the Persian originals will be found in the third volume of E. G. Browne.

Khvājū:

Our elder has left his mystic robe as a pledge in the vintner's shop,
O my friends all, disciples too of our goblet-seizing elder.
If wine has made us infamous the world over, what can we do?
So ran the writ of our destiny on the primal day of the world.

We have bound our mad heart in the chain of your tresses;
many a man of reason has become mad for our chain.
Be not heedless of the shaft of our world-consuming sigh,
for very hard flies our arrow from its gently-striking bow.

Ḥāfiẓ:

Last night our elder set forth for the tavern out of the mosque:
friends of the mystic way, henceforward what can we do?
Let us also become fellow-drinkers in the Magian inn,
for so ran the writ of our destiny on the primal day of the world.
If Reason knew how happy the heart is in his tresses' bond,
the men of reason too would become mad to wear our chain.
The shaft of our sigh surpasses heaven: Ḥāfiẓ, be silent!
Have compassion upon your soul: beware of our shaft.

It will be noticed that in the final couplet of this poem Ḥāfiẓ has introduced Rūmī's second 'signature' of Khamūsh ('Silent').

Khvājū:

O eastern breeze, bring me tidings of that certain one thou knowest;
over that land be passing at that certain time thou knowest.
Soar on wings like a bird, and when thou reachest the zenith
upon that nest then alight in that certain manner thou knowest.
Go not such wise that the dust be strewn on him in thy passing;
when thou arrivest, convey him that certain message thou knowest.

Ḥāfiẓ:

O breath of felicity's dawn, by that certain token thou knowest
pass over So-and-so's street at that certain time thou knowest.

A royal messenger thou; lo, my eyes are fixed on the highway;
courteously, not abruptly, in that certain manner thou knowest
say: 'My feeble spirit has slipped away; now for God's sake
give of thy quickening ruby that certain thing thou knowest.'
These two words I have written such wise that none else knoweth;
recite them too, of thy bounty, in a certain fashion thou knowest.

Khvājū:

What care if in Hell or Heaven we alight, if the Friend be there?
What care if in mosque or church we kneel, if our prayer be true?

Ḥāfiẓ:

What care if sober or drunk, every man is seeking the Friend;
what care if in mosque or church, each place is the house of Love.

Khvājū:

How shall I tear my heart away from the Darling's face? For His love
entered my heart with my mother's milk, and will leave it with my life.

Ḥāfiẓ:

Thy passion dwells in my whole being, Thy love inhabits my heart;
entered my body with my mother's milk, and will leave it with my life.

Salmān:

Since ever on the world fell the rumour of Thy beauty
in quest of Thee unceasing through all the world men wander.

My passionate abstaining is scattered like dry stubble;
strike up a song, O minstrel! O saki, bring the wine-bowl!
We have attached our hearts to Thy heart-unloosing ruby;
part in a smile those lips, that our hearts may be unloosened.
The lovers of Thy tresses have joined a circle round Thee;
distracted for Thy ringlets, they fall upon each other.

Ḥāfiẓ:

This is the feast, the rose's season: bring wine, O saki!
Who ever saw a flask without wine in the time of roses?
The rose has bloomed: my companions, why do you sit heedless
with no sound of psaltery, no friend, no wine, no flagon?
With all this pious abstaining my heart has become quite frozen;
saki, give me the goblet, that my heart may be unloosened.
When the morning cup is circling you know how sweet an image
the soft cheek of the saki casts in the shining wine-bowl.

THIRTEEN

Ḥāfiẓ

'In the time of the coming down of the banners of the Sulṭān of earth's inhabitants, the world-protecting Emperor, Amīr Tīmūr Gūrkān, and in the days of the overthrow of the realm of Sulṭān Zain al-'Ābidīn, immunity was granted to the people of Shīrāz. As the poet Ḥāfiẓ was amongst those who dwelt in that city, being a householder in a certain quarter of the town, his name appeared on the list of those required to pay indemnity, and the tax-collector received instructions to exact a certain sum from him. In this situation the poet appealed to the afore-mentioned Amīr, declaring himself to be bankrupt and penniless. The aforesaid Amīr remarked, "You are the man who uttered the verses:

My Shīrāz Turk if she but deign
To take my heart into her hand,
I'll barter for her Hindu mole
Bukhārā, yea, and Samarqand.

A man who is prepared to barter Bukhārā and Samarqand for a single mole cannot be a bankrupt." Ḥāfiẓ replied, "It is on account of such extravagances that I am a bankrupt." Because of this impromptu answer his majesty cancelled the impost and the aforesaid Ḥāfiẓ was discharged.'

This famous anecdote of Ḥāfiẓ' last years makes as good a point of departure as any. It is true that E. G. Browne, who knew of no earlier authority for the incident than Daulatshāh (and his garbled account involves a chronological impossibility), described the story as 'probably entirely apocryphal.' However, the version given above rests upon a more ancient text; it is drawn from a rare book entitled *Anīs al-nās*, composed after the fashion of the *Qābūs-nāma* by a certain Shujā' of Shīrāz about the year 1427, within one generation of Ḥāfiẓ' death; and assuredly, *se non è vero, è ben trovato*. That meeting between the mighty Tamerlane and Persia's greatest lyric poet is beyond question one of the most memorable encounters in the history of literature.

Shams al-Dīn Muḥammad Ḥāfiẓ was born at Shīrāz most probably in 1326. His father Bahā' al-Dīn (or Kamāl al-Dīn), who had migrated to Shīrāz from Iṣfahān, died when Ḥāfiẓ was a mere child, so that it was left to his mother to care for his education. It seems that he enjoyed the best all-round training that Shīrāz could offer, and among his teachers Qiwām al-Dīn 'Abd Allāh (d. 1370) is mentioned. We have no certain means of knowing at what age Ḥāfiẓ first tried his hand at composing poetry, but it may be assumed that he will have followed the fashion prevailing amongst bright boys brought up in royal capitals and looked early to letters as a promising career. At all events we find in his *Dīvān* several poems in honour of Qiwām al-Dīn Ḥasan, vizier to Shāh Abū Isḥāq Injū, who died in 1353, as well as a full-length panegyric in the name of Abū Isḥāq himself, executed by Mubāriz al-Dīn's orders in 1357. What profit these exercises brought him we cannot say; but chance has preserved in Tashkent a manuscript of the *Khamsa* of Amīr Khusrau which Ḥāfiẓ made, completed on February 9, 1355, and this suggests that he may have been supplementing a precarious livelihood by working as a professional copyist at that time. Later he composed a nostalgic poem commemorating the brilliance of Abū Isḥāq's court-circle:

In the days of the Sultanate of Shāh Shaikh Abū Isḥāq
the kingdom of Fārs was adorned with five wondrous personages—

first, an emperor like him, a distributor of provinces,
who bore off the prize of pre-eminence for justice, bounty and equity;
second, the last of the Substitutes, Shaikh Amīn al-Dīn,
admitted amongst the Poles and the congregation of Pegs;
third, the like of that just judge, Aṣīl-i Millat u Dīn,
than who heaven remembers no better judge ever breathed;
fourth, the like of that learned judge, 'Aḍud, who in composing
dedicated his commentary on the *Mawāqif* to the king;
fifth, the like of that patron, Ḥājjī Qiwām, whose heart was a sea
and like Ḥātim of old bade all men accept his munificence.
These men have departed, and left none their like behind them;
God most Great and Glorious grant to them all forgiveness!

Ḥāfiẓ next enjoyed the protection of Burhān al-Dīn Fatḥ Allāh, minister to the austere and strictly orthodox Mubāriz al-Dīn. But it was the accession of the latter's more liberal-minded son Shāh Shujā' which marked the turning-point in Ḥāfiẓ' fortunes; during his long but far from tranquil reign, which closed in 1384, his poetic genius discovered scope for its full consummation. Ḥāfiẓ died six years later, having survived long enough to witness the ruin of the Muẓaffarids and the advent of Tīmūr's terror. It may have well been those last convulsions that moved him to cry:

Again the times are out of joint; and again
For wine and the loved one's languid glance I am fain.
The wheel of fortune's sphere is a marvellous thing:
What next proud head to the lowly dust will it bring?
Or if my Magian elder kindle the light,
Whose lantern, pray, will blaze aflame and be bright?
'Tis a famous tale, the deceitfulness of earth;
The night is pregnant: what will dawn bring to birth?
Tumult and bloody battle rage in the plain:
Bring blood-red wine, and fill the goblet again!

It is certain that Ḥāfiẓ enjoyed great fame even during his lifetime. The invitations which he received from Uvais the Jalā'irid to visit Baghdad, and Maḥmūd Shāh the Bahmanid to join him in the Deccan, attest the esteem in which he was held by royal connoisseurs of art. Documentary evidence confirms the tenor of these reports. Thus, in a manuscript of Shams-i Qais's *al-Mu'jam* which was compiled by Ibn Faqīh at Baghdad in 1379 a poem of Ḥāfiẓ was deliberately substituted for one by 'Imādī in the section on how to write good lyrics. In 1380 a group of scholars resident in Shīrāz were commissioned by the vizier to compile an anthology of choice poems; Ḥāfiẓ was cited four times. Mu'īn al-Dīn Yazdī the historian of the Muẓaffarids quoted from Ḥāfiẓ, though not by name, in a composition written in 1387. Even more remarkable, Shāh Shujā' himself in the course of a letter addressed to Sulṭān Uvais of Baghdad quoted the famous line:

What lies behind the curtain, who knows if it be fair or foul?

The first editor of Ḥāfiẓ' collected poems, his lifelong friend Muḥammad Gulandām, in his preface to the *Dīvān* expatiates 'on the poet's incomparable genius, his catholic sympathy, and the celebrity attained by his verse even in his lifetime, not only in Persia, from Fárs to Khurásán and Ádharbáyján, but in India, Turkistán and Mesopotamia.'

What were the qualities in Ḥāfiẓ' poetry which secured for him such high regard amongst his contemporaries, and have established his reputation down the succeeding centuries as the greatest lyric poet of Persia? Gertrude Bell, who early in her adventurous life conceived an enthusiasm for Ḥāfiẓ which compelled her to write a volume of very fine translations, remarked by way of introduction: 'I am very conscious that my appreciation of the poet is that of the Western. Exactly on what grounds he is appreciated in the East it is difficult to determine, and what his compatriots make of his teaching it is perhaps impossible to understand.' These words were written sixty years ago; since then many Persian scholars have put pen to paper in the endeavour to analyse and elucidate the fascination which Ḥāfiẓ' poems have continued to exercise over his countrymen. Before reviewing a selection of these observations, it will be convenient to summarize the history of Ḥāfiẓ studies and interpretation in the West.

News of Ḥāfiẓ' unique fame seems first to have reached Europe in the seventeenth century, being reported by those intrepid travellers, among them Sir Thomas Herbert, who were laying the foundations of East–West trade. It was probably about 1690 that Thomas Hyde (1636–1703) while Bodley's Librarian transcribed into roman characters and translated into Latin the first of Ḥāfiẓ. In 1771 Count C. E. A. de Rewiczki published at Vienna his *Specimen Poeseos Persicae* containing sixteen lyrics of Ḥāfiẓ, complete with Latin translation and commentary. He had then been corresponding for some years with William Jones on the subject of their common enthusiasm, and on March 7, 1768, he had informed him: 'Ghazelam *agar ān Turk-i Shīrāzī* non verti Latino carmine ob versuum incohaerentiam.' This essay in literary criticism was destined to have important consequences. Jones appears to have accepted the theory of Ḥāfiẓ' incoherence, and when he published in his *Grammar of the Persian Language* (1771) and again in his still more influential *Poems consisting chiefly of Translations* (1772) his celebrated paraphrase of the ode which the Persian nobleman had discarded, he made Ḥāfiẓ say in the concluding stanza:

> Go boldly forth, my simple lay,
> Whose accents flow with artless ease,
> Like orient pearls at random strung:
> Thy notes are sweet, the damsels say;
> But O! far sweeter, if they please
> The nymph for whom these notes are sung.

Incidentally, Jones had already printed in 1770 thirteen poems of Ḥāfiẓ done into French rhyme; he also made versions in Latin and Greek verse. In 1774 J. Richardson issued his *Specimen of Persian Poetry*, admittedly based on the work of Count de Rewiczki, and in 1787 J. Nott published his *Select Odes*. These versions by Jones, Richardson and Nott, like others by T. Ford and T. Law printed in the *Asiatick Miscellany* (Calcutta, 1785–6), are characteristic products of the eighteenth century; they flow with easy elegance, and they are not scrupulously faithful. These qualities are well illustrated in the work of Thomas Law (1759–1834), who later settled in the United States and married George Washington's step-granddaughter.

My bosom grac'd with each gay flow'r,
I grasp the bowl, my nymph in glee;
The monarch of the world that hour,
Is but a slave compar'd to me.

Intrude not with the taper's light,
My social friends, with beaming eyes;
Trundle around a starry night,
And lo! my nymph the moon supplies.

Away, thy sprinkling odours spare,
Be not officiously thus kind;
The waving ringlets of my Fair,
Shed perfume to the fainting wind.

My ears th' enlivening notes inspire,
As lute or harp alternate sound;
My eyes those ruby lips admire,
Or catch the glasses sparkling round.

Then let no moments steal away,
Without thy mistress and thy wine;
The spring flow'rs blossom to decay,
And youth but glows to own decline.

Then in 1791 appeared the *editio princeps* of the *Dīvān* of Ḥāfiẓ, printed in *nasta'līq* characters at Upjohn's Calcutta press. Nine years later J. H. Hindley, using manuscripts in the Chetham Library at Manchester, dedicated to Sir William Ouseley (who had published some prose-translations of Ḥāfiẓ in his *Persian Miscellanies* and *Oriental Collections*) his *Persian Lyrics*, a selection of eleven poems from Ḥāfiẓ with prose and verse paraphrases. In a long and thoughtful preface Hindley discussed many problems confronting the translator of Persian poetry, and his remarks merit respectful attention still.

'To give a literal or perfect translation of our author metrically, or even prosaically, into *English*, may be confidently pronounced impossible. An obvious proof of this assertion will be found, on considering for a moment those oppugnancies, which occur so generally in the idiomatic construction of the languages of ENGLAND and IRAN, and which must ever most effectually militate against such closeness of version. Whatever might be looked for from favourable analogies, the frequent and varied allusions from words of similar sound and formation, though generally of exactly opposite signification, as well as the lively and often recondite *lusus verborum*, so common in the *Arabic* and *Persian*, and which, though strange, if not trifling, to a *European* ear, are, to the habitual feelings of the *Asiatic*, both choice and exquisite. These obstacles, I say, must alone render every chance of translative imitation in this case completely hopeless.'

Hindley next passes to another difficulty—the frequent use of compound words in Persian poetry, impossible to reproduce in elegant and idiomatic English. He also refers pertinently to the problems raised by Ḥāfiẓ' habitual use of Ṣūfī imagery. Then he discusses the most fundamental issue of all, the very construction of the Persian lyric with its repetitive monorhyme. 'The constant recurrence of the same rhyme,' he remarks, 'is not suited to our language, which, as has been often observed by critics, will not bear reiterated monotonies.' In such cases the translator must perforce dispense with the minutiae of punctilious imitation, 'provided he strictly confine himself to the prominent ideas of his original, where no eccentricities oppose him.' Later Hindley takes up the charge of incoherency which had been levelled against Ḥāfiẓ, maintaining that he is in fact far less guilty than most of his compatriots; what looseness and variety of images do occur in his poems can be readily condoned in a lyric poet.

'If we attend only to the time, the place, the object, the intention and the imagery of each *Ghazal*, the ideas for the most part appear to flow naturally, and without any absurd or harsh transition: and surely in these lighter rhapsodies, the coruscations of wit, the effusions of tenderness, and the luxuriant sallies of an unrestrained and impassioned imagination, may be fairly presumed to have been aided by the delicious wines, by the joyous symposiacs, and by the instructive and delightful *Macamat* of *Shiraz*, just as similar poetical beauties are reported to have arisen from similarly stimulating and exhilarating causes in that truly *Hafizian* poetry so immediately present to classical recollection, which sings the praises of *Teios*, *Mitylene* and *Falernum*. Under these circumstances, therefore, the translator will only have to allow our author, what he finds in the Grecian and Roman lyric poets, and what we should be willing to allow any poet of our own, the liberty of glancing with the frenzied eye of inspiration from earth to heaven, from heaven to earth, in search of objects adapted to the subject of his composition; and, after attending to the minute turns of the versification, we suspect, it will be his own fault, if he finds an unsurmountable difficulty in explaining his author's meaning in a manner so perceptibly connected as to avoid exciting disgust in an English reader.'

Putting theory into practice, Hindley transmuted into English verse (among other pieces) a poem which Sir William Jones had previously put into French. Jones's translation is a remarkable *tour de force.*

O toi, léger et doux Zéphire,
Quand tu passes par le séjour
Où l'objet de mon tendre amour
Entouré des grâces respire,
Fais qu'au retour, selon mes voeux,
Ton haleine soit parfumée
De cette senteur embaumée
Qu'épand l'ambre de ses cheveux.

Que de son souffle favorable
Mon être seroit ranimé,
Si par toi de mon bien-aimé
J'avois un message agréable!
Si trop foible tu ne peux pas
Porter ce poids, à ma prière
Jette sur moi de la poussière,
Que tu recueilles sous ses pas.

Mon âme languit dans l'attente
De son retour si désiré;
Ah! quand ce visage adoré
Viendra-t-il la rendre contente?
Le pin fut moins haut que mon cœur,
A présent au saule semblable,
Pour cet objet incomparable
Il tremble d'amoureuse ardeur.

Quoique celui que mon cœur aime,
Pour ma tendresse ait peu d'égards,
Hélas! pour un de ses regards
Je donnerois l'univers même.
Que ce seroit un bien pour moi,
Puisqu'à ses pieds le sort m'enchaîne,
De n'avoir d'autre soin ni peine,
De ne vivre que pour mon Roi.

Here for contrast and comparison is Hindley's version.

Zephyr, should'st thou chance to rove
By the mansion of my love,
From her locks ambrosial bring
Choicest odours on thy wing.

Could'st thou waft me from her breast
Tender sighs to say I'm blest,
As she lives! my soul would be
Sprinkl'd o'er with ecstasy.

But if Heav'n the boon deny,
Round her stately footsteps fly,
With the dust that thence may rise,
Stop the tears which bathe these eyes.

Lost, poor mendicant! I roam
Begging, craving she would come:
Where shall I thy phantom see,
Where, dear nymph, a glimpse of thee?

Like the wind-tost reed my breast
Fann'd with hope is ne'er at rest,
Throbbing, longing to excess
Her fair figure to caress.

Yes, my charmer, tho' I see
Thy heart courts no love with me,
Not for worlds, could they be mine,
Would I give a hair of thine.

Why, O care! shall I in vain
Strive to shun thy galling chain,
When these strains still fail to save,
And make Hafiz more a slave.

So far the interpretation of Ḥāfiẓ had been virtually a British monopoly. But the turn of German scholarship was coming presently. In 1812–13 the industrious and indefatigable Joseph von Hammer-Purgstall published at Tübingen a prose rendering of the entire *Dīvān* in over a thousand pages. Two years later, on June 7, 1814, Goethe inscribed in his diary for the first time a reference to the poems of the Persian 'Korankenner.' From 1816 to 1818 the great man was energetically pursuing his oriental studies; in 1819 he published his *West-östlicher Divan* with its elaborate apparatus of 'Noten und Abhandlungen zu besserem Verständniss.' It is surely of the highest interest to examine the impression made by the greatest Persian lyrical poet on the greatest literary genius of Germany, and it will not be superfluous to reproduce here the text of Goethe's 'An Hafis.'

Was alle wollen weisst du schon
Und hast es wohl verstanden:
Denn Sehnsucht hält, von Staub zu Thron,
Uns all in strengen Banden.

Es tut so weh, so wohl hernach,
Wer sträubte sich dagegen?
Und wenn den Hals der eine brach,
Der andre bleibt verwegen.

Verzeihe, Meister, wie du weisst
Dass ich mich oft vermesse,
Wenn sie das Auge nach sich reisst
Die wandelnde Zypresse.

Wie Wurzelfasern schleicht ihr Fuss
Und buhlet mit dem Boden;
Wie leicht Gewölk verschmilzt ihr Gruss,
Wie Ost-Gekof' ihr Oden.

Das alles drängt uns ahndevoll,
Wo Lock und Locke kräuselt,
In brauner Fülle ringelnd schwoll,
Sodann im Winde säuselt.

Nun öffnet sich die Stirne klar,
Dein Herz damit zu glätten,
Vernimmst ein Lied so froh und wahr,
Den Geist darin zu betten.

Und wenn die Lippen sich dabei
Aufs niedlichste bewegen:
Sie machen dich auf einmal frei
In Fesseln dich zu legen.

Der Atem will nicht mehr zurück,
Die Seel zur Seele fliehend,
Gerüche winden sich durchs Glück
Unsichtbar wolkig ziehend.

Doch wenn es allgewaltig brennt,
Dann greifst du nach der Schale:
Der Schenke läuft, der Schenke kömmt
Zum erst- und zweitenmale.

Sein Auge blitzt, sein Herz erbebt,
Er hofft auf deine Lehren,
Dich, wenn der Wein den Geist erhebt,
Im höchsten Sinn zu hören.

Ihm öffnet sich der Welten Raum,
Im Innern Heil und Orden,
Es schwillt die Brust, es bräunt der Flaum,
Er ist ein Jüngling worden.

Und wenn dir kein Geheimnis blieb
Was Herz und Welt enthalte,
Dem Denker winkst du treu und lieb,
Dass sich der Sinn entfalte.

Auch dass vom Throne Fürstenhort
Sich nicht für uns verliere,
Gibst du dem Schach ein gutes Wort
Und gibst es dem Vesire.

Das alles kennst und singst du heut
Und singst es morgen eben:
So trägt uns freundlich dein Geleit
Durchs rauhe milde Leben.

About the year 1845 E. B. Cowell, later to be Professor of Sanskrit at Cambridge but at that time a lad of nineteen living in Ipswich, began to publish in literary magazines occasional prose versions of Ḥāfiẓ. He showed these to his friend Edward FitzGerald (whom he would begin to teach Persian in 1852), and some time in 1846 FitzGerald told him, 'Your Hafiz is fine: and his tavern world is a sad and just idea. . . . It would be a good work to give us some of the good things of Hafiz and the Persians; of bulbuls and ghuls we have had enough.' On June 8, 1854, FitzGerald was staying with Alfred Tennyson in Freshwater, and announced to Cowell: 'Tennyson and I have been trying at some Hafiz in Sir W. Jones' Poeseos. Will you correct and send back the enclosed as *soon as you can*—giving us the *metre* and sound of any words very necessary to the music—Also tell us of any Odes to be got at in the Poeseos and Elsewhere, giving us the *metre*. A. T. *will* only look at Hafiz—in whom he takes some interest.' On October 14, 1854, FitzGerald brought Cowell's versions of Ḥāfiẓ to the notice of Thomas Carlyle: 'Please to look at the September Number of Fraser's Magazine where are some prose Translations of Hafiz by Cowell which may interest you a little. I think Cowell (as he is apt to do) gives Hafiz rather too much credit for a mystical wine-cup, and Cupbearer; I mean taking him on the whole. The few odes he quotes have certainly a deep and pious feeling; such as the Man of Mirth will feel at times; none perhaps more strongly.' But neither Tennyson nor

Carlyle reacted to Ḥāfiẓ as Goethe had done. FitzGerald persevered longer in his interest, and on January 22, 1857, he was able to report: 'I have gone carefully over two-thirds of Hafiz again with Dictionary and Von Hammer.' But 'Umar Khaiyām now monopolized his attention, and Ḥāfiẓ soon afterwards dropped out of his life and letters.

In those same years H. Brockhaus had been busy on his edition of *Die Lieder des Hafis* with Sūdī's commentary (3 volumes, Leipzig 1854–60); V. von Rosenzweig-Schwannau was active on another edition, this accompanied by a German verse-translation of the whole *Dīvān* (3 volumes, Vienna 1858–64). In 1875 the selections with metrical renderings made by H. Bicknell, who had been to Mecca disguised as a pilgrim and had resided in Shīrāz 'with the object of clearing up doubtful points, and becoming personally acquainted with the localities mentioned by the poet,' were posthumously edited by C. E. Wilson; and in 1891 H. Wilberforce Clarke printed in over a thousand large pages a prose translation of the entire *Dīvān* which is curious rather than reliable. These are the highlights in the story of a continuing preoccupation with Ḥāfiẓ in a number of countries. But the most successful nineteenth-century interpretation was the *Poems from the Divan of Hafiz* published by young Gertrude Bell in 1897, an extract from whose prefatory remarks has already been quoted. In the following year that celebrated Homeric scholar Walter Leaf produced his *Versions from Hafiz* which he sub-titled 'An Essay in Persian Metre.' In his introduction he gave reasons for departing from the kind of views on how to translate Ḥāfiẓ which J. H. Hindley had advanced nearly a century before.

'Those who want them have not far to seek for translations of Hafiz. . . . They may scent in our Western winds the aroma from his Eastern garden, perfumed with musk of Tartary; they may gaze on the flame of rose and tulip, or taste of the tart and heady Persian wine, and wind their fingers in the ringlets of the beloved. But to the fifth sense of hearing not one, I think, has attempted to appeal, and the song of the Bulbul of Shiraz has fallen upon European ears only in measures transformed at best, often only in the wingless words of prose. But for Hafiz, at least as much as for any poet, form is of the essence of his poetry. More indeed than for the poets whom we know best. We have learnt from our Greek masters to seek the unity of a poem in the thought or mood developed in it. Whether sensuous or intellectual, the unity is internal and essential. To a Persian poet this is not so; and that is a hard lesson which we must learn before we can do full justice to Eastern art. In the Persian ode we find a succession of couplets often startling in their independence, in their giddy transitions from grave to gay, from thought to mood. . . . It is from the common metre and common rhyme alone that an ode gains a formal unity. . . . For all these reasons it seems worthwhile to make an attempt, however poor, to give English readers some idea of this most intimate and indissoluble bond of spirit and form in Hafiz. And with it all, one must try to convey some faint reminder of the fact that Hafiz is, as few poets have been, a master of words and rhythms.'

Leaf consequently made his experiment of translating eighteen of Ḥāfiẓ' lyrics into English verse, monorhymed and metred in conformity with their originals.

All bounds my heart is breaking; friends, haste to my salvation!
Woe's me! My secret hidden cries loud for proclamation.

'Mid reefs my bark is grounded; blow fair, O breeze of mercy;
Mayhap we win the Friend yet, Love's goal of navigation.

This ten-day smile of heaven swift passes like a tale told!
Be gracious while thou mayest, brook not procrastination . . .

More sweet to me than kisses, more soft than maiden's cheeks
are,
That bitter named of Sufis 'Dam of abomination.'

When comes the hour of sadness, turn thou to wine and gladness;
Kārūns of beggars maketh wine's chemic transmutation.

Wine-flecked is HAFIZ' cassock, yet not of choice he dons it;
Ah, Shaikh of hem unspotted, hear thou my exculpation!

It seems extraordinary that so eminent a critic of Greek literature could have been complacent to convey such a totally misleading and unworthy impression of Ḥāfiẓ to the unsuspecting public. But much more in this line was to follow very quickly. In 1901 John Payne, already widely known for his versions of the *Arabian Nights*, Boccaccio and Villon, brought out in three elegant volumes *The Poems of Shemseddin Mohammed Hafiz of Shiraz*, 'now first completely done into English verse from the Persian, in accordance with the original forms.' His picture of Ḥāfiẓ was certainly not lacking in sentimentality.

'Unbound by our laws and unfettered by our prescriptions, above our approof and beyond our blame, such as Hafiz are not to be tried by our standards or condemned by our limitations; they have an inalienable title to the privilege which forms the foundation of our English judicial system; they can only be judged by their peers. Like Shakespeare, like Socrates, like Mendelssohn, Hafiz was one of the children of the bridechamber, who mourn not, for the bridegroom is with them. Happy, thrice happy those rare elect ones among the servants of the Ideal, to whom it is given, through shower and sunshine and without default against their august vocation, to cull the rose of hilarity from the storm-swept meads of life, who are gifted to respire with impunity the intoxicating breath of the lilies and jessamines of love and joy. . . . These are the Parthenogeniti of life; they need no purification, as do those who have come out of great tribulation and have made white their robes in the blood of the

Lamb; intemperate and free were they born, as the flowers of the field, and pure and incontaminable shall they abide for ever. Like Ben Jonson's lily of a day, they are the plants and flowers of light; they toil not, neither do they spin; yet eternity is full of their glory.'

One wonders what Ḥāfiẓ would have thought of the suggestion that he toiled not at his exacting craft. So Payne insensitively twisted his delicate and entrancing originals into the most extraordinary contortions of forced rhyme and laboured rhythm.

> For our pain no cure, ywis, is. Help! oh help!
> For our woes no end in bliss is. Help! oh help!
>
> Faith and heart they've ta'en and threaten now the soul:
> 'Gainst these cruel cockatrices Help! oh help!
>
> Help, against the heart-enslavers pitiless,
> Souls who seek in price of kisses! Help! oh help!
>
> See, our blood they drink, these stony-hearted trulls!
> Muslims, say, what cure for this is? Help! oh help!
>
> Day and night I fare distracted, weep and burn,
> As the wont of me, Hafiz, is. Help! oh help!

Other versions from Ḥāfiẓ have appeared sporadically over the last fifty years; but it may be fairly said that, the great endeavours of a number of hopeful Victorians having failed to secure for the Shīrāzī poet even a tithe of the popularity so surprisingly and belatedly enjoyed by the much less considerable 'Umar Khaiyām, their successors have largely given up the struggle and accepted the unpredictable verdict of public taste. Meanwhile during the second quarter of the twentieth century the comparative neglect which Ḥāfiẓ has suffered in Europe has been more than offset by the renewed and enhanced enthusiasm with which he has been studied in Persia. Today it is no longer permissible to protest, as Gertrude Bell justly did in 1897, that 'it is difficult to determine exactly on what grounds he is appreciated in the East,' and 'perhaps impossible to understand what his compatriots make of his teaching.' Yet as recently as 1944 a writer in *Essays and Studies by Members of the English Association* was still echoing what de Rewiczki had said in 1768; discussing *Agar ān Turk-i Shīrāzī* and Jones's version of it, Professor R. M. Hewitt remarked that 'this poem of Hafiz is more than usually incoherent, and what unity it possesses comes from the rhyme which is the same throughout and occurs ten times.'

It would not be difficult, or superfluous, to compile a book out of the things that Persians have written about Ḥāfiẓ since 1925. His *Dīvān* has employed the best energies of several learned editors; his life and writings have been discussed in a multitude of erudite and not-so-erudite articles. Here it is only possible to make a very small selection; but the selection has been made with some discrimination. Some passages now quoted briefly will be found set out at greater length in my *Fifty Poems of Ḥāfiẓ* (Cambridge), where specimens illustrating the work of many English translators have also been given.

In 1942 Dr. Qāsim Ghanī, who with Mīrzā Muḥammad Qazvīnī had the previous year produced what must be regarded as the most reliable text so far of the *Dīvān* of Ḥāfiẓ, brought out the first volume of what was to have been an extremely extensive (and most valuable) study of the life and works against the background of political and literary history. A second volume appeared almost simultaneously, but the key section on the poet's biography and the critical appraisal of his poems has never seen the light of day; and Dr. Ghanī has now, alas, been dead for some years. In a preface to the first volume Mīrzā Muḥammad reports a conversation which he once had with Qāsim Ghanī.

'I remember one day we were talking about the poets of Persia, and Dr. Ghanī asked me whom I considered to be the greatest of them. "As is well known," I replied, "poetry is made up of two elements—words, and meaning. The true poet and skilled artificer maintains a proper balance between the two factors of words and meaning, and does not exceed or fall short in respect of either. That is, he does not devote himself more than is necessary to beautifying his words and ornamenting his expressions, by employing elegant verbal artifices such as *tajnīs* (play on words), *ishtiqāq* (prosonomasia), *tarṣīʿ* (correspondence), *takrīr* (repetition), *qalb* (anagram), *taṣḥīf* (change of points), *taushīḥ* (acrostic), *siyāqat al-aʿdād* (proposition of multiples), *luzūm mā lā yalzam* (double rhyme), letters *ʿuṭl* (unpointed) and *manqūṭ* (pointed), *muttaṣil* (joined) and *munfaṣil* (unjoined), and similar devices that are more like children's pastimes than rules governing elegant prose and poetry for serious men. Neither does the true poet so concern himself with refining his meaning by indulging in fine-spun fancies, involved ideas, highly abstruse similes and unintelligible references as to complicate his language and obscure his intention, making it necessary for the hearer to think hard guessing what he is driving at—such for example as characterizes the so-called 'Indian' poets. Moreover, he does not exaggerate the employment of such elegant artifices as *murāʿāt al-naẓīr* (parallelism), *ṭibāq* (matching), *īhām* (amphibology), *ibhām* (ambiguity), *tafrīʿ* (evolution), *istiṭrād* (feigning), *talmīḥ* (allusion), *jamʿ* (combination), *taqsīm* (discrimination) and the like, to the point of overloading his expression and fatiguing the hearer. It is obvious of course that the skilful use of any of these artifices, either singly or in combination with one or two others, contributes definitely to elegance of style; but when these devices are multiplied to excess, and above all when a number of them are crowded together in a single verse, or in close proximity, they produce an exceedingly artificial appearance and are in fact an affront to the very art of poetry; and they will end by wearying and exhausting the audience. If we study the works of all the Persian poets of the first class, attentively, it will become clear that every one of them, in addition to his own inborn faculty and God-given genius, has paid scrupulous observance to this point, namely, the maintenance of a balance between words and meanings, and the avoiding of excess or deficiency in either respect. . . ."

'After this statement, Dr. Ghanī asked, "Suppose for instance we now wish to choose from among all these masters of the first class, including every variety and group, moderns and ancients alike, and suppose we intend to exhibit before the world the greatest of them all—whom would you choose?" This was my answer. "The reply to this question has been generally agreed on for centuries, and the problem has been finally disposed of. Despite all differences of individual inclination and preference, despite the general divergence of opinion entertained by people on most matters, practically all are agreed on this one question; that the greatest poets of the Persian language since the coming of Islam to the present time (each one in his special variety) are the six following—Firdausī, Khaiyām, Anvarī, Rūmī, Sa'dī, Ḥāfiẓ. In my view, one can confidently add to these six the great philosopher Nāṣir-i Khusrau, since all the characteristic merits and artistic qualities that have established these six in the front rank of Persian poets are completely and in every respect present in the person of Nāṣir-i Khusrau. . . ."

'Again Dr. Ghanī persisted in his inquisition. "If," he said, "for the sake of example, some foreign country, say England, proposed to us that it was desired to erect a statue—in Hyde Park maybe—to the greatest poets of every nation on earth—the greatest, that is, by the general consensus of his compatriots—and that only one poet, and no more, was to be chosen by each nation; which of these six would you personally select as being in your view, and that of most men, the most truly poetical of the poets of Persia?" "In my view," I answered, "and I think this view coincides with the opinion held by the great majority of Persian scholars, as well as by non-Persians who have either known Persian or become acquainted with Ḥāfiẓ through the medium of translations, it may be that out of all the Persian poets of the first class—I have already named a great number of them to my good friend, and I leave you to find the names of the rest in the biographies and anthologies—without any exception whatsoever, the man whose poems embrace and contain every beauty alike of language and meaning to be found in poetry, every quality of image and reality that exists in fine speech, and who is at the same time the most eloquent and melodious writer of every age, ancient and modern included, the man who, compared with all the poetic stars of the first magnitude, is as a shining sun—without any doubt or hesitation that man is Khvāja Shams al-Ḥaqq wa'l-Milla wa'l-Dīn Muḥammad Ḥāfiẓ Shīrāzī, may God sanctify his great soul! As another great poet, Jāmī, who was also almost his contemporary, declares in his *Bahāristān*, his poetry, with all its sweetness, delicacy, freshness, ease, elegance, flow, agreeableness and unaffectedness, is something very near a miracle; it is a just object of pride not only for Persians, it is a source of glory for all mankind." '

In the same year, 1942, Dr. Riḍā-zāda Shafaq published his *History of Persian Literature*, a most interesting manual for Persian schools from which quotation has been made many times in these pages. In his section on Ḥāfiẓ the following passages occur.

'With the fine sensitivity and acute susceptibility which irradiate the Khvāja's poetry, it is remarkable how this liberal-hearted poet preserved the strength and serenity of his poetic imagination in the face of the bloody events of his time. All Persia was in the throes of insurrection and conflict; Fārs, and Shīrāz itself, did not escape this battle; and Ḥāfiẓ with his own eyes witnessed the slaying of kings, the devastation of houses, the wars of pretenders, even the quarrels between members of a single family, such as for instance the Muẓaffarids; yet he seems to have regarded these events from some spiritual eminence as if they were the little waves of an ocean; his gaze was rather fixed on the unity of the ocean of nature, the meaning and purpose of the world. It is true that on occasion his mind rebelled, and in deep emotion he would say:

> What is this anarchy that I see in the lunatic sphere?
> I see all horizons full of strife and sedition.

But he always returned to his mental composure, and sought for tranquility of heart in a world tumultuous beneath the wings of his broad, celestial thoughts.

'This mystical steadfastness of Ḥāfiẓ is apparent even in his *qaṣīdas*; he belongs to that class of poets who rarely indulged in panegyric, was never guilty of hyperbole. He was not the man to flatter for flattery's sake; he never surrendered his steadfastness of purpose. Though every prince in his turn was powerful and all-conquering, Ḥāfiẓ never debased his language, nor transgressed the bounds of legitimate applause. He did not hesitate on occasion to proffer counsel, reminding them in penetrating and moving verses of the truth that every man in the end gets his deserts, that fate rewards and punishes every act, and reckons king and beggar equal and alike.

'Ḥāfiẓ' spiritual greatness and mental power proceeded from that mystical consciousness which in him attained perfection. That path of life of which Sanā'ī, 'Aṭṭār, Jalāl al-Dīn and Sa'dī had spoken each in turn and in his own way, was by Ḥāfiẓ described in language that plumbs the depths of feeling and soars to the heights of expression. Subjects of which others had spoken in detail, in his choice, brief lyrics found better and sweeter treatment. So deeply immersed was he in the mystic unity, that in every ode and lyric, whatever its formal subject, he included one or more verses expressive of this lofty theme. This indeed is perhaps the greatest individual feature of Ḥāfiẓ' poetry. . . .

'His true mastery is in the lyric. In Ḥāfiẓ' hands the mystical lyric on the one hand reached the summit of eloquence and beauty, and on the other manifested a simplicity all its own. As we have already said, in short words he stated ideas mighty and subtle. Quite apart from the sweetness, simplicity and conciseness which are apparent in every lyric of Ḥāfiẓ, a spirit of genuine sincerity pervades every line. It is evident that the master's lyrics come straight from the heart; each poem is a subtle expression of the poet's innermost thoughts. . . .

'Especially in his lyrics, Ḥāfiẓ in addition to the spark he borrowed from the fire of the *ghazals* of 'Aṭṭār and Rūmī, also took something from the style of his own age. In this respect he showed himself a disciple particularly of the style of such predecessors and contemporaries as Sa'dī, Khvājū, Salmān-i Sāvajī, Auḥadī and 'Imād-i Faqīh; many of the master's verses and lyrics are parallel to theirs. . . . Yet for all this Ḥāfiẓ was by no means content to be a mere imitator: he had his own style, and imparted a new lustre to the words. If his poetry is more often quoted than that of Khvājū and Salmān, this is due not solely to his spirituality, his greatness and his mystical influence; its celebrity is explained in part by the sweetness of his melody and the fluency and firmness of his verse. The poet himself, with that fine talent, that subtlety of taste and gift of revelation which he indisputably possessed, was well aware of the merit of his own composition, and it was in full and sure belief that he said:

> O Ḥāfiẓ, I have not seen anything lovelier than thy poetry;
> I swear it, by the Koran thou hast in thy bosom.

Indeed Ḥāfiẓ, with that high talent, spiritual subtlety, natural gift of language, minute meditation, mystical experience and passionate gnosis which were vouchsafed to him, evolved such a construction of words and a mingling of varied expressions and ideas that he created an independent style and characteristic form of mystical lyric; so much so that connoisseurs of Persian literature can immediately recognize his poetry and identify his accent. . . .'

At the end of the previous chapter some examples were given of poems in which Ḥāfiẓ quoted from or imitated the work of earlier poets. Many more instances of this poetic emulation are to be found in the long introduction of Ḥusain Pizhmān to his edition of the *Dīvān* of Ḥāfiẓ. While conceding the particularly strong influence which the work of Khvājū exercised on the development of Ḥāfiẓ—so strong that some critics have called Ḥāfiẓ Khvājū's pupil—Pizhmān has also established references to many other poets including Sa'dī, Auḥadī, Kamāl al-Dīn Ismā'īl, Mas'ūd-i Sa'd, Firdausī, Sanā'ī, 'Imād-i Faqīh, 'Irāqi, Humām al-Dīn Tabrīzī, Salmān-i Sāvajī (though as he was a contemporary of Ḥāfiẓ it is impossible to determine for certain which poet borrowed from which), Ẓahīr al-Dīn Fāryābī and 'Umar Khaiyām. A good proportion of the passages quoted disclose verbal correspondences so close that it cannot be doubted that Ḥāfiẓ was intending that his borrowings should be recognized. This indeed, far from being thought a fault, would be accepted as proof of an admirable erudition, and moreover—if the later poet could sensibly improve on his predecessor's turn of thought or language—as certain evidence of artistic superiority. Sometimes the connection is rather more tenuous, and can perhaps be dismissed as an accidental coincidence of phraseology. But neither Pizhmān nor Shiblī Nu'mānī has dealt with a far more pervasive phenomenon, the incessant emulation which was the inevitable consequence of the acceptance by all Persian poets of a comparatively narrow repertory of themes and images. Readers interested to have more on this subject may care to glance at my article 'Orient Pearls at Random Strung' contributed to the Sir William Jones bicentenary issue of the *Bulletin of the School of Oriental and African Studies*.

Thus, let us glance once more at the opening couplet of the most famous and most frequently translated of all Ḥāfiẓ' lyrics.

Agar ān Turk-i Shīrāẓī ba-dast ārad dil-i mā-rā
ba-khāl-i Hindu-y-ash bakhsham Samarqand ū Bukhārā-rā

It is incidentally fascinating to examine what the various translators have made of this. First, Jones himself:

Sweet maid, if thou wouldst charm my sight,
And bid these arms thy neck infold;
That rosy cheek, that lily hand,
Would give thy poet more delight
Than all Bocara's vaunted gold,
Than all the gems of Samarcand.

More than a century later Gertrude Bell, taking in the second couplet as well, gave this rendering:

O Turkish maid of Shiraz! in thy hand
If thou'lt take my heart, for the mole on thy cheek
I would barter Bokhara and Samarkand.
Bring, Cup-bearer, all that is left of thy wine!
In the Garden of Paradise vainly thou'lt seek
The lip of the fountain of Ruknabad,
And the bowers of Mosalla where roses twine.

Walter Leaf made the same passage into the following:

An if yon Turk of Shīrāz land this heart would take to hold in fee,
Bokhārā town and Samarcand to that black mole my dower should be.
Ho, Sākī, pour the wineflask dry; in Eden's bowers we ne'er shall find
Musallā's rosy bed, nor streams of Ruknābād's delightsome lea.

John Payne put the two couplets this way:

So but that Turk of Shiraz take My heart within her hand of snow,
Bokhara, ay, and Samarcand On her black mole will I bestow.

Give, cupbearer, the wine that's left; For thou'lt not find in Paradise
The banks of Ruknabád nor yet Musella's rosegarths all a-glow.

Richard Le Gallienne in his *Odes from the Divan of Hafiz* (London, 1905) required to gather the first three couplets of the original to form the first stanza of his paraphrase.

You little Turk of Shiraz-Town,
Freebooter of the hearts of men,
As beautiful, as says renown,
As your freebooting Turcomen;
Dear Turco-maid—a plunderer too—
Here is my heart, and there your hand:
If you'll exchange, I'll give to you
Bokhara—yes! and Samarcand.
Indeed, I'll give them for the mole
Upon your cheek, and add thereto
Even my body and my soul.

The wordy paraphrase spills over into a further twenty-one lines which can be easily spared in this brief review. E. G. Browne offered his own version of the ode, beginning thus:

If that unkindly Shíráz Turk would take my heart within her hand,
I'd give Bukhárá for the mole upon her cheek, or Samarqand!

P. L. Stallard in his *Renderings from the Dewan of Khwaja Shamsu'ddin Muhammad Hafiz Shirazi* (Basil Blackwell, 1937) opened frivolously enough:

Should that little chit of Shiraz
    Bear my heart within her hand,
For her cheek's swart mole I'd barter
    Bukhara and Samarcand!

The phrase *Turk-i Shīrāzī* was obviously borrowed from a line of Sa'dī:

No one suffers such cruelty at the hand of a Turk of Cathay
as I suffer at the hand of the Turk of Shīrāz.

The idea of calling a mole 'Hindu' and contrasting its blackness with the famous and attractive pallor of a Turkish complexion was also thought of by Sa'dī:

A stranger much beloved is the Hindu mole
alighted on the Turkistan of her face.

The same contrast of Indian and Turk, combined with the conceit of bartering even more extensive territories in exchange for the beloved's beauty, was already invented by Sa'dī:

They yield the dwellings of India and all the climes of the
    Turks
when they behold your Turkish eye and your Indian tress.

But a whole chapter would be required to bring out all the echoes and subtle implications of this miraculous poem; and this is only one of five hundred lyrics, each equally beautiful and each equally charged (for the understanding reader) with a superfluity of marvellous overtones. To return to what Persians have lately written about Ḥāfiẓ: among the Master's most devoted and original admirers is the contemporary scholar and poet Mas'ūd Farzād, who planned long ago but has not yet accomplished what would be a most valuable aid to future studies, a variorum edition of the *Dīvān*. He has published a number of papers in Persian and English on various aspects of his work, but here we shall quote only from his lecture *Haafez and his Poems* delivered at the Islamic Cultural Centre, London, on January 6, 1949.

'What are the seven poetic wonders of the world? Shakespeare's and Milton's Works are certainly two of them. Dante's *Divine Comedy* and Goethe's *Faust* are in all probability two others. May I suggest that Jelaaleddin Mowlavi Rumi's *Masnavi* and Haafez's *Divan* (or collected lyrics) should receive serious consideration in this connection? True, the suggestion comes from one who *happens* to have the honour of being a compatriot of Rumi and Haafez, but this, let me hope, will not give rise to a charge of Chauvinism, for no less a scholar-poet than Sir William Jones many decades ago expressed the opinion that "Masnavi" was comparable in worth with Shakespeare's works. After such a verdict it would follow almost automatically that the collected lyrics of Haafez, too, belong to the same exalted company.

'We are all familiar with the common English saying to the effect that in any English home where there is a Bible there is to be found a Shakespeare also. Significantly enough, the Persians have an exact counterpart of this saying for the Qor'an and Haafez respectively.

'We have little positive indication that Shakespeare was famous outside England in his lifetime; and we learn from the scholars that even after his death (particularly before the last ten or fifteen decades) there were periods during which the general public did not know Shakespeare adequately. Is it not, therefore, a remarkable fact that (in spite of the undoubtedly less favourable state of communications in fourteenth century Persia as compared with Elizabethan England) the poems of Haafez, even in his life-time, reached the hearts of many thousands of people, commoners as well as kings, in towns many hundreds of miles apart; and furthermore, that the moon of this popularity has never waned, but has steadily gained in brilliance ever since?

'Two facts may enhance the sense of wonder which some of us would feel because of this stupendous historical phenomenon. One is that the interval of time between the writing days of Haafez and ourselves is considerably longer than the corresponding period in the case of Shakespeare; these, in round figures, being six centuries and three and a half centuries respectively. The other is that the printing press, as an aid to the dissemination of knowledge, rendered definite and early service to Shakespeare, but not to Haafez. Some of Shakespeare's plays, as everyone knows, were published even in his lifetime; and no longer than seven years after his death, a collection comprising as much as two-thirds of his writings was published by his personal friends. The first printed edition of Haafez's poems, however, appeared more than four centuries after his death: while the first serious attempts at publishing a *critical* edition of his poems were made only about fifty years ago. I should, of course, emphasize that I am not making a comparison between Shakespeare and Haafez. No such comparison would be relevant, for Shakespeare was essentially and mainly a dramatic, and Haafez exclusively a lyric poet. I am merely trying to convey, through comparison with cultural and social phenomena well-known to the Western world, the measure and extent, in time and place, of the popularity and the influence of this prince of Persian, and perhaps of all, lyric poets.'

In his interesting paper Farzād inevitably takes up the familiar paradox of 'Umar Khaiyām's greater vogue through FitzGerald's mediumship, and 'wonders why FitzGerald who did try his hand at the translation of two other Persian poets (Jaami and Attaar) did not choose Haafez also for the purpose.' He reviews the problems facing the would-be translator of Ḥāfiẓ, chief among which is the lack of a really satisfactory edition of the *Dīvān*. In the course of setting out the prerequisites for such an edition, Farzād makes some important and original remarks on what he calls the 'miracle of continuity' in the structure of the Ḥāfiẓian lyric.

'In connection with the problem of the order of the lines, which I was perhaps the first person to stumble upon and to declare, I should like to mention that formerly the ghazal was likened to a pearl necklace, each pearl representing a beyt (or verse-unit) and the string representing the rhyme and metre. It was pointed out that there was no link, other than the string, between the pearls; and that the pearls could be rearranged, and even have their numbers reduced or increased, without destroying or even damaging the identity of the entity, the necklace. . . . I agree that, at first glance, some of the best Persian ghazals would seem to be of loose construction; and that many mediocre and inferior Persian ghazals, especially later ones, are so in fact. At the same time I should declare that I have not found this loose construction at all true in the case of a single one of the ghazals of Haafez. . . . One fundamental fact seems to me to be that in the ghazal of Haafez there exists an unuttered but clearly suggested train of thought (or silent verse, as it were) between each verse-unit and the next. If we do not recognize this, then indeed the written beyts or verse-units may seem somewhat disconnected, and we may justifiably agree with a Haafezian critic who described as a "model of incoherence" one of Haafez's ghazals which appeared to him to be a particularly bad offender in this respect. If, however, we do realize the existence of this latent and suggested thought-content, we will find that, by the simple process of association of ideas (which "modern" psychology "discovered" and labelled several centuries after Haafez knew about it and used it) he has linked every verse with the next in every single one of his poems, ghazal or otherwise; and has thus created within the poem a complete literary sequence which is as solid as a steel chain, and as beautiful as a golden one.'

Much more in this fascinating lecture is deserving of the closest attention, and much must be omitted in this necessarily brief epitome, which will be concluded with Farzād's portrait of 'the man Haafez.'

'We have heard much about the scantiness of material for a biography of Haafez. We are, however, in possession of certain facts and certain significant fables concerning his life. We know more than a little about his times. A special study of his poems will, I believe, add to this mass of information considerably, and supply us with most of the points we wish to know about the inner life of his heart and mind, and about the type of facts and incidents that affected him so deeply as to result in the writing of his existing poems. Before such a study is completed, the answer to the all-important question "What manner of man was Haafez?" must necessarily be fragmentary and conditional.

'So far as we can see now, Haafez was one of the many people who combined a religious life with the writing of poetry. One almost immediately thinks of John Donne as an English parallel to him. Yes, there are many resemblances between the two men, and these include not only the poetry they both wrote but also the unorthodox and, if you like, the irregular life they both led. The most Haafezian of the English authors, however, is I believe Charles Lamb, although he was chiefly a prose-writer. A whole talk could be devoted to the scores upon scores of passages in Lamb's essays which bear striking testimony to the similarity of attitude between him and Haafez. A pun on such an occasion may not be quite respectable but I hope to be pardoned if I cannot refrain from calling Haafez the Persian Lamb.

'What strikes me as the most essential characteristic of the man Haafez is that his emotional and intellectual reactions in the face of life's situations were, above all, rational. And being lord both of language and literary design, he succeeded in transforming the dictates of this crystalline common sense into poems of unsurpassable beauty in a language that is second to none in the beauty of her poetry. . . .

'Like all men of good sense and deep sensibility, Haafez finds himself on more than one occasion a stranger among his fellows; at war with some of his social superiors; hating, and hated by, hypocrites; struck dumb by loud, unscrupulous, mendacious mediocrities; wondering why such people and things should be. He finds that (to borrow an immortal phrase from Shakespeare) "cold reason" has, in his own case at least, failed to solve the problem of life's complexities, where all the most essential facts seem perpetually and deliberately to be hidden behind a psychological curtain more solid and more effective than any iron curtain. Furthermore, no means other than this same poor, inadequate reason has been vouchsafed to man for the solution of this painful riddle.

'Finding himself and his fellow-humans incapable of answering these burning questions he tries two diametrically opposite solutions. One, as symbolized by Wine (and sometimes Love) is the path of unreason, of the unconscious. The other as symbolized by the Elder of the Wise Men (*piir e morghàn*) is objective; for this is the path of Pure Reason, and he is the Complete Man who knows the truth, and the secret of life; and is incidentally (or perhaps consequently) cheerful, tranquil, and tolerant: a man, in short, whom every seeker should strive to resemble as nearly, or at least to follow as closely, as possible.'

It is obvious that the last word on Ḥāfiẓ is very far from having been written as yet. In my *Fifty Poems of Ḥāfiẓ* I have offered some speculative analyses of the structure of his lyrics, and attempted to deduce a stylistic criterion for dating the individual poems. Others have expressed and will express very different views. We shall remain, as we have been hitherto, benighted wanderers in this wilderness of thought and expression until the whole vast desert of Persian poetry has been expertly surveyed and signposted. Some questions of a primary and fundamental nature are still unanswered. What, for instance, is the origin and significance of the poet's signature, so curious a feature of the Persian lyric? Why did the lyric displace the ode in popularity during the fourteenth century? To what extent is it permissible to regard the lyric as a personal confession? Or is the lyric in fact merely a shorter panegyric, designed for singing instead of recitation? How authentic is the mysticism which now becomes the dominant characteristic of these poems? What is the true meaning of the references to love and wine, to roses and nightingales?

It can be plausibly argued that many of the lyrics of Ḥāfiẓ which appear at first sight to record the poet's private emotions and experiences are after all disguised elaborations of the oldest motive in Persian poetry—adulation of the royal patron and a begging for his very material favour. It is well to remember that the Ṣafavid rulers of Persia, from Ismā'īl I who established that powerful dynasty at the beginning of the sixteenth century down to the infant 'Abbās II whose death in 1737 encouraged Nādir Shāh to extinguish the line, boasted of their descent from a certain Shaikh Ṣafī al-Dīn, a Ṣūfī claimant of 'Alid blood, who died in 1334. Were the contenders for Empire in Ḥāfiẓ' lifetime buttressing their pretensions to a divine right of kings by similar devices? The disappearance of the Baghdad caliphate had left a political vacuum which many would be ambitious to fill. Ṣūfīs thought that they had attained union with God, or (as in the poetry of Ibn al-Fāriḍ) with the eternal Spirit of Muḥammad, at the height of their ecstasies, making them Perfect Men; and chiefs of these multiplying Orders did not hesitate to call themselves, even if with a new connotation, caliphs. Might not the ambitious man of affairs, by playing the mysterious charade of likening his court to a mystic circle, with himself as the head of the brotherhood, rest his title to be obeyed on divine election, now that the old pontificate had been exploded?

These are searching and exciting questions which will, it may be hoped, engage the attention of future researchers. But even if they all come to be answered, whatever the outcome of the great investigation, the magic of Ḥāfiẓ' poetry will continue to cast its spell, and men will still wonder at the inner meaning of his wonderfully melodious and simple but baffling words.

I

Monarch of firs that stately rise,
Of honeyed lips sole emperor,
The arrows of whose flashing eyes
Transfix the bravest conqueror—

Lately in wine as passing by
This lowly beggar he espied,
'O thou,' he said, 'the lamp and eye
Of such as make sweet words their pride!

How long of silver and of gold
Shall thy poor purse undowered be?
Be thou my slave, and then, behold!
All silver limbs shall cherish thee.

Art thou a mote, my little one?
Be not so humble: play at love!
And thou shalt whisper to the sun,
Whirling within its sphere above.

Put not thy trust in this world's vows;
But if thou canst a goblet get,
Enjoy the arched and lovely brows,
The bodies soft and delicate!'

II

Then spake the elder of the bowl
(Peace to his spirit Allah grant!):
'Entrust not thy immortal soul
To such as break their covenant.

Leave enemies to go their road;
Lay hold upon the Loved One's hem;
As thou wouldst be a man of God,
Such men are devils: heed not them.'

III

I walked where tulips blossomed red,
And whispered to the morning breeze:
'Who are yon martyrs cold and dead,
Whose bloody winding-sheets are these?'

'Hafiz,' he answered, "tis not mine
Or thine to know this mystery;
Let all thy tale of ruby wine,
And sugar lips, and kisses be!'

FOURTEEN

Tīmūrid Historians

The storming and bloody career of Tīmūr the Lame and the wide empire which he bequeathed to his successors might well have been calculated to furnish chroniclers with rich material for weaving the tapestry of marvellous and terrible tales; and chroniclers were not slow to exploit their opportunities of making history pay. We shall now consider some of the books written in the fifteenth century to glorify the new dynasty, books which took their inspiration from the already famous work of Juvainī and Rashīd al-Dīn Faḍl Allāh and would supply models for the later historians of Moghul India. But first it is necessary to recall in passing that the so-called *Memoirs* and *Institutes* of Tīmūr, long supposed to have originated (in Chaghatay Turkish) from the emperor's pen, are now generally recognized for the impostures that they are. For what, for instance, is to be said of an autobiography which concludes, 'At night, on the 17th of the month of Sha'bān, calling upon the name of God, I lost my senses, and resigned my pure soul to the Almighty and Holy Creator'? It is a pity, for the *Memoirs* at least make fascinating reading and are not unworthy of a conqueror.

'About this time there arose in my heart the desire to lead an expedition against the infidels, and to become a *gházi*; for it had reached my ears that the slayer of infidels is a *gházi*, and if he is slain he becomes a martyr. It was on this account that I formed this resolution, but I was undetermined in my mind whether I should direct my expedition against the infidels of China or against the infidels and polytheists of India. In this matter I sought an omen from the Kurán, and the verse I opened upon was this, "O Prophet, make war upon infidels and unbelievers, and treat them with severity." My great officers told me that the inhabitants of Hindustán were infidels and unbelievers. In obedience to the order of Almighty God I determined on an expedition against them, and I issued orders to the *amírs* of mature years, and the leaders in war, to come before me, and when they had come together I questioned the assembly as to whether I should invade Hindustán or China, and said to them, "By the order of God and the Prophet it is incumbent upon me to make war upon these infidels and polytheists." Throwing themselves upon their knees they all wished me good fortune.'

C. E. Chapman's version of Muḥammad Afḍal's version of the alleged *Malfūẓāt* has here been cited. It is unfortunate that the careful and esteemed translations of Major W. Davy (Oxford, 1783) and Major C. Stewart (London, 1830) must now be discarded as of no more than secondary importance.

The oldest extant biography of Tīmūr is the *Ẓafar-nāma* of Niẓām al-Dīn Shāmī, undertaken in 1401 at the emperor's commission and completed in 1404, one year before Tīmūr's death. This text was edited by Dr. F. Tauer (Prague, 1937). Far more famous—for all that the work of Niẓām al-Dīn is, in E. G. Browne's words, 'conciser and less florid'—is the later recension, also called *Ẓafar-nāma*, executed in 1424 by Sharaf al-Dīn 'Alī Yazdī. This book has been known and widely used in Europe since Pétis de la Croix translated it into French (Paris, 1722) and J. Darby (London, 1723) performed the simpler labour of turning the French into English. The later historian Mīr Khvānd declared that this *Ẓafar-nāma* 'surpassed everything that had up to his time enlightened the world in the department of history'; Edward Gibbon, confessing that de la Croix's version had 'always been my faithful guide,' remarked that 'his geography and chronology are wonderfully accurate; and he may be trusted for public facts, though he servilely praises the virtue and fortune of the hero.' Sir Henry Elliot took a less favourable view, calling the work 'a very partial biography' and 'interspersed with fables.' Yazdī was close to Tīmūr's son Shāh-Rukh (reigned 1405–47) and enjoyed the more particular favour of his grandson Ibrāhīm Sulṭān (d. 1435); later he was suspected by Shāh-Rukh of complicity in the rebellion of Sulṭān Muḥammad, but was saved from execution through the interposition of Ulugh Beg's son Mīrzā 'Abd al-Laṭīf, who gave him shelter in Samarqand. The death of Shāh-Rukh encouraged Sulṭān Muḥammad to invite Yazdī back to his native Yazd, and there he died in 1454.

The text of Yazdī's *Ẓafar-nāma* was edited by Muḥammad Ilāhdād at Calcutta in 1887–8, but no modern translation has so far been made. Some passages however were included by J. Dowson in *The History of India as Told by its own Historians*; in making his extracts he relied mainly upon an abridgment which he judged to be identical with that described by Duncan Forbes as 'Another curiosity . . . a very plain and sensible paraphrase of the *Zafar-náma*, done, by command of Jahángír, by 'Abdu-s Sattár Kásim in the city of Ájmír, A.H. 1024 (A.D. 1617). The doer of the thing says very sensibly in his introduction that Yazdí's book is very flowery and pedantic, written in the *'ibárat-i munshiyána*, which we may felicitously translate the Jedediah Cleishbotham style, which he, 'Abdu-s Sattár aforesaid, improves marvellously by leaving out all Arabic and Persian verses that are not to the point, and enriching the narrative from other sources.' Even in its expurgated form the history makes sufficiently vigorous reading, as for instance this description of Tīmūr's capture and sack of Delhi in the last days of 1398.

'After their defeat, Sultán Mahmúd and Mallú Khán went to Dehlí and repented of the course they had pursued and of the rashness they had displayed. But repentance after a disaster is of no avail. No resource but flight was left. So in the darkness of the night Sultán Mahmúd left the city by the gate of Hauz-rání and Mallú Khán by the Baraka gate, both of which are to the south of the Jahán-panáh. They fled into the desert. When Tímúr was informed of their flight he sent Amír Sa'íd and other officers in pursuit of them. These officers captured many fugitives and secured a large booty. They also made prisoners of Mallú Khán's sons, Saif Khán entitled Malik Sharfu-d dín, and Khudá-dád. On the same evening orders were given to Allah-dád and other officers to take possession of the gates of the city and to prevent the escape of any one.

'On the 8th Rabí'u-s sání, Tímúr hoisted his victorious flag on the walls of Dehlí. He then went to the gate of the *maidán* and took his seat in the *'Ídgáh*. This gate is one of the gates of Jahán-panáh and opens towards the *Hauz-i Kháss*. There he held his court; and the *saiyids*, the *kázis*, the nobles and the great men who were in the city, hastened to pay their homage to him. Fazlu-llah Balkhí, deputy of Mallú Khán, with all the officers of the *díwán*, proceeded to make their submission. The *saiyids*, the *'ulamá*, and the *shaikhs* sought for protection through the intervention of the princes and officers. Prince Pír Muhammad, Amír Sulaimán Sháh, Amír Jahán Sháh, and others interceded for them in due season, and gained their object. The standard of victory was raised and drums were beaten and music played to proclaim the conquest to the skies. . . . The elephants and rhinoceroses were brought forth with all their trappings and paraded before the emperor. The elephants all in token of submission bowed their heads to the ground and raised a cry altogether as if they were asking for quarter. . . .

'On the 16th of the month a number of soldiers collected at the gate of Dehlí and derided the inhabitants. When Tímúr heard of this he directed some of the *amírs* to put a stop to it. But it was the divine pleasure to ruin the city and to punish the inhabitants, and that was brought about in this way. The wife of Jahán Malik 'Aghá and other ladies went into the city to see the palace of the Thousand Columns (*Hazár-sutún*), which Malik Jauná had built in the Jahán-panáh. The officers of the Treasury had also gone there to collect the ransom money. Several thousand soldiers, with orders for grain and sugar, had proceeded to the city. An order had been issued for the officers to arrest every nobleman who had fought against Tímúr and had fled to the city, and in execution of this order they were scattered about the city. When parties and bands of soldiers were going about the city, numbers of Hindus and *gabrs* in the cities of Dehlí, Sírí, Jahán-panáh, and Old Dehlí, seeing the violence of the soldiers, took up arms and assaulted them. Many of the infidels set fire to their goods and effects, and threw themselves, their wives and children, into the flames. The soldiers grew more eager for plunder and destruction. Notwithstanding the boldness and the struggles of the Hindus, the officers in charge kept the gates closed, and would not allow any more soldiers to enter the city, lest it should be sacked. But on that Friday night there were about 15,000 men in the city who were engaged from early eve till morning in plundering and burning the houses. In many places the impure infidel *gabrs* made resistance. In the morning the soldiers who were outside, being unable to control themselves, went to the city and raised a great disturbance. On that Sunday, the 17th of the month, the whole place was pillaged, and several palaces in Jahán-panáh and Síri were destroyed. On the 18th the like plundering went on. Every soldier obtained more than twenty persons as slaves, and some brought as many as fifty or a hundred men, women, and children as slaves out of the city. The other plunder and spoils were immense, gems and jewels of all sorts, rubies, diamonds, stuffs and fabrics of all kinds, vases and vessels of gold and silver, sums of money in *'ala'í tankas*, and other coins beyond all computation. Most of the women who were made prisoners wore bracelets of gold or silver on their wrists and legs and valuable rings upon their toes. Medicines and perfumes and unguents, and the like, of these no one took any notice. On the 19th of the month Old Dehlí was thought of, for many infidel Hindus had fled thither and taken refuge in the great mosque, where they prepared to defend themselves. Amír

Sháh Malik and 'Alí Sultán Tawáchí, with 500 trusty men, proceeded against them, and falling upon them with the sword despatched them to hell. High towers were built with the heads of the Hindus, and their bodies became the food of ravenous beasts and birds. On the same day all Old Dehlí was plundered. Such of the inhabitants as had escaped alive were made prisoners. For several days in succession the prisoners were brought out of the city, and every *amír* of a *túmán* or *kushún* took a party of them under his command. Several thousand craftsmen and mechanics were brought out of the city, and under the command of Tímúr some were divided among the princes, *amírs*, and *ághás* who had assisted in the conquest, and some were reserved for those who were maintaining the royal authority in other parts. Tímúr had formed the design of building a *Masjid-i jami'* in Samarkand, his capital, and he now gave orders that all the stone-masons should be reserved for that pious work.'

In 1414 Shāh-Rukh received into his library a copy of a celebrated Arabic treatise on geography (doubtless the *Ṣuwar al-aqālīm* of al-Iṣṭakhrī after al-Balkhī), and was so impressed with it that he decided to have a Persian translation made. He entrusted the task to a man who had been with him on a number of campaigns, including the capture in 1400 of Aleppo and Damascus: Shihāb al-Dīn 'Abd Allāh ibn Luṭf Allāh al-Khwāfī, known as Ḥāfiẓ-i Abrū. The commission was completed by 1420; but meanwhile in 1417 Shāh-Rukh had given Ḥāfiẓ-i Abrū the further labour of compiling a history of the world. He simplified this daunting charge by copying word-for-word large portions of Bal'amī's version of Ṭabarī, the *Jāmi' al-tawārīkh* of Rashīd al-Dīn Faḍl Allāh, and the *Ẓafar-nāma* of Niẓām al-Dīn Shāmī; adding a few personal touches, an introduction, some connecting passages and supplements, he was able to finish his *Majmū'a* in record time. Then in 1423 Shāh-Rukh's third son Bāisunghur, a famous patron of the arts who is best known for having caused to be prepared a critical edition of Firdausī's *Shāh-nāma*, requested

Ḥāfiẓ-i Abrū to write another universal history of a more original kind. The industrious compiler immediately embarked on the first of the four volumes in which he planned to tell his long tale, having set up on his shelves all the texts that could be ransacked for reliable or amusing information—commentaries on the Koran, collections of the Traditions of the Prophet, Ṭabarī again, Mas'ūdī, Firdausī, 'Utbī, Ibn al-Athīr, Jūzjānī, Juvainī, Vaṣṣāf, Rashīd al-Dīn, Ḥamd Allāh Mustaufī and the rest. He finished the first volume of this *Majma' al-tawārīkh* (from the Creation down to the death of the last Sāsānian king) on 8 Dhu 'l-Qa'da 826 (October 13, 1423). The second volume, recording the life of Muḥammad and the history of the Caliphate from beginning to end, was completed three years later. The third volume took up the affairs of Persia following the fall of Baghdad, and described the empires of the Saljūqs and the Mongols down to the death of Abū Sa'īd. The fourth volume, which was given the separate title *Zubdat al-tawārīkh*, corrected and expanded the *Ẓafar-nāma* of Niẓām al-Dīn Shāmī and then went on with the story of Shāh-Rukh; Ḥāfiẓ-i Abrū had reached the year 1427 when he died on June 25, 1430.

Relatively little has so far been printed of all these extensive writings, preserved in widely-scattered manuscripts. Dr. Tauer in 1934 published the thin supplement to Niẓām al-Dīn Shāmī as contained in the *Majmū'a* in the sixth volume of *Archiv Orientální*. In 1939 Dr. Khān-Bābā Bayānī issued at Teheran the more substantial supplement to Rashīd al-Dīn as *Dhail Jāmi' al-tawārīkh*; three years earlier he had put out at Paris, as the second volume of his admirable enterprise, *Hâfiẓ-i Abrû: Chronique des Rois Mongols en Iran*, described on the title-page as an annotated translation of the original Persian. However, the text runs to 256 pages while the translation occupies only 156 pages, terminating at a point which occurs on page 188 of the edition. Both these monographs have drawn upon Ḥāfiẓ Abrū's *Majmū'a*; of the *Majma' al-tawārīkh* a considerable passage relating to a mission sent to China in 1419 was edited in the seventh volume of the *Oriental College Magazine* (Lahore, 1930).

How Khān-Bābā Bayānī pricked the balloon of Ḥāfiẓ-i Abrū's verbose rhetoric is neatly demonstrated by his treatment of the opening paragraphs of the account of Amīr Chūpān's fall from Abū Sa'īd's favour. Bayānī translates:

'Arrivé à l'apogée du pouvoir et de la considération générale, Emir Tchûpân prit toutes les affaires d'état à sa charge. Ce qui devait exciter la jalousie de l'entourage du Sultan et être la cause de sa disgrâce.

'Le roi Abû-Saïd ayant atteint la fleur de l'age, c'est-à-dire vingt ans (725/1324), tomba amoureux de la ravissante Baghdâd-Khatûn, la propre fille de Tchûpân. Or, deux ans auparavant, c'est-à-dire en 723/1323 elle s'était mariée avec Sheikh Hasan, fils d'Emir Husein.

'La tradition mongole décrétée par le grand conquérant Tchangiz était la pour satisfaire la jeune ardeur de l'impétueux et royal amoureux.

'En effet celle-ci voulait que si le choix royal était porté sur une "beauté mariée," le propre époux devait quitter volontairement sa femme pour en faire cadeau aux caprices du tout puissant.

'Mettant cette tradition à profit le Sultan informa le malheureux père de son intention.

'Lorsqu'Emir Tchûpân apprit la nouvelle il en fût extrêmement irrité, et son inquiétude ne fut pas moindre que sa colère.

Si quelqu'un se permet de renouveler devant ma personne de telles
insinuations, je l'acculerai à la ruine, aux pires châtiments, il ne pourra plus goûter à la joie et à la tranquillité.

'La réponse négative de Tchûpân désespéra le jeune roi qui prit la décision de s'imposer la terrible séparation de l'idole, et, rancunier par nature, se prit de colère contre son dévoué serviteur, et lui voua une ḥaine terrible.'

A literal version of this sentimentally-rendered passage would be:

'Amīr Chūpān took all the realms of Sulṭān Abū Sa'īd into the grasp of his authority and the hand of his control, and by the attainment of his purposes and the success of his designs, the contriving of the means of rulership and the exaltation of the ranks of propinquity, he attracted to himself the envy of the princes and the jealousy of the pillars of the state.

When a thing is perfect, then the hour of its diminishing is near;
expect a decline, as soon as men say, "Everything is perfect."

'Now the cause of the change in Sulṭān Abū Sa'īd's disposition towards Amīr Chūpān had its origin in the following circumstance. Baghdād Khātūn, the daughter of Amīr Chūpān, was extremely beautiful. In the time of the reign of Abū Sa'īd, during the months of the year 723, Amīr Chūpān gave her to Prince Shaikh Ḥasan, son of Amīr Ḥusain. But in the year 725 King Abū Sa'īd, whose age had now reached twenty years, in accordance with the saying that "youth is a kind of madness" conceived an attachment for Baghdād Khātūn that reached such proportions that he could not rest or remain tranquil.

When the heart falls for a languid narcissus-eye,
be it a king's or a slave's, it slips out of control.

Prince Abū Sa'īd, following the purport of the royal rule—for it was the wont and custom of Chingīz Khān that should any lady please the king, usage required her husband to forgo her with a good grace—sent one of his confidants to Amīr Chūpān and put before him the facts of the situation. Amīr Chūpān on hearing of this was astonished and confounded; the fire of jealous pride and indignation began to shoot out flames in his breast, and he was utterly divided between the thought of dishonour and the fear of reproach.

Thus spoke he: "If henceforward any man
dares speak to me upon this impudence,
be sure I'll follow him through all the world
nor let him find a single instant's peace."

Since the Amīr's answer was not agreeable to the Sulṭān's temperament, the Sulṭān despaired of the Amīr's co-operation in managing this affair. He put up with the pain of separation, but a dust settled upon his mind.'

Among minor Tīmūrid historians mention should be made of Faṣīḥ Khvāfī, finance minister to Shāh-Rukh and Bāisunghur, who compiled the as yet unpublished *Mujmal-i Faṣīḥī*, 'a valuable compendium of Islamic history and biography to A.H. 845/1441–2.' Of far greater interest is Kamāl al-Dīn 'Abd al-Razzāq ibn Isḥāq Samarqandī, born at Harāt in 1413, whose father was a religious and judicial attaché to Shāh-Rukh's court. At the age of twenty-five he commended himself to the Sulṭān by dedicating to him a subtle grammatical treatise; four years later, in 1441, Shāh-Rukh despatched him on a mission to South India which occupied him three years. A second embassy took him to Gīlān in 1446; his later years were spent in holy retirement, and it was as head of a *khānqāh* in Harāt that he died in 1482. 'Abd al-Razzāq is famous for his *Maṭla'-i sa'dain*, a history of the Tīmūrids spanning nearly 170 years, from the birth in 1304 of Abū Sa'īd the Īl-Khān down to the second accession of Sulṭān Ḥusain in 1470. This work was known in the West already in the seventeenth century, when Antoine Galland, more celebrated for his pioneering translation of the *Arabian Nights*, made a version from the *Maṭla'-i sa'dain* of which an extract was published in Melchisedec Thevenot's *Relations de divers voyages curieux* (Paris, 1663–72). It was the account of Shāh-Rukh's embassies to India and China that attracted especial interest in those days when European merchants were first venturing into such distant parts; the excitement long continued unabated, and in 1785 William Chambers of the East

India Company published (in the first folio volume of the handsome but short-lived *Asiatick Miscellany*) 'An Account of Embassies and Letters that passed between the Emperor of China and Sultan Shahrokh, Son of Amir Timur.' The translator, who also edited the section of his concern, prefixed to his essay 'the following account, taken from the Habib us Sier of Khondemir,' which 'shows in what degree of esteem the Author and his work have been held in Asia.'

'Kamal ud Din Abdul Rezak was a son of Jelal ud Din Ishak of Samarcand, and was born at Herat on the 12th of Shaban 816 (or 6th November, A.D. 1413). His father Ishak resided at the court of Sultan Schahrokh, in quality of Kazy and Imam, and was sometimes consulted on points of law, and desired to read learned treatises in his Majesty's presence. Abdur Rezak, after his father's death, in the year 841 (A.D. 1437), wrote a comment on Azd ud Din Yahia's Treatise of *Arabic* prepositions and pronouns, and dedicated it to Sultan Schahrokh; on occasion of which he had the honour to kiss his Majesty's hand. In the latter part of that prince's reign, he went as his ambassador to the King of Bijanagur (Visiapore), and experienced various extraordinary incidents and vicissitudes on that journey; but at length returned to Khorasan in safety. After the death of Sultan Shahrokh, he was successively admitted to the presence of Mirza Abdul Latif, Mirza Abdullah, and Mirza Abul Kasim; and in the first Jumad of 877 (or October 1472), under the reign of Sultan Abu Said, he was appointed Superintendent of the Khankah of Mirza Shahrokh, where he continued to the time of his death, which happened in the latter Jumad of the year 877 (answering to part of July and August 1482). Among the excellent productions of his pen is that useful work, the MATLA US SADEIN, which is in every one's hand, and is universally known, where he has given a general history of events from the time of Sultan Abu Said Bahadur Khan, down to the assassination of Mirza Sultan Abu Saîd Gurkân.'

Chambers had little doubt of the reliability of the matter before him. 'Apart from the authenticity of the history, the letters themselves seem to have strong marks of being genuine, both in the matter they contain, and in the stile in which they are written. Of the first every one may form his opinion; the latter must be submitted to the judgment of those who peruse them in the original language. They will perceive, that while those from Sultan Shahrokh are penned with that purity and propriety of diction, which might be expected from a Persian monarch, those from the Emperor of China are expressed in such quaint and awkward terms, as might be supposed to come from a Mogul interpreter translating each word of a Chinese letter at the peril of his life. But the simplicity and unaffected brevity of the Chinese original, seems to have been such as could not suffer any material injury from a servile translation, and much of the national character is visible in these productions.'

The correspondence opens in the year 1412, when 'ambassadors from Day-ming Khan, Emperor of Chîn and Mâchin, and all those countries, arrived at Herat.' We are told that Shah-Rukh 'ordered the royal gardens to be bedecked like the gardens of Paradise, and sent his martial and lion-like yesavals to assign every one his proper mansion. After which his Majesty himself, irradiated with a splendour like the sun, ascended his throne as that glorious luminary when in the zenith of his course, and bestowed upon the chief of his Lords, and on the ambassadors, the happiness of kissing his hand. The latter, after offering him their presents, delivered their message.' A separate missive contained a detailed list of the Emperor's offerings, while the ambassadors also carried with them 'one calculated to serve as a pass.' It is stated that 'each was written in the Persian language and character, as well as in the Turkish language with the Mogul character, and likewise in the language and character of China.' The following is Chambers's version of the 'Letter from the Emperor of China.'

'The great Emperor, Day-ming, sends this letter to the country of Samarcand to Shahrokh Bahâdur.

'As we consider that the most high God has created all things that are in heaven and earth, to the end that all his creatures may be happy, and that it is in consequence of his sovereign decree, that we are become Lord of the face of the earth, we therefore endeavour to exercise rule in obedience to his commands; and for this reason we make no partial distinctions between those that are near, and those that are afar off, but regard them all with an eye of equal benevolence.

'We have heard, before this, that thou art a wise and an excellent man, highly distinguished above others, that thou art obedient to the commands of the most high God, that thou art a father to thy people and thy troops, and art good and beneficent towards all; which has given us much satisfaction. But it was with singular pleasure we observed, that when we sent an ambassador with Kimkhâs, and Torkos, and a dress, thou didst pay all due honour to our command, and didst make a proper display of the favour thou hadst received, insomuch that small and great rejoiced at it. Thou didst also forthwith dispatch an ambassador to do us homage, and to present us the rarities, horses, and choice manufactures of that country. So that with the strictest regard to truth we can declare, that we have deemed thee worthy of praise and of distinction.

'The government of the Moguls was some time ago extinct, but thy father Timur Fûmâ was obedient to the commands of the most high God, and did homage to our great emperor Tây Zûy, nor did he omit to send ambassadors with presents. He (the emperor) for this reason granted protection to the men of that country, and enriched them all. We have now seen that thou art a worthy follower of thy father, in his noble spirit, and in his measures; we have therefore sent Duji-chûn-bay-azkasây, and Hararâ Sûchû and Dan-ching Sadasûn Kunchi, with congratulations, and a dress, and Kimkhâs, and Torgos, &c., that the truth may be known. We shall hereafter send persons whose office it will be to go and return successively, in order to keep open a free communication, that merchants may traffick and carry on their business to their wish.

'Khalil Sultan, is thy brother's son; it is necessary that thou treat him with kindness, in consideration of his rights as being the son of so near a relation. We trust that thou wilt pay attention to our sincerity and to our advice in these matters. This is what we make known to thee!'

Shāh-Rukh appears to have been by no means daunted by the lofty tone of the Chinese Emperor. 'When the affairs of the Chinese Ambassadors were settled,' continues 'Abd al-Razzāq, 'they had an audience of leave, and set out on their return. Sheikh Mohammed Bakshy accompanied them as Envoy on the part of his Majesty, and as the Emperor of China had not yet assented to the Mussulman Faith, nor regulated his conduct by the law of the Koran, his Majesty, from motives of friendship, sent him a letter of good advice in Arabic and Persian, conceiving, that perhaps the Emperor might be prevailed upon to embrace the faith.' Chambers has some sharp comments to offer on the contents of the Arabic document. 'Nothing can exceed the absurd presumption which appears in the two first paragraphs of this letter, considered as an address to a powerful monarch of an opposite persuasion. Those that reason in this manner have need of the sword to inforce their arguments. But there is so manifest a difference between this and the subsequent Persian letter on the same subject, that there seems ground to suspect the latter alone was intended to be read at Peking. The Arabic letter was probably drawn up by some of the Mussulman doctors of the court of Shahrokh, and he, perhaps, sent it with the other, merely to gratify the pride and opiniatry of that class of men in his own dominions, trusting that the Persian only would be understood in China.' The first document sent by Shāh-Rukh begins with the familiar formula 'In the name of the most merciful God' and then proceeds:

'There is no God but God, and Mohammed is his Apostle.

'Mohammed, the Apostle of God, hath said, "As long as ever there shall remain a people of mine that are steady in keeping the commandments of God, the man that persecutes them shall not prosper, nor shall their enemy prevail against them, until the day of judgement."

'When the most high God proposed to create Adam and his race, he said, "I have been a treasure concealed, but I chuse now to be known. I therefore create human creatures, that I may be known." It is then evident from hence, that the wisdom of the Supreme Being, whose power is glorious, and whose word is sublime, in the creation of the human species, was this, That the knowledge of him and of the true faith might shine forth and be propagated. For this purpose also he sent his Apostle to direct men in the way, and teach them the true religion, that it might be exalted above all others, notwithstanding the opposition of the Associaters; and that the law and the commandments, and the rites concerning clean and unclean might be known. And he granted us the sublime and miraculous Korân to silence the unbelievers, and cut short their tongues when they dispute and oppose the truth; and it will remain by his sovereign favour and far extending grace unto the last day.

'He hath also established by his power in every age and period puissant sovereigns, and masters of numerous armies, in all parts of the world from east to west, to administer justice and exercise clemency, and to spread over the nations the wings of security and peace; to direct them to obey the obvious commands of God, and to avoid the evils and excesses which he has forbidden; to raise high among them the standards of the glorious law, and to take away heathenism and infidelity from the midst of them, by promoting the belief of the unity.

'The Most High God, therefore, constrains us, by his past mercies and present bounties, to labour for the establishment of the rules of his righteous and indispensable law; and commands us, under a sense of thankfulness to him, to administer justice and mercy to our subjects in all cases, agreeably to the prophetic code and the precepts of Mustafâ. He requires us also to found mosques and colleges, alms-houses, and places of worship, in all parts of our dominions, that the study of the sciences and of the laws, and the moral practice which is the result of those studies, may not be discontinued.

'Seeing then that the permanence of temporal prosperity, and of dominion in this lower world, depends on an adherence to truth and goodness, and on the extirpation of heathenism and infidelity from the earth, with a view to future retribution, I cherish the hope that your Majesty and the nobles of your realm, will unite with us in these matters, and will join us in establishing the institutions of the sacred law. I trust also that your Majesty will continue to send hither ambassadors, and express messengers, and will strengthen the foundations of affection and friendship, by keeping open a free communication between the two empires; that travellers and merchants may pass to and fro unmolested, our subjects in all our cities may be refreshed with the fruits of this commerce, and that means of support may abound among all ranks of people.

'Peace be to him that follows the right path, for God is ever gracious to those that serve him!'

Whether or not the Emperor of China was able to understand the contents of Shāh-Rukh's Arabic missive, his Persian letter fell little short in boldness, and contained moreover a remarkable summary of recent history.

'To the Emperor Dây-ming, the Sultan Shahrokh sends boundless peace!

'The Most High God, having, in the depth of his wisdom, and in the perfection of his power, created Adam, was pleased in succeeding times, to make of his sons prophets and apostles, whom he sent among men to summon them to obey the truth. To some of those prophets also, as to Abraham, Moses, David, and Mohammed, he gave particular books, and taught each of them a law commanding the people of the time in which they lived, to obey that law, and to remain in the faith of each respectively. All these Apostles of God, called upon men to embrace the religion of the unity, and the worship of the true God, and forbade the adoration of the sun, moon, and stars, of kings and idols; and though each of them had a special and distinct dispensation, they were nevertheless all agreed in the doctrine of the unity of the Supreme Being. At length, when the apostleship and prophetic office devolved on our Apostle Mohammed Mustafâ, (on whom be mercy and peace from God), the other systems were abolished, and he became the apostle and prophet of the latter time. It behoves all the world, therefore, lords, kings, and viziers, rich and poor, small and great, to embrace this religion, and forsake the systems and persuasions of past ages. This is the true and the right faith, and this is Islamism.

'Some years before the present period, Chengêz Khân sallied forth, and sent his sons into different countries and kingdoms. He sent Jojy Khan into the parts about Sarây, Krim, and the Deshte Kafchâk, where some of the Kings his successors such as Uzbek, and Jani Khân, and Urus Khân professed the Mussulman faith, and regulated their conduct by the law of Mohammed. Hulâku Khân was appointed to preside over the cities of Khorasân, and Irâk, and the parts adjacent, and some of his sons who succeeded to the government of those countries, having admitted the light of the Mohammedan faith into their hearts, became in like manner professors of Islamism and were so happy as to be converted to it before they died. Among these were the King Gazan, so remarkable for the sincerity of his character, Aljây-tu-Sultan also, and the fortunate monarch Abu-saîd Bahâdur, till at length the sovereignty devolved on my father Amîr Tîmur (whose dust I venerate). He throughout his empire made the religion of Mohammed the standard of all his measures, so that in the times of his government the professors of Islamism were in the most prosperous condition. And now that by the goodness and favour of divine providence, the kingdoms of Khorasân, Irâk, and Maverrunnaher are come into my possession, I govern according to the dictates of the holy law of the prophet, and its positive and negative precepts; and the Tergu and institutions of Chengêz Khân are abolished.

'As then it is sure and certain that salvation and deliverance in eternity, and sovereignty and prosperity in the world, are the effect of faith and Islamism, and the favour of the Most High, it is our duty to conduct ourselves with justice and equity towards our subjects; and I have hope that by the goodness and favour of God your majesty also will in those countries make the law of Mohammed, the Apostle of God, the rule of your administration, and thereby strengthen the cause of Islamism. That this world's few days of sovereignty may in the end be exchanged for an eternal kingdom, and the old adage be verified, "May thy latter end be better than thy beginning."

'Ambassadors from those parts have lately arrived here, have delivered us your Majesty's presents, and brought us news of your welfare and of the flourishing state of your dominions. The affection and friendship which subsisted between our respective fathers, is revived by this circumstance, as indeed it is proverbial that, "the mutual friendship of fathers creates a relationship between their sons." In return we have dispatched Mohammed Bakshy as our ambassador from hence, to acquaint your Majesty with our welfare. And we are persuaded that henceforward a free communication will be maintained between the two countries, that merchants may pass and repass in security, which, at the same time that it contributes to the prosperity of kingdoms, is what raises the character of princes both in a political and in a religious view. May the grace of charity, and the practice of the duties of amity, ever accompany those who profess to walk in the right path.'

Whether or not these texts represent the actual wording of

the messages exchanged on this memorable occasion, we can feel reasonably assured, by the nearness of ʿAbd al-Razzāq's record to the events he chronicled, that what he set down was not far from the truth. Elsewhere in the *Maṭlaʿ-i saʿdain* we have lively descriptions of his personal experiences and observations when upon the mission to South India, and the following extract is taken from a version made 'by an English gentleman, probably Mr. C. J. Oldfield, B.C.S.' as revised by Sir H. M. Elliot.

'Opposite the mint is the office of the Prefect of the City [Bíjánagar], to which it is said 12,000 policemen are attached; and their pay, which equals each day 12,000 *fanams*, is derived from the proceeds of the brothels. The splendour of those houses, the beauty of the heart-ravishers, their blandishments and ogles, are beyond all description. It is best to be brief on the matter.

'One thing worth mentioning is this, behind the mint there is a sort of bazar, which is more than 300 yards long and 20 broad. On two sides of it there are houses and fore-courts, and in front of the houses, instead of benches, lofty seats are built of excellent stone, and on each side of the avenue formed by the houses there are figures of lions, panthers, tigers, and other animals, so well painted as to seem alive. After the time of mid-day prayers, they place at the doors of these houses, which are beautifully decorated, chairs and settees, on which the courtezans seat themselves. Every one is covered with pearls, precious stones, and costly garments. They are all exceedingly young and beautiful. Each has one or two slave girls standing before her, who invite and allure to indulgence and pleasure. Any man who passes through this place makes choice of whom he will. The servants of these brothels take care of whatever is taken into them, and if anything is lost they are dismissed. There are several brothels within these seven fortresses, and the revenues of them, which, as stated before, amount to 12,000 *fanams*, go to pay the wages of the policemen. The business of these men is to acquaint themselves with all the events and accidents that happen within the seven walls, and to recover everything that is lost, or that may be abstracted by theft; otherwise they are fined. Thus, certain slaves which my companion had bought took to flight, and when the circumstance was reported to the Prefect, he ordered the watchmen of that quarter where the poorest people dwelt to produce them or pay the penalty; which last they did, on ascertaining the amount. Such are the details relating to the city of Bíjánagar and the condition of its sovereign.

'The author of this history, who arrived at Bíjánagar at the close of Zí-hijja, took up his abode in a lofty mansion which had been assigned to him, resembling that which one sees in Hirát on the high ground at the King's Gate. Here he reposed himself after the fatigues of the journey for several days, and passed under happy auspices the first day of the new moon of Muharram in that splendid city and beautiful abode.

'One day messengers came from the king to summon me, and towards the evening I went to the Court, and presented five beautiful horses and two trays, each containing nine pieces of damask and satin. The king was seated in great state in the forty-pillared hall, and a great crowd of Brahmans and others stood on the right and left of him. He was clothed in a robe of *zaitún* satin, and he had round his neck a collar composed of pure pearls of regal excellence, the value of which a jeweller would find it difficult to calculate. He was of an olive colour, of a spare body, and rather tall. He was exceedingly young, for there was only some slight down upon his cheeks, and none upon his chin. His whole appearance was very prepossessing. On being presented to him, I bowed down my head. He received me kindly, and seated me near him, and, taking the august letter of the emperor, made it over (to the interpreters), and said, "My heart is exceedingly glad that the great king has sent an ambassador to me." As I was in a profuse perspiration from the excessive heat and the quantity of clothes which I had on me, the monarch took compassion on me, and favoured me with a fan of Khatáí which he held in his hand. They then brought a tray, and gave me two packets of betel, a purse containing 500 *fanams*, and about 20 *miskáls* of camphor, and, obtaining leave to depart, I returned to my lodging. The daily provision forwarded to me comprised two sheep, four couple of fowls, five *mans* of rice, one *man* of butter, one *man* of sugar, and two *varáhas* in gold. This occurred every day. Twice a week I was summoned to the presence towards the evening, when the king asked me several questions respecting the Khákán-i Sa'id, and each time I received a packet of betel, a purse of *fanams*, and some *miskáls* of camphor.

'The monarch addressed us through his interpreter, and said, "Your kings feast ambassadors and place dishes before them, but as I and you cannot eat together,

' "This purse of gold represents the repast of an ambassador." '

We turn aside from these records of high imperial affairs to glance at one of the most famous and most frequently quoted books in Persian literature, the *Tadhkirat al-shu'arā'* of Amīr Daulatshāh ibn 'Alā' al-Daula Bakhtīshāh of Samarqand, used in Europe ever since von Hammer-Purgstall made it the basis of his *Geschichte der schönen Redekünste Persiens* (Vienna, 1818). Very meagre information is available about Daulatshāh's life, though his contemporary Mīr 'Alī Shīr Navā'ī, the Turkish poet and literary historian, counted him among 'sundry gentlemen and noblemen of Khurásán and other places whose ingenuity and talent impelled them to write poetry,' adding that he was 'a wholly excellent youth, unassuming and of good parts.' His one book, this *Memoir of the Poets*, was completed in 1487, the author being at that time about fifty years old. 'This is an entertaining and inaccurate work, containing a good selection of verses and a quantity of historical errors': such was the brief verdict of E. G. Browne, who edited the text. Elsewhere he comments on its value as a record of the social background to fifteenth century Persia: 'Daulatsháh, in spite of all his faults, of which inaccuracy and an intolerable floridity of style are the worst, does succeed in depicting better than many contemporary historians and biographers the strange mixture of murder, drunkenness, love of Art and literary taste which characterized the courts of these Tímúrid princes.'

In 1909 P. B. Vachha published at Bombay 'reluctantly, against my will and principles, at the earnest request of some of the students of Elphinstone College' a translation of that portion of the *Tadhkirat al-shuʿarā*' which was currently prescribed for the B.A. examination. 'I had no wish to translate this book myself,' the candid munshi went on, 'or to see it translated by anybody else. And perhaps, I should have, after all, desisted from the undertaking, did I not think it probable, nay certain, that if I did not translate the book somebody else was sure to. It is painful to observe that in the course of my teaching, I have often met with volumes of notes and translations which display not merely scandalous inefficiency, but what can only be called downright dishonesty. I undertook the work in the hope of being at least more conscientious if not more capable. I regret I had to do the work in such haste as prevented its being accomplished with such neatness as I should desire. I have had to finish it practically in a fortnight, and I am painfully conscious of many signs of hasty and ill-considered work. But at the same time I have the consolation of not having purposely shirked a single difficulty, or having given a single explanation which I did not believe to be the correct one, or of having in a single instance attempted to disguise my ignorance in a wilderness of words.' The resulting product, though not elegant, is undoubtedly useful and its value is enhanced by some honest prefatory remarks on the nature of Persian poetry.

'In spite of the not unfounded complaint of the provoking monotony of the Persian muse, Dawlatshah's record displays a vast variety of subjects and styles. In fact Persian poetry is not characterized by a nauseating plethora of produce of one kind, so much as by rank luxuriance and overgrowth of all the kinds. The genius of the people and language of Persia is distinguished by an extraordinary fertility and facility, which have proved fatal to the due development of either. The Persian poets not merely scribbled an overwhelming amount of one kind of poetry. Rather, to use Dr. Johnson's words, they did not leave any style of writing untouched, and adorned and over-adorned all that they touched. They wrote *too much* of all kinds of poetry and not merely of one kind. That most important of arts—the art to blot—seems to have been unknown to and unpractised by them. Hence the fearful extent and bulk of Persian poetical literature. With this fullness and fertility of the literature he had to deal with, our author must have had enough to do. If he read all the works of all the authors dealt with in his book, he must have been a marvel of patience and industry. If Milton and Spenser in English literature are more talked about than read, it is doubtful if any mortal can have the capacity to go through all the sixty thousand verses of the Shahnama, and all the six *daftars* of Rumi, and all the countless millions of verses written by Anwari, and Khaqani, Jami and Emir Khusraw—of whom the last alone is said to have manufactured four hundred thousand verses of which the author of the *Atish Kadah* has the impudence to assure us that he read one hundred thousand. How any human being can write so much poetry (or for the matter of that stuff of any kind) is rather perplexing. But in a country where, according to our author, people could compose faultless verses in the press of battle, and on the brink of death after receiving mortal wounds, or while playing at a game of cards or dice, or where payment orders to a stable-keeper are given in rhyme (and a very difficult rhyme too), no wonder that the gifted and the accomplished can turn out any amount of the so-called poetry.'

The historian of Persian, as of Arabic, literature can find it in his heart sometimes to envy his colleague concerned with the writings of the Greeks and the Romans, whose task has been made so much lighter by the vanishing of all but a manageable corpus which any man may without undue discomfort read and re-read in the course of one lifetime!

Here for the sake of example is P. B. Vachha's translation of the notorious and entirely unhistorical biography of 'Umar Khaiyām, that says so much about a fictitious friendship and so little about poetry.

'He was a Nishapuri, extremely learned, and in astrology surpassed all others in his time. He was highly esteemed by monarchs, so much so, that Sultan Sanjar used to give him a seat by his own side on the throne. Khwaja Nasir-uddin Tusi referred this matter to the notice of Hulagu Khan saying that his own learning was a hundred times as much as Omar's but that the scholars had lost their consequence in the latter days. The author of *Tarikhe Isṭaẓahari* says that Nizam-ul-mulk, Hasan Sabbah and Omar were studying together at Nishapur, and were school companions. They had entered into a bond of brotherhood with one another. The star of Nizam-ul-mulk's fortune became ascendant, and he worthily became the minister of the kingdom. Hasan and Omar resolved to serve under the Khwaja, and with that intent went to Isfahan. When the three met the Khwaja greeted their arrival with a variety of favours; and after a time asked them what their intentions were. Omar expressed his desire to have a pension and his means of livelihood provided for him at Nishapur, so as to enable him to spend his life in ease. This was done. When next Hasan was asked what he desired, he replied that he wished to be employed in the concerns of the world. The Khwaja made over to his charge the revenue work of Hamadan and Daniwar. Now Hasan expected the Khwaja to give him a share in the ministry; so he took insult at the work assigned, and he conceived hostile feelings towards the Khwaja. He used to associate with the courtiers of Malikshah, and play chess and backgammon with them. He thus won over the courtiers and favourites of the king. Then he represented to the king, that he (the Sultan) had been reigning for twenty years, and it was necessary that he should require some information regarding the income and expenses of the Kingdom, and the state of his treasury.

The Sultan sent for Nizam-ul-mulk and asked him how long would it take to prepare an epitome of the state revenues and expenses. The minister replied, "By the blessing of your fortune, your empire extends from the frontiers of Kashgar to Asia Minor and Antioch; if one exerts himself to the utmost this task can be accomplished in one year." The following night Hasan told the king, that if His Majesty should entrust that work to him, and strengthen his hands, he would complete the memorandum in forty days and present it to the king. The Sultan placed the control of the record-office into the hands of Hasan, and ordered that all the accountants and auditors should be under Hasan's orders, and that the work should be accomplished in forty days. Hasan busied himself with accounts, and a little before forty days, he completed his work. When Nizam-ul-mulk saw that Hasan would accomplish the work, he played a trick. He asked his own personal attendant to make friends with the special slave of Hasan, and lavish gold and money upon him. And he further instructed his slave that on the fortieth day when Hasan should have finished his work, while he (the minister) and Hasan should be in the royal presence, he (the slave) should ask to see the catalogue prepared by Hasan under the pretext of comparing it with the one prepared by his own master; and that when the volume came into his hands, he should derange and disperse it. This was settled: and on the fortieth day, the slave dispersed the account book of Hasan. Nizam-ul-mulk and Hasan both went to the court. The Sultan asked Hasan if he had completed his epitome. Hasan said, yes, and the Sultan asked him to produce it. When the volume was opened in the royal presence, and when the Sultan would ask him about Ray, the page would indicate a statement of Ray. Hasan at once apprehended that he had been outwitted by Nizam-ul-mulk. He was confused, and his hands and feet began to shake. While he was hastily trying to rearrange his work, and the king was swearing at him, the Khwaja submitted, "O my Lord, I knew from the beginning that this man was mad. But when your majesty paid heed to him, I dared not interfere.

How is it possible to draw up the accounts of a kingdom of this extent in forty days?" The other courtiers supported the Khwaja, and reviled and ridiculed Hasan. The Sultan ordered Hasan to be slapped and driven out. He concealed himself, and fled from house to house in Isfahan. He had a friend by name Rais Abul Fazl. He sought refuge in his house, and the Rais entertained him. He won the Rais over to his heterodox and heretical opinions. One night he said to the Rais, "If I can have *one* sincere friend, I would overthrow the kingdom of this Turkoman (Malikshah), and the ministry of this boor (Nizam-ul-mulk)." The Rais considered within himself how it was possible for one man with one friend to pull down an empire extending from Kashgar to Egypt. "Verily," he said, "this man is under the influence of melancholia." That day he brought almond oil and dodder of thyme, and mixed saffron and such other drugs as have the property of removing hypochondria, with food. Hasan understood the state of things by his sagacity, and fled from his friend's house to the Fort of Almut which is situated in the Highlands of Dilam. There he absorbed himself in devotion and imposed upon the governor of the fort, so that he became his follower. He used to sit in a cave outside the fort, and occupy himself with abstinence and devotion. The governor requested Hasan to make his place within the castle. Hasan replied that he did not perform his prayers on anybody else's property, and asked the governor to sell him a plot of the size of a cow's hide so that he might perform his prayers in his own land. The Kotwal, accordingly sold him a plot of the size of a cow's hide. When he had come within the fort, he won over to his persuasion all the people of the fort, and made them his pupils. Then he cut up the cow's hide into a thin strip, and passed it round the whole fort from one gate. Next morning he sent word to the governor saying that the fort was his property and that he had bought it; that the Kotwal should no longer stay in his (Hasan's) property, and should go out. As all the inhabitants of the fort were the followers of Hasan, the poor Kotwal was quite confounded and went out. Hasan became master of the fort by this fraud. For the price of the castle he wrote to Rais Abul Fazl, saying, "I still do not possess a friend; if I should have one I would make still further progress." Then that accursed man sent out his missionaries in all directions, and misled the people. The creed of heresy and impiety (duality) was thus preached, and most of the people of Iran and Turan became involved in the troubles of these miscreants. If we said more of their history, it would be too long. The strongholds of these heretics were completely destroyed in the time of Hulagukhan and their domination came to an end.'

And that, strangely enough, is all that Daulatshāh has to say about 'Umar Khaiyām.

The fifteenth century was not yet out when a gigantic history of the world was produced in Harāt which achieved great popularity and exercised a wholly baneful influence. Muḥammad ibn Khāvand Shāh ibn Maḥmūd, better known as Mīr Khvānd (Mirchond) was born in 1433 and died in 1498; little more is known of his life than that, except that he enjoyed the patronage of Mīr 'Alī Shīr Navā'ī and produced the elephantine *Rauḍat al-ṣafā'*. Into that 'Garden of Purity' he crowded (in seven huge volumes) all that had happened since Creation in the world known to Muslim historians; he chose Juvainī as the model of how to write Persian, but he was ambitious to better his master so that his style reached heights of bombastical rhetoric only to be surpassed by his Indian imitators. Ironically enough this book has attracted more attention and employed more labour in Europe than any other Persian history. It was away to a good start when it underlay the *Relaciones de P. Teixeira d'el origen, descendencia y succession de los Reges de Persia y de Harmuz* (Amberes, 1610), a work which Captain J. Stevens put into English in 1715 as *The History of Persia*. After such scholars as B. von Jenisch, Silvestre de Sacy, Joseph von Hammer-Purgstall, F. Wilken, C. Stewart, A. Jourdain, J. A. Vullers and W. H. Morley had occupied themselves with editing or translating parts of the mammoth, E. Rehatsek in the fullness of time embarked boldly upon a version of the whole. Under the auspices of the Royal Asiatic Society five volumes totalling some 2,000 pages had been published between 1891 and 1894 before a halt was called; even then much less than a half had been accomplished. On this heroic but misguided enterprise and its harvest of disregarded tomes it suffices to quote the opinion of E. G. Browne: 'These, it must be admitted with regret, are of no great value, for, apart from the fact that any student desirous of acquainting himself with the ideas of the Muslims as to the prophets, patriarchs and kings of olden time would prefer to seek his information from earlier and more trustworthy sources, the translation itself is both inaccurate and singularly uncouth, nor is it to be desired that English readers should form their ideas even of the verbose and florid style of Mírkhwánd from a rendering which is needlessly grotesque.'

It is therefore not proposed to allow Rehatsek to stand in these pages as an illustration of Mīr Khvānd's work. Let us turn instead to an older and less ambitious attempt, that made by David Shea when he was employed in the Oriental Department of the Hon. East-India Company's College at Haileybury: *History of the Early Kings of Persia* (London, 1832). Shea gracefully acknowledges the help he received from 'Mirza Ibrahim, a learned native of Shíráz, who to an intimate knowledge of the customs and languages of Western Asia unites an extensive acquaintance with English and European literature. The Translator now regrets that he did not more frequently avail himself of such powerful aid, so cheerfully afforded on every occasion.' Mīr Khvānd's record was taken at its face value, and among the passages singled out as of particular interest 'to those who cultivate the science of Political Economy' is 'the Oration of Minucheher,' hailed as 'containing a summary of the Oriental doctrines on that subject, emanating from a patriot king, sanctioned by the Mubeds' and received 'with acclamations by a grateful people.' The opening phrases of Minuchihr's alleged speech disclose Mīr Khvānd at his most rhetorical.

'Infinite and unbounded praises and thanksgivings to the Creator, who brought out from the cell of contingency, to the bridal chamber of existence, the youthful Brides of accidental forms in the mineral, animal, and vegetable kingdoms, by the intermarriage and conjunction of elementary matter; and has organized the chain of created Beings by the fiat of the *Káf* and *Nún*—the Mighty Predestinator, who has caused a resplendent substance in a circular body to become the centre for regulating the concerns of the celestial regions, and arranging the affairs of the kingdoms of the earth!'

The maxims for rulership prove to be nothing more than the traditional 'advice to kings' contained in so many Persian books, from the *Shāh-nāma* onwards.

'Whereas human efforts are limited to providing things necessary for the support of life, and every individual is furnished with means and resources by which success may crown his efforts, and the conceptions of imagination may be arrayed in the attire of reality, all persons, therefore, in proportion as their dispositions are inclined to moderation, and the constitution of their natural temper more endowed with fortitude, will, in the same degree, gird on the zone of exertion, to attain exalted rank and praiseworthy distinction: it is therefore incumbent on the truly wise, neither to desist a moment, by reposing on the couch of indolence, from the attainment of happiness, nor to have their attention engrossed by whatever has the stamp of novelty. That monarch is the most fortunate, who, agreeably to this saying, "He is the happiest shepherd who renders his flock most happy," devotes every time and season to the care of his subjects, and never thinks it lawful to relax in the acquittal of their claims on him; but directs all his knowledge to the curbing or punishing of oppression;—the influence of whose benefits extend to the noble and the mendicant; and who esteems it a sacred obligation to redress the injured and relieve the oppressed;—he, who never demands from the subject more than the established and regular imposts; nor ever introduces new rules or capricious innovations, which are invariably attended with small gains and great losses. . . . A good prince should be possessed of three qualities: First, whatever he says should be spoken in truth: in short, he should on no account wander in the regions of falsehood. Secondly, he should be liberal; carefully avoiding penuriousness, which renders every one despicable, but particularly a prince. Thirdly, he must be clement, and not prone to anger: as the people are subject to him, and he can do whatever he pleases, he should not therefore give way to anger, as evil results invariably proceed from this reprehensible temper.'

'To the Classical Scholar,' Shea adds, 'the accounts of Darius and Alexander the Great, as transmitted by the Historians of the East, will present a striking and amusing contrast with the history of these Monarchs as recorded by the Writers of Greece and Rome.' To indicate what amusement Mīr Khvānd has to offer on this topic, here in conclusion is his description of the death of Alexander.

'The astrologers, who calculated Iskander's nativity, had announced, that when the prince's death drew nigh, the earth under him would become iron, and the heavens above him be of gold. Now, when Zu-al-Kurnain had rested from the conquest of kingdoms, he made preparations for returning into the Ionian country: in the district of Kums, being separated from his army, a great hemorrhage seized him, so that, through the urgency of the occasion, one of the nobles spread his coat of mail under him, and, in order to keep off the inconvenience of the heat, interposed his golden shield between him and the sun. Iskander, on contemplating this arrangement, exclaimed: "This is the earth of iron and the heaven of gold, which the astrologers declared to be one of the prognostics of my death; so that my life draws to a conclusion:

Alas! the tale of youth is concluded;
The blooming spring of life is turned to December:
The bird of delight, which nestled in my heart,
I know not when it came, or when it departed."

He then sent for a secretary, to write a Letter to his mother; and, by the king's direction, the commencement of it ran thus: "This Letter is addressed from the slave, the son of a slave, namely, Iskander, (who for a short time and limited space consorted with his fellow-mortals on earth, but who, during future times and countless ages, will associate with the inhabitants of eternity), to his mother, from the benefits of whose society and attentions I derived no advantage in this abode of proximity: but, if it please God, when in the world of light and honour, and the mansions of bliss and joy, I shall have the profit of being near her." Such is the purport of the long epistle, which is recorded at length in more extended histories.

'When the world-subduing monarch had folded up the carpet of life, and expressed his cheerful resignation to the summons of the Almighty, agreeably to his testament, having wrapped his body in a shroud, they deposited it in a golden coffin, which the grandees and nobles bore, and exhibited in a great assembly. On this the chief of the people rose up, and said: "Should any one feel inclined to weep over a sovereign, it may surely be over this one. Should he choose to express his admiration, it surely may be in this instance." After which, turning towards the sages, he requested them to say something sententious and concise, expressive of the regrets of the nobles, and imparting counsel to the people. . . .

'When each of the sages, according to the measure of his science and wisdom had thus spoken a few words, they then despatched towards Iskanderieh, Zu-al-Kurnain's remains, enveloped in the mercy and forgiveness of the Almighty. The people of the city went forth to meet the bier with all possible splendor: but when it met his mother's sight, she wept over him, with moans and lamentations and accents of sorrow, and spoke thus: "O delight of mine eyes! O beloved child! I behold with astonishment, how he, whose wisdom and science had mounted to the heavens, who had made the four habitable regions his kingdom, and rendered the sovereigns of the world his slaves, now sleeps so profoundly as not to awake, and has become so silent as not to utter a word. Which of you will inform Iskander, on my part, that you gave me counsel, and I accepted it; that you condoled with me, and I was comforted; that you exhorted me to patience, and I put endurance in practice?" At this conjuncture, all the wise men, coming into her presence, condoled with her in a suitable manner; and having recourse to exhortations and counsels, then committed the blessed remains of Iskander to the earth.'

It is certainly striking, if not amusing, to find Alexander in his last moments quoting the quatrain of 'Umar Khaiyām which FitzGerald rendered so beautifully:

> Alas, that Spring should vanish with the Rose!
> That Youth's sweet-scented Manuscript should close!
> The Nightingale that in the Branches sang,
> Ah, whence, and whither flown again, who knows!

FIFTEEN

Fifteenth-Century Poets

THE springs of poetry flowed as abundantly as ever under the Tīmūrids, and the fifteenth century produced one, indeed the last, of the seven Persian immortals. But before reviewing this concluding phase of the classical epoch—for after Jāmī Persian literature is generally considered to have entered its silver period, declining slowly into sterility until its sudden renaissance in modern times—it is still necessary to look at two more prose writers of distinction who made important contributions to ethical writing. Of these the first, Jalāl al-Dīn Muḥammad ibn As'ad Davvānī was one of the most productive authors Persia ever produced; so that it is strange that E. G. Browne should have said of him that 'in spite of his fame, he seems to have left little behind him besides his work on Ethics, except some Quatrains, written and commented by himself, and an explanation of one of the odes of Ḥáfiẓ.' But Browne forgot to take into consideration Davvānī's work in Arabic, of which some seventy titles survive; nevertheless he is indeed chiefly eminent as the author of the *Akhlāq-i Jalālī*, a book in direct line of descent from Ṭūsī's *Akhlāq-i Nāṣirī*.

Davvānī was born in 1427 at Davvān near Kāzarūn, stated by Yāqūt to be 'a district of Fārs noted for the excellence of its wines.' His father was a judge who claimed to be descended from the first caliph Abū Bakr; he himself served as a provincial justice, and also taught in the Orphans' College in Shīrāz; he died close by his birthplace in 1501. Ibn al-'Imād, who inexplicably puts his *obiit* in the year 1522, states that he was visited by students from as far afield as Transoxiana and Turkey, and this is little surprising; for his commentaries on the Arab philosophers and theologians exhibit a rare gift for clear exposition. The *Akhlāq-i Jalālī* (its original and more pompous title is *Lawāmi' al-ishrāq fī makārim al-akhlāq*) was composed for Uzun Ḥasan of the 'White Sheep' dynasty, supplanter of the 'Black Sheep' in Western Persia, between 1467 and 1477 under circumstances described by Davvānī as follows.

'Of his highness's exalted nature and destiny a remarkable sign is this; that in spite of the freshness of youth, and the demands of youth and royalty, unlike those headstrong wassailers in arrogance who pass their leisure time in animal enjoyments and the encouragement of their passions, the greatest part of his auspicious moments (after the discharge of his religious duties, and attention to the claims and interests of his subjects), he condescends to devote to the principles of science, the wonders of art, the exhortations and parables of the masters in wisdom and virtue, the histories of kings who were guided by justice, and of fathers who were pillars of the faith. This is sufficiently demonstrated by the book of choice precepts and rare apophthegms culled from the discourses of famous kings, pious fathers, and eminent philosophers, which (agreeably to the text, *well is it for the assiduous in study*,) he so constantly makes the companion of his enlightened mind. Doubtless it is a book of valuable uses and lofty truths; and, as such, was deservedly kept by his highness's great predecessors in the rich repository of their choicest jewels. Yet, as it was compiled by some ancient writer, and contains terms no longer known, and curious metres such as are now not current, his highness was pleased to direct even the unprovided author of the present to correct and complete it. On examining it for the purpose, it proved to be complicated and diffuse, as touching the unity of parts in the composition; and deficient, as touching its material, in not embodying the entire authorities on the science of morals and politics. Hence it was that the writer's mind became impressed with a different plan; which was to form a fresh compilation, such, as while it contained the radices of the active science, might be illustrated as to evidence and proof from the shining light of Scripture passages, from the loop-hole where the lamp of prophetical tradition is preserved, from the torches gleaming amidst the language of the Prophet's companions and followers, the elders and leaders of the faith, and from the rays of explanation scattered in the writings of the foremost divines of nature; adhering as far as possible in appropriate places to the scope of the former treatise, and, where congenial sentiments occurred, giving prelibations from the striking passages of those who look beneath the veil, in order that the whole may be supported by the conspicuous authority of the age's chiefs. Such a work, with the Almighty's assistance, and under the countenance of our glorious prince, I hope it may be rendered, that neither the principles of science, nor the ways of practical wisdom, may be inadequately or unworthily supplied to their respective votaries.'

The version quoted is that made by W. F. Thompson of the Bengal Civil Service, and published in 1839 as *Practical Philosophy of the Muhammadan People*. It is a curious and somewhat inaccurate translation of Davvānī's book, and the extensive preliminary 'Notice of the Nature, Origin and Uses' of the text is a strange mixture of prejudice and enlightenment, from which it is sufficient to quote the concluding sentence: 'Such a piece of pleading is the following Treatise: crude and extravagant perhaps in its doctrines, as compared with the productions of more favoured countries, but embodying at least some principles sacred to the interests of right; capable in most of being reduced to the purer standards we ourselves enjoy; and, above all, teeming with that ardent enthusiasm for the cause of right (however dimly apprehended) which gives to wrong itself some of the best attributes of virtue.' Though the *Akhlāq-i Jalālī* is in truth a comparatively unoriginal book, being in the main derived through the *Akhlāq-i*

Nāṣirī from Ibn Miskawaih's *Tahdhīb al-akhlāq*, it does not lack for noble and eloquent passages.

'This is that love, the watchword of the theological divines, which contributes so much to harmonizing the disposition and enlightening the mind. No sooner does this sun of the moral world, for such may love be termed, (agreeably to the text, *It illuminated the earth with the lustre of its Lord*,) dawn upon the mental horizon, than the thick darkness of natural inclination retreats in the opposite direction, and rolls itself away. This fire which inflames the universe, (and of which the mystery is thus expressed, *it abideth not*, *neither doth it pass away*,) no sooner does it enkindle the rubbish of our lives, than the propensities of disposition are altogether consumed.

Love, beaconing on these earthly shores,
Enlightens yet consumes our clay;
The frame that sinks, the thought that soars,
The faith that guides, are all its prey.

Mysterious Minister to earth,
Yet enemy of earthly leaven!
It shifts the dross from human worth,
And sublimates the soul to heaven.'

The section 'On the Management of Wives' is not without some amusing touches. Davvānī is addressing the husband.

'Let him allow his wife no musical instruments, no visiting out of doors, no listening to men's stories, nor any intercourse with women noted for such practices; especially where any previous suspicion has been raised. We have it among the Prophet's dicta, that women should be forbidden to read or listen to the history of Joseph, lest it lead to their swerving from the rule of chastity.

'The particulars which wives should abide by are five: (1) To adhere to chastity. (2) To wear a contented demeanour. (3) To consider their husbands' dignity, and treat them with respect. (4) To submit to their directions, and beware of being refractory. (5) To humour them in their moments of merriment and not disturb them by captious remarks.

'The refuge of revelation declared that if the worship of one created thing could be permitted to another, he would have enjoined wives to worship husbands. Philosophers have said, A good wife is as a mother for affection and tenderness; as a handmaiden for content and attention; and as a friend for concord and sincerity: while a bad wife is as a rebel for unruliness and contumacy; as a foe for contemptuousness and reproach; and as a thief for treacherous designs upon her husband's purse.

'When a person is afflicted with an unsuitable wife, there is no cure for it like mutual separation, provided other considerations (as the loss of children, &c.) do not militate against it. If this is not to be contrived, there is no alternative but to soothe and humour her with money and the like. The best of all expedients next to this is to commit her to the care of some person who can restrain her from wrong-doing, and then to take a long journey, and remain a long time in the taking it. It may be that the gladdener of sorrow will vouchsafe to give thee joy, in the shape of some soft message from her side.

'The Arab philosophers say there are five sorts of wives to be avoided: yearners, favourers, deplorers, back-biters, and toad-stools. The yearner is one who has had a child by a former husband, and who indulges him out of the property of her present one. The favourer is a woman of property, who makes a favour of bestowing it upon her husband. The deplorer is one who has had a husband better, as she avers, than her present one; at whose conduct, accordingly, she is incessantly exclaiming and complaining. The back-biter is one un-invested with the robe of continence, and who, ever and anon, in her husband's absence, brands his blind side by speaking of his faults. The toad-stool is an unprincipled beauty, whom they mean to liken to vegetation springing from corruption: the same idea, indeed, we find among the dicta of the Prince of Prophets.

'Now any one who cannot or does not attend to the management of his wife had better continue in celibacy.'

The other fifteenth-century moralist was a writer of elaborately decorated prose who enjoyed an even greater vogue during the long decline of Persian letters, particularly in Moghul India where countless copies were made of his most famous book, the celebrated *Anvār-i Suhailī*. Ḥusain Vā'iẓ Kāshifī, a native of Baihaq, belonged to the large circle of scholars and authors who enjoyed the patronage of Mīr 'Alī Shīr and the protection of Ḥusain Bāiqarā. Possessing great powers as a preacher, he had regular engagements three times weekly in royal Harāt; writing was therefore for him a side-line, but one which must have been very profitable, for he composed many books on a wide variety of subjects, ranging from Koranic exegesis to hagiography and poetics. Here only two of his works will be considered: the high-minded but entertaining manual of ethics which he wrote in 1495 for Sulṭān Ḥusain's son Abu 'l-Muḥsin, and the immensely verbose paraphrase of the *Kalīla wa-Dimna* compiled at the instance of Amīr Aḥmad al-Suhailī. Kāshifī died in 1505.

The *Akhlāq-i Muḥsinī* is rather more loosely constructed than the ethical treatises of Ṭūsī and Davvānī, running rapidly through the long catalogue of moral and spiritual virtues with an enlivening commentary of illustrative anecdotes. The supreme virtue, particularly in a king, is justice.

'Justice is a regent, which regulates the state; it is a ray, giving splendour and dispelling darkness. The Almighty hath ordained this quality to his servants (when he says: *Truly God gives a commandment for justice and liberality*:) and Justice is this, that they should give redress to the oppressed; while liberality is this, that they apply the ointment of ease to the wounds of the afflicted. It is recorded, that, one moment of justice, in a king, is more preponderating, in the scale of the balance of obedience, than sixty years of devotion; because the result of devotion reaches none but the performer; while the advantage of justice attaches to noble and vulgar, small and great; and the fortunes of officers in church and state, and the prudent schemes of men connected with the government or religion, are secure and well organized by the happy influence of it. Justice extends further than the boundaries of calculation; and is beyond the limits of judgment.'

This is a quotation from *The Morals of the Beneficent*, a greatly shortened version of Kāshifī's original made by the Rev. H. G. Keene and dedicated 'to the Students of the East India Company' (Hertford, 1850). 'I had the satisfaction for several years to serve as a Professor in your College,' the benevolent translator explained. 'I wish I could think that my usefulness was equal to my earnest desire for the prosperity of our Indian possessions; the welfare of the natives; and the health and happiness of those who are called, by Providence, to the important duty of governing those ancient and interesting nations.' It seems appropriate to add Keene's rendering of a passage from Chapter XI—On a Lofty Spirit.

'They have related, that, in those days when Alexander was intending that he would carry aloft the standard of empire from the confines of Greece, for the purpose of seizing the kingdoms of Arabia and Persia, and that he would set the August stirrup in motion for the design of conquering the land and the ocean of the world—he was thoughtful and sad in mind. Aristotle, the philosopher, who was his minister, when he saw signs of thoughtfulness, and marks of anxiety on the aspect of his condition, and the forehead of his affairs, said, "O king of the world! the means of prosperity are ready and prepared; troops and attendants stand in the station of service and obedience; the treasury is replenished; fortune is arrayed in the quality of continuance; the shrub of prosperity is adorned with the honour of steadfastness;

success has tied on the girdle of alliance: while dignity and glory sit at the royal threshold in attendance;—what reason is there for this distraction of thy brilliant mind, and for this disturbance of thy splendid spirit?" Alexander answered thus, "I am considering that the expanse of the world is extremely contemptible, and the extent of the Seven Climes is very contracted: I am ashamed to mount my horse for the sake of this portion of territory, and to set off for the acquisition and conquest of it.

The length and breadth of the Seven Climes would not form
 a reward for this;
That I, with the design of conquering it, should mount my
 horse;
If there were a thousand worlds of this kind, it is too little still;
That I, with the design of controul, should set off for those
 parts."

Aristotle said, "There is no doubt, that the possession and government of this bit of world is not suitable to thy high ambition, and is not worthy of thy noble desires. Unite the kingdom of eternity with it: that as by the stroke of the world-burning sword, thou bringest this perishable mansion within the limits of seizure, by the blessing of justice enlightening the world, thou mayest also bring the kingdom of eternal happiness into the grasp of a just claim; so that this imperfection may be reconciled with the blessing of that perfection, and this trifle may, by the glory of the other, become great, and receive splendour.

Seek the kingdom of futurity, for it is joyful;
An atom from that kingdom would be a hundred
 worlds;
Strive, that, in the midst of this abode;
The expanse of that world may come into thy hand."

Alexander having found consolation upon this discourse, gave excessive praise to the philosopher. And to this day the falcon of the wisdom of each perfect man takes its flight in the atmosphere of the praise of Alexander; for this reason that the phœnix of his ambition did not stoop her head to the bone of the fragments of this world.'

The *Anvār-i Suhailī*, after exercising for three centuries the best skill of calligraphers and miniaturists, took its place among the earliest Persian texts to be printed in British India: Captain C. Stewart superintended its production at Calcutta in 1804. The same scholar brought out a version of the seventh chapter at London in 1821; fourteen years more passed, and the Rev. H. G. Keene published at Hertford the first book with 'a literal translation.' It was in 1854 that *The Lights of Canopus* appeared in full splendour in our Western sky, when E. B. Eastwick (whose *Gulistān* had made so poor an impression on Edward FitzGerald) dedicated 'to Her Most Gracious Majesty Queen Victoria' 650 pages of Kāshifī in close-printed English. (Twenty-three years later Sir A. N. Wollaston would perform the self-same work of supererogation.) Eastwick admitted candidly that his *opus magnum* was intended primarily for 'those who desire to qualify themselves for examination in our Indian territories. To them the present Translation is offered with far more confidence than to the English public, for it is impossible not to perceive that those very characteristics of style, which form its chiefest beauties in the eye of Persian taste, will appear to the European reader as ridiculous blemishes. The undeviating equipoise of bi-propositional sentences, and oftentimes their length and intricacy; the hyperbole and sameness of metaphor, and the rudeness and unskilfulness of the plots of some of the stories, cannot but be wearisome and repulsive to the better and simpler judgment of the West.' It would have been more accurate to speak of the appeal of this book to a *debased* Persian taste; for Kāshifī's style bears the unmistakable hallmark of aesthetic corruption, and would have been as contemptuously spurned by a generation that had never known Juvainī and Vaṣṣāf as it is now rejected by a public educated to appreciate older and austerer models. 'The

Preface may be dismissed from consideration at once, as being a turgid specimen of the obscure and repulsive preludes with which Persian writers think fit to commence their compositions.' So wrote Eastwick; and one cannot but admire the conscientiousness with which he strove to unravel 'the gigantic toils of an endless prolixity and verboseness, which it would require a Hercules to disentangle.'

'Such is the exhortation of the Kuran, and the advice [contained in] the sacred book, which comprehends both exoteric and esoteric kinds [of knowledge], and contains all mysteries religious and mundane, and from the words and meaning of which every one, whether reader or hearer, according to his degree, reaps advantage, and "*to it the speaker alludes.*"

COUPLET

The young spring of its loveliness makes soul and spirit fresh;
Its scent delights the pious, and its hue enchants the flesh.

And this kind of speech has been poured out and sent down on not even one of the greatest prophets, except our Prophet (May blessing and peace be upon him!); nay, it is the distinctive privilege of His Holiness, the seal of prophecy; *as he* (*The blessing and peace of God be upon him!*), *indicated in this*, "*I have received the All-comprehensive Words*:" and, inasmuch as sincerity of obedience is a cause of inheriting special intimacy with God, and productive of the verification of relationship to Him, assuredly the minds of a select number of His great people (who are characterized by the mark, "*Ye are the best nation that hath been raised up unto mankind*"), have become the recipients of the lights of the most resplendent rays of that universality [of knowledge] the borrowing of which may be [affirmed to be] from the niche of the high prophetical office of that holy person; and hence they consider *that* to be perfect discourse, in the survey of the beauty of the meaning of which, the eye of the superficial observers derives benefit from the words, and is irradiated by the expressions; while the nostril of the esoteric examiners is perfumed by the sweet odours of the truths and niceties which are discoverable under its external sense; so that each individual, in proportion to his capacity, has derived a share from its table of unlimited advantages.

HEMISTICH

No seeker passes from it uncontent.

And, from the tenor of these premises, it is understood that the more the face of each word is adorned with the soft down and mole of knowledge, and the more the cheek of each advice is embellished with the cosmetic of universal wisdom, so much the more is the heart of true lovers inclined to survey its adornments.

COUPLET

The more each one is lovely 'mid the fair,
The more the gaze of all is centred there.'

In an earlier chapter a comparison was instituted between Ibn al-Muqaffaʿ and his Persian translator Naṣr Allāh, their versions of the story of the Ascetic and the Pot being chosen for this purpose. Kāshifī's verbosity is well illustrated in his elaborate treatment of the same anecdote.

'They have related that a pious man had a house in the vicinity of a merchant, and lived happily through favor of his neighborly kindness. The merchant continually sold honey and oil, and made his profits by that traffic in unctuous and sweet commodities. Inasmuch as the pious man lived a blameless life, and ever sowed in the field of his guileless heart the seed of the love of God, the merchant reposed implicit confidence in him, and took the supply of his wants upon himself. And in this very thing is the use of riches,—to win over the hearts of the poor, and to raise up a perpetual provision from perishable wealth.

COUPLET

Win, O rich man! the heart's love of the poor,
For golden treasures are a fleeting store.

'The merchant, too, considering the opportunity of doing good a blessing, sent every day somewhat from the stock, in the buying and selling of which he was occupied, for the support of the Devotee. The latter used somewhat of this and stored up the rest in a corner. In a short time a jar was filled by these means. One day the pious man looked into that jar, and thought thus to himself, "Well, now! what quantity of honey and oil is collected in this vessel?" At last he conjectured ten mans to be there, and said, "If I can sell these for ten dirams, I can buy for that sum five ewes, and these five will each have young every six months, and each will have two lambs. Thus in a year there will be twenty-five, and in ten years from their progeny there will be herds upon herds. So by these means I shall have an abundant supply, and will sell some, and lay in a handsome stock of furniture, and wed a wife of a noble family. After nine months, I shall have a son born to me, who will study science and polite manners. However, when the weakness of infancy is exchanged for the strength of youth, and that graceful cypress grows up in the garden of manhood, it is probable that he may transgress my orders, and begin to be refractory, and in that case it will be necessary for me to correct him, and I will do so with this very staff which I hold in my hand." He then lifted up his staff, and was so immersed in thought, that, fancying the head and neck of his rebellious son before him, he brought down the staff, and struck it on the jar of honey and oil. It happened that the jar was placed on a shelf, beneath which he sate with it facing him. As soon as his staff reached the jar, it broke it, and let out the honey and oil all over the head and face and vest and hair of the pious man.

HEMISTICH

And all these schemes at once dissolved away.'

The reader will observe that the foregoing extract corresponds with only the second part of Ibn al-Muqaffa''s original; the first part is even more extravagantly inflated. It would be a long time before any Persian author would have the resolution and the boldness to call a spade a spade.

The first of the poets now to be discussed survived only a little way into the fifteenth century and therefore did most of his work in the fourteenth. Muḥammad Shīrīn Maghribī, born about 1350 perhaps near Iṣfahān, is said to have owed his poetical name to the fact that he had travelled in the Maghrib; a personal friend of Kamāl al-Dīn of Khujand, he resided like him most of his life in Tabrīz, where he died in 1407. He was a passionate Ṣūfī, and his poetry follows the tradition of Anṣārī, Bābā Ṭāhir, Rūmī and 'Irāqī. 'His doctrine, 'wrote Riḍā Qulī Khān, 'is the unity of Being; his source of inspiration is the pleasure of direct vision. Only one theme is to be found in all his utterance; his refrains and lyrics are charged with the realities of unitarianism.' The *Dīvān* of Maghribī, which was lithographed twice in the nineteenth century, has been calculated to contain about 2,300 verses; the style is very fluent, but abounds in those metaphysical conceits which were the commonplaces of this school of poetry.

O centre and pivot of Being, circumference of bounty,
firm-fixed as the Pole-star, inconstant as the Sphere,
if I send 'Peace' to Thee, Thou art Thyself all peace,
or if I send thee 'Blessing,' Thou art all blessing.
How can any give Thee to Thee? O tell me that,
Thou who givest as alms Thyself and art Thyself alms.
Most utter of manifests, in manifestation most perfect,
barrier of all barriers, gatherer of dispersion,
most beauteous of the beautiful, comeliest of the comely,
most charming of the charming, subtlest of subtleties!
Both sickness and cure art Thou, both sorrow and joy;
both lock and key art Thou, both prison and release,

both treasure and talisman, both body and spirit,
both name and the thing named, both essence and attributes;
both Maghribī and the West, both Eastern and the East,
Throne, Carpet and Element, both heavens and space.

It may be noted that in the first verse the word translated 'circumference' also bears the meaning of 'ocean,' poets always liking to speak of an 'ocean of bounty' when praising munificence. Similarly in the last couplet there is a pun between Maghribī, the poet's name, and its literal signification of 'Western.' The whole poem, inspired as it is by the pantheistic (or rather panentheistic) theosophy of Ibn 'Arabī, might well have found a place in the *Dīvān-i Shams-i Tabrīz*.

Thou art a drop; speak not of the depths of Ocean;
  Thou art a mote; speak not of the Sun sublime.
Man of To-day, seek not to express the notion
  Of all the past and future spans of Time.

Since thou hast knowledge neither of earth nor heaven,
  Speak not henceforward of 'over' and 'below';
Ignorant if the Scale be of eight or seven,
  Talk not so glibly of 're' and 'te' and 'do.'

My son, have done with denial and affirmation,
  The bold 'exception' and the confident 'nay';
If thou art bidden to self-immolation,
  Go, sacrifice thy self, and nothing say!

Of 'I' and 'we' so long as naught thou knowest,
  Be silent; speak no more of 'I' and 'we';
Breathe not the names of highest or of lowest,
  Till God shall teach thee what the names may be.

He who of all things the prime source became
Bade Maghribī: 'Of things no thing proclaim!'

Maulānā Abū Isḥāq Ḥallāj of Shīrāz wrote poetry of a very different kind. A favourite of Tīmūr's grandson Iskandar, governor of Fārs until he was blinded by his uncle Shāh-Rukh, he began life as a cotton-carder and made his fortune by his wit; he had an astonishing gift for parody, and most of his compositions are amusing and sometimes obscene imitations of the poems of the eminent. In addition to his *Dīvān-i Aṭʿima* ('Food Poems'), the Galata edition of his collected works contains a 'Treatise on the Affair of the Rice and the Pasty.'

'The saffron-pilaff-gobblers of the kitchen of eloquence and the haggis-renders of the table of oratory, the macaroni-tossers of the cauldron of expression and the sheep's-tail-fat-basters of the roast of reference have so related. . . .'

A few other short essays similar in character complete the Rabelaisian collection. Busḥāq, as he called himself, died between 1424 and 1427. To attempt to convey through translation the flavour of his verse is a thankless and impossible task; here follows a poor and partial impression of his parody of a lyric by Ḥāfiẓ, the original model being given first.

Blame not the drunkard, zealot,
In pride of purity;
The wickedness of others
Shall not be charged to thee.

If I be saint or sinner,
Be thou thyself, and go!
For in the end each gathers
The harvest he doth sow.

Of God's eternal bounty
O make me not despair;
Behind the veil who knoweth
What ugly is, what fair?

Not I alone have riven
The veil of piety;
My father, too, abandoned
Supreme felicity.

Upon the tavern's threshold
Submissive I remain,
And whoso comprehends not,
Why, let him break his brain!

Ḥāfiẓ' poem speaks of mystical subtleties; Bushāq twists it into a very different shape.

Blame not the pottage, pastry,
In pride of purity;
It shall not have for leaven
The light-mixed dough of thee.

If mastic, chives and onions
Thou droppest in the dough,
Why, in the end each gathers
The harvest he doth sow.

Within the pie one cannot
Affirm the syrup's there;
Behind the veil who knoweth
What ugly is, what fair?

For bread I am not seeking;
For corn, as all agree,
My father, too, abandoned
Supreme felicity.

Go, garnish the bouillon,
The date-loaf knead again;
Who would deny this banquet,
Why, let him break his brain!

Even Ḥāfiẓ' most famous poem of all was not regarded by the Cotton-carder as sacrosanct.

> A Khurāsānī dish of paste
> If thou wouldst set before my hand,
> I'll barter for its fragrant fry
> Bukhārā, yea, and Samarqand.

These curious and clever verses provide the serious scholar with a happy hunting-ground; for not only do they abound in rare culinary terms precious to the lexicographer, they also incidentally constitute extremely early testimony—earlier than any known manuscript—to the wording and verse-order of many poems of Ḥāfiẓ.

The Ni'mat-Allāhī order of dervishes, active to this day in parts of Persia, derives its name from Shāh Nūr al-Dīn Muḥammad Ni'mat Allāh Valī, son of Mīr 'Abd Allāh, a renowned poet and a powerful saint who was born at Aleppo in 1330, being descended from Muḥammad Bāqir the fifth Imām of the Shī'a. When twenty-four years of age he made the pilgrimage to Mecca and there came under the influence of the Ṣūfī teacher and biographer 'Abd Allāh al-Yāfi'ī, whose *khalīfa* he eventually became. After al-Yāfi'ī's death he travelled into north-eastern Persia and settled at Māhān near Kirmān, where he died a centenarian on April 5, 1431. His tomb is still a centre of pilgrimage; in his lifetime he enjoyed the admiring patronage of many rulers including Shāh-Rukh, and his grandsons were welcomed to the Deccan by Aḥmad Shāh Bahmanī; his blood was mingled in the veins of the Ṣafavid kings of Persia. He is said to have written over five hundred treatises on mysticism 'on different questions of Ṣūfī doctrine. About a hundred of these have come down to us and can be identified. They are for the most part quite short treatises, generally explanations of difficult passages in the classics of Ṣūfīsm like Ibn al-'Arabī, Fakhr al-Dīn 'Irāḳī, etc.' E. Berthels adds, 'His large *Dīwān* of lyrics is more valuable; it contains much true poetry and is marked by a fervent sincerity.' Indeed it is only his *Dīvān* that has attracted interest in modern times; after being lithographed at Teheran in 1860 it was republished in 1948 by Maḥmūd Amīn al-Islām Kirmānī in 560 pages. The introduction is a piece of unusually prolix and tortuous prose, a fine specimen of post-classical survival.

'It does not remain hidden how with the onslaught and domination of the wicked Tartars over the Islamic kingdoms and the fall of Baghdad, which was reckoned the capital of the kingdoms and the centre of the mighty caliphate, the greater portion of the lands of Central Asia and the Arabian Peninsula became exposed to general slaughter and the frightful oppressions of that irreligious and lawless people, and throughout this wide expanse all the vestiges of science, literature and religion together with every good custom and laudable usage were totally destroyed and annihilated, so much so that a bridge was built over the Tigris out of scientific, religious and literary books, and because of the grief and sorrow felt over the loss of those precious treasures a veritable Tigris of tears was poured forth from the eyes of the seekers after knowledge, yet in view of the truthfulness of the promise of the greatest Lawgiver the divine grace was directed towards the Muslims and after total despair the lightning-flash of hope shone forth. On the one hand the Aiyūbid Sulṭāns with extraordinary and unimaginable courage and steadfastness, while sorely tried by the Crusades, interposed a strong and solid barrier in the face of the torrent of upheavals and smashed to pieces the irresistible attacks of the Mongols, saving Syria, Egypt and Asia Minor from cruel oppression and genocidal tyranny; on the other hand scholars and men of learning, especially esoteric theologians and the followers of the mystic way, who are reckoned the spirit within the body of the faith, by dint of unendurable labours and sacrifices through multitudinous pronouncements strove to bind the broken and reform the corrupt, and that irreligious people who were the enemies of all law and of the entire human species following those guidance-giving communications entered upon the highway of rectitude and veracity. Finally the victors were vanquished by the truth of the Islamic religion and placed about their necks the collar of the Ḥanīfite faith, and Islam too was saved from extinction.'

The editor, 'overwhelmed by the burden of sin and wickedness' as he humbly confesses, then describes how in thankfulness for this deliverance men converted in mass to the Ṣūfī way of abstinence and self-abasement, and names among the leaders of this movement 'that moon of Māhān' (a pun on 'moons'), 'that king of kings' Saiyid Nūr al-Dīn Ni'mat Allāh Valī. He explains that his *Dīvān* had already been printed once before, thanks to the initiative of pious Pārsīs, but that edition was 'full of shocking errors and defects.'

'One day, in the *khānqāh* of Āqā Saiyid Abu 'l-Qāsim Vafī 'Alī-Shāh Sīrajānī (may God continue his blessings) a group of gnostics were discussing the *Dīvān* of Ḥaḍrat-i Shāh and expressing their regret that it was so erroneous and defective. The Saiyid said, "If anyone would undertake the expense, I would labour to correct it." His Excellency Āqā Sardār Nuṣrat accepted to find a part of the outlay, and several other persons followed his lead and shared in the costs of printing. The Saiyid applied himself to the task and assembled many manuscripts from far and near, toiling for a long while until he completed the correction successfully. Āqā-yi Mīrzā Kāẓim Khān, the grandson of Raunaq 'Alī-Shāh, volunteered to transcribe the text; and by the blessing of Ḥaḍrat-i Shāh at the very time the transcription was finished the printing-press was brought to Kirmān and all means were at hand for printing the book. But owing to a number of vicissitudes the completion was delayed until the year A.H. 1336, when His Excellency Āqā Shaikh Yaḥyā (may his blessings continue) was appointed Director of Education and Bequests in Kirmān. He laboured to good purpose to extend education, so much so that nearly fifteen schools were founded in the district of Kirmān.'

Among the good works performed by Sardār Nuṣrat was his providing for the completion of the publication of Ni'mat Allāh's *Dīvān*. The poetry has been characterized by E. G. Browne as 'on the whole monotonous and mediocre, similar in style and subject-matter to that of Maghribī, and altogether lacking the consuming ardour and brilliant illustration of Shams-i Tabrīz.' This is by no means an unfair estimate, for there are very few original ideas or artifices to be found in the collection; one feature however which has escaped notice is the remarkable number of poems containing seven couplets—a curious coincidence with the sonnet which also appears in the lyrics of Jāmī.

The sea is surging and rolling towards us;
the pearls of the sea are raining upon us;
His Majesty the Sultan of Love is counting
one by one the treasure of the Names out to us.
We are the trustees, and the trust is His;
what once He committed, He now commits to us.
Our field is secure from the year of dryness;
His mercy is evermore raining on us.
My Friend plays again the game of friendship;
He is sowing well the seed of goodness in us.
I have good hopes that His bountiful grace
will not leave longer our 'ourness' in us.
Never ant had reason to fear hurt from us,
how then should our Master do hurt to us?

In this poem Ni'mat Allāh recalls three Koranic passages. The sense of new creation experienced in the mystical rapture leads him to compare himself with Adam, and Sūra II 29 records:

And He taught Adam the names, all of them.

The same thought reminds him of the divine trust which man undertook at the beginning, as Sūra XXXIII 72 states:

> We offered the trust to the heavens and the earth
> and the mountains, but they refused to carry it
> and were afraid of it; and man carried it.

In his final verse the poet is remembering Solomon's adventure as mentioned in Sūra XXVII 17:

> And his hosts were mustered to Solomon,
> jinn, men and birds, duly disposed;
> till, when they came on the Valley of Ants,
> an ant said, 'Ants, enter your
> dwelling-places, lest Solomon and
> his hosts crush you, being unaware!'
> But he smiled, laughing at his words.

He may also well have had in mind the verses of Sa'dī quoting Firdausī, which Sir William Jones translated.

> Crush not yon ant, who stores the golden grain:
> He lives with pleasure, and will die with pain:
> Learn from him rather to secure the spoil
> Of patient cares and persevering toil.

The following poem also begins with the familiar simile of the Sea.

> We are of the sea, and the sea is our essence;
> why then is there this duality between us?
> The world is an imaginary line before the sight;
> read well that line, for it was inscribed by us.
> Whatsoever we possess in both the worlds
> in reality, my friend, belongs to God.

His love I keep secretly in my heart;
the lees of the pain of His love is our cure.
Companions are we of the cup, comrades of the saki,
lest thou suppose that he is apart from us:
it is the assembly of love, and we are drunk—
who ever enjoyed so royal a party?
So long as Niʻmat Allāh is the slave of the Lord,
the king of the world is as a beggar at his door.

The imagery of wine and the tavern is far from neglected.

Last night in a dream I saw the phantom image of his face;
I saw that drunkenly he was drawing me towards him.
With a hundred coquetries the Christian child embraced me—
his waist was bound with a girdle, his hair was flowing free.
My love has the breath of Jesus, bringing new life to my heart;
with whomsoever I speak now, my conversation is of him.
The world has become irradiated by the light of his presence;
sweet-scented grows the earth from his musk-perfumed tresses.
The darling's love is a treasure hidden in the heart's recess;
if you desire the treasure, seek it in the heart's recess.
Saki, bring wine, and pour it over the crown of my head;
of your kindness wash this robe that wraps about my breast.
Like the ecstatic nightingale I fell upon the rose's face;
for love of Niʻmat Allāh he laid his cheek upon mine.

Niʻmat Allāh, as we have seen, was related to the Ṣafavid house through his descendants; his contemporary Muʻīn al-Dīn ʻAlī called Qāsim-i Anvār, also a Ṣūfī poet born near Tabrīz in 1356, was the pupil of Ṣadr al-Dīn Ardabīlī, an ancestor of the Ṣafavids. He travelled much, particularly in Gīlān, and Gīlānī expressions have been noticed in his vocabulary; later, like Niʻmat Allāh, he removed to the north-west, making his home first in Nīshāpūr and then in Harāt. When an attempt was made on Shāh-Rukh's life in 1426 by a Ḥurūfī heretic, Qāsim-i Anvār (whose poetry exhibits Ḥurūfī tendencies) fell under suspicion of complicity and was banished. Ulugh Beg the royal astronomer harboured him in Samarqand for a while, but later he returned to Khurāsān and settled in Kharjird, where he died in 1433.

Qāsim-i Anvār wrote at least two prose treatises and an epitome of Sa'dī's *Būstān* in addition to a considerable quantity of original verse, but neither his *Dīvān* nor his other work has so far been published. A few specimens of his compositions are given by Daulatshāh, and E. G. Browne has quoted and translated several poems; ten pieces are also included in N. Bland's *Century of Persian Ghazels*. Browne remarks that his poetry 'so far as a foreigner may venture to judge it, is only of average merit, and is generally of the same mystical character as that of Maghribí and other kindred poets.' V. F. Büchner cautiously assents to this opinion: 'One cannot deny his ability to write pleasing Persian verse but we look in vain for anything out of the way which would give him a claim to a place among the great names of Persian literature. A just verdict of his literary activity, however, will only be possible when his works have been published.'

Sa'dī's influence is apparent in the following anecdote told in rhyming couplets in the *Anīs al-'ārifīn* and translated by E. G. Browne.

A negro, lacking reason, faith and taste,
Whose life the demon Folly had laid waste
Had in a jar some treacle set aside,
And by mischance a mouse fell in and died.
He seized the mouse and plucked it out with speed—
That cursed mouse, whose death was caused by greed.
Then to the Qáḍí sped the unwilling wight,
Taking the mouse, and told of Fortune's spite.
The Judge before the folk, refined and rude,
Condemned the treacle as unfit for food.
The luckless negro scouted this award,
Saying, 'You make a great mistake, my Lord!

I tasted it, and found it sweet and good;
If sweet, it cannot be unfit for food.
Had this my treacle bitter been, then sure
Unlawful had I held it and impure.'
The mind perverted of this black accursed
Bitter and sweet confounded and reversed.
Sin seemeth sweet and service sour, alack!
To thee whose face is as a negro's black.
To passion's palate falsehood seemeth sweet;
Bitter is truth to natures incomplete.
When men are sick and biliously inclined
The taste of sugar alum calls to mind.
Sick for this world all hearts, both young and old,
Jaundiced for love of silver and of gold.
O captive in the snare of worldly joys,
Perish not mouse-like for the sweet that cloys!
Though bitter seems God's discipline to thee
This bitter drug is thy sure remedy.
This bitter drug will cause thine ill's surcease,
And give the patient healing, rest and peace.

In his lyrics Qāsim-i Anvār shows the same predilection which we have already observed in Niʿmat Allāh for the poem of seven couplets.

Of thy favour, Cup-bearer, fill me up that clear and crystalline bowl,
That spirit of holy sanctity, that high and exalted soul!
What day thou givest a cup of wine to settle our whole affair
Bestow, I pray, of your charity a draught on yon Preacher rare!
Would'st thou that the motes of the universe may with thee in the dance be whirled?
Then toss aside in thy dance's stride thy tresses tangled and curled!

O chiding mentor, get thee hence: desist and cease thy strain,
For never thy windy talk can drive from our heads this passion
and pain.
'Lose thyself,' thou didst say, 'that thou to thyself the way
may'st gain!'
But this riddle dark and inscrutable I cannot solve or explain.
Whenever I cast my life away, a hundred I win in its place:
Who can limit the miracles of Christ and His healing grace?
Qásim ne'er of his own free will would play the lover's part,
But what can he do when the matter lies with the Lord of the
Soul and Heart?

The ingenious translator of this Ḥāfiẓ-like poem is again E. G. Browne. Here finally is a composition in a shorter measure.

In Lovers' Road there stands a shrine,
Within, a lovely idol dwelling
Whom no man knows, but of that sign
Mysterious every tongue is telling.

Before that candle the sun's light
Is dimmed, so many moths surround it;
That tress and mole recall aright
A baited snare, as I have found it.

Saki, since I have broken troth
Pour me again a goodly beaker!
His languid glance is nothing loth
To intoxicate the thirsty seeker
Who'll find rare pearls within the sea
That is the tears of Qāsimī.

Another considerable poet of the fifteenth century whose works still await an editor is Shams al-Dīn Muḥammad ibn 'Abd Allāh Kātibī of Turshīz, a village district in the province of

Nīshāpūr. He tried his luck with the Tīmūrids at Harāt, but finding no favour there he proceeded to Mīrzā Shaikh Ibrāhīm's court at Shīrvān. Continuing westwards at a time when most poets were tending to migrate eastwards, he failed to amuse Iskandar ibn Qarā Yūsuf of Azerbaijan and leaving him with a scurrilous lampoon passed on to Iṣfahān. There he experienced a conversion; renouncing the life of panegyrist which had brought him so little satisfaction, he resigned himself to God and devoted the rest of his life (which ended at Astarābād about 1435) to Ṣūfī meditation. His literary output was considerable. In his earlier years he had written a number of romantic idylls of remarkable prosodic ingenuity as well as odes and lyrics; at Astarābād he proposed to construct a *Khamsa* in emulation of Niẓāmī, but death of the plague forestalled him before he could complete this ambitious project. 'In my humble opinion,' Mīr 'Alī Shīr Navā'ī remarks, 'his poetical talent was such that had he enjoyed the patronage of a ruler, like our own most fortunate Sovereign, capable of appreciating good verse, and had his life endured longer, he would have captured the hearts of all with his effusions.' Jāmī summed up his opinion of Kātibī by describing his verse as an assortment of 'cats and camels.' C. Huart found it in his heart to rebuke him for improvidence: 'He spent the whole of his life in poverty as a result of the foolish prodigality which made him spend in a few days the sums he received from the munificence of his patrons.'

The few lyrics of Kātibī that have been printed exhibit no extraordinary features; they reach an average high standard of competence, and they are nearly all seven couplets long.

My darling drew his dagger, and my heart is half-slain:
come gladly forth, my soul, for your desire is at hand.
That fairy-fair has returned, and draws, draws insanely;
wise is he today whosoever insanely draws.
Crimson is the needle that stitched my wounded breast,
crimson not from my blood, but from the fire in my heart.

A thousand like caravans have been lost on the road of love;
ask the caravan-leader what this halting-station may be.
My heart, crave not for the turquoise seal-ring of the sky:
forgo this bezel, for it is full of deadly poison.
Be not a prey to the world, for in the turn of heaven's bow
many a game has been slaughtered by this pebble of clay.
Fair is the script of love on the heart's tablet, Kātibī:
every proof that bears not that attestation is void.

The 'pebble of clay' hurled by malignant heaven at gullible mortals is presumably a poetic reminiscence of those strange missiles which, according to Koran CV, destroyed the 'Men of the Elephant.'

Hast thou not seen how thy Lord did with the Men of the Elephant?
Did He not make their guile to go astray?
And He loosed upon them birds in flights,
hurling against them stones of baked clay
and He made them like green blades devoured.

The man without love, though outwardly he be a human
in truth only the name flourishes—the city is waste.
Whosoever sits a guest at the table of love
is replete with the delicacies of this world and that.
Both worlds are dedicated on the altar of love,
but only the lover knows this, for he is full of wisdom.
If you consider well the sea, the pearl of love
won from that mine is the base of all elements.
Love is the *qibla* to which men pure of heart turn:
the Kaaba is a heap of sand from this wilderness.
Seek pomp and circumstance from love, for if an ant
had possession of love's ring, he would be a Solomon.
Love converts the heart's sparrow into a phœnix:
O Kātibī, this is the very speech of the birds!

The *zabān-i murghān* mentioned in the last verse of this poem is a literal Persian rendering of that *manṭiq al-ṭair* or 'speech of the birds' stated in Koran XXVII 16 to have been taught by God to Solomon. In comparing his own poetry with this language Kātibī not only flatters himself after the approved fashion, but he also conveys by implication the pleasing suggestion that his patron, by understanding and suitably rewarding the poet, will thereby prove himself to be as wise (and, it is hoped, as wealthy) as Solomon. The *qibla* to which reference is made in an earlier verse is the Mecca-ward direction faced by all Muslims when they pray.

Not a great deal needs to be said of the last poet considered in this chapter, 'Ārifī of Harāt who died in 1449 and whose tenuous claim to immortality rests upon a single and not very long poem. The *Gūy u chaugān* ('Ball and Polo-stick') is stated by its proud author to have been composed in a fortnight.

> The style that belongs to 'Ārifī's poetry
> cannot be described by every pen:
> this utterance is fancy from end to end,
> a magic that is lawful to me only.
> This new moon mounts to the highest zenith
> having taken its ray from the East of the soul;
> in two weeks, for the sake of its name, I
> completed it, like the fourteen-days moon.
> This poem, that is like a rolling pearl
> lovely as befits the ear of the Sultan—
> when I reckoned up the number of its lines
> I found the sum came to five hundred and one.

This *mathnavī*, which has been edited and translated by R. S. Greenshields, compares the life of the mystic with a game of polo; the likeness had already occurred to 'Umar Khaiyām in another context, as admirers of Edward FitzGerald will remember.

> The Ball no question makes of Ayes and Noes,
> But Here or There as strikes the Player goes;
> And He that toss'd you down into the Field,
> *He* knows about it all—He knows—HE knows!

SIXTEEN

Jāmī

'THE soothing modulations of the nightingale of Shīrāz, Khvāja Shams al-Dīn Muḥammad Ḥāfiẓ, had not yet reached the ears of mortal men when Shams al-Din Muḥammad Dashtī of Iṣfahān found shelter in Samarqand from the hands of the marauding Turks. It was in the village of Kharjird (Jām) that he finally settled, and there took to himself in marriage the daughter of one of the descendants of Imām Muḥammad ibn Ḥasan Shaibānī. Of this union a child was born named Aḥmad who also elected to reside in the same town, where he became occupied in the administration of justice. Some while later he went to Harāt to clear up certain affairs, and on his return found in his arms a five-year-old child. This child was called 'Abd al-Raḥmān; afterwards he was known throughout the lands as Jāmī. It was thirty-one years since the shining star of Ḥāfiẓ had set, and now the hand of destiny placed another candle in the lamp-stand of Persian literature.'

With these quaint but graphic words H. Pizhmān introduces to the reader (in his edition of the *Dīvān* of Jāmī) the man universally regarded as the last eminent figure in the history of classical Persian literature, 'the greatest master of verse and prose to appear in Persia during the ninth century of Islam' as Dr. 'Alī Aṣghar Ḥikmat justly claims. Mullā Nūr al-Dīn 'Abd al-Raḥmān ibn Aḥmad Jāmī was born on November 7, 1414, and died at Harāt on November 9, 1492; these dates are certain, for we possess unusually abundant and reliable materials for his biography. His life thus spanned almost the whole of the fifteenth century, as Ḥāfiẓ had the fourteenth and Sa'dī the thirteenth; his literary output matched the length of his days. 'By reason of the extreme elevation of his genius,' wrote Sām Mīrzā, Shāh Ismā'īl's son, in his *Tuḥfa-yi Sāmī*, 'there is no need to describe his condition or set forth any account of him, since the rays of his virtues have reached from the East to the uttermost parts of the West, while the bountiful table of his excellencies is spread from shore to shore.' Bābur the great Mogul inscribed in his diary that 'in exoteric and esoteric learning there was none equal to him' and that he was 'too exalted for there to be any need for praising him.'

It was in Harāt that Jāmī acquired that profound learning in all branches of the Islamic sciences which qualified him to write with authority on the interpretation of the Koran, the Traditions of Muḥammad, the biography of the Prophet, Arabic grammar, poetics and prosody, music and riddles, and made of him among the most erudite of Persian poets. But an even earlier contact made in his native Jām in 1419 destined him for the mystical life, when the Naqshbandī saint Khvāja Muḥammad Pārsā chanced to pass through the town on his pilgrimage to Mecca. Jāmī recorded in later life how 'the pure refulgence of his beaming countenance is even now, as then, clearly visible to me, and my heart still feels the joy I experienced from that happy meeting. I firmly believe that that bond of union, friendship, confidence, and love, which subsequently bound the great body of pious spirits to this humble creature, is wholly due to the fortunate influence of his glance.' Jāmī paid tribute to 'the great body of pious spirits' in his *Nafaḥāt al-uns*, composed in 1478, in which he revised and continued the biographies of the saints written long before by al-Sulamī and translated by Anṣārī; sixty years after his encounter with Muḥammad Pārsā he made a little collection of his sayings as a grateful offering to his memory.

Jāmī did not have to wait until after his death to be acclaimed as a great writer; kings and princes competed to do him honour during his lifetime. Dr. Ḥikmat, to whose admirable monograph

Jāmī (Teheran, 1942) reference has already been made, enumerates the poet's patrons in the following order. First, in 1452 Jāmī dedicated the *Ḥilya-yi ḥulal* (a treatise on riddles) to Mīrzā Abu 'l-Qāsim Bābur, grandson of Shāh-Rukh and son of Bāisunghur, who died in 1457. Secondly, he wrote occasional verses in praise of Mīrzā Abū Sa'īd, son of Khalīl Sulṭān, who ruled over the Tīmūrid empire from 1451 to 1467, but 'the Sulṭān did not recognize his merit as he should have done.' Thirdly, Sulṭān Ḥusain Bāiqarā, the last of the Tīmūrids (reigned 1469–1506) not only exchanged letters with Jāmī but applauded his genius in his book *Majālis al-'ushshāq*; in return Jāmī commemorated him in his *Bahāristān* as well as in several idylls and many odes. Fourthly, Mīr 'Alī Shīr Navā'ī (whom Jāmī initiated into the Naqshbandī fraternity), 'though countless scholars, poets and artists had gathered like moths about the candle of his munificence, himself took the initiative in seeking out Jāmī and clutched his skirts with the hand of servitude'; Ḥikmat advances as proof of the influence of Navā'ī's encouragement and admiration that the majority of Jāmī's works were composed during the last quarter of his life. Jāmī was additionally favoured by foreign rulers, among them Jahān-Shāh of the 'Black Sheep' dynasty (1437–67) who sent a copy of his own *Dīvān* to the poet, Uzun Ḥasan of the 'White Sheep' (1466–78) whom Jāmī visited in 1472 on his way back from Mecca, and his son Ya'qūb (1478–90) to whom the *Salāmān u Absāl* was dedicated. Sulṭān Bāyazīd II of Turkey urgently invited Jāmī to his court to settle a theologians' quarrel—letters exchanged between the two are preserved in the *Munsha'āt* of Firīdūn Bey—but Jāmī prudently declined, advancing it is said as excuse the report that the plague was raging in the Ottoman dominions.

The most ancient catalogue of the works of Jāmī is the list given by Sām Mīrzā, amounting to 45 separate titles. A very great part of these has survived, but only the most important books will be reviewed here; it will be convenient to glance at the prose compositions first. The *Nafaḥāt al-uns*, comprising 582 biographies of Muslim saints, edited at Calcutta in 1859 by Captain W. Nassau Lees with a valuable life of the author, is an important source for the history of Ṣūfism, especially in the later period; written in a simple and straightforward style, it abounds in interesting and informative anecdotes and is among the finest specimens, as Dr. Ḥikmat affirms, of fifteenth-century prose. Some extracts have been translated by R. A. Nicholson in his *Eastern Poetry and Prose.*

'Shiblí—God sanctify his spirit!—fell into a frenzy. He was brought to the mad-house, and a number of his friends came to see him. "Who are ye?" he asked. They said, "We are thy friends." He picked up a stone and rushed at them. They all fled. "Come back," he shouted, "hypocrites as ye are! Friends from friends take not flight or shun the stones of their despite."

He is thy friend who, wronged by thee his friend,
The more thou harm'st him loveth thee the more;
Whom thou mayst pelt with stones and only make
His love's foundations firmer than before.'

Jāmī wrote a commentary on the *Lama'āt* of 'Irāqī at Navā'ī's invitation, completing it in 1481; some years earlier he had composed the *Lavā'iḥ* in emulation of that work, offering it to the 'Shāh of Hamadān.' E. H. Whinfield, who published the text of this book in facsimile with an excellent translation, in which he was assisted by Mīrzā Muḥammad Qazvīnī, suggested that 'the person referred to is probably Shāh Manuchahr, Governor of Hamadān, who paid much attention to Jāmī when he visited the town in A.H. 877'; Ḥikmat however prefers to believe that the veiled reference is to Jahān-Shāh whose name was either omitted or subsequently excised because of the evil reputation he enjoyed in Harāt. The *Lavā'iḥ* is divided into thirty 'Flashes'; the metaphysical prose, following the tradition beginning with Aḥmad Ghazālī in his *Savāniḥ*, is interspersed with quatrains.

Flash XXI

The Absolute does not exist without the relative, and the relative is not formulated without the Absolute; but the relative stands in need of the Absolute, while the Absolute has no need of the relative. Consequently, the necessary connection of the two is mutual, but the need is on one side only, as in the case of the motion of a hand holding a key, and that of the key thus held.

O Thou whose sacred precincts none may see,
Unseen Thou makest all things seen to be;
  Thou and we are not separate, yet still
Thou hast no need of us, but we of Thee.

Moreover, the Absolute requires a relative of some sort, not one particular relative, but any one that may be substituted for it. Now, seeing that there is no substitute for the Absolute, it is the Absolute alone who is the 'Qibla' of the needs of all relatives.

None by endeavour can behold Thy face,
Or access gain without prevenient grace;
  For every man some substitute is found,
Thou hast no peer, and none can take Thy place.

Of accident or substance Thou hast naught,
Without constraint of cause Thy grace is wrought;
  Thou canst replace what's lost, but if Thou'rt lost,
In vain a substitute for Thee is sought.

It is in regard to His essence that the Absolute has no need of the relative. In other respects the manifestation of the names of His Divinity and the realization of the relations of His Sovereignty are clearly impossible otherwise than by means of the relative.

In me Thy beauty love and longing wrought:
Did I not seek Thee how could'st Thou be sought?
  My love is as a mirror in the which
Thy beauty into evidence is brought.

Nay, what is more, it is the 'Truth' who is Himself at once the lover and the beloved, the seeker and the sought. He is loved and sought in His character of the 'One who is all'; and He is lover and seeker when viewed as the sum of all particulars and plurality.

O Lord, none but Thyself can fathom Thee,
Yet every mosque and church doth harbour Thee;
I know the seekers and what 'tis they seek—
Seekers and sought are all comprised in Thee.

The *Bahāristān* is a very different kind of book. Jāmī himself explains the circumstances under which he came to compose it; the version quoted is that made by E. Rehatsek and published anonymously by the 'Kama Shastra Society' in 1887, allegedly at Benares.

'As at present my darling and beloved son Ziâ-uddin-Yusuf—may Allah preserve him from what will bring grief and affliction upon me—is engaged in studying the rudiments of the Arabic language, and acquiring various other branches of a liberal education; and as it is well-known that young boys and inexperienced youths become very disheartened and unhappy when they receive instruction in idiomatic expressions they were not accustomed to, and never heard of, I made him now and then read a few lines from the *Gulistân* of that celebrated Sheikh and great master, Muslihuddin S'adi Shirâzi.

Verses:

Nine *Gulistans*, a garden of paradise,
The very brambles and rubbish of which are of the nature of ambergris
The gates are the doors to paradise
The abundant stories are so many *Kawthers*

The sallies of wit by curtains hidden
Are the envy of the *Hûris* brought up delicately;
The poems as lofty trees are delightful
From the pleasant dew of *the rivers below them.*

On that occasion it occurred to me to compose a tract in imitation of that noble prose and poetry, that those who are present may hear, and the absent may read it.'

As Sa'dī's *Gulistān* is divided into eight chapters, so the *Bahāristān* is set out in eight 'gardens.' While Jāmī carefully imitates Sa'dī's rhyming and rhythmical prose and his interspersion of verses, the contents of his book are somewhat different; in particular the seventh 'garden' is a miniature anthology of Persian poets bringing in some pointed criticisms. 'He was much addicted to incoherent expressions' is Jāmī's verdict on the minor poet Ādharī; Kātibī 'used many expressions peculiar to himself in a peculiar manner'; Ḥāfiẓ himself 'wrote exquisite poetry, and his Ghazals are superior in fluency and elegance, but some contain errors in their versification.' The sixth book is advertised as a 'blowing of the zephirs of wit, and the breezes of jocular sallies, which cause the buds of the lips to laugh and the flowers of the hearts to bloom'; some of the anecdotes retailed are of an indecency unexpected in a man famous for his piety, and these were modestly expurgated by C. E. Wilson when he printed his *Persian Wit and Humour* in the London of 1883.

'A few short stories have necessarily been left untranslated on account of their objectionable character, and a slight degree of licence taken with a few whose coarseness rendered a perfectly literal version unsuitable. One story of some length which the translator was unwilling to omit has been partially rendered into Latin. It should be stated that the only translation of the Bahári-stán hitherto made is that by the accomplished Baron von Schlechta-Wssehrd; which, excellent as it is, omits much that by a little freedom of rendering, and the exertion of some ingenuity might have been preserved.'

In sober truth the jokes are not very mirth-provoking, though great names are freely bandied about and great insults affectionately recalled.

'A learned man of ill-favoured countenance and hideous form, on paying a visit to Farazdak, found that his face had become pale through an illness from which he had suffered. "What has happened to thee," he enquired, "that thy colour has thus paled?" "As soon as I saw thee," replied Farazdak, "I thought of my sins, and my colour turned pale as thou seest it." "Why," said the other, "at the time of seeing me didst thou think of thy sins?" "I thought," replied Farazdak, "and was fearful of the power of God Most High, should He deem me worthy of punishment, to extend His severity so far as to make me as hideous as thyself."

FRAGMENT

My soul, thy frightful face seen, breaks
The league to keep in sin it made,
In fear that for my woeful sins
God might my form like thine degrade.'

It should be remembered that Jamī was a Sunnī, and as such attracted to himself the hatred of the Shī'a; this is hardly surprising, seeing that he was prepared to write down stories like the following.

'A descendant of 'Alí being in Baghdad called to himself a certain woman, and on her demanding money of him, said: "Is it not enough for thee that a member of the house of prophecy, and of the family of saintship embrace thee?" "Speak in this manner," she replied, "to the courtesans of Kum and Káshán, but seek not without the payment of money, the accomplishment of this desire from the courtesans of Baghdad." '

Considerable as Jāmī's achievements were in prose, it is far more through his poetry that he has dwarfed all who have come after him. Coming so late in the classical tradition, he inevitably had little new to add to what the great figures of the past had said; Persia would need a new contact and a fresh and abundant source of inspiration from outside before her writers could recover the old creativeness. Jāmī's verse testifies to the thoroughness with which he had studied Anvarī and Khāqānī, Sa'dī and Ḥāfiẓ, Niẓāmī and Amīr Khusrau, all the acknowledged masters of ode, lyric, idyll. Yet he fused together these diverse elements and produced out of the amalgam an individual style of great fluency and brilliance, a diction permeated above all else by the language and the ideas of mysticism.

Amīr Khusrau had published five *Dīvāns* representing different phases of his literary activity; Jāmī did not quite rival this productivity, but for all that he put together three separate collections of odes and lyrics. The first, called *Fātiḥat al-shabāb*, was issued in 1479, the second, *Wāsiṭat al-'iqd*, in 1489, the third *Khātimat al-ḥayāt*, in 1491; each is preceded by an elegant preface written by the poet himself. Jāmī sums up his own output in this genre, and at the same time defends himself against any criticism that might have been provoked by his contributions to the ancient art of princely panegyric.

> The greater part of my *Dīvān* of poems
> consists in lyrics such as mad lovers sing,
> or else of goodly counsels and wise saws
> inspired by sensitivity and true learning.
> You will not find any mention of base men
> herein, such as would waste life's precious coin:
> kings have been praised only at their request,
> not out of predilection and self-seeking.
> If you examine them from end to end,
> turn them a hundred ways, and then return,
> you will not light, in all these panegyrics,

upon a single thought of selfish greed:
you'll not discover, in all these noble paeans,
a solitary line of servile begging.

The *Kullīyāt* of Jāmī—his odes, lyrics and occasional pieces—extends to 568 pages in the Lucknow lithograph of 1876. In making his modern edition of the *Dīvān* Pizhmān has omitted many poems judged to be of inferior merit, and yet his text required no fewer than 316 pages—a rich offering to future workers, for very few of Jāmī's lyrics have so far been translated. Sir William Jones was early in the field with an ingenious version in which he aimed to imitate the intricate rhyming pattern of the original.

How sweet the gale of morning breathes!
  Sweet news of my delight he brings;
News, that the rose will soon approach
  the tuneful bird of night, he brings.
Soon will a thousand parted souls
  be led, his captives, through the sky,
Since tidings, which in every heart
  must ardent flames excite, he brings.
Late near my charmer's flowing robe
  he pass'd, and kiss'd the fragrant hem;
Thence, odour to the rose-bud's veil,
  and jasmine's mantle white, he brings.
Painful is absence, and that pain
  to some base rival oft is ow'd;
Thou know'st, dear maid! when to thine ear
  false tales, contriv'd in spite, he brings.
Why should I trace love's mazy path,
  since destiny my bliss forbids?
Black destiny! my lot is woe,
  to me no ray of light he brings.

In vain a friend his mind disturbs,
in vain a childish trouble gives,
When sage physician to the couch
of heart-sick lovelorn wight, he brings.
A roving stranger in thy town,
no guidance can sad JAMI find,
Till this his name, and rambling lay,
to thine all-piercing sight he brings.

Stephen Weston (1747–1830), a country clergyman who amused himself with Chinese and Sanskrit as well as Arabic and Persian, made a translation of one lyric.

To unfrequented worlds I soaring fly,
Sad is the town without thy cheering eye.
Since thou art gone I've no affection known,
And tho' midst crowds, I seem to stray alone.
No dread of solitude my soul assails,
Where'er I go thy image never fails.
Bound with Love's fetters, a distracted swain,
I seek thee thro' the world, and wear thy chain.
Whether on silk or roses of the mead
I tread; all paths to aught but thee that lead,
O'ergrown with thorns, and set with briars rude,
Retard my love, and all my hopes delude.
I said, alas! my life I freely give;
Depriv'd of thee I've no desire to live.
Some spirit whisper'd patience to my heart,
That e'en today for aye I might depart.

Jāmī's *Dīvān* has attracted more interest in Germany, where Rückert, von Rosenzweig-Schwannau and Wickerhauser all occupied themselves with his lyrics a century ago. E. G. Browne put a handful into prose; otherwise this master of melody has been strangely neglected. His fondness for the poem of seven couplets encourages the attempt to reproduce him in the form of the sonnet, and the following experiments were made to that end.

Thou lookest not upon the prisoner,
Nor visitest the stranger at the gate;
Wilt thou not suffer thy glance on me to err,
That with no other heart is intimate?
Heed not the tales mine enemies relate:
Thou hast no friend than I more friendlier.
My heart's blood filled mine eyelashes of late—
That I am heartless, how canst thou aver?
Yet how shall my lamenting move thy heart
That has no symptom of fidelity?
But, do not drive me from thy door to part,
Though that I suffer is no grief to thee.
Be not ashamed of love's idolatry,
Jami; in this most virtuous thou art.

Far from thy face, my love, it is with me
As if to my own being I were dead:
I can endure, that beauty all is fled,
But I am slain, when I am lost to thee.
Upon the day we meet in amity
I'll tell thee how in absence my heart bled;
Until that hour, how can my grief be said,
My tongue being silenced by much misery?
Thou saidst, 'How fares thy heart in its great woe?'
My heart being yet with thee, how shall I know?
Nay, draw not back thy skirt, for I would pour
My lifeblood at thy feet in passionate flow.
Jami has laid his head thy gate before,
Saying, 'I am the dog that keeps thy door.'

No harbinger to take my message there,
No friendly breeze to bring his cheer to me:
How can I suffer the beloved to see,
His very name being more than I can bear?

Dust of that road is a collyrium fair
Men labour far to gather eagerly:
What joy it were his prisoner to be,
How glad the bird that falls into his snare!
When that bright moon above his roof doth rise
Heaven is envious of so fair a place;
And as the breeze towards the cedar flies,
So yearns my heart his body to embrace.
When Jami to the tavern wins the race,
Will not the Elder give him wine for prize?

But Jāmī was not ambitious only to emulate Anvarī and Ḥāfiẓ; he also aimed at matching the work of Niẓāmī in the field of more extended composition. Niẓāmī had written five epics (or idylls, as it seems preferable to call the shorter epic); Jāmī composed seven, known collectively as the *Haft Aurang* ('Seven Thrones'). It appears that Jāmī himself was responsible for publishing the seven together, for some manuscripts of the collection are introduced by an editorial preface, presumably (as Dr. Ḥikmat believes) from his pen.

'Since these seven *mathnavīs* are like seven brothers, happily born of the loins of a father (a pen of Wāsiṭī stock) and the womb of one mother (ink of Chinese origin), and have dragged the merchandise of manifestation out of the subterranean cavern of the invisible into the inhabited region of the visible world, it may be appropriate to call them the *Haft Aurang*, a term given in ancient Persian to seven brothers who are seven stars appearing in the northern quarter and circling about the Pole-star.'

Noticing that certain very ancient copies lack this preface, Ḥikmat concludes that Jāmī originally composed only five idylls in emulation of the *Khamsa* of Niẓāmī and of Amīr Khusrau, but afterwards decided to add two more. This conjecture is strengthened by the fact that in the *Khirad-nāma-yi Iskandarī*, the last of the seven, Jāmī expressly states that it was his first intention to write five *mathnavīs* in the same metres as those of Niẓāmī, but that he augmented this total by writing the *Silsilat al-dhahab* and the *Subḥat al-abrār*. We shall now consider these seven poems in the order in which they occur in the manuscripts.

First, the *Silsilat al-dhahab*, written in the *khafīf* metre after the fashion of Sanā'ī's *Ḥadīqat al-ḥaqīqa* and Auḥadī's *Jām-i Jam*, is dedicated to Sulṭān Ḥusain Bāiqarā and must have been completed between 1468 and 1472. The *terminus a quo* is fixed by the date of that Sultan's accession; the *terminus ad quem* is determined by a more interesting historical argument, for it was in 1472 that Jāmī set out on the pilgrimage to Mecca, and on his way back ran into a storm of protest at Baghdad on account of certain verses from the poem of an allegedly anti-Shī'ite complexion which were already in circulation in that city. A fairly detailed account of the contents of this didactic poem is given by E. G. Browne, who inexplicably assigns its composition to the year 1485; he assesses its length at about 7,200 couplets, speaks of 'a certain incoherence and scrappiness' and declares that 'it contains some excellent matter, but is too long, and lacks artistic unity of conception'; he also translates an episode.

A bard whose verse with magic charm was filled,
Who in all arts of eulogy was skilled,
Did for some king a flag of honour raise,
And wrought a poem filled with arts of praise.
Reason and Law the praise of kings approve;
Kings are the shadow of the Lord above.
The shadow's praise doth to the wise accord
With praises rendered to the shadow's Lord.
A skilful rhapsodist the bard one day
Brought in his verse before the King to lay.
Melodious verse melodious voice doth need
That so its beauty may increase indeed.
From end to end these praises of the King

Unto his ears the rhapsodist did bring.
A fine delivery is speech's need:
The Book God bids melodiously to read.
When to the end he had declaimed the piece
And from reciting it at length did cease,
The poet strained his ears to hear the pause
Swiftly curtailed by thunders of applause.
The man of talent travaileth with pain
Hoping the critic's well-earned praise to gain,
Yet no one breathed a word or showed a sign
Of recognition of those verses fine,
Till one renowned for ignorance and pride,
Standing beyond the cultured circle, cried,
'God bless thee! Well thou singest, well dost string
Fair pearls of speech to please our Lord the King!'
The poet gazed on him with saddened eye,
Covered his face, and sore began to cry.
'By this,' he wailed, 'my back is snapped in twain:
The praise of this lewd fellow me hath slain!
That King and beggar grudged my praises due
My fortune's face with black did not imbrue,
But this fool-fellow's baseless ill-judged praise
Hath changed to woe the pleasure of my days!'
In folly's garden every flower and fruit,
Though fair of branch and bud, is foul of root.
'Verse which accordeth with the vulgar mood
Is known to men of taste as weak and crude.
Like seeks for like; this is the common law;
How can the ripe foregather with the raw?
The crow repeats the crow's unlovely wail,
And scorns the warbling of the nightingale.
The owl to some forsaken nook doth cling,
Nor home desires in palace of the King.
He hath no eye to judge the worth of verse,
So from his praise I suffer shame and worse.'

Second, the *Salāmān u Absāl* was composed for Sulṭān Ya'qūb of the 'White Sheep,' evidently in 1479 or 1480, for Ya'qūb succeeded Uzun Ḥasan in 1478 and the poem was intended as a kind of coronation present. In it Jāmī complains of his advancing years and the necessity to wear 'Frankish spectacles.'

And yet how long, Jami, in this Old House
Stringing thy Pearls upon a Harp of Song?
Year after Year striking up some new Song,
The Breath of some Old Story? Life is gone,
And yet the Song is not the Last; my Soul
Is spent—and still a Story to be told!
And I, whose Back is crookéd as the Harp
I still keep tuning through the Night till Day!
That Harp untun'd by Time—the Harper's hand
Shaking with Age—how shall the Harper's hand
Repair its cunning, and the sweet old Harp
Be modulated as of old? Methinks
'Tis time to break and cast it in the Fire;
Yea, sweet the Harp that can be sweet no more,
To cast it in the Fire—the vain old Harp
That can no more sound Sweetness to the Ear,
But burn'd may breathe sweet Attar to the Soul,
And comfort so the Faith and Intellect,
Now that the Body looks to Dissolution.
My Teeth fall out—my two Eyes see no more
Till by Feringhi Glasses turn'd to Four;
Pain sits with me sitting behind my knees,
From which I hardly rise unhelpt of hand;
I bow down to my Root, and like a Child
Yearn, as is likely, to my Mother Earth,
With whom I soon shall cease to moan and weep,
And on my Mother's Bosom fall asleep.

The version quoted is that of Edward FitzGerald, first published in 1856 and based upon F. Falconer's edition of 1850. (E. G. Browne's bibliographical note is entirely erroneous; Falconer did not make an English translation and FitzGerald's abridgment was not in prose.) FitzGerald's versions of 1856 and 1879 have recently been republished together with a literal rendering of the whole poem, so that it would be superfluous to discuss this work here at greater length, except to remark that in it Jāmī took up a philosophical allegory which had not been treated by any previous poet. The metre is *ramal*, like the *Mathnavī-yi ma'navī* of Rūmī.

Third, the *Tuḥfat al-aḥrār* is a didactic poem in the *sarī'* metre, modelled on the *Makhzan al-asrār* of Niẓāmī and Amīr Khusrau's *Maṭla' al-anwār*. This work makes no mention of any prince and was seemingly intended as a tribute to all the saints; in particular Jāmī blesses the memory of Bahā' al-Dīn Muḥammad Bukhārī the founder of the Naqshbandī order, and prays for the welfare of his friend and contemporary Nāṣir al-Dīn 'Ubaid Allāh called Khvāja Aḥrār. In the twentieth and concluding discourse the poet addresses his son Ḍiyā' al-Dīn Yūsuf, born after his father had reached sixty and at the time of writing four years old. The educational programme outlined for the little boy harks back to the famous *ars longa vita brevis*. After recommending a thorough study of the Koran as laying the surest foundations of a religious life, Jāmī proceeds:

> Thereafter put your back into manners and customs
> and turn your face to the acquisition of learning;
> commit to heart a digest of every subject—
> gather a fragrant blossom from every garden.
> Whatever lesson you set yourself, be certain
> not to pass on until you know it completely.
> Science has ways so many and multifarious:
> see you do not transgress the essential limits.
> Life is short: long is learning and virtue—
> only acquire what is absolutely essential.

Fourth, the *Subḥat al-abrār*, yet a third didactic poem, composed in a rare variety of the *ramal* metre otherwise employed in a section of the *Nuh sipihr* of Amīr Khusrau, is dedicated to Sulṭān Ḥusain Bāiqarā and again mentions Jāmī's son Yūsuf. Since the boy is now stated to be five, and since he is known to have been born in 1477, it is possible to date the *Tuḥfat al-aḥrār* as completed in 1481 and the *Subḥat al-abrār* in 1482; both poems are preceded by prefaces in elaborately artificial prose. How differently this work has impressed different readers is well seen by comparing verdicts: 'The *Subḥatu'l-Abrár*, or "Rosary of the Pious" is a didactic poem of theological, mystical and ethical contents very similar to the last, equally lacking in coherence and even less attractive in form and matter' (E. G. Browne); 'This is a very charming and eloquent poem embracing lofty topics and written in a delightful metre never employed in any work after Jāmī' ('Alī Aṣghar Ḥikmat).

Fifth, the *Yūsuf u Zulaikhā* was composed in 1483 in the *hazaj* metre, like the *Vīs u Rāmīn* of Fakhr al-Dīn Gurgānī and the *Khusrau u Shīrīn* of Niẓāmī. Jāmī again commemorates the revered Khvāja 'Ubaid Allāh Naqshband, and eulogizes Sulṭān Ḥusain Bāiqarā; at the end he remembers his good friend and patron Mīr 'Alī Shīr. The poem is based on the story of Joseph and Potiphar's wife as told in Sūra XII of the Koran, a romantic theme (Jāmī gives it a mystical twist) which was a favourite with Persian authors; an idyll on this topic is attributed to Firdausī's old age, and among others who wrote on the same subject were Shihāb al-Dīn 'Am'aq and Mas'ūd of Qum; many Turkish poets also took it up. This is the most popular of all Jāmī's works, and deservedly so; it was published with a German verse-translation by V. E. von Rosenzweig-Schwannau at Vienna in 1824, and English metrical versions were put out by R. T. H. Griffith in 1881 and by A. Rogers in 1892; in 1910 Auguste Bricteux produced a rendering in French prose. It cannot be said that any of these translations does justice to the brilliance and subtlety of Jāmī's original. Griffith, who found Rosenzweig-

Schwannau's blank verse 'meritorious though decidedly heavy,' set himself a difficult target which he was uncertain of having reached.

'I have endeavoured in my translation to give what I can of the spirit of the poem, and at the same time to reproduce its form and manner as closely as the differing idioms of the two languages permit me to do. But Jámí's plays upon words—which are looked on as beauties in Persian poetry—I have been obliged to pass by without attempting the almost impossible and useless task of reproducing them. Most of them I omit even to notice, as they are unintelligible without the Persian text and context. . . . Jámí has employed throughout this poem the rhymed hendecasyllabic couplet, and a translation in unrhymed verse would altogether fail to give an idea of his manner. Accordingly for the introductory cantos, which are didactic and somewhat stately in style, I have used the old rhymed heroic metre, and for the rest of the poem a lighter and freer measure, in which I vary at will the number of syllables or accents. I fear that many of my lines will not read off easily at first sight: but I trust that the greater fault of monotony has to some extent been avoided.'

One of the most dramatic incidents in the story comes when Potiphar's wife invites the ladies of Egypt to a banquet and suddenly introduces Joseph into the dining-hall in order to test the effect of his beauty on them.

Like a bed of roses in perfect bloom
That secret treasure appeared in the room.
The women of Memphis beheld him, and took
From that garden of glory the rose of a look.
One glance at his beauty o'erpowered each soul
And drew from their fingers the reins of control.
Each lady would cut through the orange she held,
As she gazed on that beauty unparalleled.

But she wounded her finger, so moved in her heart,
That she knew not her hand and her orange apart.
One made a pen of her finger, to write
On her soul his name who had ravished her sight—
A reed which, struck with the point of the knife,
Poured out a red flood from each joint in the strife.
One scored a calendar's lines in red
On the silver sheet of her palm outspread,
And each column, marked with the blood-drops, showed
Like a brook when the stream o'er the bank has flowed.
When they saw that youth in his beauty's pride:
'No mortal is he,' in amaze they cried.
'No clay and water composed his frame,
But, a holy angel, from heaven he came.'
''Tis my peerless boy,' cried Zulaikha, 'long
For him have I suffered reproach and wrong.
I told him my love for him, called him the whole
Aim and desire of my heart and soul.
He looked on me coldly; I bent not his will
To give me his love and my hope fulfil.
He still rebelled: I was forced to send
To prison the boy whom I could not bend.
In trouble and toil, under lock and chain,
He passed long days in affliction and pain.
But his spirit was tamed by the woe he felt,
And the heart that was hardened began to melt.
Keep your wild bird in a cage and see
How soon he forgets that he once was free.'
Of those who wounded their hands a part
Lost reason and patience, and mind and heart.
Too weak the sharp sword of his love to stay,
They gave up their souls ere they moved away.
The reason of others grew dark and dim,
And madness possessed them for love of him.

Bare-headed, bare-footed, they fled amain,
And the light that had vanished ne'er kindled again.
To some their senses at length returned,
But their hearts were wounded, their bosoms burned.
They were drunk with the cup which was full to the
brim,
And the birds of their hearts were ensnared by him.
Nay, Yúsuf's love was a mighty bowl
With varied power to move the soul.
One drank the wine till her senses reeled;
To another, life had no joy to yield;
One offered her soul his least wish to fulfil;
One dreamed of him ever, but mute and still.
But only the woman to whom no share
Of the wine was vouchsafed could be pitied there.

The exuberance of Jāmī's poetic imagination has been transmogrified into a clumsy and rather comic garrulity. Yet Griffith is certainly superior to the pedestrian Rogers.

That hidden treasure from the private room
Came out like rosebud in its fullest bloom.
Saw Egypt's dames that rose-bed of delight,
And from that rose-bed plucked one rose of sight.
With that one sight their senses them forsook,
And from their hands the reins of power shook.
At that fair form of his were all amazed,
And, wond'ring, all like lifeless bodies gazed.
By that fair vision as was each inspired,
At once to cut her orange she desired.
From her own hand her orange no one knew,
And thus across her hand the knife she drew.
A pen made one her fingers with her sword,
Upon her heart devotion to record;

A reed, which if the sword should strike a blow,
Vermilion from each joint would quickly flow:
Out of her palm a silver page one made,
Where, as in calendars, red lines were laid:
From every line there flowed a stream of blood,
Beyond its banks o'erflowing in a flood . . .
As then his face the Egyptian dames beheld,
Their hands cut many with the knives they held.
And of those dames whose hands were cut, a part
Lost wisdom, patience, and all sense and heart.
From his love's sword their souls they could not save,
In that assembly still their lives they gave.
Another part from reason were estranged,
And from that *Pari*'s love became deranged.
Bare both in head and foot they ran around,
Nor e'er again the light of reason found.
And yet a part to reason came at last,
But pained at heart for love their days they passed,
And, like Zuleikha, drunk from Joseph's bowl,
Caught in his snare were those birds of their soul.
Of wine was Joseph's beauty as a pot,
Where each found gain according to his lot.
From inebriety one profit gained;
From thoughts of being one release obtained;
One for his beauty gave her soul for nought:
One dumb remained, absorbed but in his thought.
By her alone should pardon be obtained
Who from that wine no sort of profit gained.

The reader may well marvel at the pertinacity which could sustain bathos so long and so consistently, and wonder why Jāmī, if that was the kind of stuff he wrote, should ever have survived the ridicule so miserable a performance would richly deserve. (Yet Rogers' travesty ran to a second edition.) Poor service is rendered to Persian literature by such misguided enthusiasm. Nor is Rogers' ingenuous apology for his little-apprehended inadequacies any sort of justification for such a revolting exercise: 'It has not been a light task for the translator to put into rhyme over 7,000 couplets, whilst adhering to the literal meaning of the original. The attention paid to the latter point will, he trusts, prove a sufficient excuse for any want of smoothness the critic may find in the former.' It is well to ponder the wise observation of R. A. Nicholson on the problem of translating Arabic and Persian poetry, a problem with which he himself wrestled not unsuccessfully: 'The power of verse to fulfil its aim is limited by circumstances. While any poem can be reproduced in metre, few Arabic or Persian poems are wholly suitable for English verse: we must decide what to translate, and especially what *not* to translate, before considering how it shall be done.'

Sixth, the *Lailā u Majnūn*, composed in 1484, was a direct challenge to comparison with the poems written on the same theme by Niẓāmī and Amīr Khusrau, for Jāmī chose exactly the same metre, a jaunty variety of the *hazaj*. The poet obligingly gives us the total of the verses as coming to 3,860 and states that the poem took him 'fourteen months, more or less' to complete; he again mentions Khvāja 'Ubaid Allāh and applauds the 'Sulṭān of the Age,' without however naming him more precisely. It may be added that Jāmī's nephew Hātifī, himself a noted poet who died in 1521, also composed a *Lailā u Majnūn*; it was his version of the old desert love-story that Sir William Jones chose to publish (Calcutta, 1788), assigning whatever income might accrue from the sales to 'the poor in the Supreme Court, in trust for the miserable persons under execution for debt in the prison of *Calcutta*.' Jāmī's version has not even attracted that much attention, though it contains many fine descriptions and exhibits to the full his rhetorical virtuosity. Here is a picture of a sand-storm in the summer desert.

One day the simoom that blows at noontide
rose scorching the mountain and the plain;
the desert, with its flying sand and pebbles,
was a chafing-dish full of sparking embers;
serpents thrashed about in all directions
like hairs that have been flung in a fire.
If any wild ass had ventured in that plain
and set its foot on that burning surface,
its sole would have broken into blisters
like the hoof of a travel-worn mule.
The whole world ailed of the great heat
panting like a furnace charged with fire;
into that furnace the mighty mountains
ran melting like an unguent of quicklime;
the mountain springs noisily bubbling
were stone cauldrons of boiling water.

Seventh, the *Khirad-nāma-yi Iskandarī* ('Wisdom of Alexander'), imitating in *mutaqārib* metre and subject-matter the *Iskandar-nāma* of Niẓāmī and Amīr Khusrau, enabled Jāmī in the guise of the ancient legend of Alexander to write what is virtually a fourth didactic idyll. The poet again addresses Khvāja 'Ubaid Allāh Aḥrār, Sulṭān Ḥusain Bāiqarā, and his own son; since the Khvāja died in 1490, Dr. Ḥikmat concludes that this poem must have been composed about the year 1485, certainly after the *Lailā u Majnūn*. Jāmī repeatedly complains of the increasing weariness of old age; towards the end of the work he speaks of it as the last of his *Khamsa*, and he praises the Turkish *Khamsa* which his old friend Navā'ī had written. The wise counsel which he imparts with all of an old man's sententious repetitiveness as his final offering to the world is conveniently if improbably put into the mouths of such famous sages as Aristotle, Plato, Socrates, Hippocrates, Pythagoras, Aesculapius and Hermes. The narrative drags slowly to its close with the death of Alexander and the letter of condolence supposedly sent by Aristotle to the great conqueror's mother, a document which we encountered summarized in simple prose in Mīr Khvānd's *Rauḍat al-ṣafā'*.

When Aristotle, that lapidary of Greece
who was custodian of the Grecian treasures,
received the tidings of Alexander's death,
his heart was great with sorrow, and he sighed.
Then, having trimmed his amber-scented pen
and made a fair beginning with God's name,
mingling for ink the blood-gouts of his heart
he wrote apologetically to his mother:
'I should have made my brow into a foot
and fared directly to your private chamber,
there to outpour the blood-flecked tears of grief
and with enchantments to allay your pain;
but ah, the feebleness of old age fetters
my foot, and I cannot stir a single step.
Though Alexander, Sultan of the world
whose empire spanned the earth like heaven's arch
has now departed from this narrow plain,
grieve not, that he has quit the royal throne.
No veil of shame enshrouds his face, no will
of envious rivals brought him humbly down,
not by unrighteous men his power was broken,
not to unworthy foes his valour yielded;
the sword of the decree of God the pure
that sways the world from Fish to Arcturus—
to that he rendered up his kingly rule
and died, as living, emperor of men.'

So the immortal philosopher's missive continues, and Alexander's mother sends a suitably Stoical reply.

We have now come to the end of this necessarily incomplete

and partial review of classical Persian literature. Jāmī's death marks the conclusion of the golden age; the silver period sets in with the beginning of the sixteenth century. Much good writing continued to keep alive the courtly tradition in the homeland, right down to modern times; and meanwhile Persian letters enjoyed a long and fruitful Indian summer in the neighbouring Moghul dominions. Even in this twentieth century the school of Persian poetry in Hindustan was sufficiently active to produce an international figure whose contribution to literature has ensured him immortality as certainly as his intervention in politics; the name of Muḥammad Iqbāl, that visionary whose Persian eloquence pleaded the cause of Islam reborn and was powerful in creating Pakistan, is now inscribed on the roll of honour headed by Firdausī.

The story of these five succeeding centuries may be told in a sequel to the present volume. It is a story no less impressive than that which has now been completed; for it reveals how the creative genius of the Persian people, in the very time when it seemed to be expiring at last, suddenly in response to new impulses coming from abroad rose from its death-bed to a new life of surprising and measureless vitality.

BIBLIOGRAPHY

CHAPTER I

Arberry, A. J. (ed.). *The Legacy of Persia*. Oxford, 1953.
Arberry, A. J. (ed.). *Persian Poems*. London, 1954.
Arberry, A. J. *Immortal Rose: an anthology of Persian lyrics*. London, 1948.
Bahār, Muḥammad Taqī. *Sabuk-shināsī*. 3 vols. Teheran, 1940–44.
Browne, E. G. *A Literary History of Persia*. 4 vols. Cambridge, 1928.
Browne, E. G. *A Persian Anthology*. London, 1927.
Encyclopaedia of Islam. 4 vols. Leiden, 1908–38.
Encyclopaedia of Islam. New edition. In progress. Leiden, 1954– .
Horn, P. *Geschichte der persischen Litteratur*. Leipzig, 1901.
Jackson, A. V. W. *Early Persian Poetry*. New York, 1920.
Lane-Poole, S. *The Mohammadan Dynasties*. London, 1894.
Levy, R. *Persian Literature: an introduction*. London, 1923.
Massé, H. *Anthologie persane*. Paris, 1950.
Nicholson, R. A. *A Literary History of the Arabs*. London, 1907.
Nicholson, R. A. *Eastern Poetry and Prose*. Cambridge, 1922.
Pizzi, I. *Storia della poesia persiana*. Turin, 1894.
Robinson, S. *Persian Poetry for English Readers*. Glasgow, 1883.
Shafaq, Riḍā-zāda. *Tārīkh-i adabīyāt-i Īrān*. Teheran, 1934.
Storey, C. A. *Persian Literature: a bio-bibliographical survey*. In progress. London, 1927– .
Sykes, P. M. *A History of Persia*. 3rd ed. 2 vols. London, 1950.
Sykes, P. M. *A History of Afghanistan*. 2 vols. London, 1940.

CHAPTER II

'Aufī, Muḥammad. *Lubāb al-albāb*, ed. by E. G. Browne and Mīrzā Muḥammad Qazvīnī. 2 vols. London, 1903–06.
Daulatshāh. *Tadhkirat al-shu'arā'*, ed. by E. G. Browne. London, 1901.
Niẓāmī Samarqandī. *Chahār maqāla*, ed. by Mīrzā Muḥammad Qazvīnī. London, 1910. Revised translation by E. G. Browne. London, 1921.
Rūdakī. *Dīvān*. Teheran, 1897.
Ibn al-Muqaffa'. *Kalīla wa-Dimna*, ed. by L. Cheikho. Beirut, 1905.
Bal'amī. *Tārīkh-i Ṭabarī*. Lucknow, 1874.
Firdausī. *Shāh-nāma*, ed. by Turner Macan. 4 vols. Calcutta, 1829.
Firdausī. *Shāh-nāma*, ed. by J. A. Vullers. 3 vols. Leiden, 1877–84.
Firdausī. *Shāh-nāma*, ed. by Muḥammad Ramaḍānī. 5 vols. Teheran, 1932–34.
Firdausī. *Shāh-nāma*, abridged edition by Muḥammad 'Alī Furūghī. Teheran, 1934.
Firdausī. *Shāh-nāma*, translated by J. Champion. Vol. 1 (all published). Calcutta, 1785.
Firdausī. *Shāh-nāma*, translated and abridged by J. Atkinson. London, 1832.

Firdausī. *Shāh-nāma*, done into English by A. G. Warner and E. Warner. 9 vols. London, 1905–25.
Nöldeke, T. *Das iranische Nationalepos*. Berlin, 1920.
Firdausī. *Yūsuf u Zulaikhā*, ed. by H. Ethé. Oxford, 1908.

CHAPTER III

'Unṣurī. *Dīvān*, ed. by Yaḥyā Qarīb. Teheran, 1954.
Farrukhī. *Dīvān*. Teheran, 1932.
Minuchihrī. *Dīvān*, ed. by Muḥammad Dabīr-siyāqī. Teheran, 1947.
Minuchihrī. *Dīvān*, ed. and tr. by A. de Biberstein Kazimirski. Paris, 1886.
Asadī. *Garshāsp-nāma*, ed. by Ḥasan Yaghmā'ī. Teheran, 1939.
Asadī. *Lughat-i Fārs*, ed. by P. Horn. Berlin, 1897.
Ibn Sīnā. *Dānish-nāma-yi 'Alā'ī*, ed. by Aḥmad Khurāsānī. Teheran, 1936.
Ibn Sīnā. *Dānish-nāma-yi 'Alā'ī*, tr. by M. Achena and H. Massé. In progress. Paris, 1955– .
Tārīkh-i Sīstān, ed. by Muḥammad Taqī Bahār. Teheran, 1935.
Gardīzī. *Zain al-akhbār*, ed. by Sa'īd Nafīsī. Teheran, 1954.
Hujvīrī. *Kashf al-maḥjūb*, ed. by V. A. Zhukovski. Leningrad, 1926.
Hujvīrī. *Kashf al-maḥjūb*, tr. by R. A. Nicholson. London, 1911.
Anṣārī. *Munājāt*, ed. by Muḥammad Ḥusain Bilgrāmī. Berlin, 1924.
Nāṣir-i Khusrau. *Dīvān*, ed. by Mujtabā Mīnuvī. Teheran, 1928.
Nāṣir-i Khusrau. *Safar-nāma*, ed. by Maḥmud Ghanī-zāda. Berlin, 1923.
Nāṣir-i Khusrau. *Safar-nāma*, tr. by G. Le Strange. London, 1893.
Nāṣir-i Khusrau. *Jāmi' al-ḥikmatain*, ed. by H. Corbin and Muḥammad Mu'īn. Teheran, 1953.
Abū Sa'īd ibn Abi 'l-Khair. *Rubā'īyāt*, ed. by Sa'īd Nafīsī. Teheran, 1955.
R. A. Nicholson. *Studies in Islamic Mysticism*. Cambridge, 1921.
Bābā Ṭāhir. *Dīvān*, ed. by Āzād Hamadānī. Teheran, 1927.
Bābā Ṭāhir. *Poems of a Persian Sufi*, tr. by A. J. Arberry. Cambridge, 1937.
Niẓām al-Mulk. *Siyāsat-nāma*, ed. by C. Schefer. Paris, 1891–97.
Niẓām al-Mulk. *Siyāsat-nāma*, tr. by C. Schefer. Paris, 1893.
Niẓām al-Mulk. *Siyāsat-nāma*, ed. by Murtaḍā Chahārdihī. Teheran, 1955.
Kai-Kā'ūs. *Qābūs-nāma*, ed. by R. Levy. London, 1951.
Kai-Kā'ūs. *A Mirror for Princes*, tr. by R. Levy. London, 1951.
Rādūyānī. *Tarjumān al-balāgha*, ed. by A. Ateş. Istanbul, 1949.
Ghazālī. *Kīmiyā-yi sa'ādat*, ed. by Aḥmad Ārām. 2 vols. Teheran, 1940–42.

CHAPTER IV

Qaṭrān. *Dīvān*, ed. by Muḥammad Nakhjavānī. Tabriz, 1954.
Gurgānī. *Vīs u Rāmīn*, ed. by Mujtabā Mīnuvī. Teheran, 1935.
Mas'ūd-i Sa'd-i Salmān. *Dīvān*, ed. by Rashīd Yāsimī. Teheran, 1939.
Rūnī. *Dīvān*. Teheran, 1926.
'Umar Khaiyām. *Rubā'īyāt. Omar Khayyám: a new version*, by A. J. Arberry. London, 1952.

'Umar Khaiyām. *Naurūz-nāma*, ed. by Mujtabā Mīnuvī. Teheran, 1933.
Sanā'ī. *Dīvān*, ed. by Mudarris Riḍavī. Teheran, 1941.
Sanā'ī. *Ḥadīqat al-ḥaqīqa*, ed. by Mudarris Riḍavī. Teheran, 1950.
Naṣr Allāh. *Kalīla wa-Dimna*, ed. by 'Abd al-'Aẓīm Khān Garakānī. Teheran, 1932.
Ḥasan Ghaznavī. *Dīvān*, ed. by Mudarris Riḍavī. Teheran, 1950.
Ghazālī, Aḥmad. *Savāniḥ*, ed. by H. Ritter. Istanbul, 1942.
Ḥamīdī. *Maqāmāt*. Lahore, 1923.
Niẓāmī Samarqandī. *Chahār maqāla*, ed. by Mīrzā Muḥammad Qazvīnī. London, 1910. Revised translation by E. G. Browne. London, 1921.
Baihaqī. *Tārīkh-i Baihaq*, ed. by Aḥmad Bahmanyār. Teheran, 1938.
Rashīd-i Vaṭvāṭ. *Ḥadā'iq al-siḥr*, ed. by 'Abbās Iqbāl. Teheran, 1930.
Suhravardī. *Mu'nis al-'ushshāq*, ed. by O. Spies. Stuttgart, 1934.
Suhravardī. *Three Treatises on Mysticism*, ed. by O. Spies and S. K. Khatak. Stuttgart, 1936.

CHAPTER V

Mu'izzī. *Dīvān*, ed. by 'Abbās Iqbāl. Teheran, 1939.
Anvarī. *Kullīyāt*. Lucknow, 1880.
Khāqānī. *Kullīyāt*. 2 vols. Lucknow, 1876–78.
Khāqānī. *Tuḥfat al-'Irāqain*, ed. by Yaḥyā Qarīb. Teheran, 1954.
Khāqānī. *Mémoire sur Khācānī*, by N. de Khanikoff. Paris, 1865.
Niẓāmī. *Makhzan al-asrār*. Teheran, 1934.
Niẓāmī. *Makhzan al-asrār*, tr. by G. H. Dārāb. London, 1945.
Niẓāmī. *Khusrau u Shīrīn*. Teheran, 1934.
Niẓāmī. *Lailā u Majnūn*. Teheran, 1934.
Niẓāmī. *Lailā u Majnūn*, tr. by J. Atkinson. London, 1836.
Niẓāmī. *Iskandar-nāma*. Teheran, 1937.
Niẓāmī. *Haft paikar*, ed. by H. Ritter and J. Rypka. Leipzig, 1934.
Niẓāmī. *Haft paikar*, tr. by C. E. Wilson. 2 vols. London, 1924.
'Aṭṭār. *Manṭiq al-ṭair*, ed. G. de Tassy. Paris, 1857.
'Aṭṭār. *Manṭiq al-ṭair. The Bird-Parliament*, by E. FitzGerald. Boston, 1899.
'Aṭṭār. *Tadhkirat al-auliyā'*, ed. by R. A. Nicholson. 2 vols. London, 1905–07.
'Aṭṭār. *Ilāhī-nāma*, ed. by H. Ritter. Leipzig, 1940.
'Aṭṭār. *Asrār-nāma*. Teheran, 1881.
'Aṭṭār. *Dīvān*, ed. by Sa'īd Nafīsī. Teheran, 1940.
Nafīsī, Sa'īd. *Justjū dar aḥvāl u āthār-i Farīd al-Dīn 'Aṭṭār*. Teheran, 1942.

CHAPTER VI

'Utbī. *Kitāb-i Yamīnī*, tr. by J. Reynolds. London, 1858.
Elliot, H. and Dowson, J. *The History of India as told by its own Historians*. 8 vols. London, 1867–77.
Ibn Isfandiyār. *Tārīkh-i Ṭabaristān*, ed. by 'Abbās Iqbāl. Teheran, 1941. Abridged translation by E. G. Browne. London, 1905.

Nasafī. *Tārīkh-i Jalālī*, ed. by Muḥammad 'Alī Nāṣiḥ. Teheran, 1944.
Juvainī. *Tārīkh-i Jahān-gushāy*, ed. by Mīrzā Muḥammad Qazvīnī. 3 vols. London, 1912–37.
Jūzjānī. *Ṭabaqāt-i Nāṣirī*, ed. by W. N. Lees. Calcutta, 1864.
Jūzjānī. *Ṭabaqāt-i Nāṣirī*, tr. by H. G. Raverty. 2 vols. London, 1873–81.
Rashīd al-Dīn. *Jāmi' al-tawārīkh*, ed. E. Blochet. 2 vols. (all published). London, 1910–14.
Rashīd al-Dīn. *Histoire des Francs*, ed. and tr. by K. Jahn. Leiden, 1951.
Vaṣṣāf. *Tajziyat al-amṣār*. Bombay, 1853.
Vaṣṣāf. *Geschichte Wassaf's*, ed. and tr. by J. von Hammer-Purgstall. Vol. 1 (all published). Vienna, 1856.

CHAPTER VII

Clouston, W. H. *The Book of Sindibād*. Glasgow, 1884.
Ẓahīrī. *Sindbād-nāma*, ed. by A. Ateş. Istanbul, 1949.
Daqā'iqī. *Bakhtiyār-nāma*, ed. E. Berthels. Teheran, 1921.
Daqā'iqī. *Bakhtiyār-nāma*, ed. and tr. by W. Ouseley. London, 1801.
Varāvīnī. *Marzubān-nāma*, ed. by Mīrzā Muḥammad Qazvīnī. London, 1909.

CHAPTER VIII

Massé, H. *Essai sur le poète Saadi*. Paris, 1919.
Sa'dī-nāma. Teheran, 1937.
Sa'dī. *Gulistān*, ed. by E. B. Eastwick. Hertford, 1850.
Sa'dī. *Gulistān*, ed. by 'Abd al-'Aẓim Khān Garakānī. Teheran, 1931.
Sa'dī. *Gulistān*, ed. by Muḥammad 'Alī Furūghī. Teheran, 1937.
Sa'dī. *Gulistān*, tr. by F. Gladwin. Preface by R. W. Emerson. Boston, 1884.
Sa'dī. *Gulistān*, tr. by E. B. Eastwick. Hertford, 1852.
Sa'dī. *Gulistān. Kings and Beggars*, tr. by A. J. Arberry. London, 1945.
Sa'dī. *Būstān*, ed. by C. H. Graf. Vienna, 1858.
Sa'dī. *Būstān*, ed. by Muḥammad 'Alī Furūghī. Teheran, 1937.
Sa'dī. *Būstān*, tr. by G. S. Davie. London, 1882.
Sa'dī. *Ṭaiyibāt*, ed. by L. W. King. Calcutta, 1919–21.
Sa'dī. *Ṭaiyibāt*, tr. by L. W. King. London, 1926.
Sa'dī. *Badā'i'*, ed. and tr. by L. W. King. Berlin, 1925.
Sa'dī. *Ghazalīyāt*, ed. by Muḥammad 'Alī Furūghī. Teheran, 1939.

CHAPTER IX

Furūzānfar, Badī' al-Zamān. *Sharḥ-i ḥāl-i Maulānā*. Teheran, 1932.
Nicholson, R. A. *Rūmī, Poet and Mystic*. London, 1950.
Huart, C. *Les Saints des derviches tourneurs*. 2 vols. Paris, 1918–22.
Richter, G. *Persiens Mystiker Dschelál-eddin Rumi*. Breslau, 1933.
Iqbāl, Afḍal. *The Life and Thought of Rumi*. Lahore, 1956.
Furūzānfar, Badī' al-Zamān. *Risāla dar taḥqīq-i aḥvāl u zindagānī-yi Maulānā*. Teheran, 1954.

Furūzānfar, Badī' al-Zamān. *Ma'ākhidh-i qiṣaṣ u tamthīlāt-i Mathnavī*. Teheran, 1954.
Rūmī. *Mathnavī-yi ma'navī*, ed. and tr. by R. A. Nicholson. 8 vols. London, 1924–40.
Rūmī. *Mathnavī-yi ma'navī*. Book I, tr. by J. W. Redhouse. London, 1881.
Rūmī. *Dīvān-i Shams-i Tabrīz*. Selected poems, ed. and tr. by R. A. Nicholson. Cambridge, 1898.
Rūmī. *Dīvān-i Shams-i Tabrīz*. ed. by Asad Allāh Īzadgushāsb. Isfahan, 1940.
Rūmī. *Dīvān-i Shams-i Tabrīz*, ed. by Jalāl Humā'ī. Teheran, 1956.
Rūmī. *Rubā'īyāt*. Isfahan, 1941.
Rūmī. *Rubā'īyāt*, tr. (selections) by A. J. Arberry. London, 1949.
Rūmī. *Fīhi ma fīhi*, ed. by Badī' al-Zamān Furūzānfar. Teheran, 1951.

CHAPTER X

Shams-i Qais. *Al-Mu'jam*, ed. by E. G. Browne and Mīrzā Muḥammad Qazvīnī. London, 1909.
Shams-i Qais. *Al-Mu'jam*, ed. by Mudarris Riḍavī. Teheran, 1935.
Kamāl al-Dīn Ismā'īl. *Dīvān*. Bombay, n.d.
Kamāl al-Dīn Ismā'īl. *Dīvān. The Hundred Love Songs*, tr. by L. H. Grey and E. W. Mumford. London, 1903.
Najm al-Dīn Dāya. *Mirṣād al-'ibād*, ed. by Ḥusain al-Ḥusainī al-Ni'mat-Allāhī. Teheran, 1933.
Naṣīr al-Dīn Ṭūsī. *Akhlāq-i Nāṣirī*. Lucknow, 1869.
Naṣīr al-Dīn Ṭūsī. *Akhlāq-i Nāṣirī*, abridged and ed. by Jalāl Humā'ī. Teheran, 1941.
Naṣīr al-Dīn Ṭūsī. *Akhlāq-i Nāṣirī. Muqaddima*, ed. by Jalāl Humā'ī. Teheran, 1956.
Naṣīr al-Dīn Ṭūsī. *Akhlāq-i Nāṣirī*, tr. (ch. 1) by S. A. F. Moulvi. Poona, 1902.
Naṣīr al-Dīn Ṭūsī. *Taṣavvurāt*, ed. and tr. by W. Ivanow. Leiden, 1950.
Naṣīr al-Dīn Ṭūsī. *Zīj-i Īlkhānī*, ed. by J. Greaves. London, 1648.
Naṣīr al-Dīn Ṭūsī. *Auṣāf al-ashrāf*. Teheran, 1927.
'Irāqī. *Kullīyāt*, ed. by Sa'īd Nafīsī. Teheran, 1956.
'Irāqī. *'Ushshāq-nāma*, ed. and tr. by A. J. Arberry. London, 1939.

CHAPTER XI

Wāḥid Mīrzā, Muḥammad. *Life and Works of Amir Khusrau*. Calcutta, 1935.
Amīr Khusrau. *Kullīyāt*. Cawnpore, 1871.
Amīr Khusrau. *I'jāz-i Khusravī*. Cawnpore, 1877.
Amīr Khusrau. *Khazā'in al-futūḥ*, ed. by Muḥammad Wāḥid Mīrzā. Calcutta, 1953.
Amīr Khusrau. *Nuh sipihr*, ed. by Muḥammad Wāḥid Mīrzā. Calcutta, 1950.
Amīr Khusrau. *Qirān al-sa'dain*. Lucknow, 1845.
Ḥamd Allāh Mustaufī. *Nuzhat al-qulūb*. The geographical part, ed. and tr. by G. le Strange. 2 vols. London, 1915–19.

Ḥamd Allāh Mustaufī. *Nuzhat al-qulūb*. The zoological section, ed. and tr. by J. Stephenson. London, 1928.
Ḥamd Allāh Mustaufī. *Tārīkh-i guzīda*, reproduced and abridged by E. G. Browne. Indices by R. A. Nicholson. 2 vols. London, 1910–13.
'Ubaid-i Zākānī. *Kullīyāt*, ed. by 'Abbās Iqbāl. 3rd ed. Teheran, 1955.
'Ubaid-i Zākānī. *Mūsh u gurba*. Berlin, 1923.
'Ubaid-i Zākānī. *Mūsh u gurba. Rats against cats*, tr. by Mas'ūd Farzād. London, 1946.

CHAPTER XII

Shabistarī. *Gulshan-i rāz*, ed. and tr. by E. H. Whinfield. London, 1880.
Shabistarī. *Mir'āt al-muḥaqqiqīn*. Shiraz, 1938.
Auḥadī. *Jām-i Jam*, ed. by Vaḥīd Dastgirdī. Teheran, 1929.
Ibn Yamīn. *Dīvān*, ed. by Rashīd Yāsimī. Teheran, 1939.
Ibn Yamīn. *Muqaṭṭa'āt*, ed. and tr. by O. M. F. von Schlechta-Wssehrd. Vienna, 1852.
Ibn Yamīn. *Muqaṭṭa'āt*, ed. and tr. by E. H. Rodwell. London, 1933.
Salmān-ī Sāvajī. *Kullīyāt*. Bombay, n.d.

CHAPTER XIII

Qāsim Ghanī. *Tārīkh-i 'aṣr-i Ḥāfiẓ*. Teheran, 1942.
Ḥāfiẓ. *Dīvān*, ed. and tr. by V. R. von Rosenzweig-Schwannau. 3 vols. Vienna, 1858–64.
Ḥāfiẓ. *Dīvān*, ed. by 'Abd al-Raḥīm Khalkhālī. Teheran, 1927.
Ḥāfiẓ. *Dīvān*, ed. by Ḥusain Pizhmān. Teheran, 1936.
Ḥāfiẓ. *Dīvān*, ed. by Mīrzā Muḥammad Qazvīnī and Qāsim Ghanī. Teheran, 1941.
Ḥāfiẓ. *Dīvān*. Poems, tr. by G. L. Bell. London, 1897.
Ḥāfiẓ. *Dīvān*. Fifty Poems, ed. and tr. by A. J. Arberry. Cambridge, 1947.
Hūman, Maḥmūd. *Ḥāfiz chi mī-gūyad*. Teheran, 1938.
Farzād, Mas'ūd. *Haafez and his Poems*. London, 1949.
Roemer, H. R. *Probleme der Hafizforschung*. Wiesbaden, 1951.

CHAPTER XIV

'Alī Yazdī. *Ẓafar-nāma*, ed. by Muḥammad Ilāhdād. 2 vols. Calcutta, 1885–88.
'Alī Yazdī. *Ẓafar-nāma. The History of Timur-Bec*, tr. by J. Darby. London, 1723.
Ḥāfiẓ-i Abrū. *Zubdat al-tawārīkh*, ed. and tr. by Khān-Bābā Bayānī. 2 vols. Paris, 1936–38.
Niẓām al-Dīn Shāmī. *Ẓafar-nāma*, ed. by F. Tauer. Vol. 1. Prague, 1937.
'Abd al-Razzāq. *Maṭla'-i sa'dain*, ed. by Muḥammad Shāfi'. 2 vols. Lahore, 1941–49.
Daulatshāh. *Tadhkirat al-shu'arā'*, ed. by E. G. Browne. London, 1901.
Daulatshāh. *Tadhkirat al-shu'arā'*, tr. (in part) by P. B. Vachha. Bombay, 1909.
Mīr Khvānd. *Rauḍat al-ṣafā'*, ed. by Riḍā Qulī Khān. 2 vols. Teheran, 1853–54.

Mīr Khvānd. *Rauḍat al-ṣafā'*, tr. by E. Rehatsek. 5 vols. London, 1891–94.
Mīr Khvānd. *Rauḍat al-ṣafā'*, tr. (in part) by D. Shea. London, 1832.
J. Stevens. *The History of Persia*. London, 1715.

CHAPTER XV

Davvānī. *Akhlāq-i Jalālī*, ed. by Muḥammad Kāẓim Shīrāzī. Calcutta, 1911.
Davvānī. *Akhlāq-i Jalālī*, tr. by W. F. Thompson. London, 1839.
Kāshifī. *Anvār-i Suhailī*, ed. by J. W. J. Ouseley. Hertford, 1851.
Kāshifī. *Anvār-i Suhailī*, tr. by E. B. Eastwick. Hertford, 1854.
Kāshifī. *Anvār-i Suhailī*, tr. by A. N. Wollaston. London, 1877.
Kāshifī. *Akhlāq-i Muḥsinī*, ed. and tr. by H. G. Keene. 2 vols. Hertford, 1850.
Maghribī. *Dīvān*. Teheran, 1863.
Busḥāq. *Dīvān-i Aṭ'ima*. Constantinople, 1885.
Ni'mat Allāh Valī. *Dīvān*, ed. by Muḥammad Amīn al-Islām Kirmānī. Teheran, 1937.
Bland, N. *A Century of Persian Ghazals*. London, 1851.
'Ārifī. *Gūy u chaugān*, ed. and tr. by R. S. Greenshields. 2 vols. London, 1931–32.

CHAPTER XVI

Ḥikmat, 'Alī Aṣghar. *Jāmī*. Teheran, 1942.
Sām Mīrzā. *Tuḥfa-yi Sāmī*, ed. by Iqbāl Ḥusain. Patna, 1934.
Navā'ī. *Majālis al-nafā'is*, ed. by 'Alī Aṣghar Ḥikmat. Teheran, 1945.
Jāmī. *Nafaḥāt al-uns*, ed. by W. N. Lee. Calcutta, 1859.
Jāmī. *Lavā'iḥ*, ed. and tr. by E. H. Whinfield and Mīrzā Muḥammad Qazvīnī. London, 1906.
Jāmī. *Bahāristān*, ed. and tr. by O. M. von Schlechta-Wssehrd. Vienna, 1846.
Jāmī. *Bahāristān. Persian Wit and Humour*, tr. by C. E. Wilson. London, 1883.
Jāmī. *Dīvān*, ed. by Ḥusain Pizhmān. Teheran, 1938.
Jāmī. *Salāmān u Absāl*, ed. by F. Falconer. London, 1850.
Jāmī. *Salāmān u Absāl*, tr. by E. FitzGerald. London, 1856.
A. J. Arberry. *FitzGerald's Salámán and Absál*. Cambridge, 1956.
Jāmī. *Tuḥfat al-aḥrār*, ed. by F. Falconer. London, 1848.
Jāmī. *Yūsuf u Zulaikhā*, ed. and tr. by V. E. von Rosenzweig-Schwannau. Vienna, 1824.
Jāmī. *Yūsuf u Zulaikhā*, tr. by R. T. H. Griffith. London, 1881.
Jāmī. *Yūsuf u Zulaikhā*, tr. by A. Rogers. London, 1892.

INDEX